TRUCKING
A Truck Driver's Training Handbook

S0-CGR-890

TRUCKING:

Career
PUBLISHING INCORPORATED
P. O. BOX 5486
ORANGE, CALIF. 92667

A Truck Driver's Training Handbook

By
Ken Gilliland
and
J. Millard

Edited By
S. Michele McFadden,
M.A., Education;
Reading Specialist

CORONA DEL SOL HIGH SCHOOL
1001 E. KNOX ROAD
TEMPE, AZ. 85284

Cover Design By Briner/Whitley Design

Contributing Artist: Dennis Arneson

Adaptation of "The SQ3R' Method of Studying" from
EFFECTIVE STUDY, 4th Edition by Francis P. Robinson
Copyright 1941, 1946 Harper & Row, Publishers, Inc.
Copyright© 1961, 1970 by Francis P. Robinson

By permission of Harper & Row, Publishers, Inc.

This publication is designed to provide accurate and authoritative
information in regard to the subject matter covered. It is sold with the
understanding that the publisher is not engaged in rendering legal,
accounting or other professional service. If legal advice or other
expert assistance is required, the services of a competent professional person should be sought.
*From a Declaration of Principles jointly adopted
by a Committee of the American Bar Association
and a Committee of Publishers and Associations.*

Library of Congress Catalog Card Number: 79-90760

1st Printing, 1981
2nd Printing, 1981, Revised

Copyright © 1981 by Career Publishing, Inc.

ISBN: 0-89262-025-0

All rights reserved under International and Pan-American Copyright Conventions
No part of this publication may be reproduced, stored in a retrieval system, or transmitted,
in any form or by any means, electronic, mechanical, photocopying, recording, or otherwise,
without the prior written permission of the publisher.
Published by Career Publishing, Inc., Orange, CA 92667
PRINTED AND BOUND IN THE UNITED STATES OF AMERICA

ACKNOWLEDGMENT

We, the authors, are deeply indebted to the many individuals and companies who cooperated in the creation of this course.

Our heartfelt thanks to the editor, S. Michele McFadden, who realized the need for the many innovative learning techniques used in this course and helped us to work them into the texts. Our sincere thanks also to Career Publishing, Inc., who encouraged us to use these innovations and provided the means for us to do so. We express our thanks for their dedication to this project.

Special appreciation is due the many manufacturers and private companies who supplied a great number of the drawings and photographs used throughout the book. Their help was invaluable.

We also wish to express our deep gratitude to Helen Drill for her assistance in the preparation of the manuscript and for her coordination between the authors and publisher.

In addition, we would like to extend special appreciation to our wives who showed such marvelous patience and understanding during the long months of preparation, months when they sacrificed their holidays and weekends to the continuance of this project. Their support was essential to its completion.

Ken Gilliland &
J. Millard
Authors

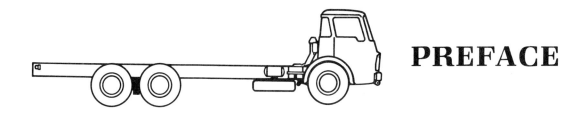

PREFACE

The professional trucker is the modern American hero. Truckers hold the place once held by ranchers, cattledrivers and farmers. Just as those men and women once helped to settle America, truckers are continuing to settle it today.

America's people are spread out. They need products from other parts of the US, just as the pioneers needed the tools, materials and medicines brought by the old stage. Workers need to ship their products too, assuring themselves of an income. As truckers move our fruits and vegetables, our lumber and oil, our cars, cattle and containers, etc., back and forth between city and country, they keep us all in touch with one another.

Truckers are like the pioneers in other ways too. They hit the road so they can feel that sense of freedom brought on by moving on down the road. They find room to breathe out on the flats. They experience joy as they drive through the red rocks and canyons of Southern Utah. They find peace and solitude as they travel the roads of Vermont. And they get in touch with America's roots in the Blue Ridge Mountains of Virginia.

Without truckers, we'd have to completely redesign our lifestyles. We'd have to produce everything we consume in our own neighborhoods. Every hour of the day, continuing while most of us sleep, truckers are helping to provide us with our luxuries as well as our needs.

As I have edited this book, my sense of respect for dedicated, professional truckers has grown and grown. Mr. Gilliland and Mr. Millard have opened my eyes to the wealth of information that a trucker needs to know.

You should be proud of yourself for choosing a career in trucking. Too often, the rest of us forget to say thank you for the job you do to keep our world running smoothly. It has been said that America runs on wheels. If that's true, it runs because truckers keep it running. Thank you. I lift my hat to the new American hero — the American trucker.

S. Michele McFadden,
Editor

HOW TO USE THIS BOOK

Learning to drive a truck is a difficult process. As a heavy duty diesel truck driver, you are in command of a huge, moving machine. Unless you're careful, the rig can run headlong down the road like a stampeding herd of cattle. You'd better know what you're doing if you want to control that herd.

This book includes a great amount of information. Much of that information will be new to you. There will be new terms, new processes, steps for you to learn to follow, regulations for you to memorize, and much more. Getting all that information under your belt will demand your dedication. You will need to study, not just read. Fortunately, your instructor is dedicated to helping you learn. You're in this together.

In writing this book, we've included sections which will help you to comprehend the subject matter. The authors have written it in a style which we hope you will find appealing. Each chapter includes a pre-reading activity (called "Before You Read"), a summary, a glossary, and three sets of questions. Let's take a look at the purpose of each of these sections.

BEFORE YOU READ

You should always begin the chapter by doing the pre-reading activity. Usually, the chapter will begin with a section called, "Before You Read." Sometimes, all you'll have to do is read this short section and start thinking about the subject of the chapter. But, more often, you'll be doing a short exercise. We designed these pre-reading activities to help you focus your attention on the subject of the chapter and to help you comprehend the information in it. Here's the purpose of these sections:

- To give you the background you need to understand the chapter.
- To help you realize what you already know about the subject and point out gaps in your knowledge.
- To help you approach the chapter with an active mind.
- To help you look for personal meaning in the chapter.
- To organize in your mind what you know or think about the subject.
- To help you study more effectively.
- To arouse your interest.

Some pre-reading activities will do some of these things for you, others will do others because the types of activities will vary from chapter to chapter. But all of the activities will make it easier for you to pick up and remember the information. Sometimes, we'll ask you to complete a study sheet as you read the chapter. Sometimes, we'll give you a quiz to take before you read it. Or, we may give you a preview of the information you'll cover in the chapter.

Once in a while, the chapter will begin with a story, rather than a "Before You Read" exercise. These stories are true. We've just changed the names of the people involved. We think these stories from the lives of truckers will start you thinking about why you need to know the information in the chapter.

Whatever the activity is, you'll find the chapter easier to understand if you do the pre-reading activity first. You'll also find it easier to answer the questions at the end of the chapter, and you should remember the information better when you become a driver.

SUMMARY

You'll find a summary at the end of each chapter. These summaries will reinforce the main ideas of the chapter. They won't cover every detail, but they will remind you of the most important things you read about.

You should read the chapter summary right after reading the chapter. And, it wouldn't hurt to reread the chapter summary quickly just before the corresponding class begins. This will remind you of what you studied the night or weekend before and help you enter into class discussion. The summaries can also help you review for tests.

GLOSSARY

The definitions of key terms are included at the end of each chapter in chapter glossaries. These words may be used several times in the book. But each word is defined in the chapter where it is first used. You may know some of these words. Others will be new to you. After all, you're entering a new field and each field has its own terminology. You may have a large vocabulary, but you can't expect to know everything about everything.

Some of the glossaries are like a second summary. When you read their definitions, you'll be reinforcing what you studied.

QUESTIONS

Three sets of questions follow each chapter. You may wish to work with your instructor to decide which questions to answer. For example, you may decide to always answer the "Checking the Facts" questions for each chapter and leave it at that. Or, your instructor may assign you some of each. But why are there three sets of questions? Each set of questions covers the same ground. But each encourages you to think in different ways.

 CHECKING THE FACTS

If you answer these questions, you'll be reminding yourself of the important points and key details of the chapter. If you have trouble answering a question, you should go back and look for that point in the chapter because you've missed something important. These questions will ask you to recall specific facts, identify correct meanings of words, match terms, list things in their proper order, and recognize true from false statements.

The types of questions vary. Some are Multiple Choice, some True-False, some Matching, some Fill-in-the-Blanks, etc.

■ GETTING THE MAIN IDEAS

If you answer these questions, you'll be sure to comprehend the main ideas of the chapter. These questions encourage you to think about the overall picture, the implications. Sometimes, we don't come right out and say something, but we imply it. So, to answer these questions, you may need to do some reading between the lines. Some of the questions will ask you to apply the main ideas to your own life, or your own trucking situation.

Again, the types of questions will vary from chapter to chapter. There will be some True-False and Multiple Choice questions. However, there will be more questions requiring you to answer, briefly, in your own words. And there will be some essay questions, so you may need to answer in a paragraph or two.

★ GOING BEYOND THE FACTS AND IDEAS

These are mainly essay questions, thought-provoking questions. You'll really have to do some thinking to answer them. You won't always find the answers in the chapter. (Sometimes you will.) In most cases, the answers will have to come out of your own head.

You'll have to analyze, synthesize, and evaluate to answer these questions. You may need to create an outline, compare two things, or see how something causes an effect. We may ask you to design a form, create a set of rules, modify something, or draw a conclusion. Or, we may ask what you'd do in a given situation or ask you to decide whether an action was right or wrong.

You may wish to answer all three sets of questions. Or, you may engage in a discussion with those who answered other questions. That way, you'll get the best reinforcement of the content. You'll get the facts, get the overall picture, and begin applying the ideas to your own career. You'll be deciding what you think as you study the course. That way, you'll have information you can really believe in when you finish the course. You won't just have a set of facts that someone else told you to believe.

A NOTE ON THE ILLUSTRATIONS

We've included a lot of illustrations in this book: commercial photographs, drawings, diagrams and charts, plus other things. Sometimes a picture is worth a thousand words, so we hope the illustrations will help to get across important points (not just make the book look handsome). You might want to carefully examine these illustrations. They will add to the information you'll pick up about trucking.

Notice one thing, however. The illustrations are numbered *by chapters.* The first picture in Chapter 1, is Figure 1-1. The first picture in Chapter 22, is Figure 22-1. The illustrations in Chapter 2 are numbered 2-1, 2-2, 2-3, 2-4, and 2-5. The next illustration in the book is Figure 3-1. We think this system of numbering is the most efficient, but it can be very confusing unless you understand what the hyphenated numbers mean.

A GOOD METHOD OF STUDY

A good system to follow in studying *Trucking* is this:

(1) Write down the reading assignment accurately.

(2) Do the "Before You Read" section. If the chapter begins with a story instead of "Before You Read," read the story. Then, do the section called, "Before You Read On," if the chapter has one.

(3) Read the chapter, using the SQ3R method. (You'll find out about this study method in Chapter 5.) If the "Before You Read" section suggested you do something as you read, do it.

(4) Read the chapter summary.

(5) Read the chapter glossary and study any words that are unfamiliar to you.

(6) Do the questions you and your instructor have assigned to you.

(7) Attend the class lecture, demonstration, or discussion. Take good notes. If you have trouble taking notes or wish to have additional study aids, tape record the lectures.

(8) After class, reread your notes. Fill in any parts where you didn't write down important points that you now remember while they are still fresh in your mind. Tidy up your notes so they will be understandable to you several weeks from now.

(9) Quiz yourself on the glossary words.

(10) Have someone else quiz you on the questions at the end of the chapter.

(11) Begin the pre-reading activity for the next assigned chapter.

This is one system of study. The "Before You Read" sections will give you other ideas for how to study. You may come up with a system that works even better for you. It needs to fit in with your own schedule — with your other course work, with your job, and with your family responsibilities. The thing is, the more you go over a subject, the clearer it becomes to you. If you follow a good, thorough system of study, like the one above, you'll comprehend all of the important information in this course of study. You'll cement it firmly in your mind. You'll find yourself earning better grades, and you'll be prepared to begin a successful career in trucking.

The Editor

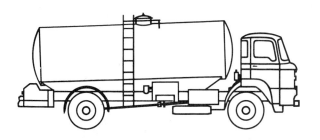

CONTENTS

Figure 1-1. You never know what you'll end up hauling as a trucker. You may haul any kind of cargo, drive any kind of rig, ride through any kind of country. This is the White Western Star Cab-over.
Courtesy of White Motor Corporation

Chapter One

INTRODUCTION

BEFORE
YOU
READ

Before you read this chapter, you might want to take a moment to think about what you already know about trucking. You could begin by asking yourself these questions:

● When were the first motor trucks produced?
● What kind of vehicles were used for transportation of goods before motor trucks?
● How has trucking changed from its early days?
● How important are trucks to our lifestyle?
● What do you have in your home that was carried by a truck?

Maybe you've thought about these things before, but you may not have put all the information together in a neat package. We'll be answering these questions in the beginning of this chapter. We'll include some other interesting facts - facts about the first transcontinental truck journey and what the first sleeper bunks were like. Then, we'll go on to some things you may not have thought about, like how much of the road taxes in the United States are paid by the trucking industry.

We'll get into the opportunities of trucking, the qualifications, and what it takes to keep out of accidents. We'll also quote what some of America's leaders have said about trucking. We'll cover all of these subjects very briefly. By reading this chapter, you'll get a bird's eye view of trucking. Then, in the rest of the book, we'll get down to specifics.

A BRIEF HISTORY OF TRUCKING | Few people realize that truck manufacturers started making motor trucks at the turn of the century. Trucks were being manufactured at the same time as cars, but they developed more slowly at first.

Figure 1-2. The first moving van in California was driven by Bill Johnson in 1909. Most vehicles were horse-drawn in those days.
Courtesy of Bekins Van Lines Company

A BRIEF HISTORY OF TRUCKING (cont.)

● *Early Truck Manufacturers*

The White Motor Corporation broke away from the White Sewing Maching Company in 1906, but even before that, White was making trucks. In fact, one company made trucks before White. Autocar started making trucks in 1899, followed by White and Mack in 1900. (White purchased Autocar in the 1950's. It also purchased two other very early manufacturers - Reo and Diamond T. Two modern White trucks are shown in this chapter.)

In the early days of trucking, makers of trucks and truck parts staged contests to show the superiority of trucks over horse-drawn delivery wagons. Car builders were staging contests in those days too. But all the automobile had to prove was that it could travel from one place to another. Trucks had to prove that they could travel over distances *and carry cargo!*

The first truck to travel coast-to-coast was a Swiss-built Sauger. It made its classic journey in 1911. The route was from Denver to Los Angeles, then by train back to Colorado, and from there to New York. The trip took a couple of months, but the truck made it and that was impressive. The next year, a Packard truck set a better record. The Packard hauled a three-ton load from New York to San Francisco in only 46 days. Contrast that with to-day's freight schedules!

As we've said, truck manufacturing started early. However, several developments had to take place before trucking became widespread. For one thing, somebody had to improve the roads, and it was hard to decide who that somebody would be. The public had to change its attitudes toward the noisy vehicles, and prices had to drop. So, while trucks were produced in the early years of this century, they were not common on the roads until after World War I.

● *Farmers and Do-It-Yourself Trucks*

You might think farmers would adopt the new vehicles quickly. After all, they farmed outside the cities and had to haul their produce to sell it. However, at first, farmers rejected the strange critters. Maybe they just didn't seem natural to the down-home men and women who used animals for power. But, eventually, something happened to change their attitudes.

By the second decade of the century, early car drivers were selling their old cars and buying newer models. For the first time, there were used cars. Farmers and haulers of goods bought many of these used cars. They cost much less than a new truck. The buyers removed the touring body, laid on a flat bed, and for the first time, hauled goods in less time than ever before.

With the growth of this type of trucking, farmers could take their produce **farther to market**. This brought about changes in the nation's lifestyle. Farmers were not as isolated as they once were. And land could be used for farms much **farther** from cities than previously. Life improved for people in the cities too. They could now buy products that used to be available only in the farm country.

Figure 1-3. One of the earliest motorized trucks in use in the United States was owned by C. Hoffberger and Company which is now Motor Freight Express and is still owned by the Hoffberger family. *Courtesy of Motor Freight Express*

A BRIEF HISTORY OF TRUCKING   (cont.)

● *The Motor Truck Versus the Horse*

In the cities, local hauling began to take a serious look at trucks too. Most delivery wagons used horses. Motor trucks were noisy and odd-looking, but horse-drawn trucks also had their problems. Horses had to have a day off for every day they hauled goods. They were expensive to feed. It cost more per ton-mile to feed a horse than to fill a truck with fuel. In the summers, many horses died from the intense heat. And, in 1911 and 1912, people began complaining bitterly about the filth caused by horses. The city streets could be clean if motor trucks were used.

● *World War I Changes Things*

During World War I, both horse-drawn trucks and motor trucks were used in Europe. Soldiers used them to carry the wounded and carry supplies to the front lines. Thousands of horses died in the war, and the Armed Forces began to see the advantage of using motor trucks in combat. Motor trucks could keep going even after being hit by many bullets, and if they were put out of commission, they didn't die. They could be repaired. Eventually, General Pershing declared that 50,000 motor trucks were needed immediately in Europe. So, in 1918, truck manufacturers produced close to a quarter of a million trucks.

When the war was over, a large percentage of the best breeding horses had been killed. In the war, many soldiers had learned to drive trucks, and the truck had proven itself as a reliable mode of transportation. By this time, many of the big truck manufacturers had gotten their start. They were geared up to produce in larger numbers than before the war. Besides those mentioned above, these included International Harvester, FWD, Oshkosh, Walter, Ford and GMC.

● *Changes in Truck Design*

A lot of changes took place during the 1920's. Pneumatic tires began replacing solid rubber tires. Truck cabs were introduced. Semi-trailers were being used, along with fifth wheels. And power-assist brakes appeared. These were all great advances for the trucker.

Earlier trucks had few creature comforts. The driver usually rode on a wooden bench and steered with a vertical steering column which was difficult to handle. There was no roof over the driver's head and no windshield. The ride was extremely rough.

Truckers were often on the road overnight even then. They slept beside the rig or in the home of a nearby farmer. Eventually, manufacturers tried adding a sleeper compartment. They tried one design that had the bunk underneath the truck's frame. Needless to say, that didn't work out. By the late 1930's, sleeper cabs were available behind the driving compartment. Some of these were accessible from the driver's seat, as they are today.

● *The Need for Good Roads*

All of these changes were wonderful. However, one more thing was needed before nationwide trucking could become a reality: decent roads. Early truck journeys were troubled by broken bridges, mud, blown tires, broken axles, and just about every trouble you can imagine - including damage to the driver's kidneys and back. Thus, the development of improved roads paralleled the development of trucks themselves.

In January of 1916, Congress passed the Federal-Aid Road Act. Over the next five years, $75 million dollars was to be spent on roads in rural areas.

The era beginning in 1921 has been called the golden age of road construction. Suddenly, billions of dollars were being spent to build roads coast-to-coast. With these new roads, with the drivers trained in World War I, with improved truck design and the public's respect for what trucks could do, trucking finally came into its own. By the late 1930's, interstate trucking was a reality of everyday life.

Today's trucks consider the comfort of the driver. The old, wooden seat and vertical steering column are gone. In their place, are air suspension seats and modern steering mechanisms. Many drivers ride in air-conditioned cabs, listening to stereo tape deck players. Some cabs feature curved instrument panels and most of them include a CB radio. Sleeper bunks are no longer

A BRIEF HISTORY OF TRUCKING (cont.)

under the truck frame. Nowadays, they are in a separate compartment and may
include things like queen-sized beds, floor-to-ceiling closets, small refriger-
ators and TV sets.

| TRUCKING'S ROLE IN THE NATION'S LIFESTYLE | National leaders in the United States have recognized the vital role that the trucking industry plays in America's lifestyle and economy. |

⬤ *Governor Finch*

Former Governor of Mississippi, Cliff Finch, worked his way through
school by driving a log truck. While Governor in 1979, he decided to investigate the problems and needs of truck drivers first hand. To do this, he drove
a rig cross-country, stopping and talking with truckers at truck stops all
along the way. After completing his trip, he had this to say:

> Since I had not driven a truck in over twenty years, I was
> fascinated to see the modern-made trucks that make truck driving
> a very exciting and interesting life. I met some of the nicest
> people in the world and I was fascinated to see so many beauti-
> ful places in each state that I traveled. Everybody I met was
> willing to help and my fellow truckers were interested in seeing
> that I made good on my trip. I found that my fellow truckers
> were hardworking, dedicated and true-blue Americans. In fact, I
> was impressed to find that not a single one wanted any type of
> handout; not a single one wanted violence; and not a single one
> wanted a guaranteed profit. The only thing that they wanted was
> an opportunity to earn a living by the "sweat of their brow."
> These are people who are the backbone of our society.

⬤ *Congressman Langrebe*

In 1971, Congressman Earl F. Langrebe of Indiana made the following
statement:

> It is time for each of us to reflect on the trucking industry's
> great contribution to our national economy. The most obvious con-
> tribution is found, of course, in the slogan, "If you've got it, a
> truck brought it." The American trucker represents both the first
> and final phases of all modes of transportation. Even items which
> travel by air, water, or rail depend on trucks to reach their final
> destination.

> But trucking contributes much more to our national economy
> than transportation. In 1969, over eight million people were em-
> ployed by the trucking industry, which means that trucking is the
> second largest employer in America. Only agriculture employs more

Figure 1-4. White Western Star Conventional Tractor hauling a dry freight van trailer. Dry freight vans are often called the work horses of the industry because they haul so many different commodities. *Courtesy of White Motor Corporation*

TRUCKING'S ROLE IN THE NATION'S LIFESTYLE (cont.)

people. In fact, one out of every ten paychecks comes from trucking.

Also, the trucking industry buys more than two million new trucks and trailers every year. In 1968, truckers bought 21 million tires, 1.4 billion quarts of oil, and 21 billion gallons of fuel.

Taxes? Truckers pay more than their share. Although trucks make up only 16 percent of all vehicular traffic, trucking pays 40 percent of the taxes that support the highway trust fund. Unlike other modes of transportation that are depending on government subsidy, the trucking industry is paying its own way.

... The courtesy and Good Samaritan tradition of the American trucker is well known to every motorist. According to the National Safety Council, the truckers' safety record is admirable. While trucks make up 16 percent of the nation's vehicle fleet, only 8.7 percent of all vehicles involved in traffic accidents were trucks.

... In short, America's got it. And a truck brought it.

7

● *The Scope of Trucking*

What do you think of when you think of trucks? You may be tempted to think only of heavy duty diesels and forget about local delivery trucks, such as bread and milk delivery vehicles. Or, you may think only of local vehicles like small parcel delivery trucks and refuse trucks and forget about the large, interstate tractor-trailer combinations. All of these vehicles are a part of the trucking industry. The industry as a whole includes large freight companies, produce haulers, moving vans and storage companies, fuel companies, food chains, heavy equipment haulers, mail and delivery companies, and every other kind of hauler you can imagine. The industry includes single-unit vans that deliver your new washing machine or bakery goods and the large triple-unit vehicles that haul electronic equipment from California to Nevada. Federal, state, and local agencies all employ trucks of one kind or another in their daily chores.

As Congressman Langrebe said, there isn't a thing that you eat, wear, or use that doesn't come by a truck somewhere along the line from the manufacturer to its final destination.

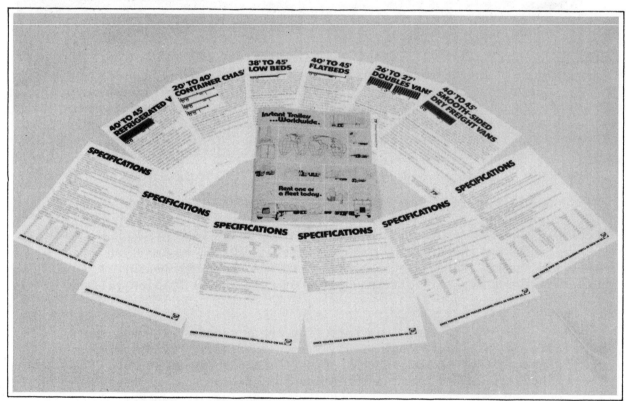

Figure 1-5. When a trucker or trucking company buys a new trailer, major consideration is placed on what will be hauled. Different trailers are suited to different types of cargo. The buyer looks closely at the specifications of the trailer to see that the trailer will be right for the job. *Courtesy of Transport International Pool*

THE	Many of the jobs in the trucking industry are not driving
DRIVER'S	jobs. However, the trucking industry revolves around the
ROLE	driver. The driver is the one who has to meet schedules,
IN	keep maintenance costs down, and see that the freight
TRUCKING	arrives safely. If it is true that if you have it, a

truck brought it, then it's true that without truck drivers, you wouldn't have it. This is where you, the driver, fit in.

● *Variety*

Being a driver today doesn't mean just driving one truck or carrying one type of load. Over the years in a driver's life, there will be loads of just about everything from fresh flowers to tankfuls of fuel. You may do specialized jobs, such as hauling automobiles, boats of all sizes, and even hogs, or "go go girls," as truckers call them. The average driver

Figure 1-6. Modern trailers are well-suited to the types of loads they will carry. *Courtesy of Hobbs Trailers, Division of Fruehauf Corporation*

may carry all of these things during a career of 30 years or so. It's the variation that makes a driver's life interesting.

You may even carry some very unusual, expensive, electronic equipment. For example, you might carry a panel board for installation at a satellite tracking station. How would you like to be responsible for the loading, hauling and installation of such a unit?

Some companies will make you responsible for everything from loading to unloading to installation. Other companies will limit your responsiblity to driving the truck, and you'll have no concern for the loading or unloading. However, with many companies, you'll have many duties besides driving. Sometimes, the driving will be the least important part of the job.

● *Expectations*

Companies need to be able to trust their drivers with expensive rigs and valuable cargo. If the driver is proficient and careful, she or he is a credit to the profession. If not, she or he is a hazard to you and me.

DRIVER'S ROLE
(cont.)

Trucking companies have to keep costs down. To do this, they pay attention to drivers' safety records, including amount of damage to company vehicles and the customer's cargo. If a customer makes a freight claim for damaged or lost cargo, it costs the trucking company money. So, companies look for drivers who are careful and honest. They also look for drivers who know how to keep maintenance costs down by driving properly.

Figure 1-7. Sometimes a driver will move on to becoming a truck mechanic after many years of driving. Rilla Raml, above, now trains truck mechanics for ICS. *Courtesy of ICS Truck Mechanics Training, Scranton, PA 18515*

Besides being careful and honest, drivers should be able to think on their feet (and on their seats). Drivers do most of their work on their own. There is no supervisor nearby to make decisions most of the time. If you arrive at the scene of an accident or encounter a leaking tanker on the road, you need to know what to do. If your brakes go out on you as you're traveling down a hill, you have to make a quick decision. Or what happens if you're driving through the mountains and a blizzard starts, what do you do then? Truck drivers make hundreds of decisions alone everyday. You have to be able to size up situations and decide what action to take whether it's traffic you encounter or an angry customer.

If an employer is going to trust a man or woman with valuable equipment and cargo and pay the kind of money truckers get paid, then the employer can rightly expect that person to know something. The remaining chapters of this book are designed to help you develop this knowledge.

WHO BELONGS ON THE ROAD?

Don't think all drivers are experts. Many drivers on the road don't belong there because they don't know their equipment and don't understand the hazards involved in operating it at freeway speeds. But a truck driver does not have to speed to be dangerous. Any number of things can cause an accident. The driver's attitude, health, degree of concern for safety and courtesy to others - all of these can contribute to an accident.

The best insurance a driver can have is this: a good night's sleep and a cheerful attitude. These two are a necessity if a driver is to succeed. The *rest* will give you the strength to cope with long hours. The *cheerful attitude* helps you deal with traffic conditions and with customers and the many other people you'll deal with in a long day's work. As a driver, you cannot work all day and play all night. You'll pay for it the next day. You'll pay in loss of quickness in your reactions and in irritation over small matters. Driving is a very demanding job. Treat it as such.

● *A Few Words About Accidents*

No one seems interested in how experienced a driver is until there has been an accident. Then it's a little late to say you should have known more about the potential dangers involved in operating a 35-ton rig at 60 mph in heavy traffic or on mountain roads in snow and ice. It is what you *don't know* about possible mechanical failures and dangerous road situations that may cause an accident.

There are three basic deterrents to accidents:

1. Initial good training

2. Experience

3. A clear head

Experience only comes with age and practice. Therefore, you need expert, qualified help to stay alive and out of trouble from the very beginning. And, you need to keep a clear head by getting the proper rest you need before beginning a run, keeping alert, and stopping to rest if you are fatigued. Keep these things in mind; keep working hard at improving your skills, and you will develop into a seasoned pro.

● *Are Drivers A Dime A Dozen?*

Driving a rig is one thing, but knowing your rig and all its components, or parts, is another. This knowledge makes the difference between a fair driver and a good, experienced one. If you owned an $80,000 or $100,000 rig wouldn't you want to hire the best drivers? Wouldn't you want your drivers to understand how the truck worked?

Ever heard the old saying, "Drivers are a dime a dozen?" Well, *drivers* may be a dime a dozen, but *good drivers* are not. Good, capable drivers are scarce. Ask any truck owner how hard it is to find a good one.

SUMMARY | Motor trucks developed at about the same time as cars. At first, people thought they were a fad, but gradually, they began to prefer them over the horse-drawn delivery wagon. One thing that helped change attitudes was World War I. Motor trucks proved that they were dependable and efficient during the war in Europe.

SUMMARY (cont.)

Farmers could not afford to buy trucks. However, when a used car market arose, farmers converted cars into trucks. Now, they could travel farther to sell their goods and sell things only available on the farm previously.

Early trucks were uncomfortable and hard on a trucker's body. By the 1920's, manufacturers were already improving things. They began using pneumatic tires, semi-trailers, and even power-assist brakes. Seats were becoming more comfortable and truck makers began enclosing the driver in a cab.

Good roads had to be built before trucking could become widespread. So, in 1916, the US Congress began providing funds for highway building. The era beginning in 1921 has been called the golden age of road construction.

Trucking has made a huge impact on the American economy and lifestyle. A great many people earn their livings from truck driving. Everything we eat, wear and use travels by truck somewhere along the line.

There are many kinds of careers open to a competent driver. She or he may choose from such jobs as long distance or local hauling, driving or managing, and being an owner-operator or working for a company. There are many different types of loads - too many to list - and most drivers will carry a great variety of loads during a lifetime career.

Finally, a lot is expected of a driver. Good drivers know a lot about the mechanical workings of their rigs. They have received good training from the start, and they have learned as much as they can through experience - through lots of practice. They keep cheerful attitudes while driving and delivering and get plenty of rest. They're concerned about safety and courtesy. Good, capable drivers are as scarce as hens' teeth and as valuable as gold.

GLOSSARY

accessible: Easy to enter or approach; reachable.

component: A part of a whole. A spoke is a component of a bicycle wheel. A piston is a component of a truck engine.

deterrent: Tending to hinder or discourage; having the power to prevent.

interstate: Across state lines or national boundaries. If you carry a load from Maryland to Delaware, or from Seattle to Vancouver, BC, you are involved in interstate commerce.

owner-operator: A driver who works as an independent carrier of goods, not working as an employee of one trucking company. Sometimes called an independent.

pneumatic: Worked by or filled with compressed air.

GLOSSARY   (cont.)

proficient: Expert; very skilled at something; highly competent.

vehicular: Having to do with vehicles. Vehicular laws have to do with vehicles.

▶ CHECKING THE FACTS

Circle the letter of the phrase that best completes each sentence or best answers each question:

1. Autocar produced the first trucks in
    A. 1886
    B. 1899
    C. 1911
    D. 1921

2. Horse-drawn wagons had some problems. Three of the following things were problems. Which one was not a problem with horses?
    A. Horses were expensive to feed.
    B. Horses had to have a day off for every day they worked.
    C. Horses were noisy in the city streets.
    D. Horses died in the hot summer and in battles during wars.

3. One out of every _____ paychecks in America comes from trucking.
    A. 2
    B. 10
    C. 75
    D. 1,000

4. What do we mean when we speak of the trucking industry?
    A. primarily large freight companies
    B. primarily local delivery trucks
    C. vehicles of federal, state and local government agencies
    D. primarily trucks driven by owner-operators
    E. all of the above

Put a plus (+) before the statement if it is true. Put a zero (0) before the statement if it is false.

_____ 5. Trucks are continually becoming more comfortable.

_____ 6. Unfortunately, truckers cannot say that they pay their share of road taxes.

_____ 7. Everything you eat, wear or use was carried by a truck somewhere along the line.

_____ 8. Most drivers haul one kind of cargo throughout their lifetimes.

_____ 9. Drivers are a dime a dozen. The best way for a beginner to get a job is to work for less money than other drivers expect.

13

■ GETTING THE MAIN IDEAS

Circle the letter of the phrase that <u>best</u> completes each sentence or <u>best</u> answers each question:

1. Two things that helped to get the trucking industry rolling were
   A. World War I <u>and</u> improved roads.
   B. a disease during the 1920's and 30's that killed many horses <u>and</u> invention of the internal combustion engine.
   C. the industrial revolution <u>and</u> growth of large cities.
   D. World War II and the discovery of diesel fuel.

2. The driver plays a big role in
   A. safety.
   B. losses from freight claims.
   C. maintenance costs.
   D. all of the above.

3. What are three things which will help you avoid accidents? (Choose the letter of the <u>best</u> answer. All four answers may be correct.)
   A. reducing speed, shifting gears properly, and knowing your rig
   B. getting enough sleep, eating the proper diet, and driving at a speed which suits road conditions
   C. good initial training, experience, and keeping a clear head
   D. not being afraid to speed up when you have to, being a better driver than the other guy or gal, and knowing your rig

4. What makes the difference between a fair driver and a good, experienced one?
   A. age
   B. ability to keep on schedule
   C. understanding how the truck works
   D. gear shifting and braking ability

You might want to answer the next two questions on a separate sheet of paper.

5. In your own words, describe what this slogan means: "If you've got it, a truck brought it."

6. Describe a good driver or list a good driver's characteristics.

★ GOING BEYOND THE FACTS AND IDEAS

1. Compare early trucks with today's trucks. You might wish to do this in a paragraph, orally, or in chart form.

2. This chapter talked a lot about what good drivers do. Compile a list of bad characteristics you have seen in some truckers. List things you've seen truck drivers do that a good driver would not do.

3. What habits do you have that you might need to change to become one of the real pros?

Figure 2-1. *From the author's own collection*

Chapter Two

DEFINITIONS OF TYPES OF
VEHICLES AND LICENSES

BEFORE
YOU
READ

Have you ever read a whole page of something and gotten to the bottom only to find that you can't remember anything you read? Your eyes were reading along all right, but your mind was off doing something else. Daydreaming. Planning your weekend. If that has happened to you, you've discovered something very important about reading. You have to be alert to do it. You need to read with an active mind. The more active your mind is while you read, chances are, the more you'll remember. So take a moment to get that brain clicking.

One way to help yourself read with an active mind is to *preview* a chapter before you begin to read it. You *look ahead* at the types of things you'll be reading about in the chapter. A quick way to do this is to read the headings (printed all in caps in this book) and the sub-headings (printed in italics preceded by a heavy dot). Let's take a few minutes to preview this chapter. Right now, look ahead at the pages to come in this chapter.

BEFORE YOU READ   (cont.)

Now that you've looked ahead, let's go on. You know that you'll be learning some definitions in this chapter - definitions of *types of vehicles* and *types of licenses*. These two subjects make up the two main sections of this chapter. You know that from the chapter title and from looking ahead at the headings in the chapter. Most of the information in this chapter is listed under those two headings.

Now locate the section, "TYPES OF VEHICLES." Look ahead. Answer this first question right here for practice in previewing a chapter: How many types of vehicles will you learn technical definitions for and what are these vehicles called?

Right. Passenger vehicles, trucks, trailers and dollies. You found that out by looking at the sub-headings. Now answer a few more questions on your own. Read each question below; then look ahead to find the answer. It should take you only a moment. Look for clues like sub-headings and words in *italics*.

What are the two kinds of truck vehicles called?
How many kinds of trailers are there and what are they called?
What kinds of dollies will we talk about?
What are the three kinds of drivers' licenses called?

This little process has probably taken you just a few minutes. What has it done? It has prepared your mind for what you are about to read, made your mind active. If you do this before you read each chapter, you'll find that you probably remember more of what you read.

A FEW WORDS TO BEGIN

A new driver often walks into a trucking company office to apply for a job, knowing full well he or she doesn't have a background of experience. But let's say the driver has learned a little of the language and plans to bluff through the interview, hoping to sound like a pro.

As time goes by in the interview, the questions get heavier. Finally, the truck supervisor says something like, "Have you ever driven a Cummins cabover with a Mack engine?"

If the driver is duped into saying, "Of course I have," he or she is on the short end of the stick. An experienced driver would automatically know the interviewer was pulling someone's leg because Cummins does not manufacture trucks. They manufacture engines. Mack is a truck manufacturer.

Later, maybe the novice is asked if she or he knows how to operate a two-wheeler. The beginner who thinks this is a motorcycle or bicycle is in real trouble because any driver knows this is a hand truck.

You can see that it is very important to know the correct terminology before you do anything else. You have to speak the language to communicate, and that is half the battle of acquiring a job. To start building your trucking vocabulary, we need to begin with the basics.

Figure 2-2. A conventional tractor towing a semi-trailer.
Courtesy of Pullman Trailmobile

TYPES
OF
VEHICLES

● *Passenger Vehicles*

A passenger vehicle is any motor vehicle, other than a motor truck or truck tractor, designed for carrying not more than ten persons, including the driver. It is used or maintained for the transportation of persons. House cars and motor homes are included in this definition.

● *Trucks*

1. A *motor truck* is a motor vehicle designed, used, or maintained primarily for the transportation of property. It is also known as a bobtail or straight truck. Try not to confuse it with a tractor without a trailer.

2. A *truck tractor* is a motor vehicle used for drawing other vehicles. It is built so that the only load it carries is part of the weight of the vehicle it is drawing. There are two kinds of truck tractors: *conventional* types and *cab-over* types.

TYPES OF VEHICLES   (cont.)

A conventional tractor has the engine under the hood and fenders. In other words, the engine is out front, under the hood, like your car engine. The cab-over has a flat face with the engine beneath the cab. The driver sits up top, over the front axle. Figure 2-1 is a cab-over and Figure 2-2 is a conventional tractor. The advantage of the cab-over is the short overall length and the good visibility since there are no hood and fenders blocking your view. (See Figure 15-5.)

⬤ *Trailers*

1. A *trailer* is a vehicle built for carrying or hauling property. It is to be pulled by a motor truck or tractor and is built so that *no part of its weight* rests on the vehicle pulling it. You will often hear people refer to trailers as "full trailers." Figure 2-3 shows a motor truck pulling a trailer.

2. A *semi-trailer* is a vehicle built for carrying or hauling people or property. It has one or more axles and two or more wheels. It is pulled by a motor vehicle and is built so that *some of its weight* and part of its load rests upon or is carried by the vehicle pulling it. A major advantage of the semi-trailer combination over the straight truck is this: the semi allows for quick and easy release of the trailer from the tractor. Thus, the driver may drop off a trailer and pick up a new one without waiting for the first trailer to be unloaded. Figure 2-4 shows a tractor pulling a semi-trailer.

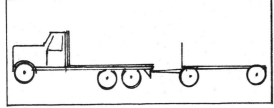

Figure 2-3

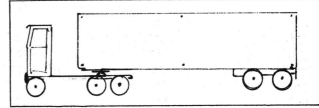

Figure 2-4

Notice the *drawbar* between the truck and trailer in Figure 2-3. A drawbar is a rigid connection between a trailer and a towing vehicle which is securely attached to both vehicles by non-rigid means. It doesn't carry any part of the load.

⬤ *Dollies*

1. A *pole* or *pipe dolly* is a vehicle pulled by a motor vehicle and is built for hauling poles, pipes, timbers, or integral structural materials. It must have one or more axles and two or more wheels. It must be connected to the towing vehicle by chain, rope, cable, drawbar or reach, or by the load, without any part of the weight of the dolly resting upon the towing vehicle. (See Figure 2-5.)

2. A *logging dolly* is a vehicle designed for carrying logs. It has one or more axles. The axles can't be more than 54 inches apart. A logging dolly is used in connection with a motor truck only to transport logs. The dolly is securely connected to the towing vehicle by a reach and by the load.

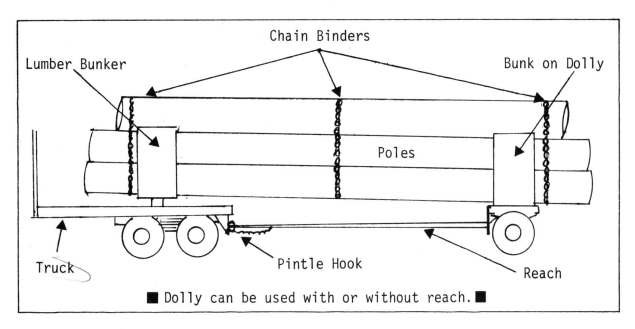

Figure 2-5. This is a pole or pipe dolly. The *reach* is the towing connection from the dolly to the back of the towing vehicle. The reach is connected to the back of the towing vehicle by what is called a *pintle hook* and a *safety chain* or *cable*, as shown. The *bunk* is nothing but a U-shaped or square saddle that the poles or pipes are set in. The *bunker* is in the same U-shape and holds the load. The *chain binder* is the lashing device. There may be a cable or strap around the load, but the chain binder cinches the load; that is, it applies pressure to tighten the load. The bunker rests on the towing vehicle on a swivel pin which secures it to the vehicle. When the poles or pipes are strapped to the bunker, they can't move out of the bunker.

TYPES OF LICENSES | From state to state, drivers' license categories will vary regarding the type of vehicle a person can drive with a specific license. For instance, in California, a truck driver's license would be rated as a "Class 1" license. In New Jersey, it is called a "Chauffeur's License," while Alaska's truck driver's license is called simply a "Driver's License," meaning, a commercial license. (An automobile license in Alaska is called an "Operator's License.") Basically, the licenses are all the same.

Age requirements and fees will change from state to state, just as the license names will. However, every heavy-duty truck driver in the United States is required to carry the proper license for his or her home state. The license indicates that the driver is qualified to handle the type of vehicle he or she is driving.

We'll describe the three main types of drivers' licenses below. In describing them, we'll use California terms and regulations as an example. As a general rule, you'll find these classifications are pretty much the same from state to state.

19

TYPES OF LICENSES   (cont.)

● *Basic Class Three*

You can find the laws relating to drivers' licenses in your state's driver's handbook. It will contain the information you need to know to get your basic, or Class 3, license. This license allows you to drive three-axle motor homes in addition to cars. It also allows you to tow a single vehicle if that vehicle weighs less than 6,000 pounds gross, that is, including everything - the vehicle and the load.

● *Class Two*

The Class 2 license permits you to drive any bus, any farm labor truck, any single vehicle with three or more axles, and any vehicle like that towing another vehicle weighing less than 6,000 pounds gross. It also allows you to drive all vehicles listed under Class 3. So how does it differ from Class 3? It removes the axle limitation and it permits you to drive buses and farm labor trucks. Sometimes it is valid for interstate driving (that is, from one state to another) of Class 2 vehicles; sometimes it is not. To be valid for interstate driving of Class 2 vehicles, it must be accompanied by a valid medical certificate which is not more than two years old. (We'll be talking about medical certificates in Chapter 4.)

● *Class One*

If you carry a Class 1 license, you can drive *any* combination of vehicles, including all of those listed under Classes 2 and 3. You can tow trailers weighing over 6,000 pounds gross, and you can tow more than one trailer. (With a Class 2 license, you can only tow one trailer.) A Class 1 license is valid for operation of Class 1 and Class 2 vehicles only when you have a valid medical certificate which isn't over two years old.

SUMMARY | There were two main things we talked about in this chapter. The first main thing was types of vehicles. We defined the major types of vehicles: passenger vehicles, trucks, trailers, and dollies. We talked about the differences between trucks and tractors and between trailers and semi-trailers. These four things may be the most important definitions in the chapter.

We talked about three types of licenses, and since their names vary from state to state, we used California names for them. A Class 3 license is the type that a regular car driver has. A Class 2 license makes it legal for you to drive a bus, farm labor truck, and a single vehicle with three or more axles. You can tow a vehicle with either a Class 3 or Class 2 license, but only one, and it has to weigh less than 6,000 pounds. The Class 1 license is the one that heavy-duty truck drivers have to have.

Finally, we said that you have to have a valid (not over two years old) medical certificate to make your Class 2 or Class 1 license valid nationwide. You get a certificate by passing a doctor's physical exam. Getting this exam every couple of years is one of your responsibilities as a truck driver.

GLOSSARY | This chapter is a lot like a glossary itself. Therefore, we haven't included a separate list of words which you should have learned from it. Instead, in the section below, "Checking the Facts," you'll be creating the glossary yourself.

▶ CHECKING THE FACTS

Fill in the blanks. Listed below are the words you will need. Use them all - just one in each blank.

cab-over	conventional	pole dolly
Class 1	semi-trailer	tractor
Class 3	straight truck	trailer

1. A tractor in which the engine is out front, under the hood, is called

   a _____.

2. Motor trucks are used mainly for transporting property. A motor truck

   is sometimes called a bobtail or _____.

3. A tractor with a flat face and engine underneath the cab is called a

   _____.

4. A _____ is a vehicle which is
   pulled by a motor vehicle, built for hauling various things. It is
   connected to the towing vehicle by a chain, rope, cable or drawbar, **or**
   by the load.

5. A license which allows you to drive a heavy-duty rig of any size is

   called a _____.

6. A _____ is a vehicle used to tow other
   vehicles. It is designed so that the only load it carries is part of
   the weight of the vehicle it draws.

7. A vehicle which is built so that some of its weight and part of its

   load rests upon the towing vehicle is called a _____

   _____.

8. A vehicle built for hauling property is called a _____

   _____ if none of its weight rests on

   the towing vehicle.

9. The license most car drivers hold is a _____.

21

■ GETTING THE MAIN IDEAS

1. The rig in Figure 2-1 is made up of two vehicles. What are these two vehicles called? Be as specific as you can.

2. What kind of license do you need to drive the rig shown in Figure 2-2?

3. Say your car breaks down and you have to tow it yourself. A friend says he has a chain and he'll tow it for you. You say you think you should rent a drawbar instead, even though it'll cost money. What advantages does a drawbar have over a chain?

4. Does a vehicle have to have a motor? If not, list two vehicles that don't.

5. How is a dolly different from a trailer?

★ GOING BEYOND THE FACTS AND IDEAS

1. You deliver topsoil for Yorba Linda landscaping. The typical amount delivered is 15 - 30 cubic feet. What type of vehicle or vehicles do you think you'll drive? Can you figure out why?

2. You drive coast to coast. You carry lobster from Maine to Chicago, beer from Chicago to Tennessee, and textbooks from Tennessee to San Francisco. You have it well worked out and carry other products back to Maine and begin the whole process over again. Describe the type of vehicle or vehicles you use.

3. Why are there special vehicles for hauling lumber? Couldn't you just stack lumber in a regular trailer?

Chapter Three

REGULATING AGENCIES

Figure 3-1.

Photo by H. Haase

BEFORE YOU READ In this chapter, we'll be discussing the agencies which regulate the trucking industry. These regulating agencies include city, county, and state governments and the federal government. You'll find that each government is responsible for specific types of laws. (These laws are frequently called ordinances or statutes.) For example, counties set laws regarding their roads and the federal government sets laws about federal highways.

We'll discuss port of entry forms when we discuss state laws. And when we get into federal regulations, we'll discuss the DOT (Department of Transportation) and the ICC (Interstate Commerce Commission).

We'll wrap up the chapter with a few words on trends in truck regulations. But first, a story of a typical driver. We'll call the driver Rudy. But we could have called him by a thousand different names because this story happens over and over, every day.

A STORY ABOUT RUDY One of the basic problems that confronts the trucking industry and the government is this: How do you eliminate the abuses of the regulations and the abuses of the human element, the truck driver? As a perfect example, let's look at Rudy.

Rudy is a husky guy, 35 years old, well-experienced in his trade and very skillful in handling big rigs. He works for a small company that has only four trucks in its fleet.

Rudy was called in on a Monday morning to work at the usual time: 3:00 AM. This is the hour most drivers start the day. He hooked up his rig and was out of the yard within the first half hour. Being on a short line run this trip, Los Angeles to Phoenix, he could expect the run to take about eight hours.

Rudy arrived in Phoenix on schedule, about noon. After a quick lunch, he unloaded the freight. This took him approximately another two hours. Anyone working in an office or a plant would consider eight hours a full day and go home. But not Rudy. He had to get home, so he made the return trip to his starting point, Los Angeles. This meant being on the clock for approximately 18 hours.

When Rudy arrived in Los Angeles, his boss told him there was another load waiting for him.

If Rudy's boss were following DOT guidelines, Rudy would have been off the truck and resting at a motel after he reached the end of his run in Phoenix. Why? Because the DOT limits drivers to 10 hours of driving or a total of 15 hours on the job overall. After that, they must be off work for at least eight hours.

A number of carriers some-times ignore these rules, so drivers like Rudy end up driving too many hours in a row. These

Figure 3-2.   *Photo by H. Haase*

companies are working their drivers too hard and too long. Drivers become fatigued and driving becomes unsafe. *Safety* - it's an important word. It will certainly be important to you as a driver, won't it? And it's important to the public. Safety is one reason for regulations. We'll be talking about others.

THE NEED FOR REGULATIONS

Trucking is a closely regulated industry. Throughout your career of heavy-duty diesel truck driving, you can expect to be involved with regulations. At times, it may seem that there are too many regulations. At other times, you will find them working for your benefit. Either way, a professional attitude toward trucking regulations is part of being a professional driver. A professional attitude begins with an understanding of the reasons for regulations and a basic knowledge of the different regulating agencies.

Imagine for a moment that there were no regulations governing the trucking industry. What kind of situations might then occur?

● Schedules which could only be met by requiring drivers to follow dangerous driving practices

THE NEED FOR REGULATIONS (cont.)

- Unsafe equipment - endangering drivers, the public, the cargoes

- Overloaded vehicles which could not be operated safely and which would damage the highways

- Loads of explosives parked in residential areas

You can probably think of some others. But these are some of the hazards that trucking regulations are intended to avoid.

HOW MANY GOVERNMENTS ARE THERE? As we said above, many different government agencies are concerned with these problems. Because of alphabet names like DOT, and sometimes because of differing standards and rules from city to city and state to state, some people think this part of trucking is the most confusing part. However, if you take a few moments to sort it all out and understand the way this part of the US government is organized, it becomes fairly simple.

How many governments are there in America? If you say, "One," you are wrong. If you say, "51" (50 states and one federal) you are on the right track. If you say, "About 80,000," you will be just about right. Counting all of the school districts; water, fire, and irrigation districts; the city and county governments; the state governments, and the federal government, there are about 80,000 governments in the United States.

While you, as a driver, may haul a load of desks to a school district, or chemicals to a water district, as a general rule, these types of governments are not direct concerns of truck drivers. However, city, county, and state governments, as well as the federal government, make regulations concerning trucks. They *are* a concern of truck drivers.

CITY GOVERNMENT REGULATIONS City governments can make ordinances such as establishing truck routes, speed limits, loading zones and truck parking regulations. These laws are usually enforced by city police officers and the municipal courts.

The amount of independence each city has to make ordinances is different in each state. Therefore, as any professional driver knows, you can expect to find different rules in different cities. For example, one city may permit trucks to be parked on the main street, while another city 30 miles down the road, enforces an ordinance restricting truck parking to special areas.

COUNTY GOVERNMENT REGULATIONS | Roads outside city limits which are not designated as state highways are usually the concern of county governments. Truckers making rural deliveries or hauling agricultural products are involved with county roads.

County roads are usually patrolled by deputies from the sheriff's office. County governments are mostly interested in truck speeds, weights and cargo which may fall from the trucks while they are hauling agricultural products.

Heavy trucks on bridges are a particular concern of county officials. Many rural bridges will not support the weight of a heavy-duty diesel rig traveling at the speed limit. In these cases, the county engineers often post reduced weight or speed limits for trucks. (See Figure 3-3.)

Figure 3-3. One of many covered bridges still used in Vermont and New Hampshire. *Photo by M. McFadden*

When you travel on county roads, you, as a professional driver must read these signs carefully. If you are not sure the bridge will support your rig, you can call the county road department. The people there will be able to help you.

STATE GOVERNMENT REGULATIONS | State governments play an important part in truck regulations. Most state regulation of trucks comes from one of these two:

1. The state agency which regulates motor carriers in the state

2. The state vehicle laws

● *State Regulatory Agencies*

Almost all states have agencies which regulate motor carriers operating within their borders. Since the states are different, it follows that the agencies would be different. Some of the names these agencies call themselves are The Public Service Commission, The Public Utilities Commission, the Railroad Commission, and the Department of Motor Vehicles.

STATE GOVERNMENT REGULATIONS   (cont.)

These agencies regulate other activities besides trucking too, but where trucking is concerned, they are usually interested in three things:

1.   The *number* of trucks operating within the state

2.   *What* the trucks are hauling

3.   The *rates* being charged for hauling within the state

Ports of entry.   At the borders of each state, these agencies issue operating permits, called *port of entry* forms.   These forms allow trucks to use the roads of the state.   The fees collected from the sale of the forms help the state to collect fuel taxes.   These taxes are figured according to the number of miles each truck traveled in the state.   The permits also help prevent unfair competition among truckers.   If the truck only occasionally travels through a state, the driver can buy a *one trip permit*.   If the truck often travels through the state, the agency may issue the truck a *permanent permit number*.

Port of entry forms are standard state forms in quadruplicate.   They show the port of entry (which one you drove in), the weight and type of rig being operated and your destination.   They also show the *carrier's* name. ("Carrier" is a word you'll be hearing a lot.   It actually means the name of the person or company that owns the rig.   A commercial carrier is the same as a trucking company.   Thus, the name listed on the port of entry form is the carrier's name with the driver's signature beside it).

One-trip permits are issued for periods of from 24 hours to 72 hours. You should always find out if the cost of a 72-hour permit is the same as a 24-hour permit, as in most cases they are the same.   If the cost is the same, it's a good idea to buy the 72-hour one.   This way, you may not have to buy a second permit if you end up staying in the state over 24 hours.

For example, you get a permit for 24 hours.   Something happens and you can't pick up your load until the following day.   You go over your 24-hour period.   So, when you return through the port of entry, you have to buy a permit to cover the next 24-hour period.

By law, these forms cannot be copied.   Therefore, we haven't reproduced a port of entry form here.   However, so you know what to expect, here's a description of what the forms are like.   There's no standard size so they vary, from 4" x 8" to 6" x 8" to 8½" x 11".   The information they require varies a little too, but basically they'll ask you for these things:

● Type of vehicle (straight truck, tractor-trailer combination, flat-bed, etc.)

● Type of towing unit (tractor or truck type)

● Weight and license numbers

STATE GOVERNMENT REGULATIONS (cont.)

- Trailer or trailers' license numbers and weight of each

- Commodity carried (tires, furniture, flammables, etc.)

- Port of entry (city, town, etc.)

- Port of exit destination

- Approximate number of miles to be traveled within state

- Duration of the permit (12 to 72 hours)

- Date of entry

- Date of exit

- Fee charged by state to carrier (based on number of miles traveled in state, gross weight of rig and the commodity carried)

Figure 3-4.   *Photo by H. Haase*

Permit numbers and gross weight limit numbers. Most of the numbers you see painted on the sides of interstate trucks are *permanent state permit numbers*. Right next to these numbers, you'll usually see gross weight limit numbers. From these numbers, you can tell which state the truck often travels in. The numbers are issued by the state, but the system of numbering is controlled by the *ICC (Interstate Commerce Commission)*, a federal agency. (We'll talk about it in a moment.) Some truckers will refer to these numbers as their ICC numbers. The weight limit numbers show what the truck's gross weight limit is for each state.

STATE GOVERNMENT REGULATIONS (cont.)

The *Public Utilities Commission*, or *PUC*, is a state organization. Every state has one although it may be called by another name such as the Public Service Division. The PUC regulates trucks which operate solely within their home state boundaries. It also issues truck permit numbers and gross weight limit numbers and stencils them on the side of intrastate trucks.

To review, the PUC numbers or ICC numbers stenciled on the side of the cab are usually assigned to carriers that run regularly through a state. If a truck does not regularly run through a state, it won't have an assigned number. Instead, it will just get a temporary permit which allows it to enter and exit. As a professional driver, you'll get to know the different requirements made by the states you run through. You'll also know that as you enter a state, you must stop at the port of entry and complete the necessary paper work before proceeding through the state. Try not to confuse an ICC carrier (which travels nationwide) with a PUC carrier (which operates within the boundaries of one state).

● *State Vehicle Laws*

Each state has a set of vehicle laws which governs motor vehicles operating within that state. These laws provide for licensing of drivers and vehicles. Here again, as a professional driver, you'll need to be aware that the vehicle laws are not the same for each state. Some of the outstanding differences which the truck driver must watch for are *variations in truck speed, weight and length limits*, and *requirements regarding safety equipment*.

If you, as a driver, have a regular run through only a few states, you soon learn the different laws which are in effect at various points along your run. If you drive in many different states, you might want to buy a reference book which contains the latest vehicle laws and regulations for each state. These books are usually available at truck stops.

FEDERAL GOVERNMENT REGULATIONS | The federal government regulates trucking through the Interstate Commerce Commission which we discussed above, and the DOT or Department of Transportation which we briefly mentioned in the story about Rudy. These are two separate agencies within the federal government.

The ICC is a special commission which was set up in 1887 to regulate commerce among the states. The *Motor Carrier Act of 1935* authorized the federal government to regulate interstate trucking. From 1935 to 1967, federal regulation of interstate trucking was carried out by the ICC. At the present time, the ICC is the federal agency which issues interstate operating permits and oversees interstate freight rates.

The DOT was created in 1967. It is the fourth largest department in the federal government. Two of its subdivisions, the *Bureau of Motor Carrier Safety* and the *Office of Hazardous Materials*, make regulations affecting truck drivers. Motor carrier safety used to be a part of the ICC's work. Now, the Bureau of Motor Carrier Safety publishes and enforces the *Motor Carrier Safety Regulations*, often called simply the *MCSR* or the *DOT regulations*.

FEDERAL GOVERNMENT REGULATIONS   (cont.)

● *The Motor Carrier Safety Regulations*

As you read on in this book, you'll be reading many of the DOT regulations. We've changed the wording slightly in some places to clarify the meaning of the regulations. For now, it's important for you to know two things about the MSCR. (The designation *"MCSR,"* followed by a number, for example, *MCSR 391.5*, refers to the place in the MCSR where this rule appears. You'll be seeing these numbers many times in future chapters of this textbook.) Here are the two important things:

- ● MCSR 391.5 requires truck drivers to be familiar with these regulations, and

- ● MCSR 392.2 says, "Motor vehicles must be operated in accordance with the local state, county and city laws. However, if the federal law sets a higher standard than the local law, the driver must comply with the federal law."

What was that? First, you need to *know* these regulations. Second, you need to *follow* them. So, as we said, we'll be giving you some of the key rules from the DOT book in this text. But we won't be giving you all of them. That means you'll have to get yourself a copy of the *Motor Carrier Safety Regulations* book. After you've studied it, you should carry it in the cab with you in case you need to look up some detail. It's a little book and it's inexpensive. You can order one from the American Trucking Association in Washington, DC. Before you begin driving as a professional, you are required to know the DOT regulations.

Every driver who works in interstate commerce has to follow the DOT regulations. Interstate commerce is the hauling of any commodity *across state lines* or *across national boundaries*. A driver is working in interstate commerce when she or he carries a load from Oregon to Florida, from Maine to Quebec, and even from Maryland to Delaware. The rules apply to drivers who work for an employer (large or small) and to owner-operators.

What types of regulations will you find in the DOT book (or MCSR)? Among the subjects covered are driver qualifications, regulations on driving, parts and accessories, securing cargo, hours of service, and how to report accidents. One very important section deals with *log books* which drivers use to record their hours on and off duty. The DOT specifies a standard form for log books and expects all drivers to keep them current up to the last change of duty. We'll cover driver's qualifications in the next chapter, and we'll be referring to many of the other MCSR topics as we go along in this book.

● *The Office of Hazardous Materials*

The DOT's Office of Hazardous Materials administers the regulations covering the transportation of hazardous materials. This office sets standards for classifying and coding dangerous cargo. Trucks carrying dangerous cargo must have DOT placards attached to them.

A *placard* is usually a small cardboard or metal sign, 10 inches by 10 inches, stating that dangerous cargo (like acids, flammables, or explosives) is being carried. In case of an emergency, these placards quickly tell the fire or emergency officials what kind of dangerous cargo is in the truck.

1. The ICC and the DOT are two separate organizations in the federal government. The ICC is concerned with operating rights and with interstate freight rates. The DOT is concerned with safety and regulates interstate drivers.

2. The Bureau of Motor Carrier Safety and the Office of Hazardous Materials are both under the DOT.

3. The Motor Carrier Safety Regulations (MCSR) and the DOT Regulations (as they are called in everyday truckers' conversation) are two names for the *same rule book.*

Figure 3-5. Garrett Freightlines Inc., one of the oldest major motor carriers in the US, made this working duplicate of their first truck. The original was made in 1913 by the Reo Motor Truck Company of Lansing, Michigan. Clarence Garrett paid $525 for it in 1913. *Courtesy of Garrett Freightlines Inc.*

TRENDS IN TRUCK REGULATIONS

When trucking began, local governments passed their own rules regarding trucks. This practice created many different rules. Having many different rules caused problems when the trucks began moving greater distances and from state to state. Since the Motor Carrier Act of 1935, the trend has been toward having the same rules everywhere.

The Bureau of Motor Carrier Safety Regulations has been especially helpful to truck drivers as it has helped bring about a similarity of regulations. The MCSR are mostly made up of the best state regulations. Many state agencies, having seen that they are good regulations, have adopted them as the laws their state courts enforce for intrastate drivers too. Thus, there become fewer differences in laws affecting trucks, and the driver's job is made easier.

THE TRUCK DRIVER AS A DIPLOMAT

In this chapter, we have explained that there are many different agencies regulating truck drivers. The rules of the agencies are not always the same. As trucks and their drivers carry their cargoes through different cities, counties and states, the rules change depending on where the truck is and what it is doing.

As a professional driver, you're going to have to be part *diplomat*, meaning you'll have to work well with people. You'll have to use tact. The official at the weigh scale in California is part of a different organization than the official doing the same job in Washington, and possibly has a different rule book. You won't expect them to be using the same rule book or doing things in the same way. With this understanding, comes patience and an ability to deal effectively with the representatives of many governments.

SUMMARY

The laws that regulate the trucking industry are made by over 80,000 different governments. These include the federal government and state, county and city governments. The various laws are made to protect the public as well as the truck driver. The rules also help to maintain government property, such as bridges and road surfaces, keeping them from damages caused by vehicles too heavy for them. Trip permits and payment of road taxes help to support the highway systems.

Each government body sets rules for trucks traveling in its geographical area. Cities and towns usually pass laws about routes, speed limits, and truck loading and parking. Counties also set rules about these things, but they are especially interested in weight limits and size limits on county roads. State governments and the federal government also set rules about these things.

State governments have two concerns: regulating motor carriers and setting vehicle laws. They decide how many trucks may operate in their states, how much and what the trucks may carry, and how much to charge carriers for the privilege of hauling. Interstate truckers deal with the state officials mainly at the ports of entry. To travel in a state, a trucker needs either a permanent permit number or a one trip permit. Vehicle laws have to do with speed limits, weight and size limits and safety equipment. Intrastate drivers are regulated by the Public Utilities Commission.

Two branches of the federal government regulate interstate truck drivers. These two are the Interstate Commerce Commission (ICC) and the Department of

Transportation (DOT). The ICC oversees interstate freight rates and issues operating permits. The DOT publishes and enforces the Motor Carrier Safety Regulations and the hazardous materials regulations. Interstate drivers must know and follow these regs. Truckers call this book the MCSR or the DOT book.

GLOSSARY

carrier (motor carrier): An individual or company in the business of transporting goods or persons.

commodity: Goods shipped; any article of commerce.

DOT: The Department of Transportation. This department of the federal government publishes and enforces the MCSR and hazardous materials regulations.

ICC: The Interstate Commerce Commission. A federal commission set up in 1887. In 1935, it began regulating interstate trucking. Today, it issues operating permits and sets interstate freight rates.

intrastate: Operating solely within one state.

log book: A book which all truck drivers must carry with them. In it, they record their daily records of hours, route, etc. The federal government specifies the form of the book and how to complete it.

MCSR: Motor Carrier Safety Regulations. These are the regulations which the federal Department of Transportation has set for truck drivers regarding safety. The regulations are published in a book which truckers often refer to as, simply, the MCSR or the DOT book. All interstate drivers are required to know and follow these rules.

one trip permit: A permit which allows a truck driver to haul cargo in a state. The driver purchases the permit at one of the ports of entry in the state.

ordinance: A law or statute.

permanent permit number: A number assigned to a truck by a state a truck travels in often. Carriers pay a fee for the number. Drivers often call these numbers their ICC numbers. The numbers are stenciled on the side of the cab.

placard: A small cardboard or metal sign displayed on a vehicle. It shows that some type of dangerous cargo is being carried. For example, it may say, "Flammable," "Dangerous," or "Oxygen."

port of entry: Any place where officials check the entry of goods into a state or country.

PUC: Public Utilities Commission. A state agency which regulates intrastate truck drivers.

statute: A law; an established rule or law.

33

► CHECKING THE FACTS

Circle the letter of the phrase that <u>best</u> completes each sentence or
<u>best</u> answers each question.

1. The DOT limits interstate drivers to
   A. 10 hours of driving or a total of 15 hours on the job at a time.
   B. 16 hours on the job, whether it's driving, loading or anything else at a time.
   C. 10 hours of driving and no more than 20 hours of combined driving and riding in the cab at a time.
   D. 8 hours of driving at a time. There are no limits on non-driving activities.

2. City governments are mainly concerned with setting
   A. rates for hauling in their city.
   B. weight limits and size limits for hauling in their city.
   C. truck routes, speed limits and truck loading and parking rules.
   D. speed limits.

3. What should you do if you aren't sure a bridge will support the weight of your rig?
   A. Call the county road department and ask.
   B. Look up the weight limit in your DOT book.
   C. Phone your dispatcher for instructions.
   D. Ask a local person what the weight limit is.

4. Who sets weight limits on county roads?
   A. the city
   B. the county
   C. the state
   D. the ICC

5. Who regulates intrastate commerce?
   A. the ICC or a similar agency
   B. the DOT
   C. the PUC or a similar agency
   D. the port of entry officials

6. Who regulates safety of interstate vehicles?
   A. the ICC or a similar agency
   B. the DOT
   C. the PUC or a similar agency
   D. the Department of Motor Vehicles or a similar agency

7. Where do you buy a one trip permit?
   A. at the county road department
   B. at the Department of Motor Vehicles
   C. at the State Capitol
   D. at a state port of entry

8. How do states decide how much to charge a carrier to travel in the state?
   A. Fee is based on the number of miles traveled in the state.
   B. Fee is based on the weight of the rig.
   C. Fee is based on the commodity carried.
   D. Fee is based on all of the above.

9. An interstate driver hauls freight
   A. within only one state.
   B. between one state and another, but not between one country and another.
   C. between states and/or between countries.
   D. in at least half of the states each year.

10. Every driver has to record hours on duty in his or her
    A. MCSR book.
    B. DOT book.
    C. port of entry book.
    D. log book.

■ GETTING THE MAIN IDEAS

Circle the letter of the phrase that <u>best</u> completes each sentence or <u>best</u> answers each question.

1. Rudy's company encouraged him to
   A. drive in violation of the DOT rules.
   B. follow the DOT rules.
   C. rest when he was tired by letting his co-driver take over.
   D. record his hours on duty in his book.

2. The main reason for the DOT regulations is
   A. to encourage competition in the trucking industry.
   B. to hold freight rates down.
   C. safety.
   D. to give the federal government something to do.

3. All truckers have to
   A. memorize the DOT rules.
   B. memorize the MCSR.
   C. carry their MCSR book at all times.
   D. know and follow the MCSR.

4. Who fills out the port of entry form?
   A. the driver
   B. the owner of the trucking firm
   C. only independent owner-operators
   D. only intrastate drivers

5. If a driver travels in a state often, he or she probably has
   A. a book of one trip permit coupons.
   B. a port of entry permit.
   C. a placard.
   D. a permanent permit number.

35

6. Interstate truck drivers have to follow
   A. city and county regulations.
   B. state speed limits and weight and size limits.
   C. the MCSR.
   D. all of the above.

7. Coast to coast, US laws regarding trucking
   A. are very different between areas and getting more different all the time.
   B. are more complex in populated areas than out in the country.
   C. are the same in each state, but minor rules vary from county to county.
   D. are becoming more similar all the time.

8. What does this statement mean: A trucker has to be part diplomat.
   A. You should know how to settle arguments between people.
   B. You are your company's public relations representative.
   C. You will be traveling to many different places.
   D. Be polite and don't sound like you know everything.

9. It's probably a good idea to
   A. teach other drivers what you know about the DOT rules and regs.
   B. carry the DOT book with you in the cab.
   C. drive only intrastate.
   D. carry a book of port of entry forms for states you travel in often.

10. The two branches of the federal government which regulate interstate truck drivers are
    A. the PUC and the ICC.
    B. the ICC and the DOT.
    C. the DOT and the PUC.
    D. the MCSR and the DOT.

★ GOING BEYOND THE FACTS AND IDEAS

1. What would you have done in Rudy's situation and why?

2. We have listed four hazards the trucking regulations are intended to avoid under the heading, "The Need for Regulations." What other hazards or problems might arise if we did away with all regulations?

3. This chapter touched on a lot of different types of regulations - speed limits, hours of service, weight limits, etc. Are there any types of regulations that you feel are unnecessary? If so, which ones might be eliminated and why? If not, why not?

4. Design a port of entry form that would have room for all of the information usually required on one.

Figure 4-1.   *Courtesy of Utility Trailer Mfg. Co.*

Chapter Four

THE DRIVER'S QUALIFICATIONS

BEFORE YOU READ | Most of the information in this chapter comes from the MSCR which we talked about in the last chapter. To help you read with an active mind, we've given you a study sheet on the next page. If you fill in the blanks as you read, you'll pick up the key ideas in the chapter, and you should find the questions at the end of it quite easy. You'll find the answers to these questions in the same order as these fill-in-the-blank questions. You should be able to answer questions one and two now as we covered the ideas in the last chapter. Can you?

BEFORE YOU READ   (cont.)

1. The Motor Carrier Safety Regulations (MCSR) apply to all drivers working

    in _____   _____.

2. Before a truck driver actually drives, she or he must become familiar

    with the whole _____.

3. A driver has to take three tests before he or she can driver for a carrier.

    These three tests are (1) _____

    (2) _____, and (3) _____.

4. What can you take with you and use when you take the written examination?

    _____.

5. What percentage of correct answers do you have to get on the written exam

    to get a "Certification of Written Examination"? _____

6. Who can give you a road test? (There are two answers.) _____

    _____ or _____.

7. What are the seven things you'll be tested on during the DOT road test?

    _____

    _____

    _____

    _____

    _____

    _____

    _____

8. How old must you be to qualify as an interstate driver? _____

9. You can lose your driving privilege as a trucker if you drive under the

    influence of _____.

10. Can a carrier set higher standards than those set by DOT? _____

11. What three documents must you have with you whenever you are driving?

    _____

| THREE REQUIRED TESTS | The Motor Carrier Safety Regulations require three tests of all drivers. Before driving a vehicle, a driver must take a *written* examination, a *road* test, and a *physical*. |

| THE WRITTEN TEST | MCSR 391.35 says that a person may not drive a motor vehicle unless she or he has first taken a written examination and has been issued a certificate of written examination. |

You will not have to take this test, however, until you are employed, or in some cases, about to be employed. The carrier will give it to you or designate someone else to give it to you.

The purpose of the exam is to *instruct*. Its purpose is to teach you the rules and regulations which apply to commercial vehicle safety. Since its purpose is instruction, you are allowed to take a copy of the MCSR with you and use it during the test. You may also take any other information sheets with you that your employer, instructor, etc., may have given you that pertain to the regulations. In other words, it's an "open-book" test. There is no time limit for completing the examination.

The test consists of 66 questions. They will cover your knowledge of the MCSR and hazardous materials regulations. While the exact questions on the test will vary, you'll probably find that they are very much like those on the sample exam shown in Figure 4-3.

Trailmobile offers an Asphalt and Hot Commodity Tank, available in both Steel and Aluminum design engineered with stronger bumpers, sure stepladder rungs, and, for the first time, a volume surge vent.

Figure 4-2. Commodities this tanker might carry are governed by the MSCR and hazardous materials regulations. *Courtesy of Pullman Trailmobile*

ATA Form C0690, Reorder from: American Trucking Associations, Inc.
1616 P Street, N.W.
Washington, D. C. 20036   11-74

Examinee's Name _____   Date _____

INSTRUCTIONS All of the questions contained herein are based on the United States Department of Transportation's Federal Motor Carrier Safety Regulations. Applicants for the position of commercial driver are required to take the examination.

Each question has four answers but only one is right. Your job on each question is to read all of the answers and then to pick the one answer you think is right. Write the number of the correct answer in the answer space to the right of the question. Do not pick more than one answer for each question.

Here is a sample question to show you what is to be done:

The Federal Motor Carrier Safety Regulations were written for: 1. vehicle makers; 2. drivers only 3. carriers only; 4. drivers and carriers;

Answer _____

The right answer is number 4, "drivers and carriers," so you would write a 4 in the answer space to the right of the question.

Finally, be sure to answer every question and do not skip any pages. Keep in mind that most of the Regulations covered here are different from what is required of passenger car drivers; they apply to commercial bus and truck drivers. Again, pick only one answer for each question. There is no time limit on the examination, but try to work as fast as you can.

---

1.   390.32 A motor carrier who is also a driver (owner-operator): 1. is not covered by the safety regulations; 2. must obey only those parts of the regulations which cover drivers; 3. must obey only those parts of the regulations which cover motor carriers; 4. must obey both the parts covering drivers and the parts covering motor carriers.   **Answer** _____

2.   391.11(b)(1) With only a few exceptions, the Federal Motor Carrier Safety Regulations say a driver must be: 1. at least 18 years old; 2. at least 19 years old; 3. at least 20 years old; 4. at least 21 years old.   **Answer** _____

3.   391.15(c)(2)(3) A driver cannot drive a motor vehicle: 1. For one year after a first offense conviction for a felony involving a commercial motor vehicle he was driving; 2. For one year after a first offense conviction for driving a commercial vehicle under the influence of alcohol or narcotics; 3. For one year after a first offense conviction for leaving the scene of an accident which resulted in personal injury or death; 4. For one year after a first offense conviction for any of the above.   **Answer** _____

4.   391.21(b)(7)(8)(10) Every driver applicant must fill out an application form giving; 1. a list of all vehicle accidents he was in during the previous 3 years; 2. a list of all of his motor vehicle violation convictions and bond forfeits (except for parking) during the previous 3 years; 3. a list of names and addresses of all of his employers during the previous 3 years; 4. all of the above.   **Answer** _____

5.   391.27(a)(b) At least once a year, a driver must fill out a form listing all motor vehicle violations (except parking) which he had during the previous 12 months. He must fill out the form: 1. even if he had no violations; 2. only if he was convicted; 3. only if he was convicted or forfeited bond or collateral; 4. only if the carrier requires it.   **Answer** _____

6.   391.33(a)(2) If a driver applicant has a valid certificate showing he passed a driver's road test: 1. the carrier must accept it; 2. the carrier may still require the applicant to take a road test; 3. the carrier cannot accept it; 4. the carrier may request a road test waiver from the Bureau of Motor Carrier Safety.   **Answer** _____

7.   391.41(b)(5) Persons with breathing problems which may affect safe driving 1. cannot drive; 2. cannot drive unless the vehicle has an emergency oxygen supply; 3. cannot drive unless another driver is along; 4. cannot drive except on short runs.   **Answer** _____

8.   391.41(b)(7) Persons with arthritis, rheumatism, or any such condition which may affect safe driving: 1. cannot drive unless they are checked by a doctor before each trip; 2. cannot drive; 3. cannot drive except when they are free of pain; 4. cannot drive unless another driver is along.   **Answer** _____

9.   391.41(b)(8) Persons who have ever had epilepsy: 1. cannot drive unless another driver is along; 2. cannot drive; 3. cannot drive on long runs; 4. cannot drive without monthly medical examinations.   **Answer** _____

10.   391.41(b)(9)(12)(13) In order to be able to drive, a person: 1. must not

14.   392.5(a)(1) A driver may not drink or be under the influence of any alcoholic beverage (regardless of alcoholic content): 1. within 4 hours before going on duty or driving; 2. within 6 hours before going on duty or driving; 3. within 8 hours before going on duty or driving; 4. within 12 hours before going on duty or driving.   **Answer** _____

15.   392.7 A driver must satisfy himself that service and parking brakes, tires, lights, and reflectors, mirrors, coupling and other devices are in good working order: 1. at the end of each trip; 2. before the vehicle may be driven; 3. only when he considers it necessary; 4. according to schedules set by the carrier.   **Answer** _____

16.   392.8 Which of the following must be in place and ready for use before a vehicle can be driven? 1. at least one spare fuse or other overload protector of each type used on the vehicle; 2. a tool kit containing a specified list of hand tools; 3. at least one spare tire for every four wheels; 4. a set of spark plugs.   **Answer** _____

17.   392.9(a)(3) If any part of the cargo or anything else blocks a driver's front or side views, his arm or leg movements, or his access to emergency equipment, the driver: 1. can drive the vehicle, but must report the problems at the end of the trip; 2. cannot drive the vehicle; 3. can drive the vehicle, but only at speeds under 40 miles per hour; 4. can drive the vehicle, but only on secondary roads.   **Answer** _____

18.   392.9(a) Any driver who needs glasses to meet the minimum visual requirements: 1. must drive only during daylight hours; 2. must always wear his glasses when driving; 3. must always carry a spare pair of glasses; 4. must not drive a motor vehicle.   **Answer** _____

19.   392.9(b) A driver may drive with a hearing aid: 1. if he always has it turn on while he is driving; 2. if he always carries a spare power source for it; 3. if he can meet the hearing requirements when he has it turned on; 4. if all of the above requirements are met.   **Answer** _____

20.   392.10(a) A driver required to stop at a railroad crossing should bring his vehicle to a stop no closer to the tracks than: 1. 5 feet; 2. 10 feet; 3. 15 feet; 4. 20 feet.   **Answer** _____

21.   392.10(a) Shifting gears is not permitted: 1. when traveling faster than 35 miles per hour; 2. a when moving across any bridge; 3. when crossing railroad tracks; 4. when traveling down a hill steeper than 10 degrees.   **Answer** _____

22.   392.13 Drivers of motor vehicles not required to stop at drawbridges without signals: 1. must drive at a rate of speed which will permit a stop before reaching the lip of the draw; 2. must sound their horn before crossing; 3. can proceed across without reducing speed; 4. must slow down only if directed to by an attendant.   **Answer** _____

23.   392.15(a) A driver turning his vehicle should begin flashing his turn signal: 1. at least 50 feet before turning; 2. at least 60 feet before turning; 3. at least 75 feet before turning; 4. at least 100 feet before turning.   **Answer** _____

24.   392.16 Which of the following is true? 1. if a seat belt is installed in the vehicle, a driver must have it fastened before beginning to drive; 2. a driver may or may not use the seat belt, depending on his judgment. 3. seats belts are not necessary on heavier vehicles; 4. a driver must use his seat belt only if required to by the carrier.   **Answer** _____

25.   392.21 When a motor vehicle cannot be stopped off the traveled part of the highway, the driver: 1. must keep driving; 2. may stop, but shall get as far off the traveled part of the highway as possible; 3. may stop, but shall make sure that the vehicle can be seen as far as possible to its front and rear; 4. may stop if he has to, but should do both 2 and 3 above.   **Answer** _____

26.   392.22(b)(1) If a vehicle has a breakdown the driver must place one emergency signal: 1. 100 feet in front of the vehicle in the center of the lane it occupies; 2. 100 feet in back of the vehicle in the center of the lane it occupies; 3. 10 feet in front or back of the traffic side; 4. at all of the above locations.   **Answer** _____

27.   392.22(b)(1)(i) If a vehicle has a breakdown on a poorly-lit street or highway, the driver shall place on the traffic side: 1. a reflective triangle; 2. a lighted red electric lantern; 3. a red reflector; 4. any one of the above.   **Answer** _____

28.   392.22(b)(2)(iii) No emergency signals are required for a vehicle with a breakdown if the street or highway lighting is bright enough so it can be seen at a distance of: 1. 100 feet; 2. 200 feet; 3. 500 feet; 4. 750 feet.

Figure 4-3. This is a standard DOT written exam that is used throughout the US. It is an open-book test and must be corrected to 100%. You are seeing only part of the test here. The entire test has 66 questions.

THE WRITTEN TEST (cont.)

When you have finished the test, the person who gave it will tell you which questions, if any, you answered incorrectly. Then, if you have some incorrect answers, the person can give you additional instruction as needed, based on the results of the exam. Whether you do it the first time you take the test, or after you've had additional instruction, you will eventually get 100% on the written exam. This shows that you know the MCSR regulations and the regulations about hazardous materials.

When you have received a score of 100% on the test, you will be given a "Certification of Written Examination." It may be like the one which appears opposite. This is one of three certificates which you must carry whenever you drive.

The test itself is not a big obstacle. The real test is MCSR 391.5 which says each motor carrier and each driver shall know and be familiar with the rules given in the DOT regs, chapter 391.1 through 391.4 which cover qualifications, duties, exemptions and definitions. This puts the responsibility for knowing the rules right onto your shoulders. In a tight spot, the excuse, "I didn't know the DOT rules," is not going to be acceptable.

CERTIFICATION OF WRITTEN EXAMINATION

THIS IS TO CERTIFY THAT THE PERSON WHOSE SIGNATURE APPEARS BELOW HAS COMPLETED THE WRITTEN EXAMINATION UNDER MY SUPERVISION IN ACCORDANCE WITH THE PROVISIONS OF SECTION 391.35 OF THE MOTOR CARRIER SAFETY REGULATIONS.

_____   _____
(SIGNATURE OF PERSON TAKING   DATE OF
        EXAMINATION)   EXAMINATION)

_____
          (LOCATION OF EXAMINATION)

_____   _____
(SIGNATURE OF EXAMINER)   (TITLE)

_____
(ORGANIZATION AND ADDRESS OF EXAMINER)

CTA Form - Sa58c Rev. 572

Figure 4-4.

| THE ROAD TEST | Now let's go through what MCSR 393.31 has to say about the road test. We'll stick pretty close to their wording so you begin to become familiar with the way the DOT says things. |

MCSR 393.31 A person shall not drive a motor vehicle without having first successfully completed a road test and having been given a certificate of driver's road test in accordance with this section.

A. The road test shall be given by the motor carrier or a person designated by the motor carrier. However, a driver who is a motor carrier must be given the test by another person. The test shall be given by a person who is competent to evaluate and determine whether the person who takes the test has demonstrated capability in operating the vehicle and associated equipment that the motor carrier intends to assign.

B. The test must be of sufficient duration to enable the person giving the test to evaluate the skill of the person taking it in handling the motor vehicle. As a minimum, the person taking the test, must be

Figure 4-5. This is an International Cargostar straight truck or bobtail. Is it a conventional or cab-over? *Courtesy of International Harvester*

THE ROAD TEST (cont.)

tested while operating the type of motor vehicle to be assigned by the motor carrier, and on the skill demonstrated at performing each of the following operations:

1. Performing a pre-trip inspection

2. Placing the vehicle in operation and smoothness of handling the vehicle

3. Coupling and uncoupling combination units if the equipment the driver will be operating includes combination units

4. Backing and parking the vehicle

5. Braking and slowing the vehicle by means other than braking

6. Operating the vehicle in traffic and while passing other vehicles

7. General driving ability and habits, handling freight, and knowledge of rules and regulations

10-77

ATA Form C0790

American Trucking Associations
1616 P Street
Washington, D.C. 20036

RECORD OF ROAD TEST

Instructions to Evaluator: Check (✔) items which the driver performs satisfactorily, use ''X'' where performance is unsatisfactory. Any item not evaluated, leave blank.

Driver's Name _____ Home Address _____

Social Security No. _____ License No. _____ State _____ Class _____

Equipment Driven: Tractor Truck _____ Trailer(s) _____
                          (Make & Model)   (Body Type & Length of Each)

Length
of Test _____ Mi. From/In _____ To _____

Start Time _____ Finish Time _____ Weather Conditions _____

PART 1 — PRE-TRIP INSPECTION AND EMERGENCY EQUIPMENT

Checks general condition approaching unit _____

Checks fuel, oil, water and for excessive oil on engine _____

Checks around unit — Tires, Lights, trailer hook-up, brake and light lines, doors and inspects for body damage _____

Tests steering, brake action, tractor protection valve, and parking brake _____

Checks horn, windshield wipers, mirrors, emergency equipments; reflectors, flares, fuses, tire chains (if necessary), fire extinguisher _____

Checks instruments for normal readings _____

Checks dashboard warning lights for proper functioning. _____

Cleans windshield, windows, mirrors, lights and reflectors _____

PART 2 — PLACING VEHICLE IN MOTION AND USE OF CONTROLS

A. MOTOR

Places transmission in neutral before starting engine _____

Starts engine without difficulty _____

Checks instruments at regular intervals _____

Maintains proper engine rpm while driving _____

B. BRAKES

Knows proper use of and checks tractor-protection valve (trailer air supply valve) _____

Tests service brakes _____

Tests parking brake before starting _____

Builds full pressure in air tanks before starting _____

C. CLUTCH AND TRANSMISSION

Starts unit moving smoothly _____

Selects proper gears _____

Uses clutch properly _____

D. LIGHTS (If tested at night)

Adjusts speed for range of headlights _____

Dims lights when approaching another vehicle or following other traffic _____

PART 3 — COUPLING AND UNCOUPLING

Connects glad hands to trailer to apply trailer brakes before coupling _____

Connects glad hands and light line properly _____

Couples without difficulty _____

Raises landing gear fully after coupling _____

Visually checks king pin assembly to be certain of proper coupling _____

Checks coupling by applying hand value or tractor-protection valve (trailer air supply valve) and gently appling pressure by trying to pull away from trailer _____

Assures himself that surface will support trailer before uncoupling _____

PART 4 — BACKING AND PARKING

A. BACKING

Gets out and checks area before backing _____

Understands and utilizes mirrors properly _____

Signals when backing (if appropriate) _____

Avoids backing from blind side _____

B. PARKING (CITY)

Parks without hitting any other vehicles or stationary objects _____

Parks correct distance from curb _____

Secures unit properly — sets parking brake, transmission in correct gear, shuts off engine, blocks wheels (when necessary) _____

Carefully enters traffic from parked position _____

C. PARKING (ROAD)

Parks off pavement _____

Uses emergency warning signal or devices when necessary _____

Secures unit properly _____

Figure 4-6 (Front side). A form similar to this one may be used to test your driving skills. Are there some areas in which you can already claim proficiency?

PART 5 — SLOWING AND STOPPING

Uses clutch and gears properly   _____
Gears down properly before descending hills   _____
Starts without rolling back   _____
Test brakes at top of hills   _____
Uses brakes properly on grades   _____
Makes proper use of mirrors   _____
Plans stop far enough in advance to avoid hard braking   _____
Stops clear of crosswalks   _____

PART 6 — OPERATING IN TRAFFIC, PASSING AND TURNING

A. TURNING

Signals intention to turn well in advance   _____
Gets into proper lane well in advance of turn   _____
Checks traffic conditions and turns only when intersection is clear   _____
Restricts traffic from passing on right when preparing to complete right hand turn   _____
Completes turn promptly and safely and does not impede other traffic   _____

B. TRAFFIC SIGNS AND SIGNALS

Plans stop in advance and adjusts speed correctly   _____
Obeys all traffic signals   _____
Comes to a complete stop at all stop signs   _____

C. INTERSECTIONS

Yields right of way   _____
Checks for cross traffic regardless of traffic controls   _____
Enters all intersections prepared to stop if necessary.   _____

D. GRADE CROSSINGS

Stops at a minimum 15 feet but not more than 50 feet before crossing if stop is necessary   _____
Selects proper gear and does not shift gears while crossing   _____
Knows and understands BMCS rules governing grade crossings   _____

E. PASSING

Allows sufficient space ahead for passing   _____
Passes only in safe locations   _____
Signals changing lanes before and after passing   _____
Warns driver ahead of his intention to pass   _____
Passes only when appropriate to avoid impeding other traffic   _____
Returns to right lane promply but only when safe to do so   _____

F. SPEED

Observes speed limits   _____
Drives at speed consistent with ability   _____
Adjusts speed properly to road, weather and traffic conditions   _____
Slows down in advance of curves, danger zones and intersections   _____
Maintains consistent speed where possible   _____

G. COURTESY AND SAFETY

Yields right of way   _____
Consistently strives to drive in safe manner   _____
Allows faster traffic to pass   _____
Uses horn only when necessary   _____

PART 7 — MISCELLANEOUS

A. GENERAL DRIVING ABILITY AND HABITS

Consistently alert and attentive   _____
Consistently is aware of changing traffic conditions   _____
Anticipates problems   _____
Performs routine functions without taking eyes from road   _____
Checks instruments regularly while driving   _____
Personal appearance is professional   _____
Remains calm under pressure   _____

B. USE OF SPECIAL EQUIPMENT (SPECIFY)

_____ _____

_____ _____

_____ _____

REMARKS:

_____

_____

_____

_____

GENERAL PERFORMANCE: Satisfactory _____ ; Needs Training _____ ; Unsatisfactory _____

QUALIFIED FOR: Straight Truck ☐;   Tractor-Semitrailer ☐;   Twin Trailers ☐;   Other Combination ☐

Special Equipment _____
(Specify)

_____ Date_____
Signature of Examiner

Figure 4-6 (Back side)

THE ROAD TEST (cont.)

C. The motor carrier shall provide a road test form on which the person who gives the test shall rate the performance of the person who takes it. (A sample *road test form* is shown in Figure 4-6). After the form is completed, it shall be signed by the person who gave the test.

D. After successful completion of the road test, the person who gave it shall complete a "Certification of Road Test." It may be like the one which appears in Figure 4-7.

The "Record of Road Test" shown in Figure 4-6 is used by a number of motor carriers. This form, or something like it, might be the one your examiner uses to test your driving skills. Therefore, you might want to study it and be sure that you become proficient in all of the areas listed on it. We will be covering all of these areas in future chapters of this book. Therefore, you might check off skills listed on it as you gain them. For example, after studying Chapters 6, 7, and 9, you should have gained proficiency in Part 2, "Placing Vehicle in motion and use of controls." After studying Chapters 9 and 13, you should be able to check off all of the skills in Part 5, "Slowing and stopping," etc. If you use the chart this way as you study this book, you'll be using it opposite from the way your examiner would use it because he or she will check off only the areas where your skills are *unsatisfactory*. However, it should help you to make sure you are prepared for the test when you go to take it.

CERTIFICATION OF ROAD TEST

DRIVER'S NAME _____
SOCIAL SECURITY NO. _____
OPERATOR'S OR CHAUFFEUR'S LICENSE NO. _____
_____ STATE _____
TYPE OF POWER UNIT _____
TYPE OF TRAILER(S) _____
IF PASSENGER CARRIER, TYPE OF BUS _____

THIS IS TO CERTIFY THAT THE ABOVE-NAMED DRIVER WAS GIVEN A ROAD TEST UNDER MY SUPERVISION ON _____ 19 _____ CONSISTING OF APPROXIMATELY _____ MILES OF DRIVING.

IT IS MY CONSIDERED OPINION THAT THIS DRIVER POSSESSES SUFFICIENT DRIVING SKILL TO OPERATE SAFELY THE TYPE OF COMMERCIAL MOTOR VEHICLE LISTED ABOVE.

_____   _____
(SIGNATURE OF EXAMINER)   (TYPE)

_____
(ORGANIZATION AND ADDRESS OF EXAMINER)
CTA Form Sa58b Rev. 572

Figure 4-7.

THE PHYSICAL EXAM | The DOT is also concerned with the health and physical condition of interstate drivers. MCSR 391.41 requires applicants to have a physical exam by a physician to see if they meet the physical requirements.

As you read in Chapter Two, you must have a valid medical certificate if you expect your Class 1 or Class 2 license to be valid. This medical certificate must be approved. Who approves it? The Federal Highway Administration of the US Department of Transportation does, and your state's Department of Motor Vehicles (although the department may have a slightly different name in your state). That's it. No one else can approve it.

One of your responsibilities as a driver is to have a medical examination every two years. The first time you'll need one is just before you apply for your Class 1 or Class 2 heavy-duty truck driver's license. Then, you must be re-examined *every 24 months*. In addition, MCSR 391.45 says this: If a driver's ability to perform normal duties has been lessened by a mental or physical injury or disease, the driver must be re-examined even though the two-year period may not be up.

Here's how you go about getting the exam. Get a medical examination from a doctor. Have the doctor complete a Physical Examination Form like the one shown in Figure 4-8. If the Physical Examination Form doesn't include a Medical Examiner's Certificate, have the doctor complete one of them too. (Notice the certificate in the lower, left-hand corner of the form, Figure 4-8.) Then, take both forms to the place where you apply for your Class 1 or Class 2 license.

● *Physical Requirements*

The physical requirements for interstate drivers are listed in the DOT book (MCSR). You might wish to refer to it right now to be sure that you meet all of the qualifications. Some handicaps disqualify a person from driving interstate. The types of things which do are those which might interfere with safe driving.

However, even if you do have a handicap which would normally disqualify you from driving interstate, you may be able to get an exception declared in your case. That is, you may be able to obtain a *waiver* from the Department of Transportation. MCSR 391.49 says that if a person is handicapped, but the handicap does not interfere with the safe operation of a motor vehicle, the DOT may issue a waiver allowing the person to drive in interstate commerce. However, a person with a waiver is not allowed to drive vehicles transporting passengers or carrying hazardous materials.

QUALIFICATIONS
FOR
DRIVERS │ MCSR 391.11 lists the following qualifications for drivers:

A. A person must be qualified to drive a motor vehicle. Motor carriers may not hire or permit a person who is not qualified to drive a motor vehicle.

B. A person is qualified if he or she -

   1. Is at least 21 years old;

   2. Can read and speak English well enough to *talk to the public, understand highway traffic signs and signals, respond to official inquiries,* and *make the required entries on reports;*

   3. Can, by reason of experience or training, safely operate the type of motor vehicle which she or he will drive;

PHYSICAL EXAMINATION FORM

(MEETS DEPARTMENT OF TRANSPORTATION REQUIREMENTS)

ATA Form C0730
American Trucking Assns., Inc.
1616 P Street, N.W.
Washington, D.C. 20036   4-74

To Be Filled In By Examining Physician *(Please Print)*:

New Certification ☐

Recertification ☐

Driver's Name _____

Soc. Sec. No. _____ Date of Birth _____ Age _____

Health History: Height _____ ft. _____ in.   Weight _____ lbs.

Yes	No		Yes	No		Yes	No	
☐	☐	Asthma	☐	☐	Nervous Stomach	☐	☐	Head or spinal injuries
☐	☐	Kidney disease	☐	☐	Rheumatic Fever	☐	☐	Seizures, fits, convulsions, or fainting
☐	☐	Tuberculosis	☐	☐	Muscular disease	☐	☐	Extensive confinement by illness or injury
☐	☐	Syphilis	☐	☐	Psychiatric disorder	☐	☐	Any other nervous disorder
☐	☐	Gonorrhea	☐	☐	Cardiovascular disease	☐	☐	Suffering from any other disease
☐	☐	Diabetes	☐	☐	Gastrointestinal ulcer	☐	☐	Permanent defect from illness, disease or injury

If answer to any of the above is yes, explain: _____

General appearance and development: Good _____   Fair _____   Poor _____

Vision: For Distance: Right 20/ _____   Left 20/ _____
☐ Without corrective lenses   ☐ With corrective lenses, if worn
Evidence of disease or injury: Right _____   Left _____
Color Test _____
Horizontal field of vision: Right _____ °   Left _____ °

Hearing: Right ear _____   Left ear _____
Disease or injury _____

Audiometric test: *(if audiometer is used to test hearing)*   _____ Decibel loss at 500 Hz _____ at 1,000 Hz _____ at 2,000 Hz _____

Throat: _____

Thorax: Heart _____
If organic disease is present, is it fully compensated? _____
Blood pressure: Systolic _____   Diastolic _____
Pulse: Before exercise _____   Immediately after exercise _____
Lungs _____

Abdomen: Scars _____   Abnormal masses _____   Tenderness _____
Hernia: Yes _____   No _____   If so, where? _____   Is truss worn? _____

Gastrointestinal: Ulceration or other disease   Yes _____   No _____

Genito-Urinary: Scars _____   Urethral discharge _____

Reflexes: Rhomberg _____
Pupillary _____   Light R _____   L _____
Accommodation Right: _____   Left _____
Knee jerks: Right: Normal _____   Increased _____   Absent _____
Left: Normal _____   Increased _____   Absent _____
Remarks: _____

Extremities: Upper _____   Lower _____   Spine _____

Laboratory and Other Special Findings: Urine: Spec. Gr. _____   Alb. _____   Sugar _____
Other Laboratory Data (Serology, etc.) _____
Radiological Data _____   Electrocardiograph _____

General Comments: _____

MEDICAL EXAMINER'S CERTIFICATE
I certify that I have examined

_____
[Driver's name (Print)]

in accordance with the Motor Carrier Safety Regulations (49 CFR 391.41-391.49) and with the knowledge of his duties, I find him qualified under the regulations.
☐ Qualified only when wearing corrective lenses
☐ Qualified only when wearing a hearing aid
A completed examination form for this person is on file in my office at

_____
Address

_____
(Date of examination)   (Name of examining doctor (Print))

_____
(Signature of examining doctor)

_____
(Signature of driver)

_____
(Address of driver)

The following to be completed only when the visual test is conducted by a licensed optometrist.

_____
[Date of Examination]

_____
[Name of Optometrist (Print)]

_____
[Address of Optometrist]

_____
[Signature of Optometrist]

Figure 4-8.   The physician who examines you may use a form very similar to this one.   She or he will be looking especially for any disability which might interfere with the safe operation of a vehicle.

4. Can determine if the cargo is safely loaded and secured against movement;

5. Is familiar with the professional methods of securing cargo;

6. Meets the physical requirements stated under MCSR 391.41;

7. Has a valid operator's license;

8. Has provided the employer with a list of any violations for the previous 12 months (this is done every year after the initial employment);

9. Is not disqualified to operate motor vehicles;

10. Has completed the road test;

11. Has completed the written test; and

12. Has completed and given to the motor carrier which employs him or her an application for employment in accordance with the DOT requirements.

● *Reasons for Disqualification*

As rule number nine suggests, a driver can be disqualified from driving in interstate commerce. A driver who fails to pass the physical examination might be disqualified from driving interstate. However, that driver may still be allowed to drive locally. MCSR 391.15 lists some other reasons for disqualifying a driver. If any of the following things have happened to a driver, a carrier is barred from hiring him or her, and she or he may not drive a motor vehicle in interstate commerce:

A. The driving privilege has been lost. (MCSR 392.42 says that if your license to drive has been either revoked, suspended or withdrawn, you *must* let your employer know *by the end of the next business day*.)

B. The potential driver has been convicted of criminal misconduct. Examples of criminal misconduct are -

    ● Driving under the influence of alcohol or an amphetamine or narcotic drug

    ● Committing a crime involving the known transportation, known possession, or unlawful use of an amphetamine or narcotic drug

    ● Leaving the scene of an accident which resulted in injury or death

    ● Committing a felony involving the use of a motor vehicle

    (These are only *examples* of criminal misconduct. There are many others that will also disqualify a person from driving interstate.)

QUALIFICATIONS FOR DRIVERS   (cont.)

● *Setting More Rigid Standards*

The standards for drivers given in the MCSR are *minimum* standards for interstate drivers. In other words, all interstate drivers must at least meet these qualifications and standards. If a motor carrier, an employer, wants to set *higher* or *more rigid* standards, it can. MCSR 391.1 allows for this.

DRIVERS'
RECORDS | MCSR 391.51 requires *carriers* to keep specified records in the drivers' personnel files in the company office. These records are -

1. The driver's employment application, including

      ● A list of traffic *violations* for the previous 3 years

      ● A list of traffic *accidents* for the previous 3 years

2. Information received from past employers, including reports on

      ● Reliability,

      ● Honesty,

      ● Good moral character,

      ● Ability to get along well with others, and

      ● Previous accident record.

3. Driving record as furnished by state motor vehicle agencies

4. Completed road test and certificate or alternative evidence of driving ability

5. Written examination on safety regulations and certificate

6. Physical examination certificate

7. Any other pertinent information related to the driver's performance and qualifications

In addition, the DOT requires that the driver also carries specified documents. The driver must have the following things in his or her possession:

      ● Certificate of written test   (MCSR 391.35)

      ● Certificate of road test   (MCSR 391.31)

      ● Medical examiner's certificate   (MCSR 391.41)

A driver also has to carry a log book while on duty. We haven't listed it here because it isn't a *document*. It is a *record* of the driver's on-duty hours.

SUMMARY

In this chapter, we summarized the qualifications which the US DOT has set for interstate drivers. We began by discussing the three tests which a driver has to pass before driving interstate and then talked about basic qualifications like age.

The first test a person has to pass is a written test on the MCSR. It is "open-book" and untimed. To pass it, you must get 100% correct because it is designed to teach you the DOT rules. If you don't get 100% the first time you take it, you can take it again later. You don't want to just learn the rules for the test and forget them, because as an interstate driver, you must know all of the DOT rules at all times.

The second test, the road test, is given to you by someone who can do a good job of testing your skills as a driver. Usually, your new employer will give you the test. You'll be tested on the type of vehicle you'll be driving. Besides testing your driving skills, the road test examines other skills needed by truckers. For example, it tests your ability to do a pre-trip inspection on your rig and to handle cargo. (Many of the chapters in this book coincide with the skills tested on the road test.)

The final exam takes a look at your health and physical condition and it is given by a medical doctor. The DOT lists a number of disabilities which a person can't have if he or she is going to drive interstate. The types of disabilities listed are those which would interfere with safe driving. Every two years, drivers have to be re-examined by a doctor. They also have to be re-examined if they become ill.

Besides passing the above three tests, drivers have to meet some other qualifications. They have to be at least 21 years old. They must have the correct driver's license. They must be able to speak English up to a standard set by the DOT. And, they have to fill out an employment application which includes a list of all their traffic violations and accidents for the previous three years.

We ended the chapter by listing some records which the employer has to keep on file and naming the three documents which truckers have to carry in the cab: the certificate of written test, the certificate of road test, and the medical examiner's certificate.

GLOSSARY

combination: In trucking, this word refers to more than one unit which have been hooked together, or "coupled." A combination might be a truck and trailer, a tractor and semi-trailer, a tractor and two trailers, or some other "combination."

long-line: Long-line is usually used to refer to interstate trucking. A long-line driver is an interstate driver.

waiver: A written statement which does away with a previous claim or right. A waiver usually refers only to one person or one specific situation.

Circle the letter of the phrase that <u>best</u> completes each sentence or <u>best</u> answers each question.

1. Drivers are required to be familiar with
   A. the freight rate rules.
   B. insurance rules.
   C. the DOT rules.
   D. the truck stop rules.

2. Which of the following is <u>not</u> a required DOT test?
   A. written test on regulations
   B. essay test on mechanical knowledge
   C. road test
   D. physical examination

3. Which of the following is <u>not</u> tested during the road test?
   A. performing a pre-trip inspection of vehicle and equipment
   B. coupling and uncoupling the tractor or truck and trailer
   C. general driving habits
   D. performing routine maintenance such as oil changes, tire changes

4. Interstate drivers must have a physical exam
   A. every 24 months.
   B. every 18 months.
   C. every 12 months.
   D. every 6 months.

5. A driver engaged in over-the-road interstate commerce must be at least _____ years old.
   A. 16
   B. 18
   C. 21
   D. 25

6. Which of the following is <u>not</u> a reason for disqualifying a driver from driving interstate?
   A. loss of driving privilege
   B. conviction of a felony
   C. being over 40 years old
   D. conviction for drunk driving

7. When hiring drivers, a motor carrier
   A. may not set requirements above MCSR standards.
   B. may make up its own driver qualifications.
   C. must send all drivers to the local authority for testing.
   D. may adopt requirements above MCSR standards.

8. Whenever a driver is driving, she or he must carry
   A. the original or copy of his or her employment application form.
   B. the original or copy of his or her current medical examiner's certificate.
   C. a list of state police locations in the states where he or she will drive.
   D. a copy of the vehicle's last vehicle condition report.

■ GETTING THE MAIN IDEAS

Put a plus (+) before the statement if it is true. Put a zero (0) before the statement if it is false.

_____ 1. If you haul things across state lines or national boundaries, you must follow all the regulations in the DOT driver's hand-book.

_____ 2. If you don't get 100% on the written examination, you can take it again as many times as you need to pass it.

_____ 3. Truck drivers have to take their DOT road tests at the same place where car drivers take their drivers' test. The people who work there are the only ones qualified to give the test.

_____ 4. Interstate owner-operators do not have to follow the MCSR regulations.

_____ 5. The purpose of the DOT road test is to allow the driver to demonstrate that he or she can safely operate the type of vehicle he or she will be operating.

_____ 6. The purpose of requiring the driver to perform a pre-trip in-spection is to demonstrate that she or he is a skilled truck mechanic.

_____ 7. Any good car driver can probably pass the road test for truck drivers. It is primarily a test of road courtesy.

_____ 8. All three DOT tests (written, road, physical) are designed to see that unsafe drivers do not become interstate truck drivers.

★ GOING BEYOND THE FACTS AND IDEAS

1. Describe a handicap which the DOT might waive so that a person might qualify as an interstate driver. Explain why it should be waived.

2. Evaluate the importance of the seven skills tested on the road test. Can you find one that is less important than the other seven? If you can, you might list the reasons why it is less important. If you can't, why can't you?

3. In the last chapter, we suggested that you carry the MCSR book with you in the cab. In this chapter, we said you can take it to the written exam with you. Would it be better to memorize all of the rules and regulations so that you wouldn't have to keep carrying it around? Why or why not?

4. There are a lot of rules and regulations in this chapter. Are there one or two you disagree with? If so, you might want to explain which ones you think should be disregarded or changed and why.

Figure 5-1.   *Courtesy of Pullman Trailmobile*

Chapter Five

GETTING TO KNOW YOUR RIG

BEFORE
YOU
READ We've already talked in this book about the importance of reading with an active mind. A man called Robinson understood the importance of this, and back in the 1940's provided us with a method of picking up information when we read.

Robinson called his method the SQ3R method of study. Over the years, a great many students have proven to themselves that it helps them to remember what they read. So we thought we'd suggest it here as a way of tackling some of the key chapters in this book - like this one. Before you read about specific truck components, systems and operations, you'll want to get a bird's-eye

view of the rig from the outside, the inside, and the bottom. That's why we've
called the three major sections of this chapter -

   A LOOK OUTSIDE,
   A LOOK INSIDE, and
   A LOOK UNDERNEATH.

Using the SQ3R approach as you read this chapter will help you to get the full
bird's-eye view. So, what is the SQ3R, and how do you do it?

● *Survey*

   To survey a chapter, you simply read each heading - major headings and
minor (or sub) headings. You don't want to spend a long time doing this - just
a couple of minutes. Remember, you are just doing a quick survey to get an
idea of what the chapter is going to cover.

● *Question*

   Now, go back to the beginning of the chapter and turn the first heading
into a question. Make it a question that makes sense to you. It doesn't have
to make sense to anyone else. And make it a question that you'd like to have
the answer to. For example, take the first heading above, "A Look Outside."
You might turn that heading into one of several questions. You might ask -

   "What's the outside of a rig like?"
   "What important parts are on the outside of a rig?"
    - *or even* -
   "Is there anything I don't know about the outside of a rig?"

Make it a question that makes sense to you. You're going to ask one kind of
question if you know a lot about rigs already, and a different kind of question
if you are a real novice. Maybe your question will arouse your curiosity, or
maybe it will help you realize how much you already know about the topic.

● *Read*

   Next, begin reading the section. Now you are reading with a purpose in
mind. What purpose? To answer the question you asked in Step Two. You're
going to be reading with an active mind, actively searching for an answer to
your own question.

● *Recite*

   Once you have finished reading the section, Robinson suggests as the
second "R" in his method, that you *recite* what you read. What he means by
recite is this: in your own words, say the answer to your question. You can
do this out loud if you are alone or studying with a friend, or you can do it
"in your head." The idea is to sort of compose an answer to your question.
Make it as good an answer as you can - the type you'd write on a test. This
will tell you if you really understood what you read.

BEFORE YOU READ (cont.)

You have now completed Steps 2, 3, and 4 for one section. (It should be a short section. If you've turned every minor heading into a question, and not just the major sections, it will be short.) Now, follow the same steps for each section in the chapter. If you wish, you can take notes as you go along. You could write the answers to your questions instead of actually reciting them.

● *Review*

The last obvious step is to review. A good way to do this is to ask the questions you asked in Step Two; then, answer each one - from memory - just as you did in Step Four.

That's it. *Survey, Question, Read, Recite, Review* - SQ3R. Now you can begin using it. So, what's your first question going to be? How about, "Why is it important to know the language?"

THE IMPORTANCE OF KNOWING THE LANGUAGE	The most important part of a new driver's training is willingness to get to know the terminology or language of the industry thoroughly. We've mentioned this before. You already know the terms for the major types of vehicles and licenses. Now, you'll get to know the names of the various parts and systems of the rig.

If you don't recognize or understand the terms being used by the professional drivers around you, you are going to find yourself outside looking in and wondering what all the conversation is about. It will sound like Greek. Basically, almost anyone can learn to *drive* a truck, but it's a real professional who knows every inch of the rig.

Suppose you're going down the road and suddenly you hear a rumbling noise from the rear differential. Unless you know what a rear differential is, there is no way that you can report the malfunction to the shop. Or, suppose you hear a squeal coming from the area around the alternator or generator. You can't very well call the shop and say, "That little round thing that sits on the side of the engine and has a belt driving a pulley is making funny noises." We guarantee you'll look ridiculous, and doubt if you'll be driving much longer.

Very few companies or owners will let a person take a truck out of a yard unless they are reasonably sure that the driver knows something about the mechanical equipment of the vehicle. Let's take a brief look at the outside, the inside, and underneath the vehicle to get the big picture. Then, in later chapters, we'll deal with some of these parts in more depth.

A LOOK OUTSIDE	To get to know your rig, you need to know the placement of several important items. All of these need to be checked periodically to see that they are functioning properly.

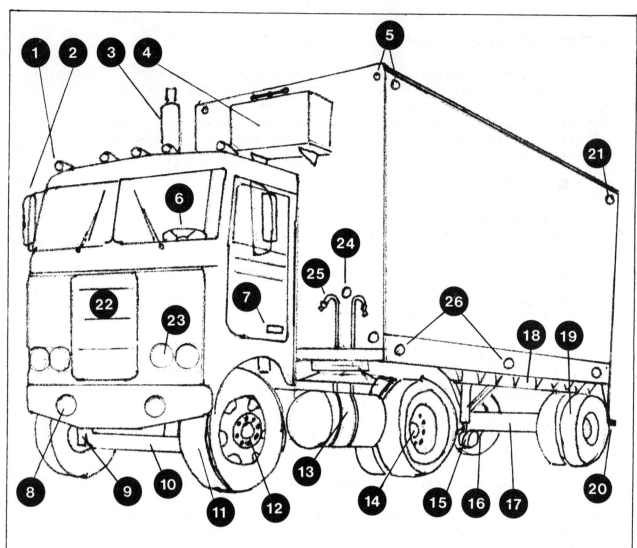

1	Cab marker lights	15	Landing gear
2	Mirror	16	Rear brake shoes
3	Muffler	17	Rear axle
4	Refer (Cooling unit)	18	Trailer frame
5	Trailer clearance lights	19	Trailer axle and wheels
6	Steering wheel	20	Dock bumper
7	Door handle	21	Rear clearance light
8	Driving lights	22	Radiator shutters
9	Axle spindle	23	Headlights
10	Front axle	24	Electrical plug connector
11	Front tire	25	Air hose couplings (Glad hands)
12	Lug nuts and studs	26	Front and side reflectors
13	Fuel tank (Saddle tank)		
14	Axle hub		

NOT VISIBLE

Trailer kingpin, located bottom center, two feet behind nose of trailer

Fifth wheel jaws and release lever on rear of tractor - connects with trailer kingpin

Figure 5-2.

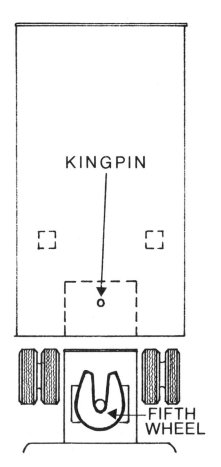

KINGPIN

FIFTH WHEEL

Figure 5-3. Kingpin on semi-trailer and fifth wheel on tractor, top view.

A LOOK INSIDE

● *Five Basic Systems*

There are five basic systems that go together to make up the total operation of the vehicle. For the rig to operate smoothly, all of these systems must be operating properly. A malfunction in one system will affect the proper operation of the other four systems as well.

The Air Brake System. The air brake system is the basic means for stopping the vehicle. It consists of everything which

A LOOK OUTSIDE (cont.)

Take a look at the diagram in Figure 5-2. As you read through the list of parts, try taking a mental walk around the rig. We sugtest that you ask yourself questions about each item. What's it for? These questions will get you thinking about why all of these parts exist on a truck. You may be surprised to figure out how much you already know, or can figure out on your own.

You may feel kind of silly asking yourself, "What's the door handle for?" But some questions will take more thought, like, "What's the rear axle for?" If you can't figure some of the answers out, or aren't sure of your answer, write the question down. Then, look for the answer as you read on in this book.

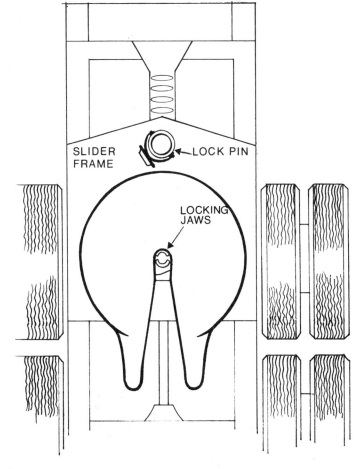

SLIDER FRAME   LOCK PIN

LOCKING JAWS

Figure 5-4. Slider-type fifth wheel, top view.

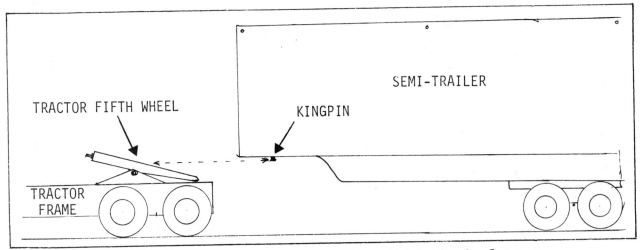

Figure 5-5. Trailer kingpin inserts into fifth wheel of tractor.

A LOOK INSIDE (cont.)

is involved in braking. The brake system is one of the most important, if not *the* most important system of any vehicle. It takes an engine to get a vehicle moving, but once it is moving the centrifugal force and weight of a vehicle becomes much more difficult to stop than it ever was to start.

WEDGE BRAKE

For example, let's say we have a 50,000 pound truck. We can start that truck with a 100 hp (horsepower) engine. That's a very small engine. It may take the truck quite a while to reach top speed, but stopping the truck often has to take place much quicker. While we had a mile and a half to build up road speed, we may be forced into coming to a complete stop within a distance of only 300 feet. Roughly speaking, it takes *ten times* the amount of hp to stop a rolling vehicle as it takes to start it. So, you can see how vital the braking system is to a vehicle.

The average air brake system functions by means of various *valves*, *gauges*, and *control levers* such as foot brakes and hand brakes. Some valves are more important to your safety and the safety of your vehicle than some other, minor valves. The "tractor protection valve" and the "RE4 valve" (relay emergency valve) on the trailer act as braking valves. They also act as safety valves in case of an emergency such

S CAM BRAKE

Figure 5-6. Two different types of air brakes. *Photographs courtesy of Rockwell International Corporation*

as loss of air pressure. The remaining fundamental parts of the braking system are the *brake shoes, brake drums, diaphragms, air tanks and lines.* (See
Figure 5-6.) We will discuss all of these parts in Chapter 9. They all play
an important part in the make-up of the air brake system.

The Electrical System. Without a doubt, the most complicated system contained in all vehicles is the electrical system. This system includes everything from the *batteries* to the individual *lights* on a rig. The complexity of
the electrical system creates a real problem for the average driver due to the
fact that the system is so technical that it "blows your mind." You have elec-
trically functioning instruments (such as the *generator* or *alternator*). You
have a *voltage regulator* which controls the surge of electricity flowing
through the system from the batteries, generator, regulators and dashboard instruments. So it becomes very complicated to try to follow the circuits in
case of shorts or other problems. Sometimes, the truck just won't start.

Unless it is a simple short circuit, it usually doesn't pay the driver to
start pulling wires apart or relocating wires. This will tend to create more
problems than are already there. Some very sophisticated instruments are required to check out any electrical system. Most drivers do not have them, and
wouldn't know how to use them. So, unless you are trained in trouble shooting
electrical problems, you should be very careful in making *any* electrical repairs.

We have mentioned, above, some of the major parts of the electrical system. Some of the other components are the *gauges* in the cab of the truck and,
of course, the *wiring* which connects everything (including the air conditioner,
heater and CB radio) to the power source. We will discuss the electrical system in more detail in Chapter 14.

The Lubricating System. The lubricating system of most engines functions
basically the same - whether the engine is a gasoline or diesel engine. The
primary purpose of a lubricating system is this: *to keep a film of oil between
all moving metal parts of an engine.* This film of oil cuts down friction.
That is, it keeps metal from rubbing against metal.

Oil is as essential to the engine as blood is to the human body. Your
body cannot function without blood, and the engine cannot function without oil.

Oil has other functions besides lubrication of the engine. Oil helps to
cool the engine internally, and it helps to keep the internal parts of the engine clean. Oil cools an engine through a *splash system.* As the oil drains
off the hot metal parts, it carries the heat back into the pan. From there,
it is circulated through an *oil cooler* that reduces the temperature of the oil
and returns it to the engine. The cleaning effect comes in when you drain the
oil from the engine at proper service intervals. As the oil drains from the
engine, it carries with it the contaminants that were inside the engine. Regular oil changes, at set intervals, are necessary because of this cleaning function. If you don't change the oil at the proper intervals, you will shorten
the life of your engine.

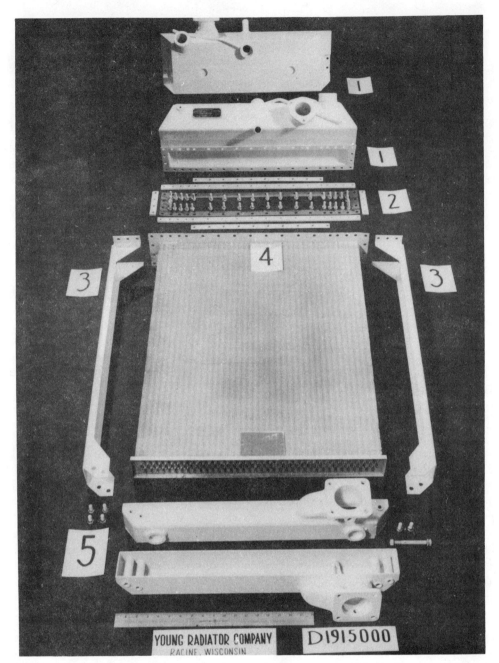

1. Radiator reservoir - top view of upper tank and bottom view of upper tank

2. Bolts and gaskets for assembly

3. Outside frame

4. Radiator core

5. Twin views of lower tank of radiator reservoir

Figure 5-7. A disassembled heavy-duty truck radiator. (Mono-Weld Model) *Photograph courtesy of Young Radiator Company, Racine, Wisconsin*

Figure 5-8. Radiator for heavy-duty truck. Includes patented deaerating top tank, efficient heavy-duty core with double lockseam tubes for extra strength and patented header joinings. *Photograph courtesy of Young Radiator Company, Racine, Wisconsin*

A LOOK INSIDE (cont.)

The Cooling System. The cooling system of any vehicle, regardless of the size of the truck, is very important. A minor water leak in a radiator or water pump, or a broken water hose could very well cause the loss of an engine. Loss of an engine will cost the owner several thousand dollars to replace it.

When we talk about a cooling system, we are talking about a number of important parts. Among the important parts are the *radiator, engine, water pump, thermostats, water hoses, fan belts* and *shutters*. Although most people think of the radiator when they think of the cooling system, the radiator is only one small part of the entire system.

The Fuel System. A diesel fuel system is basically a simple system, considering the size of the engine. You might think of the fuel system as beginning with the *fuel tank*. Then, there are *fuel lines* which carry the fuel to a *fuel pump*. The fuel pump supplies the fuel, under pressure, to the *fuel injectors*. The fuel injectors spray the fuel into the engine cylinders, creating the combustion that powers the engine. (See Figure 5-9.)

The fuel that goes into the injectors is not all used for ignition. Only a small percentage of it is used. The balance of the fuel goes through a *return line* from the injectors back to the fuel tank to be used again. There is a reason why the engine is designed to send an excess amount of fuel through the injectors. The injectors have very close tolerances and need to be lubricated during each combustion cycle. That is what the balance of the diesel fuel is used for; it actually lubricates the injectors.

Most diesels will have at least one or two *fuel filters* built into the system. These take out any dirt. Fuel filters are needed to protect the working parts of the fuel pump and injectors. It is very important that you make sure that you use clean fuel. We will discuss this system further when we talk about the gasoline and diesel engines in Chapters 12 and 13.

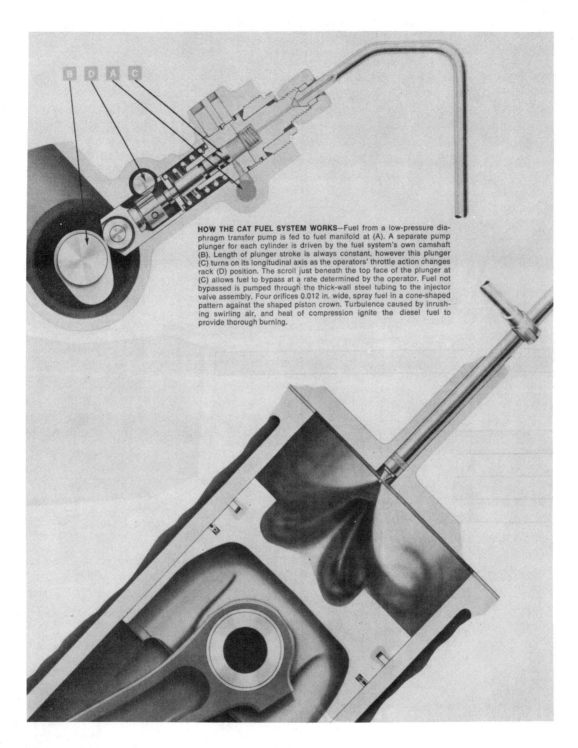

HOW THE CAT FUEL SYSTEM WORKS—Fuel from a low-pressure diaphragm transfer pump is fed to fuel manifold at (A). A separate pump plunger for each cylinder is driven by the fuel system's own camshaft (B). Length of plunger stroke is always constant, however this plunger (C) turns on its longitudinal axis as the operators' throttle action changes rack (D) position. The scroll just beneath the top face of the plunger at (C) allows fuel to bypass at a rate determined by the operator. Fuel not bypassed is pumped through the thick-wall steel tubing to the injector valve assembly. Four orifices 0.012 in. wide, spray fuel in a cone-shaped pattern against the shaped piston crown. Turbulence caused by inrushing swirling air, and heat of compression ignite the diesel fuel to provide thorough burning.

Figure 5-9. The top portion of this illustration is an individual fuel pump - one of a series of fuel pumps which makes up the complete fuel injection system. Fuel is pumped out the tubing on the right and into the cylinder shown in the lower half of the drawing. Combustion takes place there. *Courtesy of Caterpillar Tractor Company, Engine Division.*

A LOOK INSIDE (cont.)

● *The Instrument Panel*

A truck's dashboard (or instrument panel) monitors the operation of the truck's various systems and components for the driver as she or he moves down the road. It is the means of calculating the *positive* or *negative* function of any and all components in the vehicle. This monitoring function is the purpose of the gauges. Should a malfunction occur, the gauge is often the driver's only means of becoming aware of it. For example, the air pressure gauge will start to drop upon loss of air pressure anywhere in the rig's system. It doesn't matter how minute the loss of air pressure may be. The loss will be apparent on the gauge, regardless of the air loss amount. Thus, you can see that it is extremely important for every driver to check the gauges frequently while driving.

The numbered explanations are number-keyed to the picture of the Dodge cab interior in Figure 5-10. Like everything else, instrument panels will vary from truck to truck. Some truck interiors will be more complex, some simpler. Some will appear almost "space-age" compared to this older model. But you can use this panel to learn the types of gauges, valves, etc., which you will find in the trucks you drive.

1.	High Engine Temperature	Lighted when engine temperature rises above safe, normal temperature which is usually about 200° F (94° C).
2.	Low Oil Warning Light	Will flash when oil pressure has dropped below safe minimum which is 60 lbs.
3.	Speedometer	Indicates speed of travel.
4.	Water Temperature	Indicates the engine cooling system temperature. This gauge registers the temperature. The warning light (#1 above) lights up if the temperature has gone above the safe temperature in case you're not paying close attention to the gauge.
5.	Oil Pressure (in Engine)	Indicates the amount of oil pressure maintained by the engine while it is operating.
6.	Air Pressure	Shows the amount of pressure in the air reservoir.
7.	Ammeter	Shows the charging rate of the alternator.
8.	Transmission Heat Gauge	Shows the transmission temperature.
9.	Tachograph (RPM x 100) (Abbreviated "tach")	The rpm (revolutions per minute) are shown in numerals times 100. For example, 21 on the tach would mean 2100 rpm, 19 on the tach would mean 1900 rpm.

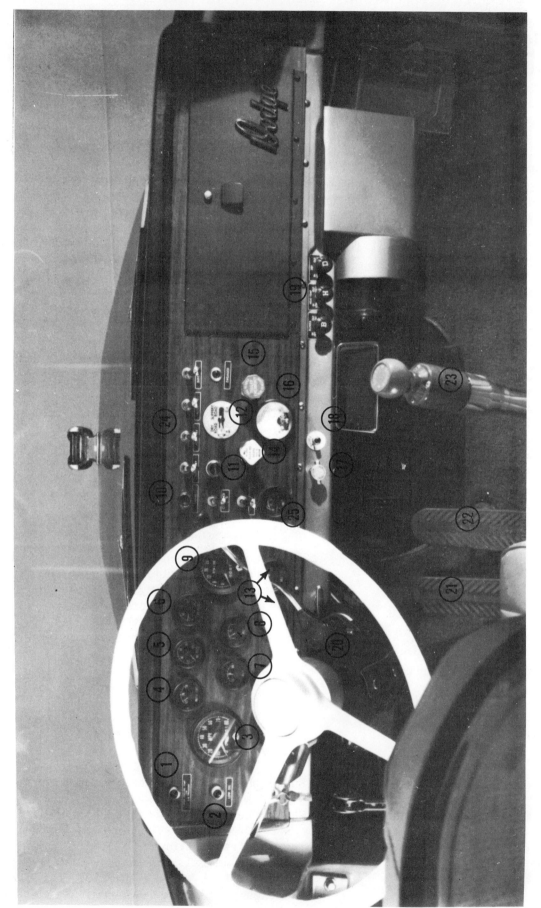

Instruction panel (also called control board or dashboard) of a Dodge 950. The numbers point to important gauges, buttons, switches, valves and pedals, each of which are briefly explained on the preceding and following pages. *Photo courtesy of Chrysler Corporation*

Figure 5-10.

10. Differential Lock Indicator

When the light is *on* it indicates that the differential lock is engaged between the rear ends (rear differential and front differential). The driver activates the lock from the cab. She or he locks both differentials when the truck is running on ground having poor traction, such as on a wet highway or a desert road with loose sand. The differentials are normally run in the unlocked position, so the light indicates to the driver that the lock is still engaged. (See Figure 5-17.)

11. Starter Button

Starts the engine.

12. Front Axle Air Limiting Valve

Limits the air pressure to the front wheel brakes. When the ground is slippery, the front wheel brakes will receive only 50% of the normal air pressure. The reduced air pressure keeps them from locking up and causing the driver to lose steering control.

13. Rear Axle Temperature Gauges

Registers the temperature of the rear differentials (or rear ends). (See Figure 5-17.)

14. Parking Brake Valve (Also called "Maxi Brake")

Driver operates this valve to set and release the parking brakes.

15. Tractor Protection Valve (Also called "Dynamite Valve" or "Trailer Emergency Valve")

Normally controlled by the driver who will push the valve in to charge the trailer with air when the air pressure hoses are hooked up to the trailer. When the driver drops the trailer (disengages it) and is bob tailing home in the tractor, he or she reverses the procedure. The driver pulls the valve out, stopping the air pressure from going out the open hoses.

16. Pyrometer (Engine Exhaust Temperature Indicator)

Indicates the engine exhaust temperature.

17. Windshield Wiper Valve

Operates the windshield wipers. There is usually one valve for each side of the windshield because the area is large. Thus, in a truck, the driver can set the wipers independently and can select fast or slow for each.

18. Windshield Washer Switch

Operates the windshield washer applicator.

A LOOK INSIDE   (cont.)

19. Heater/Defroster Switches   Operates heater and defroster.

20. Trailer Hand Valve   Operates the brakes on the trailer (or
     (Sometimes called the   trailers) only. This valve does not
     "Trailer Dolly Hand Brake")   affect the brakes on the truck or trac-
                                         tor at all; it is strictly for the towed
                                         units, regardless of the number of units
                                         being towed.

21. Brake Pedal   Operates all of the brakes in all of the
     (Also called the "Service   units under normal conditions.
     Brake Pedal")

22. Throttle Pedal   Controls the engine fuel.

23. Gearshift Lever   Used to shift the gears.

24. Dash and Truck Light Switches   Control the lights on the dashboard and
                                         exterior of the truck. (The dimmer
                                         switch is not shown in the picture, but
                                         it occupies a normal position on the
                                         floor, to the left of the driver and for-
                                         ward. It switches high and low beams.)

25. Voltmeter   Basically, shows the charging rate of
                                         the alternator and the condition of the
                                         battery. Shows whether they are in a
                                         condition of charge or discharge.

26. Hand Throttle   Used to increase the idling speed of the
     (This is the T-handle lever   engine. You pull the throttle out and
     located behind the steering   then give it a slight twist clockwise in
     wheel, inside, next to the   order to lock it in place. Unless the
     trailer hand valve.)   throttle is locked in place, it may slide
                                         back in, allowing the engine to idle back
                                         down.

Figure 5-11. *Photo by H. Haase*

Figure 5-12. Another shot of a Dodge interior. You might notice the *electrical terminal block* which, in this model, fits beneath the heater. This is the terminal where all electrical wires connect. From the terminal block, the wires run into the engine compartment, and from there, into the trailer. All wires running from the terminal block are usually color coded or numbered for easy identification throughout each rig. Where the wires leave the terminal block, they are usually incorporated into what is called a *loom* or *harness*. From the tractor, the harness will sometimes travel back to where the trailer plug connects. The wires in the trailer plug take care of the trailer lights, operate the directional signals and stop light switch. In other words, they supply power for the entire light system on the trailer. *Courtesy of Chrysler Corporation*

A LOOK UNDERNEATH There's a lot to get to know in a rig. The following illustrations are what a driver's eye sees as she or he approaches a vehicle. These illustrations show the component parts that are beneath the vehicle - parts the average person is unaware of. The average person may not even know what suspension is, let alone know how many different kinds there are. And the same goes for many other parts of a rig, from different kinds of fuel tanks to different types of construction. To the average person, a truck is a truck, and they are all alike. But to the experienced driver, each truck is different.

Heavy-duty diesel tractors are an assembled unit with many different components. Today, you have a choice of three basic engines, *an in-line six-cycle diesel, a V-8 diesel,* or *a V-12 diesel.* (The V simply means that the engine block is shaped like a V.) When it comes to transmissions, again you have a choice of two or three kinds. Some of the most commonly used transmissions are those manufactured by Eaton Corporation and Spicer. The list of component parts goes on and on. Even though you may have a Mack truck, you won't necessarily have Mack components in it. You could have a Cummins engine and Timken rear ends. It's strictly who specs out (or selects parts for) the truck at the time of purchase. The component parts in the truck will depend on the buyer's own preference for engines, gear trains, suspension systems (or "undercarriage"), etc.

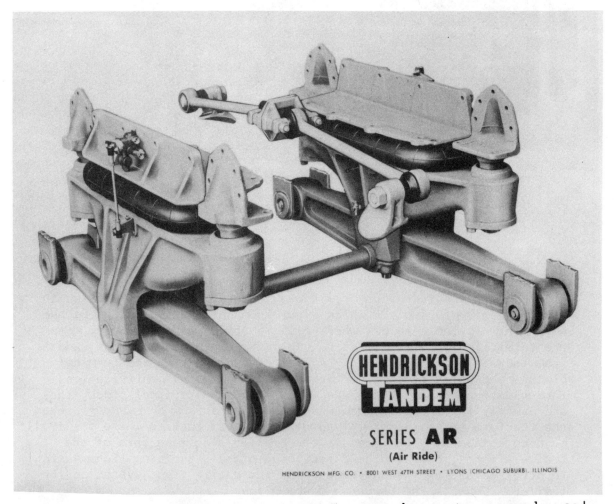

Figure 5-13. Hendrickson's "Air Ride" suspension system commonly used on three-axle road tractors and trucks. *Courtesy of Hendrickson Mfg. Co., Tandem Division*

68

A LOOK UNDERNEATH (cont.)

● *Suspensions*

The *suspension system* on a truck is similar to the suspension system on a pickup truck. It supports the body and frame of the truck and consists of the *springs* and the *mounting brackets* or *hangers*. The lower part rests on the rear or front axles, allowing the axles to move up and down with the ground changes. The suspension system must be many times heavier for a truck than for a pickup. It must be heavier because it has to handle the much greater weight of the vehicle.

There are a number of different suspension systems. The type needed on a rig depends upon what the driver is going to haul. It is necessary to select the specific type of suspension for the operation in which the driver will be engaged. Such things as whether the truck will be used on-highway or off-highway need to be considered. (When we refer to "off-highway" or "off-the-road" operations, we're referring to trucks, such as dump trucks, which spend a good part of the driving time off the road over rough ground. A dump truck requires a much heavier suspension system than a truck being driven entirely on a super highway.)

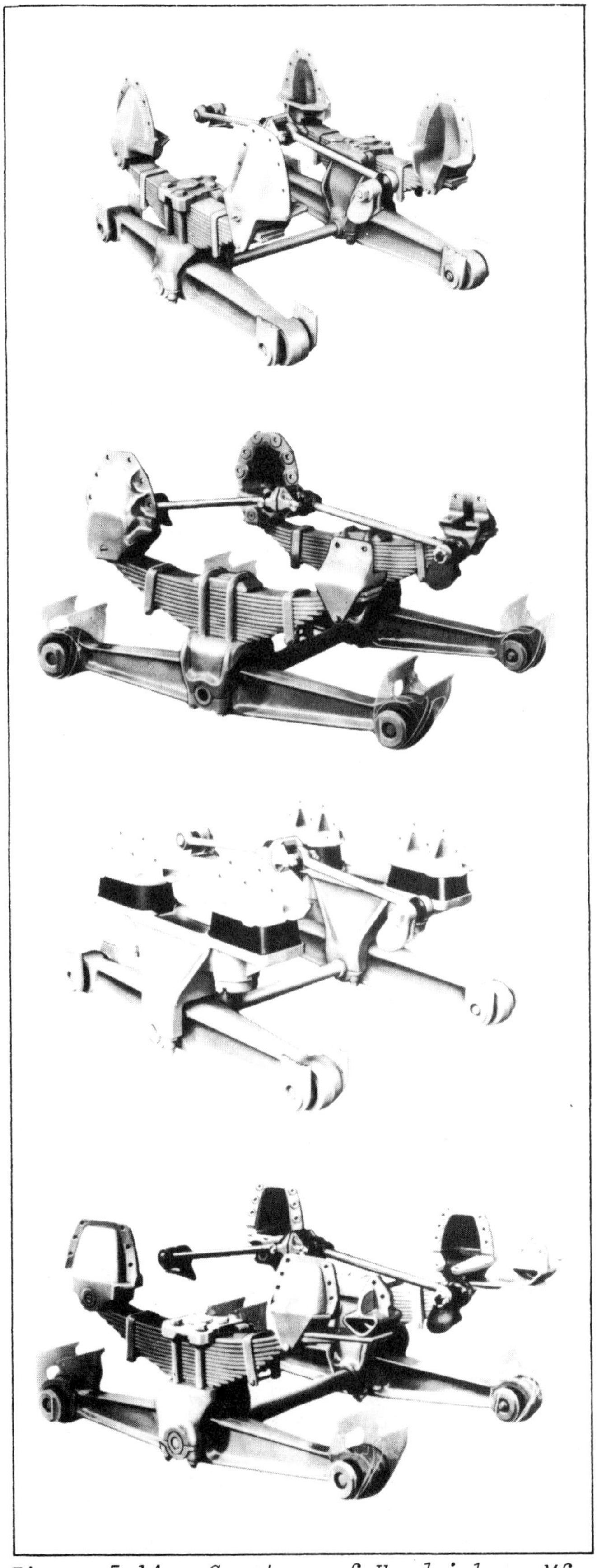

Figure 5-14 illustrates four common types of Hendrickson suspensions. Figure 5-13 shows another. These are all steel leaf, spring suspension systems designed for heavy-duty trucks. In many cases, a buyer may specify the type of suspension he or she wants when ordering a truck.

Figure 5-14. *Courtesy of Hendrickson Mfg. Co., Tandem Division*

69

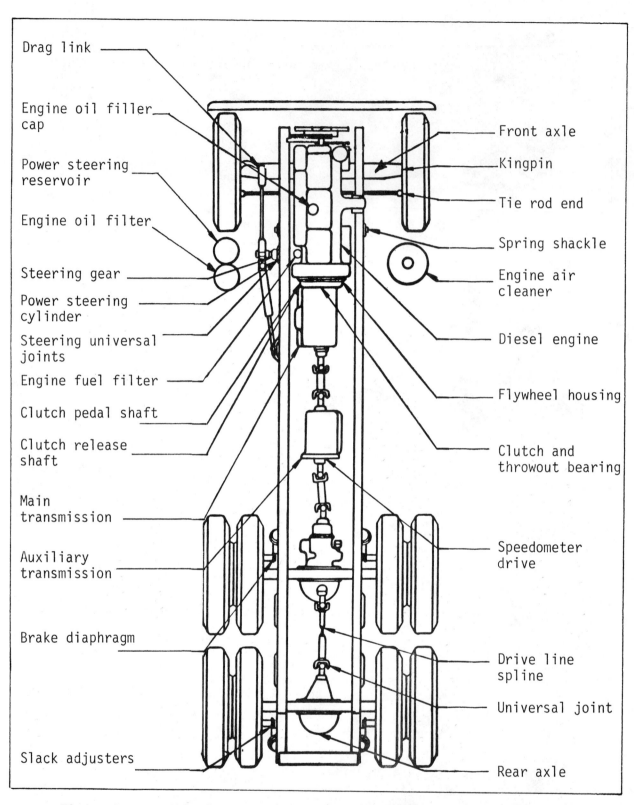

Figure 5-15. This illustration shows the location of several key components. The chart is a lubrication chart for a Peterbilt conventional truck tractor. The *kingpin* shown is a steering axle kingpin. This is the main pin that connects a wheel hub to the rigid axle. This is where the front wheels swivel. Don't confuse a front axle kingpin with a trailer kingpin, as there is no relationship between the two and what they do. *Chart courtesy of Peterbilt Motors Co.*

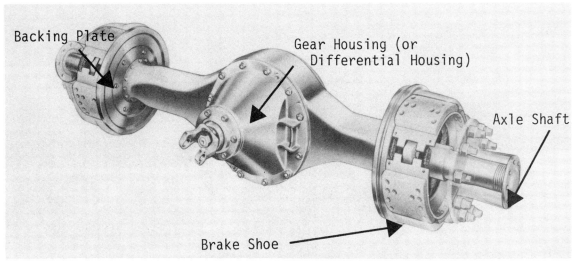

Figure 5-16. Single rear axle by Eaton, Model #23121.
Courtesy of Eaton Corporation, Axle Division.

A LOOK UNDERNEATH (cont.)

● *Axles*

On a car, an axle is a support bar which runs from one side of the car to the other to hold the two wheels on. A car has two axles: front and rear.

The truck's axles do basically the same job as the axles on a car. The axles (helped out by the suspension system) do the bulk of the job of supporting the truck's enormous weight. However, because the heavy-duty truck is much heavier than a car, two axles are not always enough to carry the great weight of the rig. Thus, many trucks and tractors are *three-axle trucks*. A three-axle truck has *one* axle in the front and *two* axles in the back. Because the emphasis is usually placed on the number of rear (or drive) axles, a three-axle tractor may be called a *tandem*-axle tractor. "Tandem" means "one placed behind another." So remember, a tandem-axle tractor has three axles - two at the rear (in tandem) and one in front. Each of the rear axles will have four wheels - two on each side. Not all trucks and tractors are three-axle trucks. Some, such as those in Figure 5-2 and Figure 4-5, have only one rear axle. Trucks with only one rear axle are called *single-axle trucks*, meaning that they only have *one* drive axle.

The next time you pass a tractor bob tailing on home down the highway, look for the eight wheels at the back. When a tractor is bob tailing, it's easy to tell whether it is a single-axle or tandem-axle tractor.

By selecting heavier axles and suspensions, a truck is capable of hauling more weight than if it had all light-duty axles. For example, you won't want to choose a front axle for your tractor that is rated at 10,000 lbs if you know your axle weights will probably run as high as 13,000 or 15,000 lbs. The heavier the axle, the longer it will last. If you overload your equipment, you will shorten the life of your axles. Using an axle intended for a light-weight load for a much heavier load is like trying to put three quarters of a ton of weight into a half-ton pickup! How long do you think the axles, tires and springs would last if you did that? The same rule applies to a heavy rig.

71

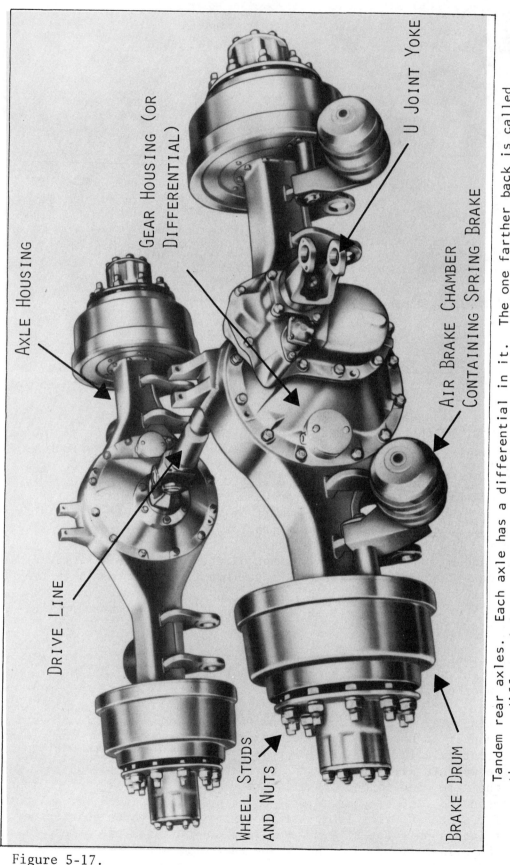

AXLE HOUSING

GEAR HOUSING (OR DIFFERENTIAL)

U JOINT YOKE

DRIVE LINE

AIR BRAKE CHAMBER CONTAINING SPRING BRAKE

WHEEL STUDS AND NUTS

BRAKE DRUM

Tandem rear axles. Each axle has a differential in it. The one farther back is called the rear differential, and the one closer to the front of the tractor is called the front differential. Under normal conditions, the rear differential only supplies the traction to the ground so that the wheels turn. The front differential is in a free-wheeling condition normally. However, when the ground is slippery, the driver locks the differential lock. When the differential lock is in place, both differentials supply traction and both become "drive axles." *Courtesy of Eaton Corporation, Axle Division.*

Figure 5-17.

A LOOK UNDERNEATH (cont.)

Each diesel rig is a specialized type of truck and is manufactured for a specific job. Anyone who shortcuts this principle by "under spec-ing" a vehicle is asking for trouble and a large number of repair bills.

Most states limit the amount of weight which can be transported by a set of wheels on a truck. (We'll talk about these laws in Chapter 19, "Permit Hauling.") If you intend to haul maximum loads (things like logs, construction equipment, etc.) you'll need to know the laws. They will specify such things as the number of wheels you need to have and the distance between the axles. The more axles and wheels a truck has, the more weight it can carry. Actually, it's a matter of common sense. If you were going to haul 20 tons, would you put it on a five-axle semi rig (triple-axle tractor plus a double-axle trailer), or would you try to haul it in a three-axle dump truck?

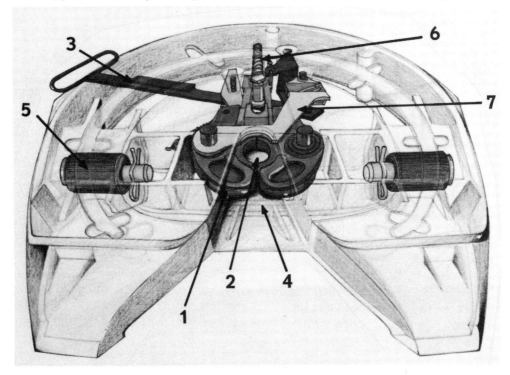

1   Coupler arms.

2   Kingpin tolerance of this unit is 35 to 40/1,000". Accurate kingpin tolerance on any fifth wheel should be within 30 to 50/1,000 of an inch.

3   Pull handle for uncoupling tractor and trailer.

4   Fifth wheel locking jaws.

5   Steel-on-rubber pivots to smooth ride.

6   Rod which projects from an unlocked fifth wheel. This projecting rod cautions you to check your rig because it is so easy to notice.

      Automatic slack adjuster.

Figure 5-18. Fifth wheel. *Courtesy of Dayton-Walther Corporation.*

A LOOK UNDERNEATH (cont.)

● *Kingpin and Fifth Wheel*

The trailer *kingpin* is located in the center, underneath the front end of the semi-trailer. The *fifth wheel* is located at the rear of the tractor. Together, they make the connection between the tractor or truck and semi-trailer, as illustrated in Figure 5-5. The kingpin inserts into the rear of the fifth wheel by a set of steel jaws. (See Figure 5-18, #4.)

You must use caution when you back underneath a trailer. You want to be sure that the kingpin is *lined up with the center slot of the fifth wheel* so that in backing the tractor into the trailer, the kingpin doesn't miss the slot. If you miss the slot, the kingpin will ride up the face of the fifth wheel, completely missing the locking jaws. If you do this, it's possible to back far enough underneath for the kingpin to run up over the fifth wheel and fall down in the front of it, leaving you completely stuck.

Making the connection properly between the towing unit and the trailer is extremely important, as you can well imagine. You don't want to drop a trailer as you ride on down the road. Therefore, we're devoting a whole chapter to this subject (Chapter 16, "Engaging and Disengaging Trailers").

SUMMARY

The professional driver knows quite a bit about the truck's various systems and components. Before one goes into detail about these systems and their operations, however, one has to get "the big picture." So that's what we've done in this chapter by taking a look at the outside, inside, and bottom side of the truck.

In "A Look Outside," we located important components on a diagram of a typical tractor-trailer combination. Then, to figure out what you already know about various truck components, you asked yourself questions about what each part is for.

In "A Look Inside," we looked first at the five basic systems of the truck and said that all five have to be functioning properly for the rig to run smoothly. The five systems are the air brake system, the electrical system, the lubricating system, the cooling system and the fuel system. Then, we located and described the purpose of each of the gauges, valves, etc., on the instrument panel. We said that the purpose of these gauges, etc., is to keep a check on the operation of the truck's systems. By monitoring the instrument panel, the driver can find out if anything goes wrong somewhere in the rig.

Finally, in "A Look Underneath," we looked at the following components: the suspension system, the axles, and the kingpin and fifth wheel. We mentioned that trucks can be purchased with many different types of suspension systems, axles, engines, etc. It is up to the buyer to select the type of rig and its components which will suit the types of cargoes which he or she is planning to haul.

GLOSSARY

axle: The axle is the steel shaft which connects the differential with the wheels. The words "axle housing" are often used to mean the entire component, including differential, housing, and steel shaft. (See Figure 5-17.)

bob tailing: Running the tractor without a trailer.

centrifugal force: An arcking force; a force which causes a rotating object to tend to move away from the center of rotation. If you swing a ball around on the end of a string, centrifugal force makes it fly away from you if you let go.

differential (rear end): The differential contains the gears that convert the rotation of the drive shaft to turn the wheels and axles.

drive axle: The axle with gears. It may be the front axle or the rear axle.

fifth wheel: The tractor support plate and locking jaws for the trailer kingpin.

lubrication: Applying oil or another fluid to reduce friction between moving parts.

malfunction: Failure to work properly.

monitor: To keep track of or to record the operation of.

off-highway (off-the-road): An off-highway vehicle is one used over rough ground a good percentage of the time.

single-axle truck: Any truck with only one axle at the rear, only one drive axle. Single-axle trucks are sometimes called bobtail trucks.

spec: To specify or request. For example, to request specified parts for a truck. A shortened form of either specify or specification.

suspension: A support system for the body and frame of a truck, consisting of springs and mounting brackets. The suspension system allows the axles to move up and down as the road surface changes. Sometimes called the undercarriage.

tandem axles: Dual axles; two axles together.

three-axle truck: A truck with one axle in front and two in the rear. Sometimes called a tandem-axle truck.

traction: Grip or pulling action such as a tire against the pavement.

In Figure 5-19, below, there are several arrows drawn to specific items on the rig. Each arrow is number keyed. Write the name of the object after each number. You might see how many you can properly identify without checking back to Figure 5-2; then, do the rest after checking.

Figure 5-19. Combination unit with a wind deflector or air shield.
Courtesy of Airshield, Division of Rudkin-Wiley Corporation

1. _____   6. _____

2. _____   7. _____

3. _____   8. _____

4. _____   9. _____

5. _____   10. _____

Note: Be sure your answers go down, like the numbers, not across.

The groups of words on the right either define or list major components of the terms on the left. Match the terms that go together best by placing the letter of the word groups in the blank before the matching term. The first one is done for you.

_G_ 11. electrical system

____ 12. air brake system

____ 13. lubricating system

____ 14. fuel system

____ 15. cooling system

____ 16. instrument panel

____ 17. differential

____ 18. fifth wheel

____ 19. three-axle truck

____ 20. V-8

____ 21. suspension system

____ 22. kingpin

____ 23. off-highway vehicle

____ 24. drive axle

____ 25. throttle pedal

A. driver uses this to control amount of engine fuel

B. monitors the operation of the truck's various systems and components

C. also called rear end

D. purpose is to keep a film of oil between all moving parts

E. the part on the semi-trailer which makes connection with tractor

F. one of the three basic engine designs

G. batteries, generator or alternator, voltage regulator, wiring, gauges, etc.

H. fuel tank, fuel lines, fuel pump, fuel filter, etc.

I. radiator, engine, water pump, fan belts, hoses, etc.

J. the basic means for stopping the vehicle

K. requires a heavier suspension system than other rigs

L. part on the tractor which makes the connection with the semi-trailer

M. has tandem rear axles

N. springs, mounting brackets, etc.

O. rear tractor axle

■ GETTING THE MAIN IDEAS

1. Explain how the lubricating system and the cooling system work together to keep the engine cool.

2. Give an example of something that might go wrong in a rig. Then, tell how the instrument panel would tell the driver about the malfunction. (You may give more than one example if you like.)

3. In your own words, explain why a dump truck might need a heavier suspension system than a tractor-trailer combination used to haul commodities like grocery items, tools, carpet or heavy ceramic floor tiles.

4. Study the diagram of the fifth wheel in Figure 5-18 and study Figure 5-5. What information do these diagrams give you about <u>how</u> tractor-trailer connections (couplings) are made and about the <u>principal</u> <u>working parts</u> of the fifth wheel?

★ GOING BEYOND THE FACTS AND IDEAS

1. Assume the driver has had trouble starting the rig. It has stalled several times, and the lights on the instrument panel are dim. What items on the instrument panel should she or he monitor especially closely? What might these items explain?

2. Describe the purpose and major components of each of the five major systems of the rig. You may do this in paragraph form or in an outline.

3. Assume that you are going to do an inspection underneath the rig to see that everything is in safe operating condition. What components will you look at and what will you look for?

Chapter
Six

STARTING
THE ENGINE
AND
SHIFTING
GEARS

Figure 6-1. Cab interior of conventional truck. Notice gearshift knob for Spicer multi-speed transmission.
Courtesy of Chrysler Corporation

BEFORE YOU READ | In this chapter, we'll be looking at two things. First, what steps are involved in starting the engine? We'll look at how to start both the gasoline and the diesel engine.
Next, we'll look at checking the tractor-trailer connection, and then at shifting up through the gears. In the second part of this chapter, we'll take a closer look at shifting gears. You'll take a look at two different shifting patterns and learn the importance of using the tach (tachometer) to determine when to shift.

There's a lot of information to digest here. So, once again, we've given you a study sheet so that you will be sure to read with an active mind. By filling in the blanks (in order) as you read, you should pick up the major facts and ideas.

1. The steps involved in starting a gasoline engine are (1) set the _____

_____ ; (2) be sure transmission is in _____ ;

(3) pull the _____ out part way; (4) depress the _____ ;

(5) turn on the _____ and operate _____ ;

(6) control engine with the _____ .

BEFORE YOU READ   (cont.)

2. Whether you're starting a diesel or gasoline engine, if you operate the
    starter for _____ and it doesn't start, stop and wait.

3. When you're starting a diesel, pay special attention to the _____
    _____ gauge and the _____ gauge.

4. To insure that your units are coupled securely, you make the power unit
    go either forward or backward in a _____.

5. How do you keep from lugging your engine? _____
    _____

6. What is double-clutching? _____
    _____
    _____

7. You aren't supposed to force the transmission into a higher gear, so what
    do you do if it won't go into gear? _____
    _____
    _____

8. What two things did the driver in the story do wrong? _____
    _____

9. What's a tachometer?_____

10. When do you shift up? _____
    _____

11. Each time you shift down, you _____ the engine speed by a set
    number of rpm per _____. Each time you shift up, you _____
    the engine rpm by a set number of rpm per _____.

12. What are twin sticks used for? _____
    _____
    _____

STARTING THE ENGINE | You've completed your vehicle inspection and you're ready to start the engine, put the vehicle into gear, and begin to function as a well-disciplined, efficient professional.

How you begin your day will often determine your overall efficiency for the whole work shift. All truckers should realize that if they don't make money for the company, the company won't be able to pay them. That thought should provide you with a reason for doing a good job throughout the day. So, with that thought in mind, let's examine some of the standard operating procedures for beginning a day with the right foot forward.

● *Starting the Gasoline Engine*

1. Be sure the *parking brake* is on.

2. Be sure the *transmission* is in neutral.

3. Unless the truck has an automatic choke, pull the *choke* out part way. How far you pull it out will depend on the weather and the condition of the vehicle. (After the engine has started, remember to push the choke all the way back in as soon as you can.)

4. Depress the *clutch* pedal. (If you leave a clutch out while you start the engine, the starter will have to turn over the shaft in the gear box as well as the engine. Therefore, to relieve the drag of turning the transmission gears over, depress the clutch just enough to disconnect the transmission from the engine. This will be the same amount as you would if you were shifting gears while moving.)

5. Turn the *ignition* on and operate the *starter*. IMPORTANT: Do not operate the starter continuously for more than 30 seconds. If the engine does not start in that time, turn the ignition off and wait several seconds. Then try again.

6. When the engine starts, watch the *gauges* to be sure they register properly. Pay close attention to the oil pressure. If it doesn't register within two to three seconds, *stop the engine* and *recheck the oil level in the crankcase*.

7. Control the engine with the *foot throttle* until it begins to run fairly smoothly.

8. When the engine will run without close attention, set the *hand throttle* at fast idle. Keep your eye on the engine temperature gauge and allow the engine to warm up to about *one-half* to *three-quarters* of the normal operating temperature before you attempt to move the vehicle.

9. If the vehicle has air brakes, make sure the *air pressure gauge* registers full pressure before you move the vehicle.

STARTING THE ENGINE (cont.)

● *Starting the Diesel Engine*

1. Depress the *clutch* pedal to relieve the starting motor of transmission drag.

2. If the engine has a *start button*, push it in firmly to start the engine. If it has a *switch key*, turn the key to "On." Don't operate an electric starter motor for more than 30 seconds at a time. If the engine doesn't start, turn off the key, or release the start button, and make another attempt after waiting 45 to 60 seconds.

3. When the engine fires, hold the speed at fast idle by depressing the *throttle* a controlled amount until the engine runs smoothly. Then, gradually reduce the speed to normal idling speed as it warms up.

4. Check the *gauges* during warm up. Pay special attention to adequate oil pressure. If the oil pressure does not register within two to five seconds, shut down the engine and find the cause of the delay.

5. Warm up the engine. Check the *air pressure gauge* to see that the air pressure for the brakes is at the normal level before you move the unit.

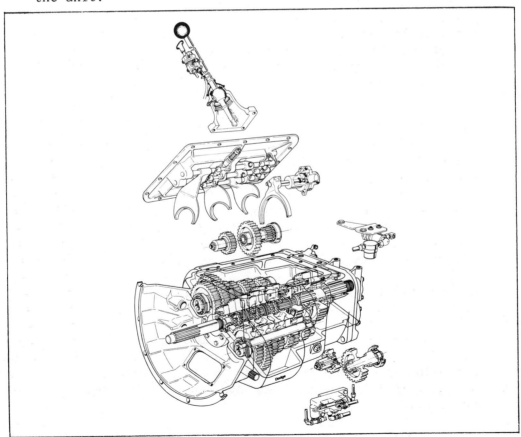

Figure 6-2. Cutaway view of Eaton Roadranger twin countershaft transmission with top cover removed, illustrating the shifting forks. *Courtesy of Chrysler Corporation*

82

TESTING THE HOOK-UP

If the rig you are driving is a combination unit, such as a tractor-trailer combination, test the hook-up in one of the two following ways before you get the unit under way.

● *Power Units with Trailer Hand Valves*

Begin by setting the *trailer hand valve* (the brake valve for the trailer). This sets the brakes on the trailer or trailers. Then, test the coupling (or hook-up) to be sure it is firm by using the following method.

Place the transmission in *reverse* and partially engage the clutch. Then, speed up the engine to make the power unit go backward in a short, sharp jerk. This is known as "hitting the pin." Now that you have set the trailer brakes, as you "hit the pin," place the transmission in the *lowest forward gear*. (Do not use underdrive on a vehicle equipped with an auxiliary transmission.) Then, partially engage the clutch and slightly speed up the engine to pull forward against the locked trailer brakes. The power unit should not move. It should be locked to the trailer pin.

Why do you do this? To be sure you are locked safely onto the trailer or trailers. To be sure that the units don't disengage from one another while you are on the road.

● *Power Units without Trailer Hand Valves*

If the power unit is *not* equipped with a trailer hand valve, place the transmission in the *lowest forward gear*. (Again, do not use the underdrive on the auxiliary transmission). Then, partially engage the clutch to give the unit a light, forward jerk. (Be sure the wheels are chocked to hold trailer.)

This will accomplish the same result as described above where you have the trailer brakes locked. Basically, in either method, you are insuring that your units are coupled together securely so that you don't drop your trailer when you are on the road.

PUTTING THE VEHICLE INTO MOTION

Now that you have tested the coupling on your combination unit, you are ready to pull out of the yard. Disengage the clutch and place the transmission in the *lowest forward gear*. If your vehicle has a trailer hand control, pull it down. This will set the trailer brakes and keep the unit from rolling backward until you are ready to move. If your unit doesn't have a hand control, leave the trailer parking brake set.

When you're starting, gradually release the clutch, and at the same time, release the trailer hand valve or parking brake as the clutch engages. At the same time, speed up the engine gradually to prevent stalling and to move the load. Speeding the engine will also keep the unit from rolling backward if you are starting on a grade; that is, a hill. Continue to release the clutch and speed up the engine smoothly until the clutch is fully engaged. When the vehicle is in motion with the clutch engaged, take the left foot completely off the clutch pedal until you are ready to shift gears or to stop.

SHIFTING UP THROUGH THE GEARS | One thing you have to beware of in shifting up through the gears is *lugging*. Lugging is premature shifting into a higher gear before the engine has reached maximum rpm (or revolutions per minute). (We'll discuss the importance of engine rpm later in this chapter.)

You certainly wouldn't shift your automobile from first gear to third gear without first increasing your road speed. If you start in first gear, just barely move, then immediately shift into second, you'll choke your car engine down. That is, you will be lugging the engine. To avoid lugging, you want to bring the engine *as close to maximum speed as possible in each gear* before you start shifting into the next higher gear.

To shift into the next higher gear, use the following steps:

1. Push down on the *clutch* pedal and release the *accelerator* (or *throttle*). Disengage the clutch as you release the accelerator.

2. While the engine speed is dropping, move the *gearshift lever* to neutral.

3. Release the clutch pedal to *engage the clutch*.

4. Quickly *disengage the clutch* by pushing down the pedal and moving the *gearshift lever* to the next higher gear.

5. *Release* the clutch pedal and *speed the engine up* at the same time.

6. Continue shifting up through the gears until the permissable road speed is reached.

The method of shifting we've just described is known as *double-clutching*. Double-clutching must be used on most manually-shifted truck transmissions - all except synchromesh transmissions.

A synchromesh transmission has thin synchronizer plates between the gears. As a gear is shifted from one ratio to another, these disks, or plates, make contact between the gears, acting like a clutch. In other words, they place a drag on a faster spinning gear just before the teeth mesh. These plates have neutralized the speed between the faster and slower spinning gear so that they will match up with each other without clashing. While we said above that you don't *have to* double-clutch if your truck has a synchromesh, you *may* double-clutch. On trucks equipped with synchromesh transmissions, shifting will be faster and smoother if you double-clutch.

> ▷ *WARNING: Never risk clashing gears by trying to force the transmission into the next gear. If the transmission cannot be shifted smoothly due to improper timing in double-clutching, then release the clutch pedal and speed up the engine again. Then, push down the clutch and start over. If the transmission cannot be shifted after two or three tries, stop in a safe place and begin again.*

SHIFTING DOWN | As you drive, you will want to be alert to changing road conditions. Sometimes, they will require you to reduce speed, and this will often require you to shift down a gear or more. Don't wait until the engine lugs before you shift down. Here's how to shift down:

1. Push down on the clutch pedal and release the accelerator as you move the gearshift knob to the neutral position.

2. Release the clutch pedal.

3. Accelerate the engine with the clutch pedal released and the transmission in neutral. Bring the engine up to a higher speed than the speed it was running when it was in the higher gear. This will help you to shift smoothly into the lower gear.

4. Depress the clutch and move the gearshift lever to the next lower gear.

5. Gradually release the clutch pedal and speed up the engine to take up the shock of engaging the clutch. (At this point, you need to check the tach for proper rpm. The reason for this will become clear later in this chapter.)

> ▷ *WARNING: Do not attempt to force the transmission into gear. If you can't shift it without clashing gears, leave the gearshift in neutral, release the clutch pedal, accelerate the engine again. Then, try the shift once more.*

SHUTTING OFF THE DIESEL ENGINE | Before you shut off, or stop, a diesel engine, there are important steps you must take so you won't damage the engine. Here they are.

1. Before you shut off the engine, allow it to run at fast idle for three to five minutes. This maintains circulation of water and oil and helps to dissipate the built-up heat.

2. Allow the engine to return to idling speed before stopping it. This cools the engine to *below normal operating temperature*. The purpose is to eliminate hot spots which will develop if there is no water circulation in the engine block. Hot spots could result in a cracked head.

3. If your engine has a *stop button*, pull it out to stop the engine. Another button, called the *emergency stop*, has a different purpose. Don't confuse them. Only use the emergency stop button if you can't stop the engine by any other means. On most types of engines, turning the key to the "Off" position also stops the engine.

4. If your engine has one, turn off the *switch key* whenever you stop the engine, as a matter of habit. This switch key controls the charging circuit. If it is left on, the battery may become discharged. The discharge of current may cause the voltage regulator points to stick so that the circuit will not charge.

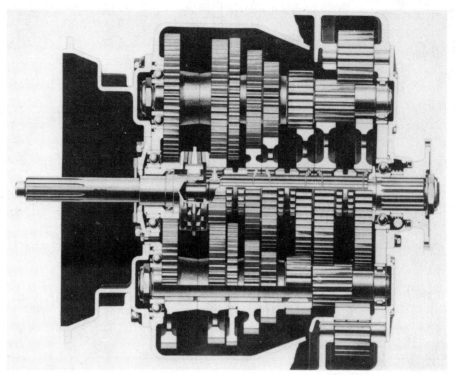

Figure 6-3.   *Courtesy of Chrysler Corporation*

KEEPING
ALERT
WHILE
SHIFTING
GEARS

One of the most important things to remember in driving may
be to keep alert. Keeping alert is especially important
when it comes to shifting gears. Remembering your gear
shift position and pattern is of prime importance. Let us
explain, by this little example, what can and will happen
if you forget. This is a true story.

First, let's make sure we know the major difference between the shifting
pattern of five and ten-speed transmissions. A truck with a five-speed transmission (with a two-speed rear end) will be identified by the red plastic button attached to the gearshift lever. A ten-speed Roadranger will have a
heavy, metal, oblong-shaped button on the gearshift. The difference between
these two is immense.

● Shifting the five-speed: For each gear you shift, you move the red axle
    button from low to high. You move it up for one gear, down for the
    next, up for the next, and so on. This is known as split-shifting.

● Shifting the ten-speed: With the button down, you shift gears one
    through five. Then, you pull the button up and return to the first
    hole, which is the sixth gear, and repeat the pattern with the but-
    ton up, shifting through gears six through ten.

To the driver, the big difference between the two transmissions is the way in
which the button is used.

KEEPING ALERT WHILE SHIFTING GEARS (cont.)

Our story begins with a driver cruising down the road at 40 mph in a truck with a ten-speed transmission. He is an experienced driver, but he's used to driving with a two-speed axle (a five-speed transmission).

A traffic signal one block ahead of him changes, and he starts a gradual slowdown. Before he has slowed down very much, the light changes to green again, and he starts to get back on the throttle. Since he had lost quite a few rpm as he slowed, he hurriedly begins another shift down. Unconsciously, with his mind only half on the job, through habit, he moves the button down and shoves the stick down a gear, jamming it into what he thinks is the next lower gear. By moving the button down, he has unfortunately shifted his ten-speed from ninth to third gear, in low range.

Since the transmission is a synchromesh, the stick goes into third gear without too much trouble. And since the driver has a habit of popping the clutch out (relaxing the pedal too quickly), the engine speed about doubles as the clutch comes out. The sudden engine speed breaks off some of the valves in the engine. It also breaks the crankshaft, tears the clutch out of the truck, and almost turns the engine over in the frame. To top it off, the fan snaps off and goes through the radiator.

What caused the accident? First, the driver didn't have his attention fully on what he was doing. He was on automatic pilot. Second, had he not had the habit of popping the clutch, he might have pulled out of the situation before major damage was done. Had he released the clutch more slowly (a better driving habit) he would have been aware of the problems.

This little mistake cost the company almost $6,000, and that was when the price of an engine was about half, or even a third, of what it is today. The truck had been scarcely a week old. And so, this is just one reason why experienced truckers will tell you, *"Keep your mind on your gears."*

THERE ARE MANY DIFFERENT GEAR SHIFT PATTERNS

A great many different gear shift patterns exist in trucks. Different transmissions have different gear ratios, and there are 30 or more different gear box combinations which you might come across. (Compare Figures 6-2 and 6-3.) There are many different shifting patterns. Two of them are shown in Figures 6-4 through 6-7 to give you a feel for what we're talking about when we speak of gear shifting a huge diesel tractor.

If there are so many different gear box combinations and shifting patterns, how can a new driver ever hope to learn to drive every possible engine which she or he may encounter. The answer? It can't be done. You must learn in the rig itself. And that means that until you become really skilled, you will have to have someone show you what to do when you actually get into each truck or tractor which you will be driving. Unless you can put your hands on the gearshift, it is impossible for you to visualize what you will be doing. Generally, there will be a diagram on the sun visor or dashboard which indicates the gear shift pattern.

Don't expect to understand all of it, but if you want to get a bit more of a feel for how shifting is done in a diesel, read through the instructions in Figures 6-4 through 6-7. These instructions and illustrations are for several Fuller Roadranger transmissions. Figures 6-4 and 6-5 explain how to shift eight different ten-speed Roadrangers. You use the same pattern for each. Figures 6-6 and 6-7 introduce the shifting pattern for the RTO-9513, RTOO-9513, RTO-12513 and for "F" model transmissions. (The "O" in "RTO" stands for "overdrive.")

Gear Shift Lever Pattern
and Range Control Button Positions

RT-610 Series   RT-1110 Series
RT-910 Series   RT-12510 Series

General Instructions

The 10-speed Roadranger Transmissions provide ten selective ratios, evenly and progressively spaced and shifted with one lever. But you do NOT shift the Roadranger as you would a conventional transmission with an auxiliary or 2-speed axle, because there is *no* split-shifting.

RT (direct) Models

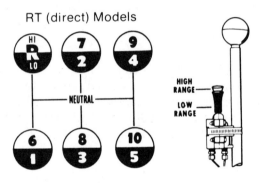

Shift 1-2-3-4-5 in low range.
Repeat pattern in high range and shift
6-7-8-9-10

The shifting of the 10-speed Roadranger Transmissions is *much simpler . . . much easier.*

ALL SHIFTS ARE MADE WITH ONE LEVER . . . you use the RANGE CONTROL BUTTON ONE TIME ONLY during a sequence of up-shifts . . . and ONE TIME ONLY during a down-shift pattern.

Why is the Roadranger different?

The Roadranger is a 2-RANGE transmission consisting of a 5-speed front section and an automatic 2-speed auxiliary section in ONE CASE. The ten forward speeds are secured by using a 5-speed shifting pattern TWICE — the first time with the transmission engaged in low gear or low range; the second time engaged in high gear or high range.

RTO (overdrive) Models

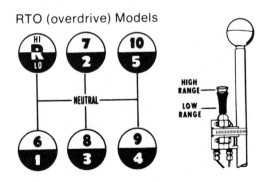

By using the same shifting pattern twice, the shift lever position for 6th speed is the same as 1st . . . 7th the same as 2nd, 8th the same as 3rd, 9th the same as 4th, and 10th the same as 5th.

Figure 6-4. *Reprinted through the courtesy of Eaton Corporation, Transmission Division*

Detailed Shifting Instructions

In the following instructions, it is assumed that the driver is familiar with motor trucks and tractors, and that he can coordinate the necessary movements of the shift lever and clutch pedal to make progressive and selective gear engagements in either direction, up or down.

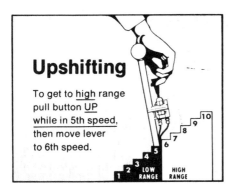

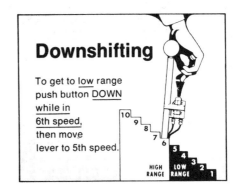

Upshifting

Let's step into the cab.

1. Move the gear shift lever to the neutral position.

2. Start the engine.

3. Wait for air system to reach normal line pressure.

4. Now look at the Range Control Button. If it is *up* push it to the down position. (With the downward movement of the button, the transmission will shift into low range.) If the button *was* down when the truck was last used, the transmission is already in low range.

5. Now start the vehicle and shift progressively through 1st, 2nd, 3rd and 4th to 5th.

6. When in 5th and *ready for the next upward shift,* PULL the Range Control Button UP and move the lever to 6th speed. As the lever *passes through the neutral position,* the transmission will automatically shift from low range to high range.

7. With the transmission in high range, you may now shift progressively through 7th, 8th and 9th to 10th.

Driving tip: always start vehicle moving in first speed gear.

Downshifting

1. When shifting down, move the lever from 10th through each successive lower speed to 6th.

2. When in 6th, and *ready for the next downward shift,* PUSH the Range Control Button DOWN and move the lever to 5th speed. As the lever *passes through the neutral position,* the transmission will automatically shift from high range to low range.

3. With the transmission in low range, shift downward through each of the four remaining steps.

Use Range Control Button only as described

Don't shift from high range to low range at high vehicle speeds.

Don't make range shifts with the vehicle moving in reverse gear.

Note: These instructions also apply to models with the "forward" positioned gear shift lever. These models are designated RTF-910, RTOF-910, etc.

Figure 6-5. These instructions are for shifting the transmissions listed in Figure 6-4. The gear shift pattern for all of these transmissions is the same. *Reprinted through the courtesy of Eaton Corporation, Transmission Division*

Gear Shift Lever Pattern and Selector Valve Positions

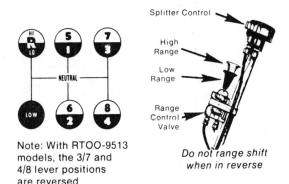

Note: With RTOO-9513 models, the 3/7 and 4/8 lever positions are reversed

Do not range shift when in reverse

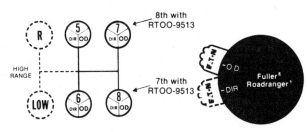

High range ratios are split with an overdrive splitter gear

These transmissions have thirteen forward and two reverse speeds, consisting of a five speed front section and a two speed range, or auxiliary, section with an overdrive splitter gear located directly behind the range section.

One ratio in the front section is used only as a Low or starting ratio. The remaining four ratios are used once through low range of the auxiliary and once through high range (direct) of the auxiliary. However, each of the four speeds in high range can be split with the overdrive ratio of the splitter gear. Ratios cannot be split while the transmission is in low range.

The overdrive gear selection is used only when the transmission is operating in high range to split the 5th, 6th, 7th and 8th speed ratios.

Shifting Sequence

While in low range, shift this pattern . . .

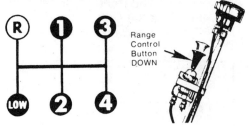

While in 4th speed of low range, pull up range control button, and shift this pattern . . .

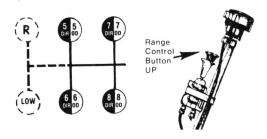

. . . Using splitter valve to split the high range ratios . . .

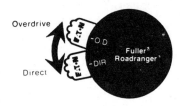

Caution:

1. Never move the gear shift lever into the low position of gear shift pattern while in high range.
2. Unless making downward range shift from 5th to 4th, never move range control valve to down position while operating in high range — splitter will become inoperative.
3. Never move splitter selector while in neutral.
4. Do not pre-select splitter valve — move the selector and complete shift immediately.

Figure 6-6.   These gear patterns are for the RTO-9513, RTOO-9513 and RTO-12513 Roadranger transmissions. These transmissions each have 13 forward speeds and two reverse speeds. The thirteen speeds are - Low, 1st, 2nd, 3rd, and 4th, plus, 5th direct, 5th overdrive, 6th direct, 6th overdrive, etc., adding up to 13. *Reprinted through the courtesy of Eaton Corporation, Transmission Division.*

Detailed Shifting Instructions

In the following instructions, it is assumed that the driver is familiar with motor trucks and tractors, and that he can coordinate the necessary movements of the shift lever and clutch pedal to make progressive and selective gear engagements in either direction, up or down.

Upshifting

1. Start engine with transmission in neutral . . . and bring vehicle's air to normal.

2. Make sure Range Control Valve on gear shift lever is in DOWN position, and splitter control is in the DIR. position.

 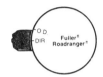

Range Control Button DOWN

3. Shift into the Low position.

4. Start vehicle moving and shift upward through 1st, 2nd, 3rd and to 4th.

Range Shift

5. While in 4th and ready for the upshift, to 5th . . . pre-select HIGH RANGE by moving Range Control Valve to HIGH position.

Range Control Button UP

6. Complete normal shift by moving shift lever to the 5th speed position. Transmission will shift automatically to high range as lever passes through neutral.

Upshift from DIRECT (5th) to OVERDRIVE (5th) in the same gear position. You do not have to move the gear shift lever.

7. Flip selector from DIR. to O.D. . . . .

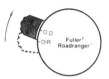

8. Then, immediately release accelerator and depress clutch. Transmission will shift when synchronous is reached.

Upshift from OVERDRIVE (5th) to DIRECT (6th) in next higher ratio.

9. Start normal shift by moving gear shift lever to the 6th speed position . . .

10. But, flip selector from O.D. to DIR. just prior to . . .

11. Making final clutch engagement and accelerating engine.

12. Complete upshift sequence. Continue shifting upward through the shift pattern to 8th overdrive.

Figure 6-7. Notice that to get from the lower to the higher gears, the driver must move the range control button up. Then, when the driver moves the shift lever to the 5th speed position, the transmission will automatically shift to high range. The splitter valve (or selector) is used to shift from direct to overdrive. You don't have to move the gearshift lever. It works the same way dropping from overdrive to direct. For example, to get from 8th overdrive to 8th direct, you simply flip the selector. *Reprinted through the courtesy of Eaton Corporation, Transmission Division.*

GEAR
SHIFT
TECHNIQUES | Now that we've explained why we won't be going into gear shifting and gear shift patterns in depth, let's talk about some of the gear shift *techniques* that will affect the life of your engine and possibly even *your* life. Every gear shift technique will affect the longevity of a transmission and other components, such as the drive line and clutch.

● *Proper Timing in Shifting*

Every new driver shifts either too fast or too slowly. The driver will shift too fast because he or she is afraid of missing the shift. We call this forced shifting. Or, the driver will shift too slowly. This allows the gears to become unsynchronized and the driver hears a loud, grinding noise. The noise is caused when one gear rotates faster than its mating gear. Unfortunately, shifting too slowly or too quickly will have a very definite side effect; it will shorten the life of the gears and synchronizers of any gear box. Therefore, it is to be avoided.

A good way to figure out what you're doing wrong is this:

● If you get a *clank*, you are probably shifting too fast.

● If you have a tendency to shift too slowly, you'll hear a *grinding noise*.

There is a rhythm attached to shifting every gear box. This rhythm (or timing) is developed by watching the tachometer at each shift. When you actually get on the road, you'll become familiar with how your tach works and you'll develop the proper rhythm.

● *Driving by the Tach*

Any drag racer can tell you what a tach is - a tachometer. A *tachometer* is an engine rpm indicator. It is an instrument which records engine rpm (revolutions per minute) so that the driver knows when it is time to shift gears - either up or down.

However, when truckers talk about the tach, they may mean a *tachometer*, or they may mean a *tachograph*. Often, the tachometer and tachograph will be combined in one unit, as in Figures 6-8 and 6-10. So, many times, a trucker will be referring to the combined instrument when he or she speaks of the tach. You'll want to become familiar with these two instruments and how they function so that you are not confused when truckers toss around the words. First, we'll talk

Figure 6-8. This instrument is a combined road speed tachograph and engine rpm indicator (or tachometer). To determine engine rpm, you multiply the number on inner circle by 100. *Courtesy of Argo Instruments Corp.*

92

GEAR SHIFT TECHNIQUES   (cont.)

about the tachometer. Then, at the end of this chapter, we'll discuss the tachograph. We'll try to help you keep them straight.

The number of revolutions per minute which an engine can make is very different for gasoline and diesel engines. An average truck *gasoline* engine can make up to 3500 revolutions per minute. On the other hand, the average *diesel* line engine (high horsepower diesel) only goes to 2100 rpm, tops. The range of a diesel is typically from an idle speed of 500 rpm to 2100 rpm. But the typical *operating range* is even shorter. For example, it may be from 1200 to 2100 or from 1200 to 1900. It may even be as short as from 1700 to 2100 rpm. Therefore, with a diesel engine, you are restricted in your shifting pattern. Why? Because you must operate your vehicle so that the rpm stay within the operating range.

A range from 1700 to 2100 is called a *close tolerance operating range*. In other words, it's not a very large range. The 10-speed Roadranger gear box, illustrated in Figure 6-2, has this range. (This is the same transmission for which shifting directions are given in Figures 6-4 and 6-5.) As the engine has a short operating range, you must compensate for it by having a transmission with very short steps in rpm between the gears. In fact, not only this gear box, but all diesel gear boxes have short steps in rpm between gears. Most multi-speed transmissions have an approximate 19% rpm drop between gears.

Engine speeds in most engines are *governed*. This means that, in any gear, you are limited in the number of rpm that the engine will make. As you have just read, the tach tells you the number of rpm that your engine is doing at any time. Thus, if you want to know how many rpm your engine is doing, all you have to do is look at the tach. (See Figure 6-8.) When you have gotten to the top governed speed for your gear, it's time to shift. This is what we mean by driving by the tach.

Let's look at an example of how this works in shifting the Roadranger ten-speed gear box. Remember, this gear box has a close tolerance operating range of 1700 to 2100 rpm.

Shifting the Roadranger 10-Speed. Example One. You are in second gear. You rev the engine up to 2100, the maximum. However, you've only increased your truck speed by 5 mph. You want to go faster. There's only one way to go faster: Shift to a higher gear. Why? Because the governor won't let your engine turn any faster. You have to pick up the next gear - third. (Of course, some engines will have different shifting patterns.)

When you shift into third gear, your rpm drop to approximately 1700 - the low end of the operating range. This drop in rpm happens automatically in any engine as you shift into a higher gear. In the Roadranger 10-speed, each time you *shift down*, you *increase* the engine speed by 400 rpm *per gear*. Each time you *step up* a gear, you *decrease* the engine speed by 400 rpm *per gear*. Once again, you wind the gear out to top rpm, 2100. Again, you've reached the top rpm, so the engine won't go any faster because of the governor which protects the engine against overspeeding. Now, you're ready to shift to the next higher gear - fourth.

GEAR SHIFT TECHNIQUES (cont.)

You see, each gear is only capable of a limited road speed due to the governed speed of the engine. This is the thing that seems to give new drivers the most problems. Remember, the diesel has a very short operating range and it should not be pulled below that. That is, it should not be operated below its normal *operating* range. If it is pulled below that, the engine will be in a lugging condition, and the engine will be damaged. Remember this rule too: Each time you shift any diesel engine down, you increase the engine speed by a set number of rpm per gear. Each time you shift any diesel engine up, you decrease the engine speed by a set number of rpm per gear. Since the operating range is short, it doesn't take much to lug your engine.

Shifting the Roadranger 10-Speed. Example Two. Let's look at another example. You're cruising down the road at 55 mph and, because of traffic, you have to slow down. You're in tenth gear. You look at your tach and see that your engine is turning at 1200 rpm because you slowed down without first shifting into a lower gear. (You are driving below the normal operating range.)

You know that you have a drop of 400 rpm between each gear step. So, what gear would you downshift to in order to get your engine speed up into the proper operating range? You should be able to shift from tenth gear down to eighth gear. By doing this, you increase your rpm by 800. So, your tach (or engine speed) should come up to 2000 rpm. Since you are dropping two gears, the rpm will increase by 400 times 2, or 800 rpm. Therefore, if you made your downshift at 1200 rpm, you would go from 1200 to 2000 and could come right into eighth gear at an ideal cruising speed of 2000 rpm.

If you don't check the tachometer first, you won't know if you are able to upshift or downshift without lugging or overwinding your engine. A 15% overwind is where the engine may come apart because it has overspeeded its governed rpm. Since many diesels are governed from idle to 2100 rpm, if you go beyond 2100, you are overwinding the engine. It is not built to withstand that speed. *Watch that tach!*

SHIFTING
TWIN
STICKS

A good many trucks are equipped with twin sticks. (See Figure 6-9.) Twin sticks are often used in trucks which have a main transmission and an auxiliary transmission. The auxiliary box is often called the Brownie.

With twin sticks, for every gear you shift in the main box, you shift the Brownie through three gears. That is, for each gear you pick up in the main box, you shift the Brownie through the same three steps: *under*, *direct*, and *overdrive (OD)*. This differs from a 13-speed Roadranger where the driver merely moves a splitter button control on the gearshift knob. (See Figures 6-6 and 6-7.) The shifting on the 13-speed is done by *air pressure*. The shifting on a vehicle equipped with twin sticks is done *manually*.

Many of the heavy-haul trucks have four-speed Brownies which have a *low-low* (or granny) *gear* as well as under, direct, and over. In these twin stick set-ups, the low-low gear is in the auxiliary box, unlike the 13-speed Roadranger where the low-low gear is in the main transmission.

TWIN STICKS (cont.)

● *It's Not Easy*

Twin stick operations are extremely involved. Take Larry Allen, for example. He's just started learning to drive a rig with twin sticks. He gets four hours of training every day. He can plan on being very busy - with both feet and both hands - for the next four weeks. It will take him that long just to master the shifting patterns well enough to pass his driving test. And even then, he'll be just barely proficient. It seems you need to be a mental computer to learn the downshift.

Figure 6-9. Interior cab view showing two gearshift levers, known as *twin sticks* or as a *5&4* or *4&4* combination. *From the author's collection*

● *Don't Wait Too Long Before Starting the Downshift*

When you are driving twin sticks going into a steep upgrade, don't wait until the last minute to make a shift down! If you do, it will be too late to pick up engine speed. Once again, assume the operating range is 1800 to 2100 rpm. Don't wait until the engine is at 1800 and then try one gear down. By the time you catch the lower gear, your engine speed will have dropped so far below 1800 that even when you catch the lower gear, your engine will be lugging.

Here's how the problem arises. As the road speed of the truck decreases, the engine speed will decrease. You have to allow a second or so to make the gear change. This will cost you rpm in engine speed. While you assume that you have pushed the clutch in to begin your shift with the tach at 1800, it is actually another 200 or 300 rpm below that point.

So what's the answer? Start early if you expect to downshift without skipping any gears. Also, have another gear ready in your mind in case you miss the one you started for. Let's say you're in third over going for third direct (one gear below). If you scratch third direct or miss it completely, don't hesitate to go right for third under or second over. While you're playing with third direct, you may lose the next two gears below it because of the grade.

KEEP
AN
OPEN
MIND

As you can see, there are many different kinds of transmissions, and new ones are being developed all the time. A lot of veteran drivers who started with an old 150 hp engine years ago still drive every other engine the same way. Sometimes they do this because they don't want to show ignorance by asking what the difference in the new equipment is. Their ears should note the difference in the engine's sound, and they should ask

KEEP AN OPEN MIND (cont.)

how their driving should be modified to suit the new engine. But, too often, they won't ask for fear of looking stupid. Remember that no one can be expected to really know an engine he or she's never driven. Don't fall into this rut. The intelligent go-getter gets that way from keeping an open mind to changes and from asking questions.

TACHOGRAPHS

A tachograph is a multi-purpose service recorder. Different models record different things. However, some things are typically recorded by tachographs. These things are engine rpm, engine running time, miles per hour, miles traveled, high and low speed limits that the vehicle has reached, and stopping time. Within the instrument is a circular card which records all of these functions. This is why a tachograph is often called "a squealer." It records on the chart every movement of the vehicle, including stopping time. (See Figure 6-10.)

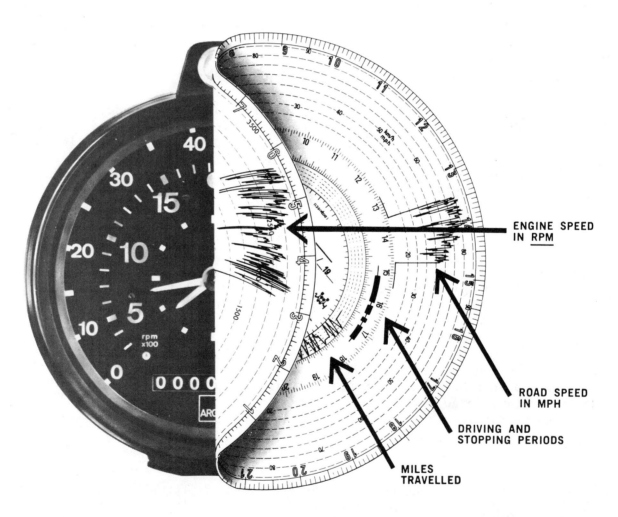

ENGINE SPEED
IN RPM

ROAD SPEED
IN MPH

DRIVING AND
STOPPING PERIODS

MILES
TRAVELLED

Figure 6-10. Many companies use tachs like this to obtain accurate, revealing records of each driver's daily performance. Things like lugging, over-revving, coasting, and taking too long a coffee break show up on the tach. *Courtesy of Argo Instruments Corporation*

96

TACHOGRAPHS (cont.)

The driver doesn't have to know how to read a tach. (That is, a tachograph. Drivers certainly have to know how to read a tachometer.) All the driver has to know is how to insert the chart in the tach and start it. Even experienced drivers should not be messing with the tach once the chart has been put in. Then, they don't disturb it. In most companies, the driver is not given a key for the tach. Only the dispatcher has that key.

As we said above, a tachograph is a tattletale device. The companies use them to keep tabs on the driver. Many drivers will quit a company before they let it install a tach in the truck. However, the tach can be more than a "squealer." It can be a protection for a driver in case of an accident, provided that the driver wasn't speeding. The tach can tell what speed the vehicle was doing at impact and whether the brakes were applied, and if so, how strongly. It can also catch errors in handling that new drivers are making so that the drivers' skills can be improved immediately. They can also help a supervisor to analyze routes because they can pinpoint slow-down areas, poor road conditions, steep hills, and similar things. Of course, if you're using poor driving techniques - such as those we've discussed in this chapter - they will show those things too.

SUMMARY | The first thing we discussed in this chapter was how to start the engine. We outlined the steps for starting both a gasoline and diesel engine. We stressed that you should never operate the starter, in either engine, for over 30 seconds. If it is a diesel engine, you want to watch the oil pressure and air pressure gauges very closely while you are starting the engine.

Next, we described two methods of testing the connection between the towing unit and the trailer or trailers. This is a safety measure you take so your trailer doesn't break loose from your truck.

After you've tested the hook-up, you may head on down the road, slowly releasing the clutch and speeding up the engine gradually so it doesn't stall. Then, you begin shifting up through the gears. Your engine may have five gears, or it may have as many as 10 or 13, depending upon what kind of transmission you have.

Each gear has a maximum speed. Once you've reached maximum speed in one gear, it's time to shift up to a higher one. The best method of shifting is called double clutching. You must use it on most manual truck transmissions, and it's good to use on any transmission. Double-clutching adds a step to gear shifting. You depress the clutch pedal, then pull the gearshift lever into neutral before you move into a higher or lower gear. Once you're in neutral, you immediately depress the clutch pedal again and shift into the gear you want.

We talked about the importance of keeping your mind on your gear shift patterns. The patterns vary from truck to truck, and if you use the wrong one, you might ruin your engine. Since there are many different patterns, you will have to learn to shift your truck when you get into it. However, we looked at two different shifting patterns as examples of what you can expect.

SUMMARY (cont.)

If you shift too soon (or even too late), you can lug your engine. Thus, we suggest that you shift by the tach. A tach (or tachometer) records engine rpm (revolutions per minute). The operating ranges of diesel engines vary, but all of them are short compared to a gasoline engine. When a trucker drives by the tach, he or she shifts gears so that the rpm are always kept within the operating range. In upshifting, the driver shifts when the tach reads close to the upper limit of the operating range. In downshifting, the driver shifts when the tach gets close to the lower limit of the operating range.

The last thing we touched on in this chapter was the tachograph. A tachograph usually combines a tachometer with a recording system. It prints information about the driver's driving habits and the route on a card. The tachograph in Figure 6-10 records typical things: engine speed in rpm, road speed in mph, driving and stopping periods and number of miles traveled.

GLOSSARY

auxiliary transmission: Another transmission which is coupled with the main transmission. It is usually referred to as a Brownie.

choke: A plate in the carburetor which shuts off the air supply to the engine. (*Carburetor* is defined in Chapter 12.)

clutch: The clutch is a group of disks that allows the engine to be disconnected from the gear box. The word "clutch" is also used to mean the clutch pedal which the driver depresses when changing gears.

coupling: The act of connecting the truck (or tractor) and trailer. Also called engaging. The word is also used to mean the connection between the two vehicles, that is, the kingpin and fifth wheel connection.

dispatcher: A person who schedules and controls truck pickups and deliveries and handles other similar jobs. The dispatcher often assigns drivers and vehicles to jobs, records information like departure and expected return times, and investigates overdue vehicles. The dispatcher may also issue equipment, establish routes and do many other tasks.

dissipate: To get rid of, to scatter or drive away.

double-clutching: A method of shifting gears. The driver depresses the clutch, moves the gearshift lever to neutral, then depresses the clutch again and moves the gearshift lever to the desired gear.

gear box: The transmission.

gear ratio: A comparison of the number of teeth on one gear to the number of teeth on another gear, expressed in two numbers. The gear ratio determines the amount of speed reduction or increase which will take place when you move from one gear to another. For example, if one gear has 25 teeth and another has 75 teeth, the ratio is 1:3. The first gear makes three turns for every one turn of the second.

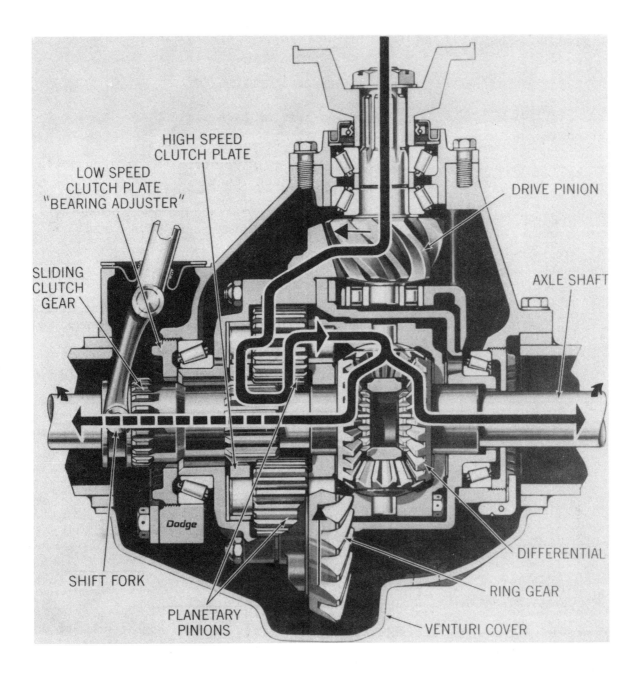

Figure 6-11. Typical heavy-duty, two-speed rear differential. The direction of rotation, shown by arrows above at the drive line, converts to a different direction at the axle shafts. *Courtesy of Chrysler Corporation*

GLOSSARY   (cont.)

gearshift lever: The "stick" used to shift the transmission, to shift the gears.

governor: A limiter, regulator or speed control device.

hitting the pin: Moving a truck or tractor back against the trailer in a short, sharp jerk to test the hook-up.

lugging: To run an engine too low in rpm in relation to the road speed or to run an engine below the recommended operating range.

operating range: The rpm range which an engine should be in when the truck is moving down the road. The typical operating range of a diesel is short, between 1800 and 2100 rpm.

popping the clutch: Releasing a clutch pedal rapidly.

rpm: Revolutions per minute, in other words, the number of turns or revolutions which something makes each minute. Diesel engines' turning speeds are rated in revolutions per minute.

synchromesh: A gear system in which contacting gears are reduced in speed to match each other before they engage.

tachograph: A clock chart that registers truck speed, revolutions of the engine, stops, starts, etc. Sometimes called a "squealer."

tachometer: An instrument which registers and displays engine rpm.

throttle (accelerator): A foot or hand unit which controls engine speed.

trailer hand valve: A hand-operated device mounted in the cab. It sets the brakes on the trailer only. It does not affect the tractor's brakes.

transmission: A box of gears that transmits power from the engine to the differential of a truck.

twin sticks: Dual gearshift levers which are used in some trucks to operate two gear boxes or "twin boxes." The two boxes, main and auxiliary, are known as the main box and the Brownie.

► CHECKING THE FACTS

Circle the letter of the word or phrase which <u>best</u> answers each question
or <u>best</u> completes each sentence.

1. The warning, "Don't operate the starter for over 30 seconds," refers
   to
   A. gasoline engines.
   B. diesel engines.
   C. both gasoline and diesel engines.
   D. engines with auxiliary transmissions.

2. The primary use of a trailer hand control valve in hooking up combina-
   tion units is
   A. to properly use underdrive in hitting the pin.
   B. to set the trailer brakes.
   C. to automatically open the fifth wheel jaws.
   D. to make sure the trailer air system has been cleared.

3. When you start a gasoline engine, you follow these steps in order:
   A. Set parking brake, put transmission in low, turn on ignition,
      operate starter, and operate throttle.
   B. Put transmission in neutral, turn on ignition, operate starter,
      depress clutch, and operate throttle.
   C. Turn on ignition, operate starter, pull out choke, depress clutch,
      move transmission to neutral, and operate throttle.
   D. Set parking brake, put transmission in neutral, pull out choke,
      depress clutch, turn on ignition, operate starter, and depress
      throttle.

4. What is the normal time for the oil pressure gauge to register during
   engine warm-up?
   A. 10 minutes
   B. 2 minutes
   C. 15 - 30 seconds
   D. 2 - 5 seconds

5. What is the best procedure to follow if your transmission can't be
   shifted smoothly because of improper timing in double-clutching?
   A. Stop immediately in a safe place and start over.
   B. Speed up the engine and continue in your present gear.
   C. Release the clutch pedal and speed up the engine again; then,
      push down the clutch and try once more.
   D. Release the clutch pedal; leave engine at idle; push down clutch,
      and try once more.

6. How long should the driver run the engine at fast idle before shutting
   it down?
   A. 30 seconds
   B. 3 - 5 minutes
   C. 15 - 20 minutes
   D. 7 - 10 minutes

7. Why do you let a diesel engine return to idling speed before shutting it down?
   A. You do this in a cold climate so it will be easier to start up again.
   B. So that you can put the engine into neutral and be ready to start back up.
   C. To avoid hot spots which could crack the engine block.
   D. So that the emergency shut-off valve opens and automatically sets the trailer brakes.

8. Which of the following is a bad practice?
   A. hitting the pin
   B. popping the clutch
   C. double-clutching
   D. driving by the tach
   E. none of the above

9. A typical close tolerance operating range would be
   A. 1700 - 2100 rpm.
   B. 0 - 2100 rpm.
   C. 700 - 2100 rpm.
   D. 1200 - 2100 rpm.

10. If you shift into a higher gear before your engine has reached maximum rpm, you will
    A. shift smoothly.
    B. overwind or overspeed your engine.
    C. lug your engine.
    D. gain speed.

11. Each time you shift down, you _____ the engine by

a set number of rpm per gear. Each time you shift up, you _____

_____ the engine by a set number of rpm per gear.

■ GETTING THE MAIN IDEAS

Circle the letter of the phrase that best completes each sentence or best answers each question.

1. Is double-clutching recommended on all manually-shifted truck transmissions?
   A. yes
   B. no
   C. all but synchromesh transmissions
   D. never

2. What is the primary reason for speeding up a diesel engine in each gear before upshifting?
   A. to maintain sufficient speed for traffic conditions
   B. to allow the transmission to be shifted more easily
   C. to avoid lugging the engine due to insufficient rpm
   D. to increase power to the drive chain

3. What is the primary purpose of downshifting?
   A. It is needed when changing road conditions require a reduction in controllable speed while maintaining proper engine rpm.
   B. It is needed to prevent loss of vehicle speed.
   C. It is needed to preserve utmost power for quick acceleration.
   D. none of the above

4. A driver watches the tach (tachometer) while driving to
   A. develop the proper rhythm for shifting.
   B. keep the rpm within the normal operating range.
   C. know when to shift gears.
   D. all of the above

5. What is the moral of the story about the driver in this chapter who ruined his engine?
   A. Don't overwind your engine.
   B. Don't lug your engine.
   C. Get a good night's rest so you can keep alert while you're shifting gears.
   D. Remember what truck you're driving and use the right shifting pattern for it.

The next five questions will help you find out how well you can get the main idea from charts. You will need to study Figure 6-6 to answer the next four questions and study Figure 6-8 to answer Question 10.

6. In the lower, left-hand corner of the chart, there is a gear shift pattern. What do "DIR" and "OD" stand for?

7. Now look at the shifting pattern in the upper, right-hand corner. When are you in neutral?

8. If you are in low range, with the range control button down, which gears can you shift into?

9. How do you shift into the high range gears?

10. Look at Figure 6-8. How do you find out how many rpm the engine is turning if you have this kind of tach?

★ GOING BEYOND THE FACTS AND IDEAS

1. How do you double-clutch? You may list the steps or describe the process in paragraph form.

2. What steps do you take in starting the diesel engine?

3. In your own words, list the steps which you must follow in shifting either the RT-910 or the RTO-9513. (See Figures 6-4 through 6-7.)

Circle the letter of the phrase which best answers each question below.

4. Look at Figure 6-4. Locate the range control button. What does the diagram mean when it points to "High Range" and "Low Range"?
   A. Some trucks will have high and some low range.
   B. You spin the button to the left for high range and to the right for low range.
   C. Most of the gears you use will be in high range.
   D. You pull the button up for high range and push it down for low range.

The last four questions refer to Figure 6-10.

5. Look at Figure 6-10. At what speed was the truck traveling just before it stopped?
   A. about 20 mph
   B. about 50 mph
   C. about 60 mph
   D. over 80 mph

6. What was the top speed the truck with this tach reached on this trip?
   A. about 20 mph
   B. about 50 mph
   C. about 70 mph
   D. over 80 mph

7. Which of the following statements is true of the driver who drove with this tach?
   A. The driver exceeded 80 mph most of the time he or she was driving.
   B. The driver allowed the engine to run at over 2500 rpm.
   C. The driver never drove over 55 mph.
   D. The driver rested between the hours of one and five in the morning.

8. Is there any other information which you can get from the tach shown in this illustration?

Figure 7-1. Single axle tractor pulling two Fruehauf beaded panel vans. Some of the features are lean beams; non-core, all-metal doors; and optional automatic support legs so you don't have to hand crank them. *Reprinted with permission of Fruehauf Division, Fruehauf Corp.*

Chapter Seven

DOT REGULATIONS ON DRIVING

MORE ABOUT RUDY | Remember Rudy from Chapter Three? When we left him, he had just arrived in Los Angeles, his home yard. It was 10:30, Monday night, and his boss told him that there was another load waiting for him.

Rudy drove home and caught a few hours of sleep. He couldn't sleep over four hours because he had to be back in the yard at 3:30 AM. This time, he has what he thinks will be an easy day, and he needs it. Just a load from LA to San Diego. He's due in San Diego at 7:00 AM.

After unloading, Rudy's routine procedure is to call the LA office to see if there's a pickup for the return trip. He makes the call.

MORE ABOUT RUDY   (cont.)

● *On to El Centro*

"There's freight we have to get in El Centro, and we have to deliver it here tomorrow morning," says the boss. Now Rudy has to go to El Centro, 110 miles east of San Diego.

By the time Rudy finishes in El Centro, it is four o'clock in the afternoon. Loading took a long time. The temperature was about 105° F (40° C) in the shade while he loaded up.

Here it is, only Tuesday, but already Rudy is running on sheer nerve - and conditioning, conditioning from pushing himself like this for a couple of years. This conditioning is the only thing keeping him awake at the wheel. He knows he has to make it into the yard with the load tonight or the boss will be on his back in the morning. So, he struggles between doing the job and doing the job well, a job he can take pride in without being a quitter. A good driver will sometimes stretch himself to the end because he is too proud to pack up and admit he's had enough.

● *What About Rudy's Log Book?*

Rudy arrives back at the home yard at ten o'clock in the evening, one more time. Already, on Tuesday, he has in over 36 hours. This is very nearly a minimum work week for anyone else.

What about Rudy's log book? Like all interstate drivers, Rudy must record his hours on duty and hours in the driver's seat in his log. So, he has to be either "Mickey-mousing" his log or carrying two. Either procedure is definitely a *violation of all good trucking practices* and a *violation of the law*.

If Rudy's schedule keeps up like this every day of the week, you can imagine the condition he will be in by Friday night. Everyone has to wind down once in a while. So, some drivers will add to this schedule a few beers after work, a little partying, a little socializing with the other drivers, and they may go some nights with no sleep at all.

● *The Ghost in the Bottle*

All drivers, at times, find themselves subject to situations similar to Rudy's. Some of them will try to push themselves beyond their physical limits and place their dependence upon a bottle full of pills - *amphetamines*. (Also called "whites," "uppers," "benies," and "speed.") The bottle may seem to be a cure-all. But in reality it becomes a monkey on the driver's back. For too many drivers, amphetamines are one of the ills of the trade.

The reason for taking pills, whatever it may be and however logical it may seem at the time, is *without merit*. Amphetamines are always unwise and, in fact, downright dangerous. They create a traffic hazard, and they injure the driver's nervous system. A driver who resorts to pills to see it through eventually loses reasoning power and normal reflexes. Plus, perhaps worst of all, the driver is subject to hallucinations of varying degrees.

MORE ABOUT RUDY (cont.)

By the time Rudy reaches Wednesday, if he decides he needs a little lift from a pill, it will be the beginning of the end. It won't be long before he will be taking more and more. Why? Because the system requires more to give the lift needed as time goes on. Then, one night, driving down the freeway, about midnight, starting to feel a little drowsy but not yet aware of it, he sees an approaching truck. It looks to him like two trucks with four lights. The question becomes, "Do I go to the right, between them, or to the left?"

● *Hallucinations*

One night, on the New Jersey turnpike, I was the co-driver in a berth when the rig came to a screeching halt. I almost fell out of the berth and asked what was the matter.

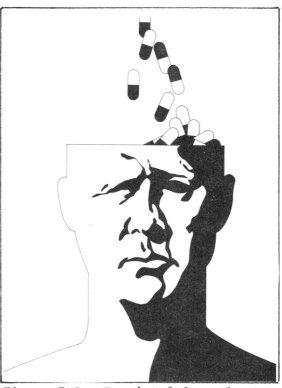

Figure 7-2. *Reprinted from the FDA Consumer, March, 1979.*

The driver said, "There's a woman with a baby buggy in the road!"

In the middle of the night? The driver had just locked it up. He had jammed on the brakes, coming to a screeching halt right in the middle of the freeway.

Another time, instead of following a curve, this same driver drove straight ahead and off the road. Fortunately, the shoulder was level. He was asleep, his eyes open, locked into position. This was a driver on amphetamines.

Another driver saw an elephant in the middle of the road. Hallucinations come in all forms. With such a driver, I and many others have sat behind the wheel for forty hours straight rather than let the other driver take a turn - for fear we'd never get to our destination if we let our co-drivers drive.

We don't have enough ICC inspectors today or state police to really watch the situation and catch the chronic violators. Sometimes, they get away with it long enough to catch themselves - often in tragic circumstances. It isn't just the driver on pills who needs checking. It might be "hot freight," an owner-operator who is running too many hours trying to make ends meet, or some other violation of the DOT rules. Remember, the DOT regs are safety precautions. They are there to protect you as a driver, and the population in general. Violate the rules and you have a very explosive situation - the kind you read about in a newspaper right after the accident happens.

107

BEFORE
YOU
READ ON The rest of this chapter gives the major DOT regulations which have to do with the actual driving of a motor vehicle in interstate commerce. It also includes the actions you are to take immediately before driving and when you stop, either to park, get fuel, or for an accident or other emergency.

As a professional driver, you are required to know these rules, yet they are sometimes detailed and difficult to remember. Therefore, we suggest that you study this chapter using the SQ3R method we discussed in Chapter 5. Remember it? Survey the chapter to see what you'll be studying. Turn each heading into a Question. Read each section to answer the question you asked yourself. Recite what you read; that is, say out loud the answer to your question. Review, or answer each question from memory. SQ3R.

BEFORE
YOU
START
WORK Some of these regulations take effect even before you start the day's work.

MCSR 392.3   If you are ill or fatigued, you cannot be required or permitted to drive.

MCSR 392.4   You cannot drive a vehicle if you are under the influence of narcotic or amphetamine drugs.

MCSR 392.5   If you have consumed an alcoholic beverage within four hours of reporting for work, you cannot drive. (Beer and wine are alcoholic beverages.) And you may not consume alcoholic beverages while on duty.

MCSR 392.9   A. If you are required to wear glasses or a hearing aid, you must be wearing the required item or items.

              B. If you wear contact lenses, you must carry a spare lens. If you are required to wear a hearing aid, you must have a spare battery.

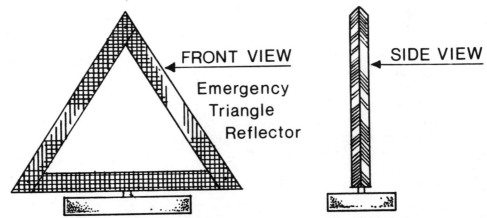

Figure 7-3. Directional triangle. Each rig must carry three of these. They are used as warning signals when a rig must be parked in an unsafe place.

108

MCSR 392.6   When your carrier dispatches you, your schedule cannot require you to exceed the speeds set by the government jurisdictions through which your vehicle travels.

MCSR 392.7   Before you leave, you must have inspected your vehicle and found the following parts in good working order:

A. Service brakes (including trailer brake connections)

B. Parking (hand) brake

C. Steering mechanism

D. Lighting devices and reflectors
Remember to wipe off the reflectors and lights. MCSR 392.33 says that motor vehicles may not be driven if any of the required lights or reflectors are obscured by dirt.

E. Tires

F. Horn

G. Windshield wiper or wipers

H. Rear vision mirror or mirrors

I. Coupling devices

MCSR 392.8   J. Emergency equipment

These are the checks of your rig which the DOT *requires* you to check during your pre-trip inspection. A good driver checks other things as well, as you will learn in the next chapter.

LOADING
AND
SECURING
CARGO

● *Safe Loading*

MCSR 392.9   Unless you are pulling a sealed van (we'll talk about these in a later chapter) or your vehicle is loaded in such a way that you cannot inspect the cargo, the regulations require that you inspect your load before you go.

Trailmobile platform trailers are available in heavy duty and extra heavy duty models. Inverted front and rear channels, along with massive "I" beam center rails offer full protection to this equipment.

Figure 7-4. Tandem axle semi-trailer. Do you think this is an accurate tie-down? *Courtesy of Pullman Trailmobile*

LOADING AND SECURING CARGO (cont.)

During the inspection of your load, check to see that

● the load is adequately distributed and properly secured;

● door tarps, etc., are secured; and

● the cargo doesn't interfere with the driver's view or free movement.

● *Accurate Tie-downs*

Sections MCSR 393.100 through 393.106 set exact requirements for tie-downs of loads. These requirements are detailed. They change from load to load. Therefore, we haven't included them here. We have included some of the more common ones in Chapter 20. When you are on the job, remember that these rules do exist and learn the ones which apply to the type of cargo you are hauling.

110

LOADING AND SECURING CARGO   (cont.)

Once on your way, you have to check your load within the first *25 miles.* Then, after the first 25-mile check, check it *at every change of duty status,* or *approximately every 150 miles.*

DRIVING ON THE ROAD

MCSR 392.10   Buses and placarded trucks must stop between 15 and 150 feet of railroad crossings. (Placarded trucks are those which are hauling explosives or other dangerous cargo. See Figure 22-7.) When it is safe, they may proceed, but the driver must not shift gears on the track.

MCSR 392.11   Interstate trucks which are *not* placarded must slow down to a speed at railroad crossings which will permit them to stop if they need to.

MCSR 392.12 & 392.13   The above railroad crossing rules apply to drawbridges too, unless they have electric traffic control signals.

MCSR 392.14   If an interstate driver comes across hazardous conditions, the driver must slow to a safe speed. Speed limits are for ideal driving conditions. That is, you're expected to observe them when the road is well-lighted, dry, free from sand or heavy winds, etc. When weather or road conditions are not ideal, you are to drive at a speed that suits those conditions.

MCSR 392.15   When you change the direction of your vehicle, you are to signal this change by flashing the turn signals. The DOT says you are to signal as follows:

A.   100 feet before a turn *and* during a turn

B.   Before and during entry into a traffic stream (such as on entering a freeway)

C.   100 feet before a lane change

MCSR 392.30   During the period between one half-hour *after sunset* and one half-hour *before sunrise* and whenever there is not enough light to see objects clearly at a distance of 500 feet, the required lamps must be lit.

MCSR 392.32   When you meet another vehicle, you are to dim your headlights as soon as the on-coming vehicle is within 500 feet. Also, you are to dim your headlights when you are following another vehicle within 500 feet.

STOPPING

● *Before You Leave Your Truck*

MCSR 392.20   Interstate drivers shall not leave their vehicles until the *parking brake has been set* and all reasonable *precautions have been taken to prevent movement.* This means *chock the wheels if necessary.*

● *Stopping on the Highway*

MCSR 392.21   Outside of business districts, pick your spot carefully. Don't stop, park, or leave your vehicle standing on the traveled part of the highway. If some emergency situation makes it impossible to get off the traveled part, make every effort to leave as much room as you can for passing traffic.

MCSR 392.22   Sometimes, an emergency forces a driver to stop on the traveled portion of the highway. If this happens to you, the DOT tells you to do this:

A. Turn on your four-way flashers.

B. Within 10 minutes of stopping, place your three required warning devices as follows:

On a Two-Lane Road.

1. 10 feet from front or rear

2. 100 feet from vehicle in the direction from which traffic is coming

3. 100 feet from vehicle in the direction in which traffic is going

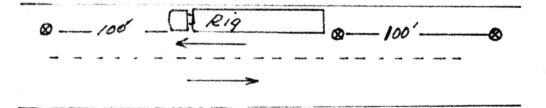

REFLECTOR POSITION
TWO-LANE ROAD

Figure 7-5. Proper placement of emergency reflectors on a two-lane road. Emergency reflectors are shown here as ⊗ . For an illustration of these reflectors, see Figure 7-3.

STOPPING (cont.)

On a Hill or Curve with Two-Way Traffic.

Two markers should be 100 to 500 feet from the vehicle, *one in each direction*. There is no set rule on curves. Your choice of placement will depend on visibility. Where will they provide other drivers with the best warning? The third marker should be placed near your vehicle. Remember, the idea is to give approaching traffic, from both directions, enough warning to safely steer around your rig.

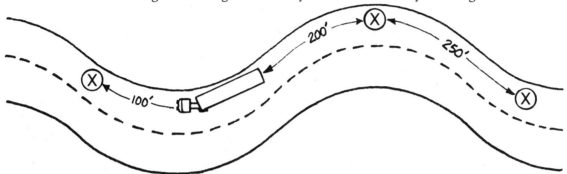

Figure 7-6. Good placement of emergency reflectors on a curve. Emergency reflectors are shown here as Ⓧ .

On a Divided Highway.

Place the markers on the *traffic side* only.

1. Within 10 feet of the vehicle

2. 100 feet from the vehicle in the direction from which the traffic is coming

3. 200 feet from the vehicle also in the direction from which the traffic is coming

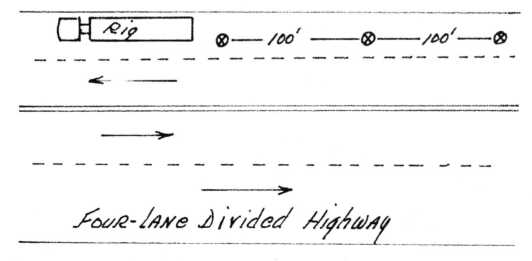

Figure 7-7. Emergency reflectors properly placed on a four-lane divided highway.

STOPPING   (cont.)

● *Stopping for Fuel*

MCSR 392.50 gives specific rules for truckers to follow when they are fueling up:

A. The engine must be turned off.

B. No one may smoke nearby. In fact, in the vicinity of the pumps, no one may do anything which might cause fire or explosion.

C. The fuel hose nozzle must be in continuous contact with the tank while the vehicle is being fueled. (This is to prevent static electricity from making a spark.)

MCSR 393.67   Fuel tanks of trucks must be securely capped. (When you are through fueling, remember to put the cap on.)

Figure 7-8. Here, a tractor pulling two new conventional tractors has stopped for fuel. You can just see one of the two tractors being towed. *Photo by. H. Haase*

PROHIBITED PRACTICES | While you are driving, you should remember that the MCSR forbid some practices. As we've said, these regulations apply to *all drivers* in interstate commerce, including owner-operators.

MCSR 392.15   This section prohibits the use of a turn signal on *only one side* of parked or disabled vehicles. It also prohibits the use of turn signals to signal to other drivers that it is safe to pass.

MCSR 392.60   This DOT section forbids interstate drivers to carry passengers without written prior approval. The only exceptions to this rule are for a few emergencies.

MCSR 392.61   Here, you are prohibited from letting an unauthorized person drive the vehicle which has been assigned to you.

MCSR 392.64   No person is allowed to ride in any closed part of your rig unless that part has a proper exit.

PROHIBITED PRACTICES (cont.)

MCSR 392.65   Most sleeper cabs have an opening between the sleeping and the
               driving portion. However, if a rig does not have this type of
               direct access between the two, a person is not to move from the
               sleeper berth to the cab while the vehicle is moving.

MCSR 392.68   You may not drive a motor vehicle with the means of power dis-
               engaged from the driving wheels, unless you are stopped or shift-
               ing gears. This means you may *not* coast.

SUMMARY | After a story about Rudy, the overworked driver, we covered
          DOT regulations relating to the actual driving of a motor
          vehicle and the actions to take before driving and when you
          stop. Let's review some of the key regulations.

As an interstate driver, you may not drive if you are ill, exhausted, or
under the influence of alcohol or a drug which might affect your driving ability. Your schedule has to be reasonable. That is, you should not be forced to
exceed any speed limits to keep it.

Before you start, you must perform the required inspection of your vehicle, and you must examine your load to see that it is secured properly. Then,
you must recheck your load at specified intervals throughout the run. If your
rig has seat belts, you have to wear them.

The DOT gives specific instructions about railroad crossings and drawbridges. Trucks carrying dangerous cargo must stop before them, then proceed carefully and not shift gears on the tracks. Other trucks must slow down as they
approach the tracks so they can stop before them if they have to.

You are to drive at a speed which suits the weather and road conditions,
but never over the speed limit. You are to use turn signals properly and dim
your headlights appropriately. Light your lamps between ½ hour after sunset
and ½ hour before sunrise *and* when needed to see things 500 feet in front.

The DOT has this to say about stopping. *Always* set your parking brake
when you leave your rig, and, if you must to be sure the vehicle won't move,
chock the wheels. If you stop on the highway, pull off to the shoulder of the
road. Don't stop or park on the traveled part of the road unless there is no
way you can drive off to the side. If you do have to stop on the traveled part
of the roadway, place your emergency warning devices in the proper places.
When you stop for fuel, don't smoke; turn off the engine, and keep the nozzle
in contact with the fuel tank as you fill it. (Remember to put the cap back
on correctly when you're finished getting fuel.)

Finally, remember that there are some things you can't do as an interstate
driver. You can't carry passengers or let a person drive your rig unless you
have received prior authorization. You can't let a person ride in some closed
part of your rig unless it is equipped with a proper exit. And, you can't
coast.

GLOSSARY

amphetamine: A drug which affects the central nervous system. Amphetamines may increase alertness for a short time. They work by short-circuiting the feeling of exhaustion. The driver using them can use up the body's reserves of energy completely. Finally, she or he experiences a sudden and total collapse. Amphetamines can cause hallucinations and can be habit-forming. Sometimes called, "uppers," "speed," "benies," or "whites."

chocking the wheels: Placing a wedge or block behind or in front of a wheel to prevent movement.

co-drivers: Two drivers who share responsibilities for a rig - driving and other duties. One will be the senior driver; the other, the helper.

disabled vehicle: A vehicle which has broken down, can't be driven.

narcotic: A drug which relieves pain and brings on sleep.

placard: A sign which is attached to a vehicle to warn of dangerous cargo. A "placarded" vehicle is one which has placards posted on it.

precaution: Caution or care taken beforehand. A safeguard.

unauthorized person: In trucking, a person who has not been approved for riding in or driving a vehicle.

▶ CHECKING THE FACTS

One of the numbers or phrases on the right goes with each of the phrases on the left. Match them correctly by putting the letter of the item on the right in the blank before its matching phrase on the left. Use each item _only_ _once_. (Notice that this exercise carries over to the next page.)

_____ 1. the number of feet before a lane change at which you signal

_____ 2. when you can't smoke

_____ 3. the number of feet from the rear of your rig where one reflector should be placed on a divided highway

_____ 4. when you can't shift gears

A. when you're near a fuel pump

B. three

C. four

D. 100

E. 500

F. 10

G. 200

H. ½ hour after sunset to ½ hour before sunrise

_____5. the number of feet from
the rear of your rig where
one reflector should be
placed on a two-lane road

_____6. the number of hours before
work during which a driver
can't drink alcohol

_____7. when you can drive up to
the speed limit

_____8. the number of emergency
reflectors you carry in
your rig

_____9. light all of the required
lamps on the rig

_____10. the number of feet between
your rig and an on-coming
vehicle when you are to
dim your headlights

_____12. the number of miles you can
drive before stopping to
recheck your load.

I. when road and weather conditions are ideal

J. 25

K. when you're driving a placarded vehicle over railroad tracks

■ GETTING THE MAIN IDEAS

1. What are placarded vehicles to do when they come to railroad
crossings? What about regular trucks?

2. You're watching the game on TV and you just opened your second nice,
cold beer. Your boss calls and says that Becky didn't show up, so
you'll have to take the Buffalo to Toronto run. What do you do?

3. What things do you need to check during your inspection of the load?

4. What do you legally use your turn signals for? Also, what are you
prohibited from using them for?

5. In your own words, list the steps you would take in refueling your
truck. Your co-driver just lit a cigarette when you pulled into the
truck stop.

★ GOING BEYOND THE FACTS AND IDEAS

1. Describe the pre-trip inspection you would make on your interstate
    tractor-trailer combination. You might want to take a few words to
    describe the rig.

2. Have you ever heard of anyone who had an experience while driving
    under the influence of amphetamines, alcohol or another drug? What
    happened?

3. You are driving a semi on a curvy, mountain road. It's a two-lane
    road, very narrow. Your tractor stops running. You push the throttle
    in further. No response. Draw a picture of the road and show your
    placement of the three emergency reflectors.

4. You drive in a hilly city. You make a lot of stops in your local
    delivery job. How do you secure your rig when you jump out to make
    a pickup or delivery?

Figure 8-1. A typical combination - a Utility dry freight van and a White Freightliner tractor - shown in the maintenance shop of Sather's Cookies in Round Lake, Minnesota. *Courtesy of Utility Trailer Mfg. Co.*

Chapter Eight

INSPECTION OF EQUIPMENT

BRENDA'S STORY | Thousands of words have been written describing proper procedures pertaining to vehicle inspections by the driver. Federal law requires it and the commercial trucking companies require it. Therefore, it is very important to take time to learn how to properly perform an inspection of the truck's equipment. Consider the case of Brenda Hoover.

Picture Brenda. In her own mind, she's the pride of the trucking industry. After all, don't we all think we are the best? She walks into the yard and does a fine inspection job on her tractor and trailer. She's systematic,

119

BRENDA'S STORY (cont.)

does everything by the numbers, just as it should be done. She's very efficient. She lifts the hood of the truck to check the oil and water before she fires off the engine. Then, with the engine warming and air pressure building up, she does a thorough job of walk-around inspection. She checks the air lines and fittings, tires and clearance lights, strutting just a bit as she walks around. All of this takes a matter of five minutes from the time she hooks up. She feels proud. She's doing a great job of impressing the fellows and gals in the yard. Finally, thinking everything is fine, she hops up in the cab, puts the truck in gear, and takes off.

Brenda did a good job as far as it went. Up to her first delivery stop, everything had gone great. Unfortunately, during her inspection, she had been thinking more about the impression she was making on the other drivers hanging around the yard than about doing the job completely. For when she hit her first stop, she found out that she had picked up the wrong trailer! Brenda had overlooked one important thing; she hadn't checked the cargo.

Brenda's situation is a very common one. Instead of trying to impress the other drivers, she should have kept her mind on her job. She would have saved herself a lot of embarrassment because the other drivers will never let her live it down. This isn't an isolated incident. It happens all the time.

WHAT IS THE PURPOSE OF THE INSPECTION? The regulations of the Department of Transportation and most state regulatory agencies, plus the operating rules of progressive motor carriers *all* require drivers to inspect their vehicles prior to the start of each trip or tour of duty. A properly performed inspection is a protection to the driver because -

- It reduces the chances of a driver taking out a vehicle which may be involved in an *accident* due to a hazardous mechanical condition, and

- It reduces the risk and inconvenience of a *mechanical failure* on the road.

In making the required inspections, you are not expected to take on the duties of the mechanic or of the maintenance department. You are simply required to observe the condition of the unit and make a brief check of parts of the vehicle which will affect its safe operation. You must be able to recognize both normal and abnormal conditions of these parts. Then, if you find any defects, you are to report them to the shop so that they may be corrected before you or another driver sets out in the vehicle.

The purpose of this chapter is to provide you with an outline for making the required inspections thoroughly and efficiently.

HOW OFTEN ARE INSPECTIONS MADE?

A professional driver will make an inspection of the equipment *before* each trip, *during* the trip, and *upon completion* of the trip. (As you read in the last chapter, the cargo should be inspected again within the first 25 miles and at every change of duty status or at intervals of approximately 150 miles.) The guidelines on frequency of inspections are slightly different for local and over-the-road drivers.

● *Long-line Drivers*

As a rule of thumb, an over-the-road driver should give the vehicle a quick visual inspection *at each stop*. Some loads require more frequent regular checks than normal. In many regular route operations, regular checks are established at which the driver is required to make an inspection.

● *Local Drivers*

In local pickup and delivery operations, the driver is required to make an inspection of the equipment *immediately before and after the meal period*. Equipment being interchanged between carriers must be inspected and a driver who operates more than one unit during a tour of duty must inspect *each* unit before driving it and make out a report on the condition of *each* vehicle after driving it.

"When did you first discover it was gone?"

Figure 8-2. *Reprinted with permission from Heavy Duty Trucking Magazine. Copyright 1979.*

The MCSR not only require you to inspect your rig before
your tour of duty; they also require you to submit a *written report* on the mechanical condition of the vehicle at
the *conclusion* of each trip. Most motor carriers also require this report, even if they don't travel interstate.

As we mentioned in Chapter 3, each driver must complete a log book showing on and off-duty hours of service. Some log books have an itemized vehicle
inspection report printed on the back of each log page. If your log book has
this type of report sheet, use it to report your post-trip inspection required
by the DOT. If you follow the instructions on it, you can be sure that your
inspection will meet DOT minimum standards. Since you will be handing in your
log sheet to your carrier at the end of each tour of duty or at the end of
each day, you will be turning in your inspection report at the same time.
Figure 8-3 shows a correctly completed "Driver's Daily Vehicle Condition Report."

When you hand in your inspection report, the dispatcher will send it on
to the maintenance shop immediately if any service is needed on the vehicle.
Then, it will be kept in the files for 90 days to one year, to conform with
the DOT regulations.

Basically, the same procedure is used for making the pre-trip check, in
checking the vehicle on the road, and inspecting it at the conclusion of a
trip before you write up the vehicle condition report. If you find a defect
in your rig on your *pre-trip inspection,* report it to the shop right away so
that they can correct it before you depart. If you find a defect during your
post-trip inspection (or if one developed during your trip) do two things:
report it to the shop <u>and</u> make a note of it on your inspection report.

Before you begin your inspection, fill in the top of the form. Write in
the name of the owner of the vehicle, for example, "Lifeline Trucking, Inc.,"
or "T.L. Garcia," or "P.T. Barnum." In the space marked, *"Vehicle Number,"*
put the number which the trucking company has assigned to your vehicle. Then,
fill in your name where it says, *"Driver,"* and fill in the date.

Now you are ready to begin your inspection "by the numbers." The easiest
way to complete your report is probably to carry it with you as you inspect
each part of your rig, checking things off as you inspect them.

As you can see, the inspection we are recommending here is
far more complete than the minimum standards set by the
DOT. As you read through this outline of a thorough rig
inspection, ask yourself why each check is important. You may feel that some
of the checks are unnecessary. If you do, be honest about it. Don't just
read them now figuring you'll disregard them when you are on the job. If you
feel a check is not needed, a waste of your time, write it down or place a
check beside it in the margin. Then, find someone you can discuss your feelings with, and determine for yourself whether or not that inspection point is
important.

DRIVER'S DAILY VEHICLE CONDITION REPORT

(TO BE COMPLETED DAILY IN ACCORDANCE WITH RULE 396.7 OF SAFETY REGULATIONS PRESCRIBED BY THE D. O. T.)

OWNER'S NAME _Del Norte Trucking Co._   VEHICLE NUMBER *T-156* *S-101*

DRIVER _Norman Crow_   DATE _1-15-_

ITEMS TO CHECK	DRIVERS REPORT	MECHANICS REPORT	ITEMS TO CHECK	DRIVERS REPORT	MECHANICS REPORT
BEFORE STARTING ENGINE	✓		COOLING SYSTEM	✓	
			ENGINE	✓	
OIL, IF ADDED INSERT NO. QTS.	✓		LEAKS	✓	
GAS, IF ADDED INSERT NO. GALS.	✓		LIGHTS, HEAD	✓	
WATER	✓		TAIL	✓	
BRAKE LINES TO TRAILER	✓		STOP AND TURN	✓	
ELECTRIC LINES TO TRAILER	✓		CLEARANCE AND MARKER	✓	
DRIVE LINE	✓		REFLECTORS	✓	
COUPLING DEVICES	✓				
TIRES & WHEELS	✓		**AFTER STARTING ENGINE (IN CAB)**		
SPRINGS	✓		AIR PRESSURE WARNING DEVICE	✓	
BODY — DOOR	X	✓	OIL PRESSURE	✓	
GLASS	✓		AMMETER	✓	
			HORN	✓	
EMERGENCY EQUIPMENT			WINDSHIELD WIPERS	✓	
TORCHES, LANTERNS, OR REFLECTORS	✓		PARKING BRAKES	✓	
FUSEES	✓		CLUTCH	✓	
FLAGS	✓		TRANSMISSION	✓	
SPARE BULBS	✓		REAR VISION MIRRORS	✓	
FUSES	✓		STEERING	✓	
FIRE EXTINGUISHER	✓		SERVICE BRAKES	✓	
TIRE CHAINS N/A			SPEEDOMETER	✓	
AFTER STARTING ENGINE (OUT OF CAB)			OTHER ITEMS *None*		
FUEL SYSTEM	✓				

DAILY MILEAGE RECORD

SPEEDOMETER READING END OF DAY _39,185_

SPEEDOMETER READING START OF DAY _39,000_

TOTAL MILES DRIVEN TODAY _185_

DATE OF TRAILER LUBRICATION IF ON THIS TRIP _____

I MADE INSPECTION AS REQUIRED ON LISTED ITEMS
DRIVER'S SIGNATURE: _Norman Crow_

I CERTIFY THAT REPAIRS CHECKED WERE MADE TODAY:
MECHANIC'S SIGNATURE: _J. M. Somers_

REPAIR ORDER NO.:

DRIVER: USE √ IF ITEM IS SATISFACTORY
USE X IF ITEM IS NOT SATISFACTORY

MECHANIC: USE √ WHEN ITEM IS CORRECTED AND SIGN YOUR INITIALS.

REMARKS: _Driver's door handle broken_

70-5A   REORDER FROM AMERICAN TRUCKING ASSNS., 1616 P ST., N.W. WASHINGTON, D.C. 20036

Figure 8-3. This is a sample of a correctly completed post-trip vehicle inspection report. As you can see, the driver who completed this report found only one thing wrong with the vehicle; the driver's door handle is broken.

HOW TO PERFORM AN INSPECTION	As you inspect each item listed on the back of your log sheet, check it off with a check mark (✓) if the item is satisfactory. An ex (✗) means that the item is *not* satisfactory; it is defective and needs repair. Every item must be marked with a check mark (✓) or an ex (✗).

The second column (see Figure 8-3) is for the mechanic's report. In most cases, the driver doesn't make any marks in this column, marked, *"Mechanic's Report,"* unless she or he personally makes minor repairs. As the mechanic repairs each item, he or she will check it off as satisfactory (✓) and then sign the lower portion of the form, certifying that the repairs have been made.

As you make your inspection, be sure to fill in every item on the report that applies to your vehicle. Thoroughly check out each component and run each check listed below. But pay special attention to three special safety areas: the *lights,* the *brakes* and the *tires.*

1. Look for leaks.

    When visibility permits, glance under the truck or power unit for signs of fresh oil, water, grease or fuel leaks. Any fresh leakage from a vehicle is a sure sign of trouble.

2. Raise the hood or complete cab (whichever you need to to get to the engine) and check these things:

    A. Oil level in crankcase.

    B. Water level in radiator. (The water should be just visible in the upper tank area.)

    C. Belts for generator water pump and air compressor. Check for tension and signs of wear. Pull on each belt by hand. If it moves, there is probably too much slippage.

Figure 8-4. *From the author's collection*

In addition –

E. Look at the engine wiring for cracked or badly worn insulation.

F. Look for loose wires. Be sure all spark plugs are on tight if it is a gasoline engine.

G. Look for signs of leaks around the engine.

H. Lower and secure cab or hood.

124

3.   Enter cab and start engine:

   A.   Watch instruments and check for normal
        readings. Watch particularly that oil
        pressure registers on the oil pressure
        gauge *within 5 seconds*. Check to see
        that the ammeter shows charge. If the
        truck is so equipped, watch to see
        that the oil pressure light and air
        pressure light go out.

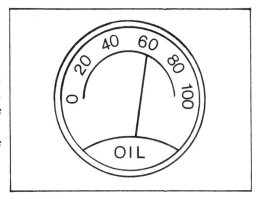

Figure 8-5.   Oil pressure gauge.

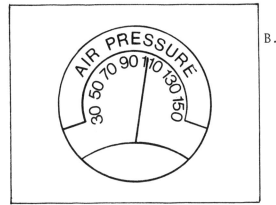

Figure 8-6.   Air pressure gauge
showing safe marginal pressure.

   B.   The air pressure gauge is the indicator
        of the supply of air in the braking
        system. Watch the air pressure gauge
        (or vacuum gauge if truck is so equip-
        ped) to be sure that air is building up.
        *Be sure that air is building up to safe
        limits - approximately 110 pounds.*
        Safe marginal pressure is normally con-
        sidered to be from 60 lbs to 110 lbs.
        However, 60 pounds is considered only
        a safe *minimum* and safe *operating*
        pressure is generally from 90-110 lbs.

   C.   When air pressure has built to maximum (110 pounds), leave the trans-
        mission in neutral and check to see that your parking brake is set.
        Then, get out to check the outside of the vehicle. Let engine idle
        to warm up gradually while you are outside.

4.   Turn on all lights and leave cab.

     Check headlights. Then return to cab and press foot dimmer switch and
     check other beam. Then push headlight switch in to halfway position to
     check parking lights on the power unit. Turn headlight switch off. Leave
     other lights on if unit has clearance and marker lights on a separate
     switch.

5.   Beginning at left front wheel, check exterior of vehicle.

   A.   Check *left front tire of power unit* for proper inflation. (Use a
        tire gauge.) *Check lug nuts.* Look at hub for signs of leaking grease.

   B.   Walk to front of unit and look up to check cab and/or front body lights.

   C.   Look under front unit for irregularities in steering mechanism.

   D.   Check *right front tire and wheel of power unit* as outlined in A above.

HOW TO PERFORM INSPECTION (cont.)

Now start down the right side of the vehicle first.

E. Check *right rear wheels of power unit* as outlined in A above, as you proceed toward rear of unit.

F. On a combination unit, check the fifth-wheel connection (jaws) at this point by looking under unit. If any light is visible between upper and lower plates of connection, the unit is not properly hooked up.

G. Check *right front side marker light and right front reflector* on trailer (on top and bottom of trailer as shown in Figure 8-8).

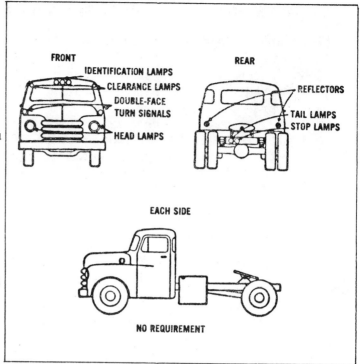

Figure 8-7. This illustration shows the lamps required by the MCSR. All interstate tractors must be equipped with all of these lights.

H. Check semi-trailer landing gear to be sure it is fully raised and that the crank handle is properly secured. (See Figure 8-9.)

I. Check *right rear tires and wheels of semi-trailer* as outlined in A above.

J. Check *right rear side marker lights and right rear reflector*. (See Figure 8-8, bottom.)

K. From rear of unit, check *rear clearance lamps* (at top of trailer) and *tail lamps and rear reflectors* (near bottom of trailer). (See Figure 8-8, top). Check to be sure rear doors are secure.

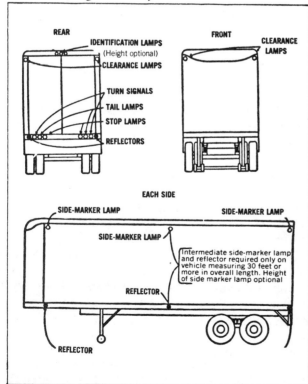

Figure 8-8. Shows lamps which the MCSR require on interstate trailers.

126

Next, start up the left side of the vehicle.

    L. Check *left* rear side marker light and *left* rear reflector on the side of the trailer.

    M. Check *left rear tires and wheels of semi-trailer* as outlined in A above.

    N. Check under the unit to be sure the fifth-wheel jaws are fully closed around trailer kingpin. Check fifth-wheel release lever to be sure it is in *locked* position.

    O. Check *left front side marker light and left front reflector.*

    P. Check *left rear tires and wheels of power unit* as outlined in A above.

6. Re-enter cab.

    A. Switch on left turn signal, checking front and rear for proper function.

    B. Re-enter and switch right turn signal and check front and rear.

    C. Honk horn to see that it operates properly.

    D. Operate windshield wipers to see that they are in good working order.

7. Check to see that all safety equipment is in the rig: three reflector triangles, two red flags, a fire extinguisher and spare fuses for each fuse used in the vehicle. The fire extinguisher must be properly filled and securely mounted where you can get to it quickly if you need it. In addition, if you are likely to encounter weather conditions requiring the use of chains, the DOT requires that you must carry one set of chains for at least one driving wheel on each side of the vehicle.

8. Wipe off all glass and mirrors. Check to see that rear vision mirrors are lined up for good visibility. (You should have wiped off all lights and reflectors when you made your check of the outside of the unit.)

9. If equipment is available, use the following procedure to check the air brake system.

    A. Check the compressor belt. (Some air compressors for truck air brake systems are driven by a belt running between the engine pulley and the compressor.) If the slack in the belt midway between the fan and the compressor is more than one inch, *or* if the belt appears to be cracked or worn, *report the condition to the shop and have it corrected before you start your trip.* (You may wish to check the belt when you're checking the oil and water levels so you don't have to raise the hood or cab again.)

    B. Check compressor action by starting the engine and letting maximum air pressure build up. This should not take more than five minutes with the engine running at fast idle. Some rigs have low pressure

Figure 8-9. An automatic trailer leg-support system by Fruehauf. The legs support the stationary semi-trailer when it is unhitched. To couple, the tractor backs its trailer-hitch plate (fifth wheel) under the trailer, and the hinged lower support legs automatically retract up and away for road-clearance (upper photo). To uncouple, the driver releases a safety latch, and as the tractor moves forward, the legs return to the correct stationary support position (lower photo). *Reprinted with permission of Fruehauf Division, Fruehauf Corporation.*

warning devices (red lights and buzzers). If you have them in your
rig, be sure they operate properly. When the system has built up
maximum pressure, the needle on the air gauge should stop rising
slightly above 100 pounds pressure. Then, allow engine to return to
a slow idle. If the air pressure gauge drops rapidly when you have
returned to a slow idle, *or* if a low pressure warning device starts
to operate, report the condition to the shop.

C.   Check for leaks. With maximum pressure built up, shut off the engine.
     Immediately, step on the brake pedal and hold it down. There will be
     a pressure drop of from 5 to 15 pounds when you apply the brakes. If
     pressure continues to drop beyond 15 pounds while your foot is on the
     brake pedal *or* if you hear air leaks, *report the condition to the shop
     and have it corrected before you start your trip.*

D.   Drain the air tanks. You must drain the air brake system periodically
     like this to remove built-up moisture and sludge. For best results,
     you should drain the air tanks at the end of each day. However, in
     cold weather, it is especially important to drain the tanks daily to
     keep moisture from freezing or obstructing the brake lines.

E.   Check the brake operation. You'll need a partner to help you handle
     this operation. One of you can operate the brakes in the cab, and the
     other one can observe the brake action on the trailer.

     (1)   Disconnect the air hoses between the tractor and trailer. The
           trailer brakes should come on at once and stay on.

     (2)   Reconnect the brake hoses and make sure the trailer brakes are
           charged. Be sure the trailer brakes release properly when they
           are charged. Then, place the *cab control valve* in the *emergency
           position* (pulled out). (See cab control valve in Figure 8-14.)
           The trailer brakes should come on and stay on.

     (3)   Return the cab control valve to the *normal position* (pushed in).
           Fan down the air pressure by rapidly applying and reapplying the
           service brakes. The trailer brakes should come on and stay on
           before the tractor pressure drops down to 20 pounds.

F.   After completing this inspection and test procedure, take steps to
     see that the trailer brakes are charged and the air pressure is up to
     the maximum as indicated on the dash gauge. Finally, make a test
     stop, preferably in the terminal yard.

(The air brake inspection will become much clearer to you after you have
studied Chapter 9.)

BE
ALERT | If your vehicle has met and passed your inspection, you
       are ready for the road. But always be alert to any unusual
       noises in your equipment, and never hesitate to pull over
to an appropriate stopping area to recheck your vehicle. *Always remember,
safety is the lifeline of the trucking industry.*

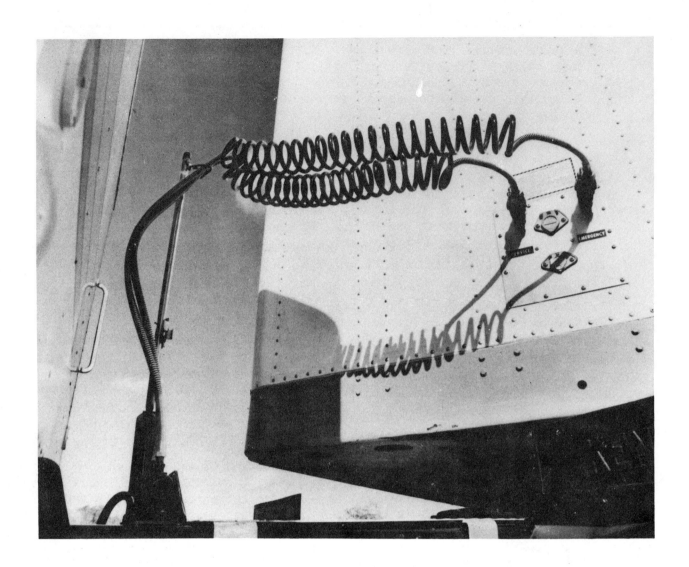

Figure 8-10. Air hoses making connection between tractor and trailer. This type of brake coil is used on extended tractors which have out-board/chassis-mounted valve ports. Notice the *pogo stick* (pole which supports the air hoses) and the *glad hands* (which connect the hoses to the trailer. *Courtesy of Parker Hannifin Corporation*

| OTHER INSPECTION FORMS | Not all carriers will have you use the inspection form which is printed on the reverse side of your log pages. Some will use others. The two forms shown in Figures 8-11 and 8-12 are common inspection forms used by shops |

and terminals for tractor and trailer units. The form in Figure 8-11 is for inspecting trucks and tractors. The form in Figure 8-12 is used when you are inspecting trailers. Both have been properly completed in these examples. "N/A" stands for "Not Applicable," and it means that the item beside "N/A" does not apply to this vehicle.

TRUCK/TRACTOR INSPECTION REPORT

TRUCK NUMBER	TRACTOR NUMBER	MAKE	YEAR	LICENSE NUMBER	MILEAGE
T 165		K.W.		J 15685	140,000

MARK EACH ITEM AS FOLLOWS: ____√____ O.K. ____0____ NEEDS WORK ____X____ ADJUSTED OR REPAIRED *(Explain on reverse side)*

INSPECT OR CHECK FOR PROPER OPERATION

1. ✓	EXHAUST SYSTEM		16. ✓	ELECTRIC LINES
2. ✓	SPRINGS, SHACKLES AND U BOLTS		17. ○	CLUTCH
3. ✓	RADIUS RODS		18. ✓	MIRRORS
4. ✓	STEERING		19. ✓	REFLECTORS
5. ✓	UNIVERSAL JOINTS		20. ✓	GLASS
6. ✓	PROPELLER SHAFT		21. ✓	FIFTH WHEEL
7. ✓	WHEELS, WHEEL NUTS		22. ✓	BODY
8. ✓	BRAKE DRUMS		23. ○	TIRES
9. ✓	FAN AND COMPRESSOR BELTS		24. ✓	AIR/HYDRAULIC LINES
10. ✓	FUEL LINES		25. ○	CAB (INTERIOR, EXTERIOR)
11. ✓	HORN		26. ○	WINDSHIELD WIPERS
12. ✓	HEADLIGHTS		27. ✓	BRAKES (SERVICE AND PARKING)
13. ○	DIRECTIONAL SIGNALS		28. ✓	LOW AIR PRESSURE INDICATOR
14. ✓	STOP, TAIL AND MARKER LIGHTS		29. ✓	ENGINE OPERATION
15. ○	GAUGES		30. ✓	HEATER/DEFROSTER

CHECK AND SERVICE THE FOLLOWING

31. X	RADIATOR COOLANT LEVEL		36. X	ENGINE OIL LEVEL
32. X	ANTI-FREEZE		37. X	TRANSMISSION OIL LEVEL
33. X	BATTERY ACID LEVEL		38. X	REAR AXLE OIL LEVEL
34. X	TIRE INFLATION PRESSURE		39. N/A	BRAKE MASTER CYLINDER LEVEL
35. X	DRAIN AIR TANKS		40. X	EMERGENCY EQUIPMENT SUPPLIES *Reflectors*

OTHER CONDITIONS REQUIRING ATTENTION NOT SPECIFIED ABOVE:

LIST REPAIRS OR REPLACEMENTS NEEDED ON REVERSE SIDE

DATE INSPECTED	INSPECTED BY
Jan 30	R. H.

C-13122 REV. 5-72 PRINTED IN U.S.A.

Figure 8-11. Common inspection form used by shops and terminals for inspecting tractors and trucks. Which items need work? Which ones were adjusted or repaired?

TRAILER INSPECTION REPORT

TRAILER NUMBER	MAKE	YEAR	LICENSE NUMBER
1069	Dobbs		X 124356

TYPE: ☒ VAN ☐ TANK ☐ FLATBED ☒ INSULATED ☐ OPEN TOP   OTHER (describe):

MARK EACH ITEM AS FOLLOWS: ____✓ O.K. ___0___ NEEDS WORK ___X___ ADJUSTED OR REPAIRED (Explain on reverse side)

FRONT

1. ✓	ELECTRIC AND AIR CONNECTIONS		3. ✓	FIFTH WHEEL PLATE AND KINGPIN
2.	HEADERBOARD N/A		4. ✓	BODY LIGHTS

LEFT SIDE / RIGHT SIDE

5. ✓	LANDING GEAR		5a. ✓	LANDING GEAR
6. ✓	BODY LIGHTS		6a. ✓	BODY LIGHTS
7. ✓	TIRES		7a. ✓	TIRES
8. ✓	BRAKE DRUMS		8a. ✓	BRAKE DRUMS
9. ✓	WHEELS AND LUGS		9a. ✓	WHEELS AND LUGS
10. ✓	REFLECTORS		10a. ✓	REFLECTORS

REAR

11. ✓	BODY LIGHTS		14. ✓	MUD FLAPS
12. ✓	STOP AND TAILLIGHTS		15. ✓	REAR BUMPERS
13. O	REFLECTORS		16. ✓	DOORS AND LATCHES

UNDERSIDE

17. ✓	FRAME AND CROSS MEMBERS		20. ✓	AIR LINES AND HOSES
18. ✓	SPRINGS AND U BOLTS		21. ✓	BRAKE RODS AND DIAPHRAGMS
19. ✓	ELECTRIC WIRING		22. ✓	BRAKE LININGS

INTERIOR

23. O	FLOOR		25. ✓	ROOF
24. ✓	SIDES		26.	SPECIAL EQUIPMENT

OTHER ITEMS REQUIRING ATTENTION NOT SPECIFIED ABOVE:

LIST REPAIRS OR REPLACEMENTS NEEDED ON REVERSE SIDE

DATE	LOCATION	INSPECTED BY
Jan 30	Rapid City, SD	R.H.

C-13121 REV. 5-72 PRINTED IN U.S.A.

Figure 8-12.   Common inspection form used by shops and terminals for inspecting trailers. What type of trailer did the shop inspect? Was anything in need of work?

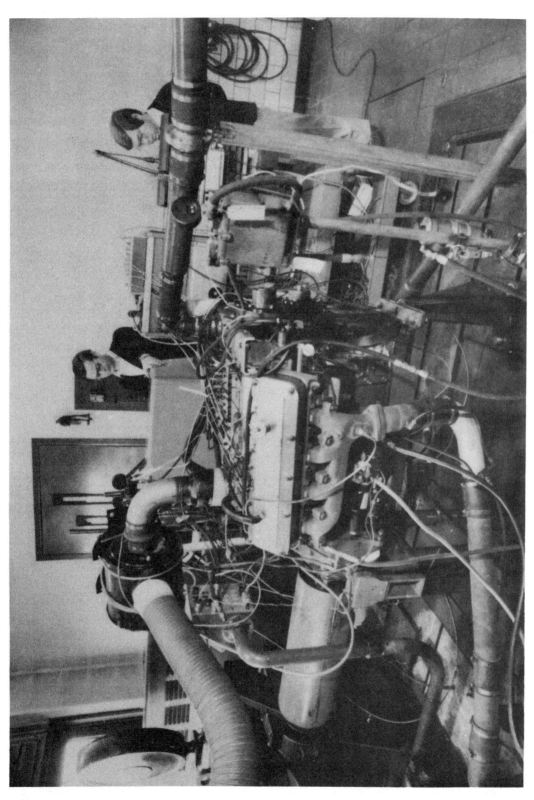

International 9.0 liter diesel engine undergoing testing procedures prior to its introduction. Manufacturers inspect their engines before they put them on the market. But it's up to the driver to keep up daily inspections to see that they keep running properly. Any irregularities should be reported to the shop. *Courtesy of International Harvester*

Figure 8-13.

SUMMARY | We began with a story about Brenda Hoover who fouled up her pre-trip inspection by hooking up to the wrong trailer.

We explained the two reasons for vehicle inspections: prevention of accidents, or safety, and reduced risk of mechanical breakdowns on the road. Then, we stated that inspections should be made *before* each trip, *during* each trip, and *immediately after* each trip. Long-line drivers make during-trip inspections at each stop, and local drivers make them before and after their meal breaks.

The post-trip inspection must be written down. Many drivers use the report form on the back of their log book pages to record it. Others use a form given to them by their carriers. When the driver has made the post-trip inspection and filled in the form, he or she gives it to the dispatcher. If the vehicle needs service, the dispatcher sends the form on to the maintenance shop.

If the driver finds anything wrong with the truck in the pre-trip inspection, she or he reports it to the shop before leaving. Some conditions need to be fixed before the driver leaves on a tour of duty.

The remainder of the chapter led you through a step-by-step vehicle inspection. The inspection you make must be thorough. Many areas of safety and maintenance need to be checked. The three most important areas to be checked are the lights, the brakes and the tires. But all of the points we mentioned in this chapter are important, so you might want to skim (re-read quickly) the section, "How to Perform an Inspection," to cement them in your mind.

In doing your inspection, you will be looking for leaks and signs of leaks. You'll want to see that the oil and water levels are sufficient, and that there is enough air pressure in the braking system. You want to see that connections are secure. For example, no loose wires, trailer doors locked shut, lug nuts on securely, fifth wheel jaws closed tightly around kingpin, and glad hands attached securely to the trailer. All lights and reflectors should work and be clean, and the windshield wipers, turn signals, and horn should work right. Your inspection includes a walk completely around the rig with your eyes fully open, and it includes starting up the power unit and checking the gauges and the whole braking system.

Finally, we said that even after you've made your inspection, you need to be alert to changing conditions of the vehicle while you drive.

GLOSSARY |

air compressor: An air pump mounted on the engine for supplying air to the air tanks. Part of the braking system.

air hoses: Flexible hoses which carry air from the air tanks in the tractor to the braking system on the trailer. They are sometimes called brake coils. See Figure 8-10.

air pressure gauge: A gauge on the truck dashboard. It tells the driver how much air is in the braking system. See Figure 8-6.

GLOSSARY (cont.)

air tank: A storage tank for compressed air. The compressed air is used to apply the brakes in the air brake system. Also called a reservoir.

ammeter: A gauge that measures the electrical energy or current flowing through the truck's electrical system.

cab control valve: A valve which opens the air brake system's air lines so air can flow back and forth between the trailer and tractor. (Air flows through a valve called the breakaway valve.) The cab control valve is also called the driver-controlled tractor protection valve.

compressor belt: A belt which runs between the engine pulley and the air compressor. It uses the power of the engine to drive (or operate) the air compressor.

glad hands: The coupling devices on each end of the tractor and trailer air brake hoses.

oil pressure gauge: A gauge on the truck dashboard. It tells the driver how much oil pressure is in the engine while it is operating.

pogo stick: An air brake hose holder. A pole with a spring swivel base which supports the air hoses and keeps them from dragging on the truck tractor frame. See Figure 8-10.

slippage: A sliding movement between two surfaces.

vehicle inspection report: A form used by a driver to report the condition of his or her vehicle upon completion of a tour of duty.

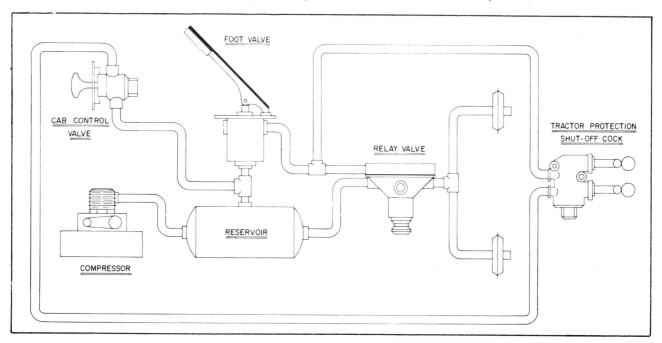

Figure 8-14. Diagram of an air brake system on a tandem-axle tractor. The air tank is labeled "Reservoir." *Courtesy of Sealco Air Controls, Inc.*

135

▶ CHECKING THE FACTS

Answer each question briefly in the space provided.

1. What are the two reasons for making a vehicle inspection? _____

   _____

   _____

2. What are the three times when a professional driver makes an inspection of the rig? _____

   _____

3. As a rule, a long-line driver should make an inspection _____

   _____. A local driver should make an inspection

   _____.

4. When are interstate drivers required to hand in a written report on
   the mechanical condition of the vehicle?

   _____

5. The report sheet you can use to report on your inspection is on the
   back of a form. What form?

   _____

6. What are the three special safety areas which you should pay attention to during your inspection?

   _____

7. When you look under the hood or cab, what are you to look for?

   _____

   _____

   _____

8. You have entered the cab and started up the engine. What three dash
   instruments should you pay special attention to? Circle one group.
   a. oil pressure, ammeter, and air pressure
   b. clutch pedal, accelerator, and brake pedal
   c. odometer, oil pressure, and air pressure
   d. ammeter, oil pressure and speedometer

9. What does the air pressure gauge indicate *and* what is the amount of air pressure you want to see when you've built it up?

_____

_____

10. When you check a tire, what do you look for? _____

_____

11. What lights do you check during inspection? _____

_____

_____

12. When you're checking out the brakes, there are three things to look for especially. If you notice one of them, you must report it to the shop right away. What are these three things?

_____

_____

_____

_____

■ GETTING THE MAIN IDEAS

Put a plus (+) before the statement if it is true. Put a zero (0) before the statement if it is false.

_____1. Vehicle inspections are a required part of the driver's duties.

_____2. Drivers who can perform good inspections and perform simple repairs are valuable because it means the company doesn't have to hire mechanics.

_____3. Companies want you to do a pre-trip inspection so that hazardous vehicle conditions can be repaired before you start out on your trip.

_____4. If air pressure isn't registering on your gauge as you warm up your engine, your brakes are probably unsafe.

_____5. When you inspect your rig, you inspect both towing unit and, if you have one, trailer.

_____6. A thorough inspection of a tractor-trailer combination takes 30 minutes or more.

_____ 7. Since we didn't mention checking your cargo or tie-downs in this chapter, you can assume that isn't part of a pre-trip or post-trip inspection.

_____ 8. All parts of the inspection are important, but the most important part is probably checking out the braking system.

_____ 9. If you've done a complete pre-trip inspection, and you've checked the rig out properly after your meal stops on the road, you shouldn't have to think about the condition of the vehicle as you drive.

Here's one last question which you may answer on a separate sheet of paper:

10. Summarize the important checks you need to make on your vehicles during a thorough inspection. Don't go into detail. (In other words, say, "Check out the braking system." Don't explain how it is done.)

★ GOING BEYOND THE FACTS AND IDEAS

1. This chapter has provided a systematic means of doing a thorough inspection of a tractor-trailer combination. Choose one of the following:
   A. Assume you drive a straight truck. Outline the systematic inspection you would make on it.
   B. Modify the inspection plan which this chapter presented. Perhaps you can see ways to save time, yet still perform an inspection which would be equally complete. Or, perhaps you would rather rearrange things to your liking. What would your inspection be? Remember, it must cover all the DOT required inspections (Chapter 7, "Before You Leave the Terminal") and must cover all safety areas.

2. Design a trip inspection report which you feel would improve on those shown in this chapter.

3. Evaluate the importance of making each of the following checks on your tractor-trailer combination. One by one, explain what the result of a breakdown in each area would be.
   A. Check air pressure build-up in the braking system.
   B. Check the lug nuts on tires.
   C. Wipe off the headlights.
   D. Check the fifth wheel/kingpin connection.
   E. Check to be sure the rear doors on the trailer are secure.
   F. See that turn signals operate properly.
   G. Be sure air pressure in the brake system doesn't drop beyond 15 pounds while your foot is on the brake pedal.
   H. Drain the air brake system daily in cold weather.
   I. Disconnect air hoses at the glad hands to see if trailer brakes come on at once and stay on.
   J. Make a test stop in the terminal yard.

Chapter Nine

THE BRAKING SYSTEM

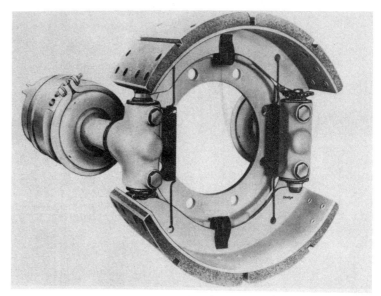

Figure 9-1. A wedge brake, showing the shoe and lining. The cylinder-shaped object on the left is the brake diaphragm. *Courtesy of the Chrysler Corporation*

BEFORE YOU READ | There are two basic kinds of brakes: disc brakes and drum brakes. Roughly speaking, *disc brakes* operate on the same principle as the brakes on a bicycle. Eventually, diesel trucks may use disc brakes. At present, however, the brakes in diesel trucks are *drum brakes*, so drum brakes are what we'll be talking about and illustrating in this chapter.

You may have worked on your own car's drum brakes or you may not. (Many cars have disc brakes.) But whether you have or haven't worked on drum brakes, you probably already know something about how drum brakes work. Each brake has a drum-shaped compartment, called a *brake drum* which rotates with the turning wheel of the vehicle. (See Figure 9-3.) To slow or stop the wheels, you have to make them stop turning around so quickly. You do this by forcing something against the brake drum to create friction. This friction makes it harder for the drum to turn. Since the brake drums are mounted on the same axles as the wheels, the wheels slow with the brake drums and the vehicle slows down. The something that you force against the brake drum is the *brake shoe*. (See Figure 9-1. Notice the lining on the shoe. It is the lining that actually contacts the drum.) So, you might say that pressure of the brake shoe against the brake drum is what stops the vehicle. This basic process is the same in a car and a tractor-trailer combination. The difference between a car and a diesel truck is in *how* the brake shoe is forced against the brake drum.

Okay, you know how the rig actually stops - by pressure of brake shoes against brake drums. But, how much do you already know about how the air brake system *applies* this pressure? Or, if you're not sure you know anything about it, how much can you figure out for yourself? Figure 9-2, on the next page, is a diagram of one type of air brake system - a Sealco Air Controls system.

139

We have labeled the major components of this system with numbers. And, below the diagram, we've provided a list of the names of these parts, but the names are not in the correct order. How many of them can you properly match with the numbers and components? The diagram is *not* to scale. For example, the distance to the trailer's brake chambers is much further than it looks in the diagram.

Take a few minutes out, now, to see how much you can figure out for yourself. It'll help you prepare your mind for what you're about to read. Then, when you've matched up all the parts and names as well as you can, read on.

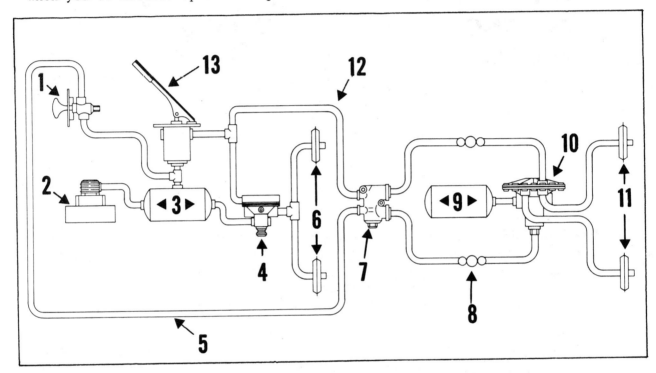

PARTS TO LOCATE

relay valve _____

glad hand _____

emergency air line_____

cab control valve _____

foot valve (brake pedal) _____

service air line _____

brake chambers on tractor _____

compressor (air compressor) _____

tractor's air tank (reservoir) _____

brake chambers on trailer _____

breakaway valve (tractor protection valve) _____

trailer's air tank (reservoir) _____

trailer valve (trailer relay emergency valve) _____

Figure 9-2. Diagram of the basic air brake system for a heavy-duty diesel combination. *Courtesy of Sealco Air Controls, Inc.*

IMPORTANCE OF THE BRAKING SYSTEM | You can't overestimate the importance of your truck's braking system. It takes a good engine to start a vehicle and maintain road speed, but, for safety, the brake system is far more important than the engine. You can travel down the highway or through mountains with a worn engine. The engine might use too much oil or sound real ratty, but it will probably get you down the road. And even if it doesn't, it's a lot less dangerous to be in a rig you can't start than to be in a rig you can't stop. If your engine is running poorly, you may damage an expensive engine or use too much fuel or have poor pickup, but if your braking system is operating poorly, your life itself is in danger.

The braking system *must be* - not can be or may be - but *must be* in good working order if you want to stay out of trouble. Any experienced driver will tell you she or he would rather have less horsepower (hp) and more braking power than the reverse. Getting a truck rolling is one thing, but you may have to stop it in one-tenth of the time it took you to start it. In other words, if it took you 30 seconds to get your road speed up, you might have to come to an abrupt stop in three seconds. Your brakes have to be in tiptop condition to make sudden stops.

Remember what you studied in Chapter 6, however. Your brakes don't do all the work. Use your gears! There is great danger in expecting your brakes to do all the work of stopping your vehicle. You must use your engine power and gears to decrease your speed. Then, you can do the rest with your brakes.

HOW YOU APPLY THE AIR BRAKES

● *The Difference Between Air Brakes and Hydraulic Brakes*

A typical car has hydraulic brakes. In a typical car, the driver applies mechanical force to the brake pedal. This mechanical force combines with brake fluid to force the brake shoe against the drum. The driver feels a build-up of pressure when he or she steps on the brake.

In a diesel truck, the driver also applies pressure to the brake pedal but doesn't feel much build-up of pressure. All the truck driver's foot is doing on the air brake pedal is opening a valve to allow air to flow through the braking system. You could do that with the pressure of one finger of one hand.

So, the feel of a truck brake pedal is entirely different from that of an automobile brake pedal. If you're driving a car, you know immediately whether you have brakes or not. You step on the brake pedal, feel a build-up of pressure under your foot, and you know you have braking power. When you apply the brakes on a diesel truck, all you'll feel is a very secure drag as the truck begins to slow down. You won't feel any pressure from the brake pedal. In other words, it takes you longer to tell whether you have working brakes or not.

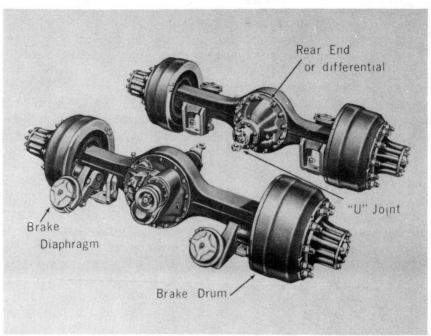

Figure 9-3. A set of tandem rear axles. Compare with Figure 5-17. *Courtesy of Rockwell International Corp.*

HOW YOU APPLY THE AIR BRAKES   (cont.)

● *The Importance of Brake Maintenance*

Say you're driving a truck, and its brake linings or brake shoes are out of adjustment. (Or, say your brake drums are in poor condition.) Suppose you need to come to a very fast stop, within a couple of hundred feet, due to an emergency. You step hard on the brake pedal, applying approximately 45 pounds of air pressure to the system. You feel that initial, secure drag as the truck begins to slow. You're used to the feel of air brakes, so you assume that the rig is going to stop properly. You assume your brakes are good. But, if your brake linings or shoes are out of adjustment, that's all you get - that slowing drag. You could shove your brake pedal to the floor boards, applying maximum pressure, and you would get no more slowing effect than what you got when you first hit the brakes. Eventually, you'll stop. But you may travel 300 to 400 feet before you do. If there is anything between you and that 400 feet, you are going to run over it, jackknife, or turn over trying to avoid that something in your path.

Air brakes are a combination of air pressure and mechanical linkage. The air pressure doesn't stop the vehicle. *The air pressure applies the force to the brake shoes, forcing them against the brake drum.* Therefore, the air pressure is not the only deciding factor in slowing down the vehicle or in making an abrupt stop. Stopping ability still leads back to the condition and adjustment of the brake shoes to the drum. Air is just one of the ingredients needed.

Ideally, you'll get to the point as a professional driver where you can adjust or at least check out your own braking system to see that everything is in good condition. But as a novice, you'll need to rely on a good maintenance department.

142

HOW YOU APPLY THE AIR BRAKES   (cont.)

● *Detecting Problems as You Drive*

For now, the important thing for you to know is this: how the air brake system works. Therefore, in most of this chapter, we'll be discussing how all the valves operate to see that air pressure gets to the brake chambers so the shoes are forced against the drum. If you understand that, you will be able to develop a good braking technique - one that will increase your road safety and extend your truck's life. As you get to know the feel of your brakes, you will be able to tell when they start to decline in efficiency. Your knowledge of the braking system will also help you to detect problems in it. If something goes wrong, you may be able to figure out what part of the air brake system failed by thinking about how your vehicles responded when you applied the brakes. This information will be extremely important. First, it will help you know what to do in an emergency situation. Second, it will help you explain the problem to the shop mechanic.

● *Two Kinds of Application Valves*

As we said above, the air brakes are a combination of air pressure and mechanical linkage. Basically, air pressure supplies the working force, and the mechanical linkage supplies the leverage and components needed to stop most heavy-duty trucks.

Let's consider an air brake system as being similar to a water system. First, we have a *compressor* (in the water system, a pump) to provide pressure. Second, we have the *reservoir* (in the water system, piping) to store the pressure. Third, we have *valves* (in the water system, a sprinkler) to release the pressure to the point of usage. (See Figure 9-4.)

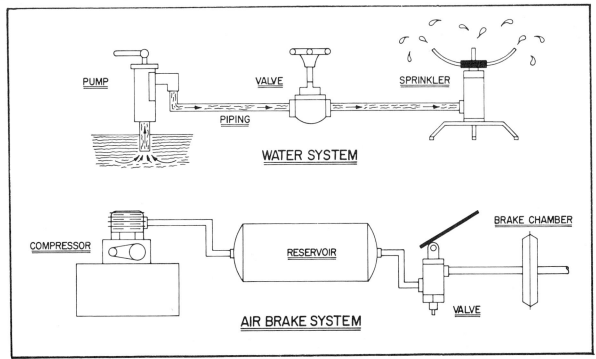

Figure 9-4. The basic air brake system can be compared to a water system. Notice the similarities. *Courtesy of Sealco Air Controls, Inc.*

143

Under normal conditions, everything begins when you, as the driver, apply the brakes. In a car, it begins when the driver steps on the brake pedal. You might call the car's brake pedal an *application valve*. In a truck, there are two kinds of application valves: foot valves (or pedals) and hand valves. A truck may have only one, or both, kinds of valves. Whether it has one or two kinds will depend upon such things as age and model of the truck. The braking system operation of the truck normally begins when the driver applies pressure to one of these valves.

You will always have some type of *foot valve*, both on straight trucks and tractor-trailer combinations. When you depress the foot valve, the truck stops. If you're driving a combination, both the tractor and trailer stop. The *hand valve* is used to stop the trailer without stopping the tractor. Since a straight truck is all one unit, there is no need for a separate hand valve.

To review, in all of today's trucks, the foot valve will stop both the tractor and trailer. The hand valve is an additional valve, used to stop the trailer only. In straight trucks, the hand valve is eliminated. Now that we know, basically, what the foot and hand valves are for, let's find out more about each one.

THE VALVES

● *The Foot Valve*

As mentioned above, the *foot valve* supplies air pressure to the straight truck, and to both tractors and trailers when they are in combination. This foot valve supplies constant pressure from the reservoirs (or air tanks) where the air is stored. A gauge in the cab (the air pressure indicator) will tell you the amount of pressure in the reservoir. Normally, a diesel truck will need 100 pounds of pressure in the reservoir. That's usually enough to supply sufficient pressure to the brake chambers.

Early Brake Systems. In the early days of trucking, many foot valves were designed to deliver only a controlled amount of pressure. For some years, foot valves delivered varying pressures, from 60 to 90 pounds. The amount of pressure delivered to the brake chambers did not depend upon the amount of pressure which the driver put on the pedal, as it does in a car. The amount of pressure was the same, whether the driver stepped lightly or heavily upon the pedal.

However, the driver could vary the amount of pressure which would be applied by adding or subtracting devices, called *spacing shims*, within the air valve. At a 60-pound setting, the valve opened when the driver applied five to seven pounds of pressure to the pedal. If the setting was raised to permit delivery of 90 pounds, the opening pressure was also raised to as much as 15 pounds. That meant that the driver had to apply 15 pounds of pressure to the pedal before the truck began to stop.

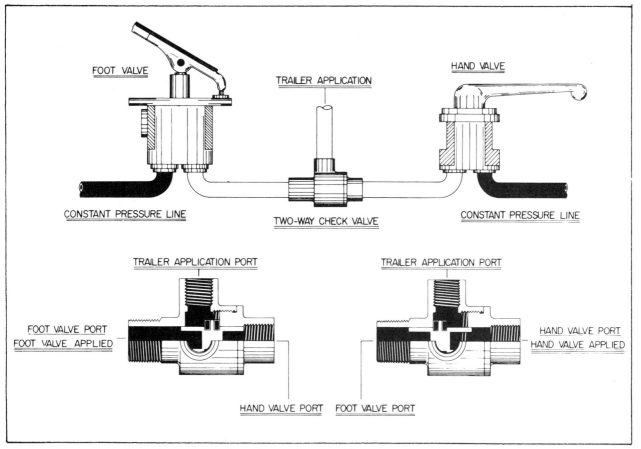

Figure 9-5. Some combinations have a hand valve, in addition to the
foot valve. The hand valve is used when you don't want to stop the
tractor, but only the trailer. You would use it, for example, to lock
the trailer brakes when you are hooking up the tractor and trailer.
Another use for the trailer hand valve is to slow the trailer before
slowing the tractor. You might want to do this when you're running in
snow, ice or rain. In such a case, you would use the hand valve to
slow the trailer just a second or two before you depress the foot
valve. This provides an even braking movement, and might prevent a
jackknife. *Courtesy of Sealco Air Controls, Inc.*

THE VALVES (cont.)

If the driver increased or decreased the shims in the foot valves, the
pressure required to operate the foot valve was also increased or decreased.
If the pressure increased, the driver would have to step down much harder on
the pedal to get a full 90 pounds of pressure. Then, the pressure would come
in a terrific surge, all at once. This great surge slugged the brake system
with too much air. What was the result? Too often, it was an immediate lockup or skid.

To avoid this, the driver had to back off the brake pedal immediately after giving it the initial thrust, so that the air pressure would be bled off,

THE VALVES   (cont.)

or fanned down, bringing about a gradual slow-down or stop. But fanning (that is, applying and releasing the brake pedal) wasn't a good practice either. It brought about a loss of air pressure, without much braking power, because every time you release the brake pedal, you're exhausting air pressure into the atmosphere. Eventually, if you keep fanning, you reduce your air pressure to dangerously low levels.

Smitty's Story. Before we go any further, let me tell you about a new driver. True story. But we'll change the driver's name to Smitty. We don't want to use the driver's real name.

Smitty was referred to a company for his first job. When he made his first trip, he complained about the rig not stopping. So, the owners sent the rig to a brake shop where it had been serviced before. The brake shop inspected the truck and reported that the trailer brakes were fried (overheated and glazed). They installed new brake shoes.

In a couple of days, Smitty reported the same situation. Again, the rig went into the shop and the report was the same as the first time.

Now, these owners kept their equipment in the best possible condition, as they were proud of their fleet. So, they questioned Smitty about the brakes. They also asked him why there was so much breakage in the trailer each trip. They were shocked when they realized what had happened.

Here's what they discovered. The route was Interstate 8, from California to Arizona, a mountainous highway. It has one grade of 6% that lasts for nine miles without a break. Being a novice, Smitty had gone off the hill loaded (a full trailer) without gearing down or slowing, and he had fanned the trailer brakes all the way down. A retarder would have been a help, but the rig wasn't equipped with one. (We'll discuss retarders thoroughly in Chapter 13. For now, it's enough to know that they help to slow the rig by slowing the engine speed.) When asked if the brakes smoked, Smitty replied, "Yes." But, he said he didn't think anything of it because he'd seen other rigs with smoke pouring out of their wheels too. As for the breakage in the trailer, each time he was asked about it, he used the excuse that he had to hit the binders (slang for brakes) to avoid hitting someone.

Smitty made a number of mistakes in his driving. Even in an old-style rig, Smitty could have used his gears to slow down as he descended the hill. He didn't. Second, since he wasn't driving an older rig, he shouldn't have been fanning his brakes. Third, he obviously was not anticipating the movement of other vehicles. If he had been reading the traffic patterns before his eyes, he wouldn't need to keep stepping on his brakes to miss hitting another vehicle. A good driver must anticipate what the other driver is going to do almost before the other driver makes the move. Smitty doesn't know how lucky he is to be alive today. It is what you don't know that may kill you.

Modern Foot Valves. Modern foot valves operate more along the lines of car brake pedals you are used to. That is, a small amount of pressure applied to the foot valve brings about a gradual braking, and a larger amount of pressure brings about a faster braking movement. This eliminates the need for fanning of the brakes and the loss of braking pressure which fanning creates.

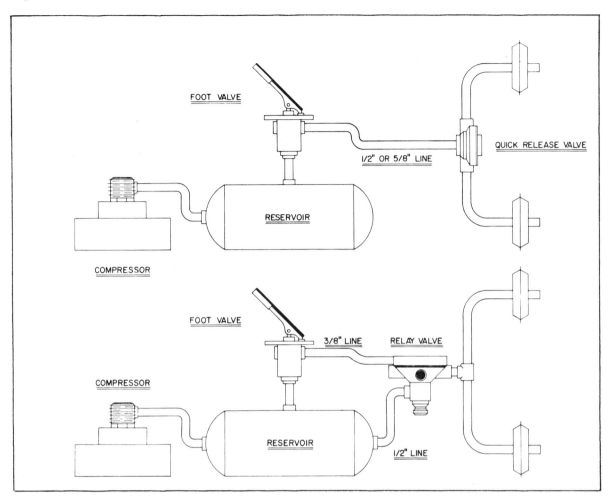

Figure 9-6. Some trucks are equipped with a "robot." Illustrated here are two kinds of robots, the quick release valve and the relay valve. *Courtesy of Sealco Air Controls, Inc.*

THE VALVES (cont.)

This fine metering in the low pressure range allows for quick brake response. It also provides especially fine brake "feel" as compared to the old-style, extreme-pressure valves which we described above.

Some truck braking systems are equipped with additional valves inside the braking system. Once installed, these valves operate automatically. Thus, they are sometimes called, "robot valves" or "robots" because they depend upon a signal from the foot application valve to operate. Two of these "robots" are the quick release valve and the relay valve. (See Figure 9-6.) As these are both options, they will not be installed, by any means, in all trucks. However, they can be very helpful, as you will see.

● *Quick Release Valves*

The *quick release valve* performs two functions. It acts as a *tee* (T-shaped junction) to provide access to the brake chambers, and, as its name implies,

THE VALVES (cont.)

allows the pressure applied to the chambers to quickly release. (See Figure 9-6.) Pressure must be released after you have applied the brakes. Normally, this is accomplished through the foot valve. However, when a quick release valve is used, the pressure is released through the quick release valve. The only advantage of a quick release valve in the system is to exhaust the applied chamber pressure *close to the point of usage.* This way, you don't have to wait for the pressure to flow back through the lines to the foot valve for exhaust. You're ready to continue much quicker after taking your foot off the brake pedal.

● *Relay Valves*

A *relay valve* is generally substituted for a quick release valve when dual rear axles are used. With a relay valve, constant pressure is made available *much closer to the point of usage.* (See Figure 9-6.) Normally, the air pressure waits in the reservoir until it is needed. When the driver depresses the foot valve, air pressure rushes from the reservoir, through the lines, to the brake chambers. However, when a relay valve has been installed, air pressure doesn't wait until the driver depresses the foot valve to rush through the lines. It constantly fills the lines and waits in the relay valve apparatus until it is needed. Then, as soon as the driver steps on the foot valve, full pressure flows to the brake chambers from a point much nearer to them. (The reservoir is actually much farther from the brake chambers than it appears in Figure 9-6 which is not to scale.) This produces a faster brake application, reducing stopping distance.

As with a quick release valve, brake pressure is released quickly at the relay valve after you've taken your foot off the pedal.

Relay valves are commonly found on straight trucks and on tractor-trailer combinations. Newer relay valves are especially recommended by the DOT for tractor-trailer use because the design provides for balanced braking and less jackknifing tendency. Relay valves provide for fast, easy control.

● *The Hand Valve*

A *trailer hand valve* is an optional valve. You will find it in about 90% of the road tractors, but there are a few that won't have one, and these are mostly found on the Eastern Seaboard of the US.

There has been a tremendous amount of discussion by the DOT about the benefits of the hand valve. A recent development has made the DOT consider the hand valve unnecessary. This development is the #121 brake system. (We'll be discussing this brake system later on in this chapter.) Besides, the DOT feels drivers don't use the hand valve anyway.

Nevertheless, hand valves can be very helpful and they can increase safety on the road. They put added control of the rig in the hands of the driver. Let's go over their basic functions.

Figure 9-7. Rear of a cab, showing the flexible air hoses (or brake coil) and glad hands, dead center. Notice the size of the air hoses. They have to be heavy-duty. They're constantly exposed, so they have to withstand desert sun and heat, ice, hail, sleet, and dust storms. If they don't work right, your trailer service brakes can't function. The two large cylinders on either side of the air hoses are exhaust pipes. Their job is to muffle the sound of the exhaust. The illustration shows the glad hands attached to the pogo stick, also known as the hose tender. *Photo by M. McFadden*

Basically, the hand valve is an assisting brake valve for the trailer service brakes when you are hooked up in combinations. By applying the trailer hand valve, you control the braking effect on your trailer or trailers. It doesn't control or interfere with your tractor or truck brakes at all. It can be used to put a slight brake drag on your trailers in snow, ice or rain.

Another major benefit of a hand valve is this: It can be used to apply the trailer brakes as you pull away from a curb after picking up a trailer. As you apply the hand valve to lock the trailer brakes, the trailer brakes should start to come on. If they don't, you know you have goofed up in hooking up your air hoses. You will probably find that you have coupled your air hoses to the trailer backward, or in reverse. In this case, use of the hand valve is a very important way to safeguard yourself against an improper hook-up.

● *The Two-Way Check Valve*

To pipe *both* the foot valve and the hand valve into the trailer application or control line, manufacturers had to tee the valves. That is, they had to form a T-shaped junction by using a two-way check valve. (See Figure 9-5.)

This valve closes one of its control ports when pressure is applied to the other control port. The valve closes so air won't be lost through the exhaust port of the application valve which isn't in use. In other words, if you apply the foot valve, the check valve stops the pressure from bleeding off in the opposite direction. If it bled off, it would be lost through the exhaust port. If you pull the hand valve, the check valve stops the pressure from bleeding off in the other direction.

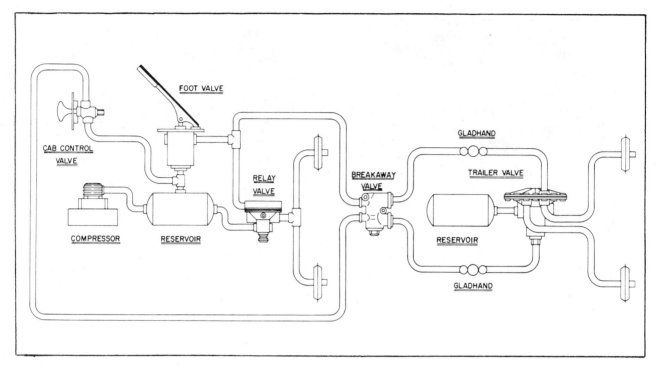

Figure 9-8. The trailer relay emergency valve must open at very low pressure to insure balanced braking between the two units. This is very important for safe braking. Most current models open at only one to two pounds of pressure, while tractor relay or quick release valves open in a four to seven pound range. This difference in opening pressure provides for a trailer brake lead which is very important in preventing jackknifing. *Courtesy of Sealco Air Controls, Inc.*

THE VALVES (cont.)

● *The Breakaway Valve*

A safety accessory included as standard equipment by truck manufacturers is the *tractor breakaway* or *tractor protection kit* or *valve*. It is required by the DOT. (Shown in Figure 9-8 as the "breakaway valve.")

This kit is made up of a *cab control valve* and a *protection valve*. The kit provides for automatic application of the emergency feature of the trailer relay emergency valve. (We'll discuss this valve next.) When tractor service air pressure drops to an unsafe level (60 pounds), the DOT regulation requires that the trailer brakes apply automatically. The DOT also requires this: If a trailer is accidentally disconnected, tractor air pressure must be protected to provide the tractor with enough air pressure to stop the vehicle. Breakaway kits provide for *automatic* operation of the trailer's brakes, in situations like those we described above. But there's also a way for the driver to apply the trailer brakes *manually* under normal conditions.

THE VALVES   (cont.)

● *The Trailer Relay Emergency Valve*

The *trailer relay emergency valve* is on the trailer. Shown in Figure 9-8 as simply, "trailer valve," it is sometimes called the RE4 valve by truckers. This relay emergency valve works hand in hand with the breakaway valve and the cab control valve.

Under normal conditions, a driver will have the cab control valve *pushed in* when the vehicle is operating. This opens the air lines so air can flow back and forth between the tractor and trailer through the breakaway valve. By pushing the cab control valve in, the driver also lets air flow through the relay emergency valve into the trailer's own air tank or reservoir.

If an emergency occurs, such as a broken air hose between the tractor and trailer, the breakaway valve automatically cuts off the air going to the trailer. (The cut-off point is 60 pounds.) As this happens, the trailer relay emergency valve also shuts off the air lines and traps the air in the trailer reservoir, protecting it against any air loss. At the same time, the relay emergency valve also sends full air tank pressure from the trailer's reservoir to the trailer's brake diaphragms. This locks up all the brakes on the trailer or trailers. This process is known as *breakaway protection*.

The relay emergency valve of today contains a check valve. This check valve makes sure that air pressure in the trailer air reservoir will be kept for the exclusive use of the trailer. Some of the older style valves did not contain this feature. If *tractor* air pressure was lost in these older rigs, the *trailer* air pressure bled down too. Then the emergency feature of the valve couldn't function. DOT regulations have required this check valve since 1956.

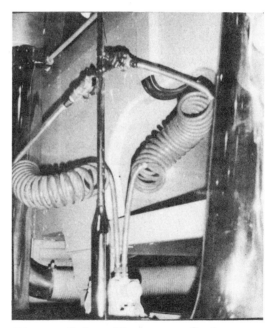

How An Automatic Lockup of the Trailer Brakes Occurs. On an emergency brake application, everything normally used in the service brake system is the same. That is, the mechanical parts, such as shoes, lining, drums are used to stop the rig. The only difference in an emergency is that the air supply comes from the emergency side of the system. The breakaway valve makes the immediate switch from the regular system to the emergency system.

If you looked inside the breakaway valve, you'd see a *shuttle valve*. This shuttle valve is balanced by brake pressure on equal sides (tractor and trailer sides) under normal conditions. However,

Figure 9-9. Close-up of the brake coil and glad hands. Many tractors have a red hose for the emergency side (or "hot side") and a blue hose for the service air. The hoses are secured to the pogo stick so they stay out of the way, free from harm and in good condition when not in use. *Photo by M. McFadden*

the instant pressure is lost on one side, the valve jumps over and cuts off the ports that lead out through the air hoses at the glad hands. When this happens, the other side of the valve opens and air rushes directly from a trailer reservoir, down to the brake chambers on the trailer's axles.

You have no control over this function once the air pressure has dropped below the 60 pounds (safe) margin. This is what we call an automatic lockup or "dynamite" situation. The air is trapped between the trailer air tank and the trailer brake diaphragm. And that is where it stays, holding the trailer brakes in the locked position.

How You Release the Trailer Brakes After an Automatic Lockup. There are only two ways to relieve a dynamite situation.

1. *If you are safely off the road*, you can repair the leak so the air pressure in the entire unit comes up to safe minimum pressures. (Safe minimum level is anything above the 60 pound mark.)

2. *If you are stuck in a traffic lane* and have to move the trailer off the road, there is only one thing you can do. Open the air cock on the air tank underneath the trailer. Then, bleed off the air until the brakes release. But, if you do this, you have *absolutely no air brakes on any of the trailers!*

> ▷ *NOTE:* *An automatic lockup affects the trailer brakes only. It is a protection for the trailer, so that it has some brakes in an extreme emergency. The tractor protection works differently. The tractor may still have normal braking after an automatic lockup has applied the trailer brakes, for example, if the air hoses came unattached at the glad hands. But, if the emergency loss of air affected the whole system - tractor and trailer - the tractor has its own emergency braking system which is altogether different from the breakaway protection of the trailer. The tractor emergency brakes are spring-applied, and we will discuss them in the section headed, "Emergency Brakes."*

● *The One-Way Check Valve*

The diagrams you have been looking at all show *one* reservoir in the tractor. Actually, many truck air brake systems have *two* reservoirs: a wet one and a dry one. The first air tank (the wet one) is the one that receives the air from the compressor. The second air tank (the dry one) receives air from the wet tank.

A *one-way check valve* is used between the two reservoirs. It protects the air supply by seeing that air can't flow back and forth between the two air reservoirs. The check valve is usually installed immediately ahead of the second (dry) reservoir. If the discharge line between the compressor and the wet reservoir breaks, the air supply in the dry reservoir is protected. The check valve also keeps air from bleeding back to the compressor.

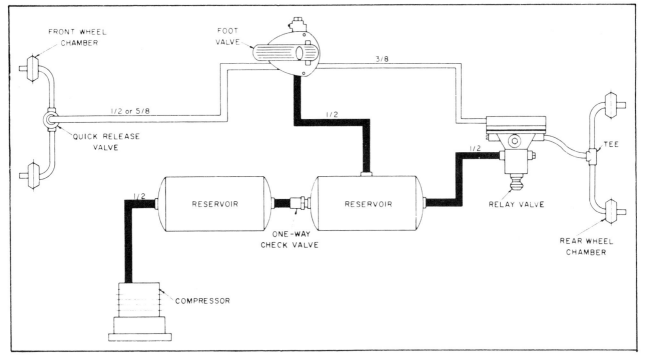

Figure 9-10. Heavy condensation will always be evident in the first air tank, known as the wet tank, because the cooling air as it reaches the first tank tends to develop quite a bit of moisture. The second, or dry tank, receives air pressure from the wet tank. By this time, much of the condensation has been eliminated and has settled in the bottom of the wet tank. *Courtesy of Sealco Air Controls, Inc.*

MAINTENANCE OF THE AIR BRAKE SYSTEM All of the components of an air brake system will, eventually, wear out. What usually happens is this. Water, dirt, varnish and sludge accumulate, and this causes the system to operate in a faulty manner. Sludge removers and air dryers help to keep the system working properly by providing a clean, dry air supply. But a good maintenance program is also needed. Proper maintenance will keep the units in a good condition, and this will allow them to function longer at near-peak performance.

● *Maintaining the Air Compressor*

An air compressor works much like a truck engine, and many of the same problems reduce its effectiveness. Heat, ring and cylinder wear, varnish and acid action all make it harder for the compressor to do its work, and they all reduce the quality of compressed air supplied to the reservoirs.

How much will the air quality be affected? It depends on the *humidity* of the area in which the truck operates. The more condensation combines with varnish and acids, the worse the air quality will be. And poor quality air is probably the biggest factor in reducing the life of your brake valves. So, if you want to make your valves last longer, you'll want to keep contaminants out. A good maintenance program will do this. (For example, most truck air compressors are lubricated with oil from the truck's engine. So, one thing you can do to maintain the air compressor is be sure the engine oil is changed regularly.)

153

MAINTENANCE OF THE AIR BRAKE SYSTEM   (cont.)

● *Maintaining the Governor*

One of the advantages of the air brake system is this: The power source or air supply is always being replenished. You can put up with small air leaks because the compressor puts back (into the reservoir) what has been used or lost to leakage. But don't let this give you a false sense of security. Breakdowns can still occur in the system.

The *air governor* controls air pressure by regulating the compressor's cut-in and cut-out points. These points are in pounds or square inches. For example, say your air governor is set for an operating range of 90 to 110 pounds. If the air pressure drops below 80 pounds, the air compressor will automatically kick in and bring the air pressure back up to the top pressure (in this case, 110 pounds). Then, the air compressor will cut out. When the air pressure drops again, it will kick in and bring the air pressure back up.

Governors generally have a range of 20 pounds between cut-in and cut-out pressures. If the governor fails to operate in this way, something is wrong. Governors do fail if they haven't been properly maintained. However, governors are not the only possible source of problems. What's wrong if your air compressor cuts in and out too often? The problem could be too many leaks in the system, calling for frequent refilling. So, a mechanic should check the piping first. If there is no problem in the piping, then the governor may need attention.

● *Maintaining the Valves*

Every so often, the operating valves need a mechanic's attention. How often? It depends on the uses made of the trucks, that is, the type of fleet operation. Normally, servicing about once a year or every 50,000 miles is sufficient.

EMERGENCY BRAKES

● *The Purpose of the Emergency Brakes*

The emergency brake system on a *tractor* is called by a number of different names. Truckers may call their tractor emergency brakes *maxi brakes, spring* or *spring-applied brakes, safety brakes,* or *parking brakes.* Regardless of their different names, the brakes all function in the same way (through spring action) and do the same basic job.

The spring-applied brakes serve two functions. The first function of the emergency brakes is *to secure the vehicle when it is stopped.* That is, they are your parking brakes. The second function is the more important one: *to stop your vehicle and hold it in case of an air loss anywhere in your brake system.* In other words, they provide a second way of applying the service brakes in case some type of malfunction in the normal air brake system prevents brake application.

● *The Design of the Emergency Brakes*

Let's backtrack for a moment. The basic braking system is operated by air. Air provides enough pressure against the mechanical linkages to bring the brake shoes in contact with the brake drums, thus stopping the truck or slowing it down.

So, what is one thing the truck must have before the regular service brakes will work? Enough air pressure. If that air pressure drops below a certain level, what will happen? You won't have any brakes. Too little air equals no service brakes. How does air pressure drop too low? Through overuse of the brakes as in fanning or snubbing, through a bad leak in an air hose, through a puncture in the reservoir, etc.

Now, if you were going to set up some type of brakes which would operate in emergencies, that is, even when the air pressure was too low, what would you do? If you thought about it, you would probably do this: You would set up a system in which a safety device would notice when air pressure dropped below a specified danger level. The safety device would then cause the auxiliary or emergency braking system to begin operating. Basically, this *is* how the emergency brake system on a tractor works.

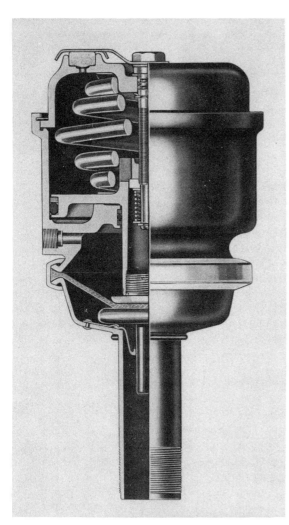

Figure 9-11.   Cutaway view of a spring brake. *Photograph courtesy of Rockwell International Corp.*

● *The Operation of the Emergency Brakes*

The emergency system has its own air tank, lever, and spring chambers. Usually, the chambers are housed in a piggyback unit atop the regular brake chamber. There is a coiled spring inside the chamber which is capable of approximately 1200 pounds per square inch. (Don't ever try pulling one apart unless you want to lose your head. That spring, if accidentally released, will go through the wall of a building.)

The emergency system operates like this: The heavy, coiled spring is held against the back of the brake chamber by air pressure. The air pressure level in the brake chamber corresponds to the air pressure level in your air reservoir. Therefore, if the air pressure drops in the reservoir, it will also drop in the brake chamber. When an air line breaks or the air pressure drops below 45 pounds, the loss of air that was holding the spring back inside the chamber

HOW MGM SPRING BRAKES WORK FOR YOU

	STOPGARD® "LD" Double Diaphragm (Cam Brakes)	STOPGARD® "E" Double Diaphragm (Cam Brakes)	MAGNUM® "M" Piston-Type (Cam Brakes)	SHORTSTOP® "SS" Piston-Type (Wedge Brakes)	STOPGARD® WEDGE "SGW" Double Diaphragm (Wedge Brakes)
The principle is basic — MGM Spring Brakes actuate your foundation brakes when there is no air pressure.	Integral Release Bolt	Detachable Release Bolt			Integral Release Bolt
1. Normal Driving A safe level of air pressure within the system holds spring brakes released, but always ready for parking or emergency application.					
2. Normal Service Brake Since the service section and spring brake section are isolated from each other by seals, the spring brake cannot interfere with the operation of the normal service brake.					
3. Parking Brakes A finger-tip control in the cab to exhaust air pressure within the spring brake gives the driver fool-proof and positive parking brakes.					
4. Manual Release MGM's manual release systems allow easy release of spring brakes to reline brakes or move the vehicle in the absence of air pressure.					

Figure 9-12. *Courtesy of MGM Brakes*

156

allows the spring to expand.   (The exact air pressure level at which this occurs varies from one tractor to another.)   Notice that at this point, the air
pressure is too low for your air brakes to work.   However, the same drop in air
pressure which put your air brakes out of commission, has allowed the coil to
expand and the spring-applied brakes to begin operating.   This mechanical
spring force sets up your brakes.   They will stay set up until enough air pressure is applied to force the spring back into a "caged" position.

   The emergency system is normally controlled by the driver except in an
emergency.   It becomes automatic upon an air loss below 45 pounds in most older
tractors.

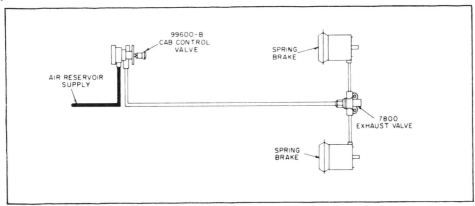

Figure 9-13.   *Courtesy of Sealco Air Controls, Inc.*

   Figure 9-13 shows the pressure-holding exhaust valve.   This valve prevents
unwanted application of the spring-applied braking system by holding sufficient
air pressure in the spring brake unit to keep the coil contracted.   It is a
one-way check valve.   However, when the reservoir air pressure is reduced by
about 65%, the valve opens, pressure is released and the coil expands.   In addition, air pressure in the chamber may be released manually by using the
spring brake valve on the dashboard.   (See Figure 9-14.)

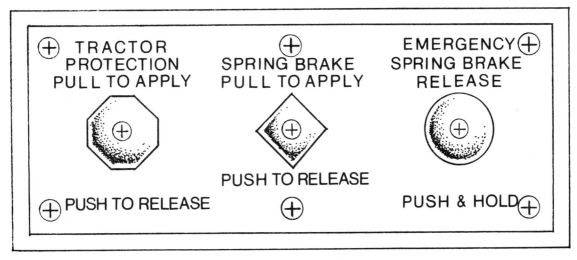

Figure 9-14.   Close-up of cab control panel, showing tractor protection valve (breakaway valve), and the two valves used to operate the
emergency brakes.

EMERGENCY BRAKES (cont.)

● *Releasing the Emergency Brakes*

Suppose you're out in traffic and you have an air pressure loss and the spring brakes go on automatically. How are you going to move the vehicle with the spring or maxi brake set up?

This is where your third tank and the valve in the truck cab, marked *"Emergency Spring Brake Release,"* come in. Look at the valve in the illustration of the dashboard. (Figure 9-14) Underneath the valve, it reads, "Push and Hold." The push and hold operation is critical for this reason: Air pressure from the third tank, sometimes called the *protected air tank* or *protected reservoir*, maintains enough air to release the spring pressure against the brakes. In other words, it pushes the spring back into a tight coil as you open the air supply from the third tank. This dash control valve is your means of supplying pressure from the third tank. If you should release this emergency valve before you have rolled clear of the road, you will allow the air to exhaust out of the spring chamber and set up the brakes again. So hold it in. There are only two or three applications of air in this small tank, so don't experiment with it. Only use it if you know what you are doing. (The third air tank is shown in Figure 9-15.)

As with the emergency air brake system, all the mechanical parts normally used to brake the truck - the shoes, lining, drums - are used when the spring brakes are applied. The only difference is that, in this case, it is *spring pressure*, rather than air pressure, which operates these mechanical parts.

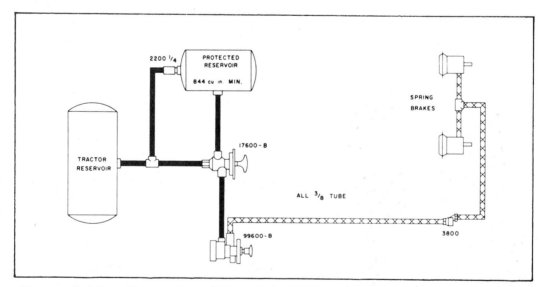

Figure 9-15. The tractor's emergency brakes are released when air from the third tank supplies enough air to force the springs back into a tight coil. *Courtesy of Sealco Air Controls, Inc.*

THE 121 BRAKING SYSTEM

Now you know how the basic braking system operates. You have just studied the braking system as it looked and worked up to January 1, 1975. Now let's talk about the changes since then. These changes affect only rigs made since 1975. If your rig was manufactured before 1975, the braking system will still be like those described above.

● *Major Changes Made*

In January of 1975, the National Highway Traffic Safety Administration (NHTSA), a division of the DOT, set new rules regarding the braking systems of trucks and buses. The major change was to set new, *shorter stopping distances*. But there were other changes too. One of these changes required rigs to remain within a 12-foot lane while stopping. Another was called anti-lockup protection or electronic skid control. Still another changed how the service and emergency air brake systems worked.

That's quite a lot of changes. However, more changes were actually required than you might guess. Many changes had to be made in truck design to get the truck to stop in a shorter distance. The air supply had to be enlarged. New valves had to be designed and installed. The brake shoes had to be enlarged, and the material in the shoes was changed. Stronger front axles were needed. All rigs had to have front axle brakes to get them to stop in time.

What is the 121 air brake system? The name comes from a number given by the DOT. Basically, the system has expanded on the basic system you've already studied. The principles of how it works are the same. The changes have been made to allow the truck to perform in the way the DOT says it must.

We'll look at a few of the specific changes in the system. But remember as you read; you really only need to know two things:

1. how to check out the system to see that it is working properly before each tour of duty, and

2. how to operate the system.

It also helps if you can tell the mechanic where the problems may lie. We're giving you this additional background so you know a little bit more than the average driver about what might go wrong, and how to best operate the system in a problem situation.

● *Review of the Single System*

Older truck air brake systems, or pre-121 systems if you care to call them that, had single air lines carrying the air to the brakes of a truck or trailer. If any part of the air system failed, it affected all the axles. The only backup was an automatic lockup of the trailer brakes and the spring brakes on the tractor axles. There were spring brakes on only one rear tractor axle and no spring brakes at all on the trailer. One thing to remember with the old system is this: If the trailer locks up due to low air pressure, the remaining air in the trailer tank is the only thing keeping the trailer brakes applied.

THE 121 BRAKING SYSTEM   (cont.)

● *The Dual Air Supply System*

The DOT requirements which began in 1975 required a dual air supply system which would be just about unfailing. The system which was created is actually a single system. However, it is made up of two interconnected systems which normally function as one. That's why it's often called a dual air supply system. If you lose one system, the other system allows you to safely stop your rig.

To do this, the 121 system has three air tanks for the service brakes on all trucks and tractors. One tank is often called the supply tank and the other two are called service tanks. The *supply tank* holds the air and feeds it to the dual service tanks.

As we said above, the brake system functions as a single unit when you use your foot pedal. That is, both *service tanks* work together because both service tanks and their air lines are interconnected and function as a single system. The so-called "dual system" comes in when there is a failure on one side of the system. Each half of the system is isolated from the other by a *double check valve* so that a failure in one side will not create a failure in the other. You, as a driver, will have only one indication of the breakdown. A drop in air pressure will show up on the air gauge. The air gauge will indicate the location of the failure because one needle of the two on your dashboard air pressure gauge will start dropping.

Each manufacturer describes its braking system in its own way. A mechanic needs a brake schematic (or drawing) to troubleshoot a leak in the system. One of these schematics is reproduced as Figure 9-16. A driver might also find the defect by blocking the foot pedal down, then getting out of the cab and checking the tractor axles to find which brake is not applied.

● *Breakdowns in the System*

What happens if something goes wrong? Let's assume you don't have any brakes on your front axles. This is not ideal, but it isn't terribly dangerous by itself. For years, three-axle tractors didn't have front axle brakes. Until the 121 system, they weren't required in California vehicles which operated only within the state. You don't need front axle brakes to stop a rig. So, if you lose your front axle brakes only, you will still have your rear axle brakes and trailer brakes and your rig will stop. It may not stop within the DOT-required stopping distance, but it will stop somewhat beyond that distance.

Second, let's assume you lose your rear tractor axle brakes. You still have the brakes on your front axle, and that system takes over to apply brakes on your trailer axles. So, you have brakes on your front axles and on your trailer axles. Again, this is enough to stop the rig somewhat beyond the required stopping distance.

That's roughly how the 121 braking system works. It's all very complex because of the many refinements like air dryers, extra valves, dual air line

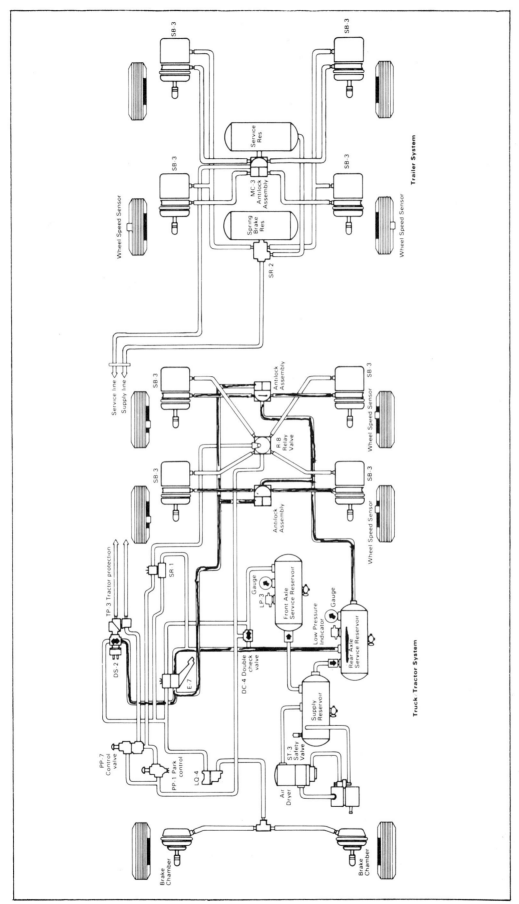

Brake schematic for a typical 121 dual tractor/trailer air brake system.
Courtesy of Bendix Heavy Vehicle Systems Group

Figure 9-16.

161

THE 121 BRAKING SYSTEM   (cont.)

systems, etc., which have been added. But, if you understand the basic design of the 121 system, you will have a beginning understanding of how it works.

> ▷ *A WORD OF CAUTION:*   *If one side or the other side of the dual system fails, don't delay repairs. Have the vehicle serviced immediately and the dual function corrected. Otherwise, you are not operating your unit safely.*

● *Anti-Lockup Protection*

As we said above, the 1975 DOT changes required a rig to remain within a 12-foot lane while stopping. If a rig's wheels lockup, the driver, of course, has trouble steering. So, to give the driver better directional control, electronic anti-lockup (or anti-skid) components were put into use.

This electronic system is separate from the air brake system. If it malfunctions, you will still have normal braking. However, you won't be protected against a wheel locking up on slippery ground - which is what the anti-lockup is designed to do. The anti-lockup also provides additional protection against jackknifing. If it goes out of order and you make a panic brake application, all your wheels may lockup and cause you to jackknife.

A yellow (or amber) light on the dashboard indicates an electronic anti-lockup malfunction. Some drivers are confused by this light and think it means they have no brakes. Not so. It means you have no anti-lockup protection.

● *Changes in Your Pre-Trip Inspection*

If you are driving a rig with a 121 braking system, you will need to make a couple of minor changes in your pre-trip brake inspection. As soon as you turn on the ignition, you should see a *red light* and a *yellow light* and hear a *buzzer sound*. The yellow light should go off within a few seconds, and the red light and buzzer should cease when both braking systems reach the 60-pound mark.

If the yellow light stays on, there is a malfunction somewhere in the anti-lockup system, as we just explained. You'll want to check this at your first opportunity. It is a danger. However, in most cases, loss of the anti-lockup won't interfere with your normal braking.

If the red light and buzzer don't go off, one of your dual systems hasn't built up to normal air pressure. Get your braking system checked immediately, before you leave on your tour of duty, because you don't have full service brakes. Your dual gauges or dual needles will tell you which system lacks sufficient air pressure.

● *Beware of Overconfidence*

Don't become overconfident if you're operating a 121-equipped truck. For example, don't start tailgating or doing some other foolish thing because you

THE 121 BRAKING SYSTEM   (cont.)

have a stronger brake system. As we said before, if you work your brakes too hard, they'll heat up on low downgrades or anyplace else. Then, it won't matter how much protection you have or how much air pressure you have. You are going to experience brake fade because of the extreme heat you're creating, and you may find yourself with a runaway truck on your hands.

● *More Changes*

As you can imagine, designing a truck's braking system which will meet all of the safety needs of a driver is not easy. Also, it's hard to get people to agree on what is safe and what isn't. So, the 121 system was controversial at the time at which we sent this book to the press. In fact, the US Courts have declared the anti-lockup portion only of the 121 system *not enforceable*. This means that if you have anti-lockup protection and it stops working, you can disconnect it and operate legally without it. (Although you're safer if you have this protection.) Most states are undecided as to what to do until DOT makes up its mind or can come up with an alternate system.

It's not easy for a trucker to keep up to date on all the new equipment and how to operate it safely and efficiently. Still, it drives home an important point. You need to keep your eyes open and keep learning about new equipment. You need to keep asking questions. Nevertheless, if your foundation of the basic operations of the truck's systems is firm, you can build upon it. You'll find picking up the information easier (whether it's in braking techniques, gear shift methods, coupling and uncoupling vehicles, inspecting a rig, or something else) if you understand the basics first.

At the time of print, each brake manufacturer has designed its dual system slightly differently, even down to the description of the truck air supply. For instance, one company will call the first tank from the compressor the "wet tank," and another will call it the "supply tank." The service tanks may be called the "primary" and "secondary" tanks by one company, and the "rear axle service reservoir" and the "front axle service reservoir" by another. So you see once again, your learning process never stops in trucking.

Figure 9-17. Proper braking techniques help to avoid accidents. This rig jackknifed and created a fire on the freeway. *Courtesy of the California Highway Patrol*

SUMMARY A heavy duty diesel slows or stops when the brake shoe (and lining) is forced against the brake drum. Normally, the driver has control over this braking. He or she applies the foot valve so that air pressure from the air tanks forces the shoes against the drum. Under emergency conditions, the brakes are applied automatically. The automatic application of the brakes occurs either through spring action or air pressure, depending upon the design of the braking system.

Your brakes are far more important than other systems of the rig. For safety, it is more important to be able to stop the rig than to start it. Your brakes must be in good, working order if you want to keep out of trouble.

Therefore, you need to learn to use good braking techniques. First, you will want to use your gears to help slow the rig. Second, you should begin applying your brakes early. You don't want to slug the brakes with air all at once. Third, you shouldn't fan your brakes. That is, you shouldn't step on and off of them to slow down. Fanning reduces the air supply in your reservoir and may reduce your braking power to dangerously low levels. Instead, you should gear down when you're going down hills or driving in traffic. Good braking techniques demand that you do three things: (1) watch the road, (2) drive at a safe speed for the roadway and weather conditions, and (3) anticipate the moves of other drivers.

Here's how your brakes work. A compressor provides air pressure, air tanks (or reservoirs) store the pressure, and valves release the pressure. You send pressure to the brake chambers when you step on the foot valve or apply the trailer hand valve. The air pressure applies force to the brake shoes. This air pressure forces the shoes against the brake drum. A little pressure on the foot valve provides a little bit of air pressure at the brake chamber. Heavier pressure on the foot valve provides more air pressure at the brake chambers, stopping the rig more quickly.

The truck's braking system has a great number of components. These components help the unit to function efficiently and effectively. Many of these components have been a part of the braking system for many years. (For example, the quick release valve, the breakaway valve, and the trailer reservoir.) Other refinements are new with the 121 braking system. Since the 121 braking system is an expansion of the older system, it makes sense to understand the older stystem first. Then, you can investigate the changes brought about by the 121 system. (The glossary serves as a good review of the many different valves, so we won't go over them again here.)

Normally, you apply all of the service brakes on the rig when you step on the foot valve. However, there are a few variations on this basic system. (1) The first variation is to apply the brakes on the trailer only by using the trailer hand valve. You might want to apply the trailer brakes to test your tractor-trailer hookup. You might also use it to apply your trailer brakes slightly ahead of your tractor brakes on a slippery roadbed. (2) The other variations of the basic service brake system work automatically. If air pressure drops below a set level, the trailer relay emergency valve traps air in the trailer reservoir and sends full air pressure to the trailer's brake chambers. The pressure automatically sets the trailer brakes. This is called

an automatic lockup or dynamite situation. The purpose is to stop the trailer
in an emergency situation. (3) An automatic lockup only affects the brakes on
the trailer, so you still need some type of emergency brakes on your tractor.
Your tractor's emergency brakes are the spring brakes or maxi brakes. If air
pressure in the tractor drops below a safe level, the spring brakes automatically set up. They do this because the air pressure that held them in a coiled up
position is gone. Thus, they expand, automatically applying your tractor's
brakes through mechanical force. You can manually apply these same spring
brakes. When you do this, you are using the spring brakes as your parking
brakes.

Many 121 systems don't have a trailer hand valve. So, in many 121 systems,
you can't apply the trailer brakes without applying the tractor brakes. Also,
the automatic braking system is different from that of pre-121 rigs. Instead,
the 121 braking system is equipped with a dual air supply system. This dual
system should keep the rig from losing braking power on all of the unit's axles
at one time.

Here's how it works. You have one supply tank and two service tanks.
That is, you have three air tanks in all. The supply tank gets air directly
from the compressor and distributes it to the two service tanks. Normally,
both of these service tanks and their air lines work together, in a single system. Together, they supply braking power to the front and rear axles of the
tractor and to the axles of the trailer.

In the 121 system, the double check valve becomes important if there is a
breakdown in the system. If one-half of the system malfunctions, the double
check valve will cut that half of the system off from the other half. The remaining, working half of the system takes over, giving you braking power to
stop your rig. If you lose your front tractor brakes, the remaining service
tank and air lines still supply air pressure to your rear tractor axles and
your trailer axles. This is enough braking power to stop the rig. If you lose
your rear tractor brakes, you will still have your front tractor brakes, and
the second half of the system takes over to supply brakes to your trailer.
Again, this is enough braking power to stop the rig.

We closed the chapter by making two important points. First, don't become overconfident if you are driving a 121-equipped rig. You still need to
use safe and effective braking techniques to keep your brakes in tiptop shape.
Second, keep learning. Trucks and truck components are constantly changing.
Ask questions and keep your eyes and ears open. In trucking, the learning process never stops.

GLOSSARY

There are 42 words in this chapter glossary. That's more than any other
chapter has, and it's just one more indication that it isn't easy to understand
a truck's braking system. With improvements and refinements happening all the
time, the list of terms just gets longer. Do your best to become familiar with
these words and their meanings, but don't expect to learn them all in a couple
of weeks.

GLOSSARY (cont.)

air brakes: A brake system using compressed air to work the brakes. Through a series of mechanical linkages, the air pressure finally forces the brake shoes against the brake drums to stop or slow the rig.

air cock (swing cock): A valve located on the end of an air line to shut off the flow of air.

anticipate: Foresee; to imagine something happening before it happens.

anti-lockup protection (electronic skid control): A feature originally included in the 121 braking system. Its purpose is to keep the wheels from locking up and causing the rig to skid all over the road when braking.

automatic lockup (dynamite situation): A situation where air brake pressure drops below 60 pounds in a tractor, causing the trailer relay valve to set up (lock up) the trailer brakes. They can't be released until air pressure returns to normal. This applies to the old, single air supply system, but not to the 121 system.

binders: In this chapter, "binders" was used as a slang term for brakes. The word also means any chain, wire rope, manila rope, steel strapping, synthetic fiber rope or nylon webbing used to secure a load to a vehicle or a detachable container. The term includes any component parts, such as hooks, attached to the chain, rope, etc.

brake chamber: An air chamber mounted near each wheel. It is connected to the brake itself by either a push rod and slack adjuster (on a cam brake) or just a push rod (on a wedge brake). Air comes to the chamber through the brake lines, but from there to the brake shoe and drum, the pressure is applied mechanically.

brake drum: A metal, drum-shaped compartment which revolves with the wheel. When the brake drums are forced to slow or stop, the wheels slow or stop turning too and stop the vehicle. (See Figure 9-3.)

brake fade: A reduction in the effectiveness of your brakes. Brake fade is usually caused by overheated brakes.

brake linings: A strong material (woven out of something like asbestos, fine copper wire, cotton, etc.) which is fastened to the brake shoe and actually contacts the brake drum during braking. (See Figure 9-1.)

brake shoe: A curved piece of heavy metal with brake lining which presses against the brake drum to slow or stop its motion. (See Figure 9-1.)

breakage: Damage of cargo caused by breaking.

breakaway protection (trailer breakaway protection): A process which applies the brakes on the trailer or trailers in case of a broken air hose or some other emergency. The trailer relay emergency valve traps air in the trailer's reservoir and, simultaneously, sends full air pressure to the brakes, setting them immediately. *See also:* automatic lockup.

breakaway valve: A valve positioned between the tractor and trailer. If air pressure drops below 60 pounds, this valve automatically cuts off the air going to the trailers, causing the trailer brakes to activate or "dynamite." The full name of the valve is the tractor protection breakaway valve, but it may also be called the tractor protection valve.

check valve (one-way check valve): A valve in an air line that allows air to flow in only one direction.

contaminants: Things that make something unclean or impure; impurities; pollutants.

diaphragm: A diaphragm is a membrane or partition that separates one thing from another. In trucking, when we use the word, it refers to a rubber partition between the two halves of the brake chamber. Air pressure in one half of the chamber pushes against the diaphragm and the diaphragm pushes against a push rod which mechanically applies the brakes.

disc brake: A brake which stops because pressure is applied on the outside of a revolving disc. Motorcycle brakes operate on this basic principle, and many automobiles have disc brakes.

drum brake: A brake which stops because pressure is applied on the inside of a revolving drum.

emergency line (hot line): A continuously charged line, supplying air to a trailer. Loss of pressure from this line causes an emergency application of the trailer brakes through the trailer relay emergency valve. (Refers to pre-121 braking systems only.)

fanning: Applying and releasing the brake pedal.

foot valve: The brake pedal. Used to apply the service brakes on all units of a combination at the same time.

fried brakes: Brakes that have become overheated and glazed, usually due to misuse. The brake linings become slick and cannot properly stop or slow the vehicle.

grade: A sloping part or hill. The word is also used in road construction to mean to make level or evenly sloping in preparation for a roadway.

hydraulic brake: A brake which uses liquid, under pressure, to apply the brakes.

GLOSSARY   (cont.)

   jackknife: A bend in the middle, or to bend in the middle. A planned jackknife is okay. It simply means to have the tractor and trailer heading at different angles while maneuvering, as in backing. However, an unplanned jackknife is extremely dangerous. The unplanned jackknife is usually created when you are braking a combination. The trailer or trailers swing around on the fifth wheel axis to about a 90-degree angle to the tractor.

   metering: Measuring or controlling, such as the flow of air to the brake system.

   NHTSA: The National Highway Traffic Safety Administration. A division of the DOT.

   121 braking system: Any braking system designed to meet the braking requirements of the NHSTA which were set in January of 1975 for the trucking industry. The new requirements included changes in air brake function and added electronic controls.

   port: An opening which allows things like steam, gas, or water to pass through. The word, of course, also means a harbor or bay, a harbor city, and is used in "port of entry" to mean a gateway or place to enter.

   quick release valve: A valve which allows air to exhaust, or release, near the brake chambers, thus providing quick air release.

   relay emergency valve (RE4 valve): This valve serves two purposes. It functions as a relay valve for the service air and, also, a quick release valve for the service air. It also automatically applies the trailer brakes upon loss of air pressure from the tractor. It is located beneath the trailer near the trailer reservoir. It is sometimes called the trailer valve or dynamite valve.

   retarders: Devices which slow or retard a truck. They provide braking action independent of, and supplemental to, the braking system.

   robot (robot valve): A valve which depends upon a signal from the foot valve to operate. Two robot valves are the quick release valve and the relay valve.

   service air: The compressed air usually used to apply the brakes on a truck. Service air is released into the brake chambers when the driver steps on the brake pedal (foot valve).

   service brakes: The primary braking system on a vehicle.

   service lines: The lines which carry service air to the brake chambers.

   slug: To hit hard, all at once.

   snub: To apply pressure to brake shoes.

GLOSSARY (cont.)

spring brake (maxi brake): A manually-controlled, spring-loaded parking and emergency brake. It automatically applies if air pressure drops below a safe level.

tee: A T-shaped junction.

valve: Basically, a valve is a device in a pipe or tube which regulates the flow in the pipe or tube by a flap, plug, lid, etc. It acts to open or block passage of liquid, air, or whatever is in the pipe. The word is used in many different ways in mechanics, but it basically always means what we have just described.

▶ CHECKING THE FACTS

Each sentence below has two words or groups of words in it in *italics*. The two words or word groups are divided by a slash mark (/). You can make the sentences true by <u>crossing out</u> one of the two words or word groups.

Example: This chapter was about the ~~*electrical system*~~/*braking system*.

1. Most brakes on a heavy-duty diesel truck are *disc brakes/drum brakes*.

2. Your air brakes can't do the whole job of slowing a huge rig. You must use your *gears/spring brakes* to help decrease your speed.

3. When you apply the foot valve, you *will/will not* feel a great build-up of pressure in a diesel truck.

4. Air brakes are a combination of air pressure and *electronic controls/ mechanical linkage*.

5. You might think of the air brake system as similar to a water system. The valves would be similar to the *piping/sprinkler head*.

6. The foot valve is the *brake pedal/way you apply the parking brakes*.

7. The foot valve applies the brakes on *the whole unit/the trailer only*.

8. The hand valve applies the brakes on *the whole unit/the trailer only*.

9. When you fan the brakes, you reduce *heat build-up/air pressure*.

10. A *quick release valve/relay valve* makes air pressure available close to the point of usage. This produces a faster brake application and reduces stopping distance.

11. Breakaway kits protect the air pressure in the *tractor/trailer*.

12. Breakaway kits automatically apply the brakes on the *tractor/trailer* when air pressure drops to an unsafe level.

13. The amount of air pressure in the system is regulated by the *compressor/air governor*.

14. In a pre-121 braking system, the spring brakes are the emergency brakes on the truck *trailer/tractor*.

15. The mechanical parts normally used to stop the truck *are the same/ are not the same* for the spring brakes and the service brakes.

16. *Air pressure/mechanical linkage* keeps the spring brakes in a caged position.

17. The protected air tank is used *for panic braking/to release the spring brakes*.

18. Under normal conditions, the two halves of the 121 braking system operate *together/separately*.

19. Each half of the 121 system is isolated from the other half by a *one-way check valve/double check valve*.

20. In the 121 system, a failure in one half of the system *will/will not* create a failure in the other half.

21. In a 121-equipped truck, when the yellow light stays on, it means this: *one half of the system has a malfunction/there is a malfunction in the anti-skid component*.

22. The component that actually touches the brake drum to slow the rig is the *brake lining/brake shoe*.

23. When you're bob tailing on home, your glad hands should be attached to the *pogo stick/steering wheel*.

24. One thing that can help to prevent a jackknife is proper use of the *relay valve/hand valve*.

25. The bottom end of the safe air pressure level is usually described as *60 pounds/90 pounds*.

■ GETTING THE MAIN IDEAS

Put a plus (+) before the statement if it is true. Put a zero (0) before the statement if it is false.

_____ 1. The system shown in Figure 9-10 has a wet and a dry air tank.

_____ 2. All tractor-trailer combinations have both a foot valve and a hand valve.

_____ 3. Air pressure enters the service line upon a normal brake application in a rig without a relay valve.

_____ 4. The hose connections from the tractor to the trailer are called the glad hands.

170

_____ 5. The spring brake uses the same brake shoes and brake drum to stop the rig as the air brake system does.

_____ 6. Figure 9-2 illustrates a pre-121 air brake system.

_____ 7. Figure 9-2 illustrates an air brake system for a straight or bobtail truck.

_____ 8. Getting a rig started is more important than being able to stop it.

_____ 9. The heavier the rig, the more build-up of pressure you will feel when you apply the foot valve.

_____ 10. As soon as you feel that initial, secure drag as the rig begins to slow, you know your brakes are good.

_____ 11. 100 pounds is a good, safe amount of pressure in the reservoir.

_____ 12. When you apply the brakes, your air pressure gauge will show a drop in air pressure. At this point, the governor will tell the compressor to produce more air pressure. Then, if the engine is running and everything is operating correctly, air pressure will return to normal.

_____ 13. In the early days of trucking, drivers had to fan the brakes if they wanted to slow their rigs gradually.

_____ 14. The main advantage of a relay valve is this: It reduces your stopping distance.

_____ 15. A trailer hand valve is an advantage in checking your tractor-trailer hook-up.

_____ 16. When air pressure drops below the 60 pound mark, air from your protected reservoir rushes to the brake chambers to apply the brakes on all axles of a combination unit.

_____ 17. The one-way check valve helps to protect the air supply which is stored in your air tanks.

_____ 18. The spring-applied brakes are held in the "OFF" position by a tension spring capable of 1200 pounds per square inch.

_____ 19. Figure 9-5 illustrates a tee.

_____ 20. With the 121 braking system in effect, hand valves are now required on all tractor-trailer combinations that drive interstate.

_____ 21. The cab control valve allows air to flow back and forth between the tractor and trailer at the breakaway valve. Under normal operating conditions, the driver should have this valve pulled out so that the breakaway valve is open.

_____22. Relay valves, hand valves and electronic skid control all help to reduce the possibility of a jackknife.

_____23. The 121 braking system is another attempt at improving safety in trucking.

_____24. In pre-121 braking systems, all valves were manually operated from the cab by the driver.

_____25. The two most important things for a trucker to know about the air brakes are (1) how to check the system out for proper functioning, and (2) how to operate the system.

_____26. Under normal conditions, this is how the dual air supply system of the 121 braking system works: The primary service tank sends air through the lines to the rear tractor axles and all trailer axles, and the secondary service tank sends air through the lines to the front tractor axles.

_____27. When a malfunction occurs, the two halves of the system work together to apply the brakes on all axles of the unit.

_____28. It is now illegal to operate a 121-equipped truck if there is a malfunction in the anti-lockup (or anti-skid) component.

_____29. 121-equipped trucks have disc brakes on the rear tractor axles.

_____30. There are many things you can do to maintain your air brake system. Here are three of them: use your gears to help slow your rig, have your brake linings and shoes inspected for proper adjustment, and have your engine oil changed regularly.

★ GOING BEYOND THE FACTS AND IDEAS

1. Divide a sheet of paper into two columns. In one column, list all of the components of the pre-121 air brake system which are needed just so the system can operate. (For example, list air lines in this column because without them no air could get to the brake chambers.) In the other column, list all of the pre-121 air brake components that are added to the system to make it more effective or efficient or safe. Be prepared to defend your choice of where to place each component.

2. Explain how the spring-applied brakes or maxi brakes work and how you release them once they are applied.

3. A fellow trucker complains that the government is meddling with the trucking industry. He says the 121 braking system is another example of this meddling, and goes on to criticize the new system as ineffective and unnecessary. The old system with its breakaway protection and maxi brakes worked fine. You want to defend the 121 system as a better system. What arguments would you use in your defense?

Figure 10-1. Early truck trailers were simple frames with springs
mounted to reduce shock to the load. Many like this were used in
the oilfields of southern California during the early Twenties.
The "truck" was an Oldsmobile. *Courtesy of Utility Trailer Mfg. Co.*

Chapter Ten

TYPES OF TRAILERS

INTRODUCTION | A semi-trailer or a full trailer, regardless of its config-
uration, is just a tool to use, like a wrench to a mecha-
nic. Each unit has its own use and capabilities. A unit can be abused by
being put into service it was not designed for - such as loading a Caterpillar
tractor onto a 40-foot flat-bed instead of using a low-bed trailer which is
designed to handle that type of equipment. There are many kinds of abuse.
Another common one is trying to haul large rocks on a flat-bed or in a trailer
that was designed for light aggregate material such as sand, gypsum, decomposed
granite or cement powder.

When you misuse any piece of equipment, you will shortchange yourself by
reducing the expected life span dramatically. In many cases, uses like those

INTRODUCTION (cont.)

we have just mentioned have resulted in breaking a trailer in half. Equipment today is very expensive. Needless to say, so are the repairs. And, many times, after misuse, it's not a matter of repairing it because the equipment is often beyond repair.

Misusing a tractor or trailer is like trying to haul a ton of freight on the roof of your car. It's just not designed for it. Get to know the many different kinds of trailers and learn to use them only for their intended uses.

BEFORE YOU READ ON This chapter is another excellent opportunity for you to practice the SQ3R method of study. There are a number of sub-headings (in italics), and each sub-section under these sub-headings describes a different type of trailer. Some are vans, some platforms, some tankers, and others. Survey the chapter. Turn each of these sub-headings into a Question. For example, you might say, "What makes a electronics van different from a warehouse van?" You might say, "What are the characteristics of an acid tank?" Read each section to answer your question. Recite (say aloud) what you read. Then, answer your questions from memory; that is, Review.

SEMI-TRAILERS AND FULL TRAILERS There are two basic trailer identifications: the semi-trailer and the full trailer. Both are sometimes called simply *trailers*. However, as you read in Chapter 2, there are important differences between the two. The semi-trailer is the one most often seen in the tractor-trailer combination. It has axles at the rear only. The front of the trailer is supported by the tractor. The full trailer is completely supported by its own axles and is drawn by a truck or a tractor. Full trailers are frequently used as the second trailers in *doubles* and as the second and third trailers in *triples*.

A semi-trailer can be converted to a full trailer by using a *dolly* or *converter dolly* under the front. (See illustration in Chapter 16.) By putting a dolly on any semi, you make a full trailer out of it.

Figure 10-2. Two tankers. Each has one *hopper*. The first trailer is a semi-trailer, the second a full trailer. *Courtesy of Pullman Trailmobile*

174

SEMI-TRAILERS AND FULL TRAILERS (cont.)

Most of the trailers discussed on the following pages are designed as semi-trailers. However, some of them can also be purchased as full trailers.

VAN
TRAILERS | The *van* is the most common type of trailer. Don't confuse van trailers ("vans") with the single-unit vans which many people drive for personal business such as camping or use as small delivery trucks. The trailer van is used in all operations where the commodity carried is *packaged or shipped in such a manner that the only protection required is a closed container*. There are a lot of different kinds of vans. They are described below.

⬤ *Dry Freight Van*

Available in lengths from 20 to 45 feet, this unit is the "work horse of the industry." The shortest units, with single axles, are commonly used in city delivery work. Two twenty-sevens (27-foot trailers) make up the usual doubles combination. The larger units - 35 to 45 feet - are normally used singly. However, some states allow drivers to use two forties as doubles on specified super roads.

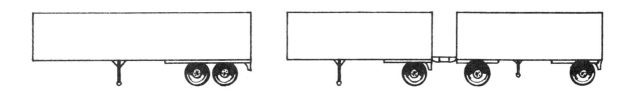

Figure 10-3. Dry freight vans, each equipped with old-style landing gear. See also Figures 8-1 and 7-1.

The *dry freight van* usually has a flat floor and has a maximum cubic capacity of approximately 2750 cubic feet. Normal *payload capacity* (or amount of income-producing cargo that can be carried) goes up to 50,000 pounds.

⬤ *Warehouse Van*

Also known as a furniture van, the *warehouse van* is a favorite of the moving industry. It has a drop in the floor, just aft (behind) of the upper coupler, where the semi-trailer is coupled to the tractor. This drop in the floor, pictured in Figures 10-4 and 10-5, provides greater cubic capacity. With a maximum drop of 27 inches, approximately 3000 cubic feet of load space is available. The drop feature also permits ease of loading.

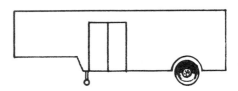

Figure 10-4. Warehouse van. See also Figure 10-5.

One problem with a drop floor is that *wheel housings* are required to accommodate the wheels and tires at the rear axle location. This is not much of a problem when

VAN TRAILERS (cont.)

the unit is hand-loaded as in moving and storage, but if the unit is loaded by forklift, the forklift may not be able to pass between the wheel housings. In this case, an electronics van should be used.

Figure 10-5. A new Utility furniture van just prior to delivery to the customer. These are also called *drop vans* because of the lowered floor area and boxed wheels. *Courtesy of Utility Trailer Mfg. Co.*

● *Electronics Van*

Similar in appearance to the warehouse van, the *electronics* van does not have as deep a drop in the floor. In this van, the drop is only about 21 inches. It is also equipped with 15-inch wheels; whereas, the warehouse van has 20-inch wheels. The smaller wheels allows for a flat floor behind the drop, doing away with the wheel-house problem. Some room is sacrificed by the shallow drop, but the loss is minor since no space is lost due to the wheel-house cube.

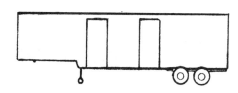

Figure 10-6. Electronics van.

This van was designed originally so the electronics industry could handle delicate equipment. Air ride or soft ride spring suspensions are commonly used to protect the load. The van is also used now to hold high-bulk, low-weight commodities known as *"balloon freight."* Potato chips, snack foods, plastics, and clothing fall into this category. Lengths run to 45 feet with up to 3100 cubic foot of space.

● *Open Top Van*

An *open top van* is basically a dry freight van without a roof. It is designed for loading under a crane. To protect the load and add stability to the sides, removable top bows are used to support a canvas or nylon tarpaulin. The tarpaulin is secured by the tie-downs at the sides and end of the trailer. The size and capacity are the same as the dry freight van.

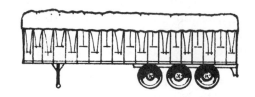

Figure 10-7. Open top van. See also Figure 10-8.

Figure 10-8. One type of open top van. This is Trailmobile's Optimum Van Grain Hopper Trailer. It is designed with two, single-gate hoppers. *Courtesy of Pullman Trailmobile.*

● *Refrigerated and Insulated Vans*

Most trailer manufacturers use their standard dry freight van as the base vehicle for a *refrigerated* or *insulated van*. They line and insulate the van with one of several types of materials. Then, they install the proper refrigerating unit. In this way, they can tailor the dry freight van to meet most refrigeration and insulation requirements. Temperature ranges are available from sub-zero Fahrenheit (-22° Celsius and colder) for frozen foods and ice cream to 35° to 45° F (2° to 8° C) for meat and produce.

Figure 10-9. Refrigerated van. See also Figure 10-10.

● *Overseas Dry Freight Containers*

In this day of modernization where the majority of freight is palletized for pickup by truck, we have progressed another stop. Now, whole van bodies are loaded with freight, and the van body itself detaches from the trailer frame (or chassis). This type of freight container is called an *overseas dry freight container* or *sea-land container*.

Overseas dry freight containers are found around the waterfront. Freight is loaded into the container. Then, the container is sealed and hauled to a dock or yard.

VAN TRAILERS (cont.)

A tractor pulls the unit to the wharf or the pier area where a huge fork-lift or an overhead crane lifts the complete van body off the trailer frame. The van body is released from the trailer frame by a set of steel pins on each corner which originally held the van in place on the trailer frame during shipment over the highway.

These types of vans are stacked two or three high at the pier awaiting a freighter. Then, these vans are loaded aboard the ship and stacked two to three high, both below and above the decks of the ship for shipment overseas. At the other port, the container is either unloaded or put on another chassis for shipment to its eventual destination. Once emptied, the container is reloaded with other commodities and completes a return trip back to the original port.

This method of shipping eliminates handling the freight from the factory to a van. It eliminates unloading at the pier, reloading on pallets and handling when the freight is put aboard ship. It is known as *containerized freight*. The van and furniture storage industry today often use the same method in shipping from one coast to the other.

Figure 10-10. A Utility refrigerated van with "reefer" unit mounted. "Reefers" are insulated vans that are kept cold by forced circulation of cold air through the cargo area. *Courtesy of Utility Trailer Mfg. Co.*

20' AND 40' DRY FREIGHT CONTAINERS

40' REFRIGERATED CONTAINERS

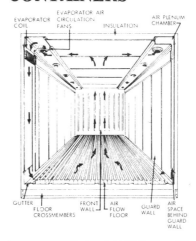

MOTOR GENERATOR SET

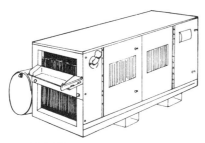

PURPOSE:

To provide auxiliary electrical supply for sea-going refrigerated containers. On board a container ship, the refrigerated container normally derives its power from the ship's generators. For over-the-road use, the M/G set is mounted beneath a container chassis and connects to the container to provide electricity which operates the container's refrigeration system.

STRIC/TEMP FLOW-THRU AIR DISTRIBUTION — Warm air is picked up by five fans on each side of container at ceiling level. Air is then directed down and inside the side wall across evaporator coils. It continues down the side wall in an air space 1" to 1½" wide, and is discharged at floor level. The floor is cross-ventilated, permitting the air to flow away from side walls toward center.

Figure 10-11. At top, is an overseas dry freight container, being lowered by a crane. On the lower left, a "reefer" unit is pictured. On the lower right, is a diagram of how air circulates from the reefer unit to cool the van. *Courtesy of Transport International Pool*

● *Platform Trailer*

Also known as a *flat-bed*, the *platform trailer* is used to haul materials that don't require the protection of, or are too large to fit in, a van trailer. Commodities such as steel, machinery, and building materials are a natural for this trailer.

The standard platform goes up to 45 feet in length. For extremely long loads, an extendable platform is offered by a number of manufacturers if you ask for it.

Normal capacities are in the 50,000 pounds range. Heavier units are available, however, on order.

Figure 10-12. Platform trailer.

● *Low-Bed Trailer*

The low-bed is the heavyweight of the trailers. Most often, they are used to haul bulldozers, cranes, and construction equipment. Low-beds are also used to transport transformers, generating plants, all types of machinery, plus just about any other heavy commodity you can think of. (See Figure 15-5.)

Normal capacities run up to 100 tons. Special combinations are available, though, where the only limit is physical size and the ability of the ground to support the load.

Figure 10-13. Low-bed trailer.

Many axle and tire combinations are offered to provide required capacities. Other options, such as removable *goosenecks* and special *deck* (or platform) configurations are available. The gooseneck is the neck section at the front of the trailer that reaches up and attaches to the towing unit.

Figure 10-14 is a multi-wheel low-bed with outriggers. *Outriggers* are swing-out brackets attached to the sides of a low-bed trailer. By swinging the brackets out, an additional plank is laid parallel with the trailer deck. This gives the driver an additional foot of deck width on each side of the trailer. Doing this, you can extend, for

Figure 10-14. Multi-wheel low-bed with outriggers and beaver tail. *From the author's own collection*

Figure 10-15. A typical **Utility** wide frame flat-bed trailer. Also called a platform trailer. All types of commodities not suited to a van can be carried if properly secured. *Courtesy of Utility Trailer Mfg. Co.*

Figure 10-16. A typical low-bed or gooseneck trailer. Low-beds are used to carry heavier materials than a flat-bed, construction equipment, components for the space and electronics industries, etc. *Courtesy of HOBBS Trailers, Division of Fruehauf Corporation*

example, an eight-foot wide trailer to a ten-foot wide trailer. By widening the load, however, you may exceed the legal width limits and need a transport permit for a wide load. You get the permit from the city, state, or county, depending on what route you are planning to travel. (We'll discuss this in depth in Chapter 19.)

The low-bed in Figure 10-14 also has a *"beaver tail."* You can just see part of it at the lower left-hand side of the picture. A beaver tail is the sloping rear section of a low-bed trailer. The purpose of it is to allow a machine (such as a bulldozer) to climb up onto the trailer from the ground.

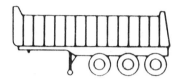

Figure 10-17. Dump trailer. See also Figure 10-19.

● *Dump Trailers*

Dump trailers range in capacity from 15 to approximately 35 cubic yards. Lengths from 20 to 30 feet are normal, but longer units are available on special order.

The dump body can be tailored for many operations. Some models are offered for normal operations, such as sand and gravel. Heavier-duty models are available for excavation, rock hauling, and unusual situations such as hot slag.

● *Pole Trailer*

Pole trailers are used to haul raw timber, and, as the name implies, poles. They're also used for anything like steel or prestressed concrete beams.

Figure 10-19. The Hobbs chassis dump. Notice the telescopic front lift. *Courtesy of HOBBS Trailers, Division of Fruehauf Corporation*

Figure 10-18. Pole trailer.

Pole trailers are made up of two racks. One attaches to the fifth wheel, and one supports the rear of the load. On some pole trailers, a telescopic pole connects the two racks. In others, the racks are secured to each end of the load. In these, the load becomes the connecting link.

OTHER TYPES OF TRAILERS (cont.)

Air hoses and electric cables are suspended from the telescopic pole or load on pole trailers. These supply brakes and lights to the rear unit.

● *Livestock Trailer*

Livestock trailers are designed to haul livestock "on the hoof." The profile of a livestock trailer is similar to a van. However, its sides are slotted for air and reinforced against animal movement.

Figure 10-20. Livestock trailer.

Double decks are common to make use of available space. Then, if a carrier needs even more space, she or he may add a "possum belly," making the trailer a triple decker.

● *Auto Transport Trailer*

A common sight, the *auto transport trailer* can carry six full-size cars and up to ten subcompacts.

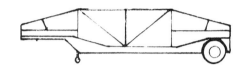

Figure 10-21. Auto transport trailer.

This type of trailer is subject to constant change because new car designs often require different methods of handling. The various sizes and arrangements have been designed mainly by the car carriers for their highly specialized field.

● *Bulk Grain and Fruit Trailer*

The *bulk grain and fruit trailer* is designed to handle a variety of bulk items. Grain, fruit, potatoes, corn and feed are easily handled. It is similar to the open top van, but it has lower sides. Removable top bows support the tarpaulin which is used to cover the load.

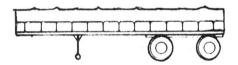

Figure 10-22. Bulk grain and fruit trailer.

The open top feature helps in chute loading. Unloading is often done by lifting the front of the trailer and allowing the load to flow off the rear.

CHARACTERISTICS OF TANKERS

Tankers are available as single compartments or compartmented. Single compartment tankers may be either *clean bore* or *baffled*. *Baffles* are obstrucing devices designed to hold back the flow of liquids, gases, etc. They keep the load from surging, but they create a cleaning problem. The *clean bore* tank design is much easier to flush out or clean. It has no corners, joints, or angles where material can build up. Clean bore tanks also drain more easily. Because it is easy to clean, the clean bore tank also offers a distinct advantage when a single tanker may be used at various times to carry different liquids.

183

CHARACTERISTICS OF TANKERS   (cont.)

There can be up to four different compartments in an average 40-foot compartmented tanker. Compartmentalization allows the driver to carry mixed loads, such as high test and regular gasoline.

Some tanks are designed for high pressure loads. They haul gases in their liquid form - liquid oxygen, hydrogen, butane, and nitrogen, to name a few. Each commodity has its own characteristics. So, you'll find many different options available for these high pressure loads. Unloading liquid gases is done by gravity feed. Either "pumped off" or "pressure" gravity feeding is used; it depends upon the commodity and the situation. Single or multiple drains are available. Where controlled unloading is required, special valving is offered.

● *Liquid Tank Trailers*

Liquid tankers carry a wide range of commodities: petroleum products, acids, chemicals, food, edible oils, waste in all forms, and just plain water, to name a few.

Figure 10-23. Hoses connect to these spouts to fill and empty the tanker. *Courtesy of Timpte-Beall, Inc.*

To handle the various liquids, tankers are offered in steel, stainless steel, and aluminum. Coatings can also be applied to the inside surface of the tank so the tanks can withstand chemical action. The tank can be insulated to handle products which require temperature control. Heaters are available if needed to keep the cargo in its liquid state. Thus, different features are available to handle different cargoes.

Two basic shapes are used in tank design: *elliptical* (egg-shaped at the end) and *cylindrical* (round at the end). Each is offered in several variations because each commodity has different needs for drainage and weight distribution. The cylindrical shape is the most versatile and the strongest. The elliptical has a lower center of gravity.

Figure 10-24. A lightweight aluminum insulated tank truck and trailer combination. This elliptical tanker is used for transporting liquids requiring temperature control. *Courtesy of Timpte-Beall, Inc.*

CHARACTERISTICS OF TANKERS (cont.)

● *Dry Bulk Tank Trailers*

Dry bulk tankers are designed to carry powdered or pelletized products, both edible and nonedible. Sugar, flour, dry milk, grain and meal are a few of the edibles. Cement, dry chemicals, fly ash, pelletized plastics, charcoal, animal feed, wood chips and limestone are some of the nonedibles.

The bulk tanker is a high-volume, low-cost means of transportation of things that would normally have to be bagged and hand-loaded. In the case of edibles, it eliminates the possibility of contamination and infestation.

Bulk tankers are usually clean bore tanks with three or four *hoppers* built into the main body. (*Hoppers* are containers, made of wood or steel, for holding grains or other products, such as those we mentioned above. They can hold either edible or nonedible products.) The hoppers are cone-shaped. The cone directs the material to the discharge outlet.

The dry bulker is loaded at the top through holes that are equipped with air-tight pressure covers. Unloading is done pneumatically. Air, under pressure, is forced through a discharge line that is attached to each hopper. Air passes through the line and forces the product into the stream. The stream of air car-ries the product from the trailer to the storage bin. Air pressure is also used to agitate the product, that is, to keep it from clogging the hopper discharge valve; and air pressure is used to pres-surize the main tank.

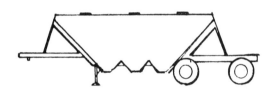

Figure 10-25. Dry bulk tanker with three hoppers.

The air for unloading can be provided by a compressor which is carried in the trailer. Or it can be provided by a turbocharger on the tractor. (We'll mention turbochargers again in Chapter 13.) On the other hand, a driver may use an outside source to force air through the discharge line.

TYPES
OF
LIQUID
TANKERS

● *Petroleum-Chemical Tanker*

You can buy a *petroleum-chemical tan-ker* with a single compartment or with three, four, or five compartments. And, they are available with or without baffles, and in all materials and shapes. Capacities go up to 9500 gallons.

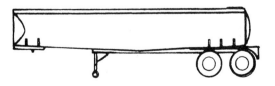

Figure 10-26. Petroleum-chemical tanker.

185

Figure 10-27. Trailmobile's Nordic Bulker is available in steel or aluminum, in a variety of lengths. There are also five separate discharge systems from which to choose. *Courtesy of Pullman Trailmobile*

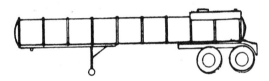

Figure 10-28. Acid tank. Notice the outside rings.

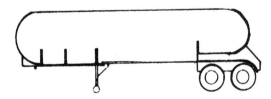

Figure 10-29. Liquefied gas tank.

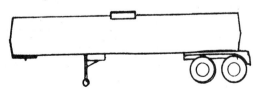

Figure 10-30. Insulated tank.

TYPES OF LIQUID TANKERS (cont.)

● *Acid Tank*

You can usually identify an *acid tank* by its smaller diameter tank and its external stiffener rings. This tank is offered in all materials. A variety of linings and baffle options are available, and acid tanks can be insulated. Their capacity is about 6000 gallons of liquid.

● *Liquefied Gas Tank*

Liquefied gas tanks come in several styles. They are designed for high pressure. They transport butane, propane, oxygen, hydrogen and other gases in their liquefied state. They can carry up to 11,000 gallons.

● *Insulated Tank*

An *insulated tank* can accept materials up to 500° F (260° C) if it is made of steel. It can carry materials up to 400° F (204° C) if it is made of aluminum.

186

SUMMARY | The main purpose of this chapter was to describe the many different kinds of trailers and the kinds of commodities each carries. It is important to use a trailer only for hauling the products it is meant to haul. Otherwise, you will harm or even destroy the trailer. Most trailer types are available as full or semi-trailers. You can also make a full trailer out of a semi by attaching it to a converter dolly. (See Figure 10-31.)

Trailers can be classified as vans, platforms, or tankers. There are also other types of trailers, however, that don't quite fit into any category. These are the dump trailer, pole trailer, livestock trailer, auto transport trailer and bulk grain and fruit trailer.

Vans are the most common type of trailer, and there are many kinds of vans. All vans are used for products that require only a closed container as protection of the load. The dry freight van is the most common type of all. Then, there are warehouse vans and electronics vans. (Both have a drop in the floor.) There are vans without roofs, called open top vans, and there are refrigerated and insulated vans. Overseas dry freight containers are also vans.

There are two kinds of platform trailers - the flat-bed and the low-bed. The flat-bed carries cargo too large for a van. It also carries cargo that simply doesn't need the protection of a van. Low-beds are the heavy-weights of the industry. They haul extremely heavy equipment, such as Cats and cranes, and other objects that would break any other type of trailer.

Haulers of special cargoes have designed trailers just right for their special needs. Among these are dump trailers, auto transports, and livestock trailers. The real oddball, however, is the pole trailer which is made up of two completely separate pieces - one for the front of the load and one for the rear.

Tankers are divided into two types: liquid tankers and dry bulk tankers (or "bulkers"). Liquid tankers can be elliptical or cylindrical. They carry many different kinds of liquids, depending upon what they are made out of, their shapes, their inner coatings, and their insulations. There are special kinds of tankers for carrying petroleum and chemicals, acids, liquefied gas, and products needing insulation. Dry bulkers carry powdered or pelletized products - edible and nonedible. The products are loaded by air pressure through holes at the top, and unloaded through "hoppers" at the bottom. Both liquid tankers and dry bulkers can be baffled or clean bore.

GLOSSARY | A complete glossary for this chapter includes all of the trailer types which we defined. This includes the large categories (vans, platforms, and tankers) *and* the smaller categories (such as open top vans, acid tanks, pole trailers and low-beds). You will be creating the glossary for all of these types of trailers if you complete the questions under, "Checking the Facts."

However, there are a lot of other words in this chapter that need to be defined. They are defined here.

GLOSSARY (cont.)

aft: Behind; toward the rear.

baffles: A device which holds back a liquid or makes it turn aside. Many tankers have baffles to keep the liquid from surging rapidly back and forth in the tank.

balloon freight: Light, but bulky commodities like potato chips and clothing.

beaver tail: The sloping rear section of a low-bed trailer. It hangs down, like a tail, and it allows construction equipment to climb up onto the platform or deck. A beaver tail is not detachable; it is permanently attached.

chassis: The frame of a motor vehicle. On a trailer, it includes the axles, wheels and suspension. On a tractor or truck, it includes all of those, plus the engine parts.

clean bore: Open, having no baffles. A clean bore tanker has no corners, joints - no areas where material can build up.

configuration: Shape, outside appearance, contour.

container (containerized freight): Usually used in trucking to mean an overseas dry freight container. A container is an entire van body (minus the chassis). It can be packed with product, hauled by truck, unloaded in one piece at the dock, and shipped overseas - all without unloading the cargo. Sometimes called sea-land containers.

converter dolly (dolly): An auxiliary axle assembly, equipped with a fifth wheel, and used to convert a semi-trailer to a full trailer. Sometimes called a converter gear or auxiliary gear.

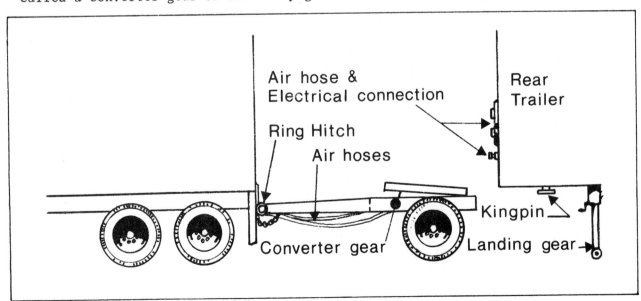

Figure 10-31. A converter dolly being used to attach a second semi-trailer to a rig, making the rig a double.

cubic foot: An area the size of a cube which is one foot, by one foot, by one foot. An area of four cubic feet could hold four of these cubes. A dry freight van might have an area of 2500 cubic feet; that is, it could hold 2500 of these cubes. Instead, of course, it is filled with cargo that takes up the same amount of space.

cylindrical: Shaped like a cylinder; that is, like a number of disks stacked on top of one another. A cylindrical tanker is round at both ends.

deck: A deck is any platform or floor shaped like a ship's deck. In trucking, it usually refers to the platform of a flat-bed or low-bed trailer.

double: A combination made up of a tractor and two trailers. It can also be a straight truck and trailer.

elliptical: Egg-shaped. An elliptical tanker is not actually egg-shaped completely. However, the ends of the tanker are egg-shaped. (See Figure 10-24.)

gooseneck: The part of a low-bed trailer that reaches up from the deck to attach to the fifth wheel. The word "gooseneck" is also used to mean a low-bed trailer itself.

hoppers: Containers made of wood or steel for holding grains or other products. In a dry bulker, separate hoppers can hold different products; each hopper is a separate container. Hoppers have openings at the bottom so the commodity can be unloaded there.

outriggers: Swing-out brackets attached to the sides of a low-bed to widen the deck.

pallets: A low, portable platform on which materials are stacked for storage or shipment. Usually made of wood.

palletized: Stacked or resting on pallets.

payload capacity: Amount of income-producing cargo that a trailer or truck can carry.

pelletized: Made into tiny balls. The tiny pieces of styrofoam in a beanbag chair have been pelletized.

reefer: A refrigerated van. A reefer is cooled by cold air forced through the cargo area by a refrigeration unit mounted to the van. The word "reefer" is also used for the refrigeration unit itself.

telescopic: Shaped like a telescope; having sections that slide one inside another. (See Figure 10-19.)

GLOSSARY   (cont.)

triple: A combination made up of a tractor and three trailers, or of a straight truck and two trailers.

wheel housing: The protrusion of the trailer deck or wall that shields or "houses" the trailer wheels in trailers where the wheels protrude into the cargo space.

▶ CHECKING THE FACTS

Each sentence below needs the name of one type of trailer to complete it. You can complete the glossary by filling in these blanks. Use each once.

1. The _____ has a shallow drop in the floor and no wheel-house problem.

2. A _____ is an insulated dry freight van with a refrigeration unit.

3. The _____ has a drop floor, a flat deck, and is used to carry very heavy equipment.

4. A tanker with external stiffener rings and a small-diameter tank is the _____.

5. _____ are usually clean bore tanks with three or four hoppers built into the main body. They are used to carry powdered or pelletized products.

6. The _____ is the work horse of the industry, meaning it's the most commonly used trailer.

7. The _____ is a dry freight van without a roof. It is loaded by crane.

8. An oil company will probably use the _____ to deliver its product.

9. Extremely hot commodities, up to 500° F (260° C) can be carried in

_____.

10. If you have a cargo which is too big to fit in a van, but not very heavy, you may choose the _____.

11. The _____ is the favorite of the moving industry. It has a fairly deep drop in the floor.

12. The _____ can be detached from the trailer chassis.

13. An open-top trailer which rises at the front and lets the cargo slide off the back is the _____.

14. The _____ is made up of two racks. One is attached to the fifth wheel; one supports the rear of the load.

15. A trailer used to carry gases in their liquefied state is a _____

_____ .

16. The _____ has slotted sides so air can flow through them. It may have one, two, or three decks.

17. The _____ is similar to the open top van, but the sides are lower. It is loaded by a chute.

18. The _____ is used to carry six or more cars or pickups at one time.

■ GETTING THE MAIN IDEAS

Part One of this section will exercise your skills at identifying types of trailers from pictures. You will find these pictures in the other chapters of this book, by figure numbers. Each figure number on the left is one of the types of trailers listed on the right. You can match the pictures by putting the letter of the correct trailer type in front of its matching figure number on the left. The types of trailer names may be used *more than once or not at all.*

_____ 1. Figure 1-1   A. double

_____ 2. Figure 1-6   B. dry freight van

_____ 3. Figure 2-1   C. dry bulk tanker

_____ 4. Figure 2-2   D. dump trailer

_____ 5. Figure 4-2   E. electronics van

_____ 6. Figure 5-2   F. warehouse van

_____ 7. Figure 7-1   G. flat-bed or platform trailer

_____ 8. Figure 7-4   H. gooseneck or low-bed

_____ 9. Figure 14-1   I. insulated tanker

_____ 10. Figure 15-2   J. livestock trailer

_____ 11. Figure 18-13   K. pole trailer

_____ 12. Figure 19-1   L. open top van

_____ 13. Figure 19-9   M. overseas dry freight container

_____ 14. Figure 22-7   N. petroleum-chemical tanker

_____ 15. Figure 25-1   O. refrigerated van

For Part Two of "Getting the Main Idea," you may answer <u>any</u> <u>four</u> of the seven questions below.

16. What is the main difference between a warehouse van and an electronics van?

17. In your own words, describe how a reefer unit operates.

18. In your own words, state the meaning of Figure 10-31. What does it show?

19. When would you choose a tanker with baffles and when would you choose a clean bore tanker?

20. What is the main difference between a van and a platform trailer? Give several examples of products typically hauled by vans and by platform trailers.

21. What is the main purpose of containerization?

22. Explain how dry bulkers are loaded and unloaded.

★ GOING BEYOND THE FACTS AND IDEAS

1. In chart form, list the characteristics of vans and tankers. You are dealing here with the large categories, not the names of individual types of trailers.

2. Select the appropriate type of trailer for each of the following commodities:
   A. a space shuttle
   B. a subway car
   C. Christmas trees
   D. cold beer in bottles
   E. boulders
   F. corn meal - loose
   G. light bulbs in packages
   H. rugs
   I. plutonium
   J. sides of beef
   K. tomatoes
   L. sheep - live
   M. chickens - live
   N. sacks of masa harina
   O. sawdust
   P. milk
   Q. gasoline
   R. liquid nitrogen

3. What type of trailer do you think would be most interesting to haul? What type would be most uninteresting? Which would be the most difficult to learn to haul? What kind of trailer would you most like to haul and why?

4. Relate a story (true or your own creation) about what happened when a driver selected the wrong type of trailer for a load.

Chapter Eleven

STEERING AND TURNING

Figure 11-1. The problems of steering and turning are compounded by conditions such as rain, snow, and ice. *Courtesy of Jim Felt Photography*

CONVOYS | Like the old record, "Convoy," rolling down the road with a rig, stacked almost bumper to bumper with a lot of other vehicles, can be a lot more hazardous than running alone. A military convoy is somewhat less dangerous, but it still requires all of a driver's skill.

The military has a lot of rigs on the road daily. Convoys are common. Did you ever notice how slowly the vehicles in a convoy run? And did you wonder why they don't roll with the rest of the traffic instead of tying everything up? Let's take a few moments to talk about the special problems of convoy driving before we get into how to steer and turn in regular traffic.

● *What a Convoy Commander Must Consider*

Every military convoy has a commander who must set the rules. Following the commander's rules is critically important. The commander considers two main things in setting the rules: *speed* and *the safety cushion*.

Speed. Why do military convoys (and other convoys) travel so slowly? Put yourself in the first vehicle, leading the pack. The convoy commander tells you, "Hold to a 35-mph speed limit." Immediately, you think, "Man alive! We're never going to get anywhere." Well, it isn't you that the commander is worried about. It's the vehicles that bring up the rear. They may have to run their wheels off to stay up with you.

An example might help you to picture what happens. Take the example of a sprinter on a track, racing with another person. The sprinter takes off at a fast pace. The second doesn't start until five seconds later. You can imagine how fast the second person has to run to catch up with the first person. Basically, this is the problem with convoy driving. In a convoy, the commander sets the speed to the needs of the last driver, not the first. By the time you get to the end of a string of 40, 50, or more vehicles, the drivers at the back are running wide open when they start off to catch up with the forward part of the convoy.

The Safety Cushion. The safety cushion (or distance between vehicles) is also important to the commander and to the lives of the drivers. Therefore, the commander tells each driver to keep a distance between vehicles, and she or he tells each driver what that distance should be. The gap between vehicles is supposed to be an *approximate* distance. The vehicles in the convoy will tend to seesaw in their positions, that is, to increase and decrease their speed and safety cushion as they drive. Too much seesawing is bad, and when it results in getting too close to the vehicle in front, it is extremely dangerous. A careful driver understands that some road conditions require him or her to increase the safety cushion, even if the commander doesn't say to. If the speed of the vehicles increases, the safety cushion should also increase. The safety cushion is critical. Too often, a driver will automatically hold the distance between vehicles set by the commander, no matter what changing safety conditions require.

● *Convoy Accidents are Big Accidents*

If you happen to be on snow and ice, too small a safety cushion and too much speed can be disastrous. I remember one convoy, late at night, heading north on the East Coast in mid-winter. The temperature was down to 28° F (-2° C). We had approximately *100 vehicles*. Jeeps led the pack, followed by heavier trucks and amphibious units. Wreckers brought up the rear. Everyone was cold and tired.

When the convoy reached a traffic circle, the leading jeep came into it too fast. Instead of making it, the jeep slid straight through the circle and up onto the grass divider. That started a chain reaction. By the time it was all over, about five short minutes later, the area looked like a gigantic parking lot in chaos. Vehicles were headed in every direction. The end result was over 60 of the 100 vehicles wrecked. Luckily, no one was injured.

Another time, we were running mountainous roads through Pennsylvania with some amphibious units. Here again, the driver in the front unit was inexperienced and we had ice underfoot. The driver failed to realize the handling characteristics of an amphibious unit which are very different from a standard truck. Why? Because each vehicle has a long bow extending out in front. This long bow has a tendency to create a centrifugal drag when you try to turn sharply.

CONVOYS (cont.)

As the first vehicle approached a curve on the ice, the driver slowed to 25 mph. Twenty-five miles per hour wasn't slow enough. The centrifugal force created by the long nose resisted the turning movement. To make matters worse, the tire tread lacked road bite due to the tread design. These two problems caused the driver to lose all steering ability and directional control. The vehicle went straight through the curve and off the road, followed by 40 other vehicles, each one duplicating the same thing on the turn. These amphibious units are made of light sheet metal. They get holes punched in them and bend and damage easily. So, the result of the accident was one huge junk pile.

In both accidents, speed was excessive, and the safety cushion was too small. These are personal examples of what happens when someone doesn't pay attention to driving. Driving is a full-time job. Your body can be relaxed, but you can't relax your vigilance.

● *Unplanned Convoy Driving*

Driving a rig over the open road often turns into an "unplanned convoy." You aren't in a planned convoy, but the congestion on the road creates many of the same problems. Unplanned convoys can be even more dangerous because you are running with little or no safety cushion between rigs. And you are often running at very high speeds.

There is no convoy commander, and, of course, you don't know who the driver ahead of you is, or what the driver's carrying. Possibly, you won't even know where your junctions are until you come up on them because the truck in front blocks your view of the road. So, you see, you have a lot of unanswered questions. Until you can come up with answers to these questions, you're in trouble.

There are trucks in front, trucks behind, trucks passing. If you have to make a quick change of lanes at a high rate of speed, everything happens in seconds. Bad weather conditions, such as snow and ice, compound the hazards. Thus, before you learn anything else about steering and turning your vehicle, remember these two things: *Watch your speed, and keep a good safety cushion between your vehicle and all other vehicles on the road.*

| STEERING YOUR VEHICLE FORWARD | The basic rule to follow whenever you're behind the wheel of a semi is, *"Whenever possible, keep two hands on the wheel, and above all, keep your thumbs from going down between the spokes of the wheel."* |

Many drivers have gotten their fingers and hands wrapped up in a spinning steering wheel and have regretted it over the years. The force of a large truck steering wheel spinning at a lightning-paced speed is enough to tear your thumb off your hand. A word of caution. This situation of getting your thumbs and fingers caught by a spinning steering wheel occurs not only at high speeds. It may also occur when you are maneuvering in and out of loading docks or freight yards - especially when you're backing in. All you have to do is

195

get the front wheel caught on a pallet or block of wood or fall in a chuck hole while your vehicle is moving slowly, and it will be enough to tear the wheel from your grip.

Whenever you take hold of the wheel, make sure you hold it firmly. Otherwise, if you hit a curb or chuck hole, the steering wheel could be pulled from your grasp. You should keep your muscles relaxed, but keep a firm grip on the wheel.

STEERING YOUR VEHICLE BACKWARD

The control of a single-unit truck (straight truck) is the same as that of a passenger car. The steering wheel is turned in the direction you wish the back of the vehicle to go. As long as you hold the wheel steady, the vehicle will back in a straight line.

However, backing a tractor-trailer combination will differ greatly because you have two units coupled together instead of one vehicle. The coupling between the tractor and trailer acts as a swivel. Even though you hold the steering wheel as straight as possible, the whole unit will seldom back up in a straight line for more than 30 feet. Normally, the trailer will take off to one side.

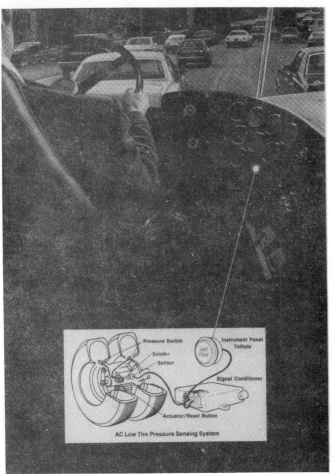

Figure 11-2. Cab interior showing instrument panel. The low tire pressure signal shown here can help save tires and fuel. Maintaining proper tire pressure reduces rolling resistance, thus helping you get more miles per gallon. *Courtesy of AC Spark Plug Division, GMC*

In backing a semi, even though you think you're going straight, the minute you sense the trailer going off on a tangent (or angle), you must compensate. You compensate by moving the steering wheel of the tractor to neutralize the angle the trailer has taken. If you turn the top of the steering wheel of a single unit, such as a car, to the left, the back of the vehicle will move to the left. With a semi, it is just the opposite. To move the back of the trailer to the left, you must move the steering wheel to the right. The process of backing a semi is known as *chasing the trailer* by truckers.

MAKING FORWARD TURNS | The most important thing a new driver must remember in controlling the vehicle in forward motion is this: *In making a turn, the rear of the vehicle follows a substantially shorter path than the front of the vehicle.* This condition exists with any type of four-wheeled vehicle - from a coaster wagon to the largest tractor or semi-trailer combination. This condition is called *off-track* or *cheating*. It is shown in Figure 11-4.

The greater the distance between the front and rear wheels and the sharper the turn, the greater the off-track will be. Thus, the path taken by the rear of the vehicle becomes every bit as important as the path taken by the front. This means that on the open highway, you must remember to keep toward the *center* of the road when turning *right*. This way, the rear wheels will not run off the highway. When turning *left*, hold the vehicle toward the *outside* of the curve so that the rear will not cut short into a lane of opposing traffic. At the ordinary right-angle intersection in a city or town, pull straight into the intersection some distance before beginning your turn. This way, the rear of your vehicle will follow a proper path and not cut too short.

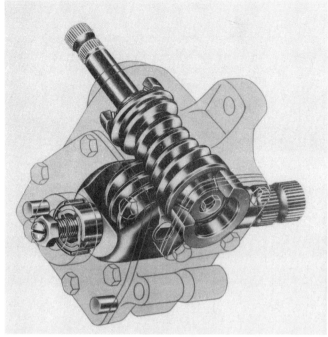

Figure 11-3. Typical Ross steering gear used on many trucks. A combination worm gear. *Courtesy of TRW, Ross Gear Division*

Figure 11-4, below, shows the turning characteristics of a semi-trailer as it attempts a right turn around a curb. From the diagram, you can tell that the track the semi-trailer follows is shorter than the track the front wheels of the tractor follows. As stated above, the solution to this problem is to pull the semi-trailer further into the intersection. This allows the "tracking" semi more room to properly avoid crossing dangerously over the curb.

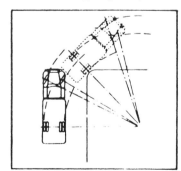 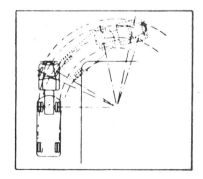

Figure 11-4. The straight truck (on the left) and the semi (on the right) both began their turns at the same point. The straight truck made the turn adequately, but the semi-trailer ran dangerously up onto the curb. What did the semi driver do wrong?

197

MAKING FORWARD TURNS (cont.)

It is easier for a set of 27-foot doubles to clear a corner than for a long, 40-foot trailer to clear it. The 40-foot semi requires a wider swing. (See Figure 11-5, below.) The division between the two trailers, in the doubles, makes the turn easier.

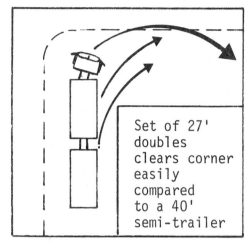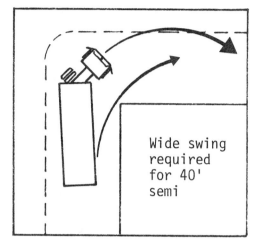

Set of 27' doubles clears corner easily compared to a 40' semi-trailer

Wide swing required for 40' semi

Figure 11-5. Set of doubles and 40-foot semi making right turns.

A rule of thumb will help you to make good turns when you are close to a curb or other vehicles. It is illustrated in Figure 11-6, opposite. Here's the rule: *Move the nose of the rig one-half rig-length into the intersection. Then, make the turn.*

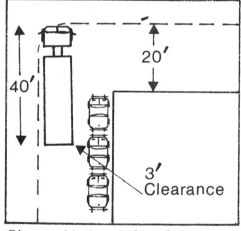

20'

40'

3' Clearance

Figure 11-6. Rule of thumb. Move one-half rig-length into intersection. Then begin turn.

MAKING BACKWARD TURNS | As we mentioned above, the control of a straight truck while backing is the same as for a passenger car. The steering wheel is turned in the direction in which you want to move the back end of the vehicle.

In backing a tractor-trailer, however, you want to remember to turn the back of your tractor in the direction *opposite* to the way you want your semi-trailer to go. In other words, if you want your trailer to back up to the *left* side (the driver's side), you must turn the rear of your tractor, and the steering wheel, to the *right* to start the jackknife. Or, if you want the rear of your semi-trailer to go off to the *right*, you angle the rear of your tractor to the *left*. That is, you turn the steering wheel to the left, which gives you the same effect.

There is a very basic reason why we refer to the rear of your tractor instead of dwelling on the steering wheel. This is because any driver backing for the first few times has a tendency to forget that the rear of the tractor is quite a distance behind the driver's seat. It protrudes out from underneath the semi-trailer where they connect. This protrusion is what causes many drivers to run over things, even automobiles, that are parked on narrow streets. *You must always be conscious of the rear end of the tractor and you must always be conscious of the wide swing of the trailer.*

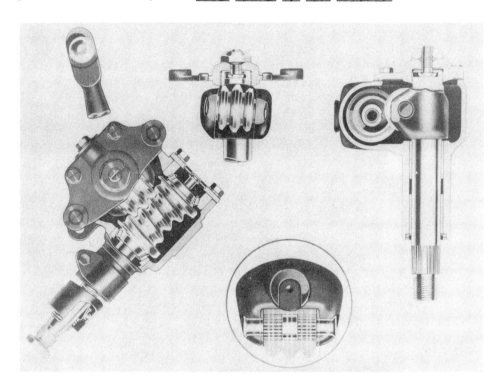

Figure 11-7. These are various cutaways of the same steering mechanism shown in Figure 11-3. Each cutaway is from a different angle. Notice how the worm gears mesh with each other without any slack between them. Any slack will cause an enormous amount of slack in truck's steering. Factory specs designate how much slack is allowed within a safe margin. *Courtesy of TRW, Ross Gear Division*

▷*NOTE:* *Interstate highways are numbered following a definite pattern. Knowing this pattern can be helpful to you.*

Odd numbers on interstate highways indicate north-south highways. Odd numbers begin small at the West Coast and increase going east with the highest numbers on the East Coast. Three digit numbers (405, 605, 805) are offshoots that route traffic around a major metropolitan area.

Even numbers on interstates are east-west highways. Even numbers begin small at the southern border of the United States and increase going north with the highest numbers near the northern border.

You might wish to take a moment to verify this information by studying a map of the United States.

SUMMARY | We began this chapter by discussing special problems in-
volved in driving in convoys - both planned ones (such as
military convoys) and unplanned ones (such as occur on congested highways).
Military convoys are guided by a commander. He or she sets speed limits and
safety cushion limits for the convoy. In setting the speed limit, the commander considers the needs of the last driver in the convoy, making sure that the
last driver doesn't have to exceed safe speeds to keep up with the convoy.
The safety cushion is the distance kept between vehicles. This must be large
enough to allow every driver to stop safely if he or she has to. Snow and ice,
and other hazardous driving conditions, require slower speeds and larger safety cushions. We ended the opening section by giving two true-life examples of
what can happen in convoys if drivers don't pay attention to their driving, to
road conditions, speed and safe distances between vehicles.

In steering forward, three things are important. One, don't let your fingers get between the spokes of the steering wheel. Two, keep your muscles relaxed. And three, keep a firm grip on the wheel.

Steering backward is different for straight trucks and combination vehicles. A straight truck backs the same as a car - very easily. A semi-trailer
combination is different. To move the back of the trailer to the left, you
turn the steering wheel to the right. To move the back of the trailer to the
right, you turn the steering wheel to the left.

In turning corners, the most important thing to remember is that the path
of the rear of the vehicle will be shorter (closer to the curb) than the front
of the vehicle. Therefore, in driving any vehicle, be sure you pull far
enough into the intersection to compensate for the shorter path of the rear of
the vehicle. The rule of thumb is to move the nose of the rig one-half rig-
length into the intersection; then turn.

In making backward turns, remember the same principal as for steering
backward. Turn the steering wheel (and the back of the towing unit) in the
opposite direction from the way you want your towed vehicle to go.

In all steering and turning, remember that you have a large vehicle. Be
aware of the amount of room it takes up in backing and turning so that you do
not run over or into anything in or near the roadway.

GLOSSARY

amphibious: Able to operate on both land and sea.

chasing the trailer: Following the nose of a trailer with the rear of the
tractor when backing a unit.

compensate: Make an allowance for; to do one thing to make up for another.
For example, to turn the steering wheel one way so that the trailer will turn
in the other direction.

convoy: A long line of vehicles. Usually, the word convoy refers to a
line of vehicles all traveling together to the same place, following the same
route.

GLOSSARY (cont.)

junction: A place where two or more roads meet.

maneuver: To manage or move skillfully.

off-track: The back of a vehicle is said to be "off-track" when it turns a corner because it follows a shorter path than the front. Some truckers say the rear of the vehicle is "cheating." It means the same thing.

protrusion: Something that sticks out.

safety cushion: A distance left between vehicles as they travel down the road. This empty space between rigs increases safety because if one rig gets into trouble, the other one should be able to avoid an accident with it.

tangent: A line going off at an angle.

traffic circle: A place in the roadway where traffic goes around in a circle in one direction. Traffic circles usually take the place of stoplights (traffic signals). (The British have many of these, but they call them round-abouts.)

vigilance: Watchfulness.

▶ CHECKING THE FACTS

Circle the letter of the phrase that best completes each sentence below.

1. In setting guidelines for a convoy, the commander
    A. considers speed and the safety cushion.
    B. sets the speed so the last vehicle can keep up with the convoy without excessive speed.
    C. expects drivers to reduce their speed if safety requires it.
    D. All of the above.

2. Good drivers steer by
    A. keeping a firm grip on the wheel, thumbs and forefinger wrapped around the major spokes of the wheel.
    B. use of their palms, gripping wheel only while turning, so that hands are not quickly tired out.
    C. keeping a firm grip on the wheel, muscles relaxed, fingers out of the way of the spokes.
    D. None of the above.

3. If you want to steer a combination unit straight backwards, you
    A. hold the wheel as straight as possible.
    B. compensate by moving the steering wheel to neutralize the angle the trailer has taken.
    C. hold the wheel straight, but if the trailer takes off to the left, turn the steering wheel left.
    D. None of the above.

4. When you make forward turns
    A. the back of your vehicle will follow a shorter path than the front.
    B. the back of your vehicle will follow a longer path than the front.
    C. the back of your vehicle will follow the same path as the front.
    D. the back of a semi-trailer will follow a shorter path than the front, but the back of a straight truck will follow the same path as the front.

5. If you want your semi-trailer to go right when you're making a backward turn,
    A. turn the rear of your tractor left.
    B. turn the rear of your tractor right.
    C. keep the rear of your tractor straight.
    D. turn the steering wheel to the right.

GETTING THE MAIN IDEA

Circle the letter of the phrase that best completes each sentence or best answers each question below.

1. One main idea in the section on convoys is this:
    A. If you ever drive in a convoy, be especially careful because convoy accidents are bad accidents.
    B. Convoys are more exciting than regular driving because of the feeling of comradery - of working with other drivers.
    C. Military convoys are more dangerous than convoys of commercial vehicles.
    D. Convoy driving is safer than regular driving because it is guided by a convoy commander and other vehicles can't get in the way of the convoy.

2. On corners, the rear wheels of a tractor-trailer unit would
    A. track the same as a straight truck.
    B. cheat less than a straight truck.
    C. cheat more than a straight truck.
    D. follow the same path as the tractor's front wheels.

3. Why is it necessary to pull straight into an intersection for a distance before beginning to turn?
    A. so the rear of the vehicle will follow a path without cutting too short.
    B. so the vehicle will not hamper on-coming traffic.
    C. so the tractor and trailer can turn into the inside lane.
    D. All of the above.

202

4. When you back a semi-trailer, why must you turn the steering wheel in the opposite direction from the way you want to move the rear of the trailer?
   A. To avoid jackknifing the vehicle.
   B. Because the rear axle of the tractor steers the trailer.
   C. The rear axle of the tractor acts as the front axle of the trailer.
   D. All of the above.

5. What does Figure 11-5 illustrate?
   A. It is easier to turn corners with a single 40-foot trailer than with a set of 27-foot doubles.
   B. A set of doubles will cheat less than a 40-foot semi-trailer.
   C. A set of doubles will cheat more than a 40-foot semi-trailer.
   D. Doubles are easier to tow than a single 40-foot semi-trailer.

★ GOING BEYOND THE FACTS AND IDEAS

1. Select one of the accidents from the section on convoys. Tell how the accident might have been avoided or if it happened, how it could have been made less severe.

2. Look at Figure 11-2. How well does the driver's grip on the steering wheel match the guidelines given in this chapter? Explain what makes it a good or poor technique.

3. This chapter explained how to back a single semi-trailer. Suppose you are towing two 27-foot trailers. You want your second 27-footer to go left. How do you do it?

4. Diagram a junction and how you would make your left turn in a combination tractor-trailer unit. Your trailer is a 40-footer. Show how many lanes each road has, and show any obstructions - such as parked cars, disabled vehicles, etc. Show how far into the roadway you will pull to make your turn.

Figure 12-1. Cutaway of a 318 cid V-8 gasoline engine for a Chrysler truck. *Courtesy of Chrysler Corporation*

Chapter Twelve

GASOLINE ENGINES

Figure 12-2. A gasoline delivery truck.
Photo by M. McFadden

BEFORE YOU READ | How much do you already know about how a gasoline engine works? Figure 12-1, opposite, illustrates a cutaway gasoline engine. Arrows point to several major parts, and each arrow is numbered. Before reading this chapter, why not try to complete the diagram by writing the correct name next to each part? The parts pointed to are listed below:

PARTS TO LOCATE

★ air cleaner   ★ push rod   ★ radiator fan

★ crankshaft   ★ distributor   ★ valve stem

★ carburetor   ★ rocker arm   ★ valve face

★ intake manifold   ★ camshaft   ★ exhaust manifold

In this chapter, we will explain how the gasoline engine works. If you correctly labeled some of the parts on the gasoline engine in Figure 12-1, you will have a head start in understanding this chapter. So, specifically, what will we be talking about here? Let us preview the chapter for you.

In the first major section, we will introduce you to the main parts of the internal combustion engine. We will describe the block and crankcase, cylinders, pistons, crankshaft and the smaller parts inside these components. For some of you, this will be a quick review of things you already know about your own car or truck engine.

In the second major section, we'll go through the four cycles of the typical gasoline engine. You can see an illustration of this operation in Figure 12-4.

The third major section explains how the valve train works. The valve train's job is to open and close the valves so four cycles can take place.

After we have explained how the gasoline engine works to create the power to turn the wheels, we'll talk about the various systems of the gasoline engine. We'll explain how each helps to keep the engine operating smoothly. As you read about these support systems, you might ask yourself how a breakdown in each system would affect the operation of the engine.

Finally, we will look at four different ways to classify engines. These four are by number of piston strokes, amount of compression, arrangement of the valves, and cylinder arrangement.

THE INTERNAL COMBUSTION ENGINE | Two internal combustion engines are used predominantly by the trucking industry: the gasoline engine and the diesel engine. We'll talk about the gasoline engine in this chapter and the diesel engine in the next.

● *The Block and Crankcase*

The largest part of the engine is made up of the block and the crankcase. The *block* is a strong, metal housing for all the parts of the engine. It is sometimes called the cylinder block. A few parts of the engine are not right inside the block, but are attached to it. (If you think of the block as a house, you might think of these things as being on the porch, in the basement, or on the roof of the house.) The *crankcase* is simply a case for the crankshaft. (We'll talk about the crankshaft in a moment.) The top part of the crankcase is usually a part of the block, and the lower part of the crankcase is the oil pan. The *oil pan* seals the bottom of the block.

● *The Cylinders*

A cylinder is anything shaped like a bunch of circles or disks, stacked on top of each other. *Cylinders* is an engine are called cylinders because that is how they are shaped. They are very smooth on the inside and the *pistons* move up and down in them. The cylinders are most often arranged in the block in either a V-type or in-line arrangement. On in-line and V-type engines, the *cylinder head* is a large casting which is bolted to the top of the cylinder block. It forms the tops of the cylinders so that a chamber (or hollow compartment) is formed. Cylinder heads are commonly called, simply, heads. The V-type engine has two heads; the in-line has one. These parts will look a little different in a diesel engine than in a gasoline engine, but you can get an idea of what the cylinders, pistons, and connecting rods look like in Figure 13-3.

THE INTERNAL COMBUSTION ENGINE (cont.)

● *The Pistons*

The chamber formed at the top of the cylinder by the head is called the *combustion chamber*. The combustion chamber is right above the pistons that move up and down in the cylinders. The pistons are also cylinder-shaped, but they are closed off at the top. They fit snugly inside the engine cylinders. The rapidly expanding gases in the combustion chamber drive the piston downward with great force, in the same way a ball is shot from a cannon. However, unlike the cannon ball, the piston is attached to a *connecting rod*, and the connecting rod is attached to the *crankshaft* (a revolving shaft).

● *The Crankshaft*

As you read above, the crankshaft is inside the block in a case called the crankcase. On this revolving shaft, there are *offsets* (or cranks). These offsets or cranks turn, or revolve. The crankshaft delivers its power through the power train to the driving wheels, and this is how the power of the engine moves the truck. (The crankshaft is Number 12 in Figure 12-1.)

● *An Engine Cycle*

Each movement, or stroke of a piston, is part of the engine's cycle. Each time there is a stroke of a piston, there is a complete engine cycle.

TYPICAL 4 CYCLE OR 4 STROKE PRINCIPLE	Gasoline engines operate on either a two-stroke or a four-stroke principle. The most common cycle is the four-stroke - two strokes up and two down. These four strokes or cycles are the *intake* stroke, the *compression* stroke, the *power* stroke, and the *exhaust* stroke.

● *The Intake Stroke*

On the intake stroke, the piston moves down in the cylinder, creating a vacuum above the piston. At the same time, the *intake valve* opens, and the fuel-air mixture is drawn into the cylinder. (See Figure 12-4.)

● *The Compression Stroke*

As soon as the compression stroke begins, both the intake and exhaust valves start to close. The piston moves upward, compressing the fuel-air mixture in the combustion chamber.

Now, fitted into the cylinder is a *spark plug*. The spark plug carries an electrical current into the cylinder. It has two electrodes in it, and a spark jumps from one electrode to the other. At the

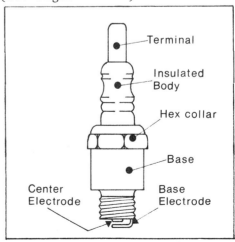

Figure 12-3. A spark plug.

207

TYPICAL 4 STROKE PRINCIPLE   (cont.)

top of the compression stroke (TDC - meaning "top, dead center"), the spark plug's electrode sparks, igniting the compressed fuel-air mixture.

● *The Power Stroke*

On the power stroke, this expanding gas mixture drives the piston down to provide the power that turns the crankshaft.

● *The Exhaust Stroke*

At the start of the exhaust stroke, the piston is at the bottom of the cylinder, and the *exhaust valve* opens. Then, the piston moves upward and forces the burned gases out of the cylinder and into the exhaust system.

This entire piston movement is called the Otto Cycle or the Four Stroke Cycle. It is the compression system used in the gasoline engines of cars and trucks.

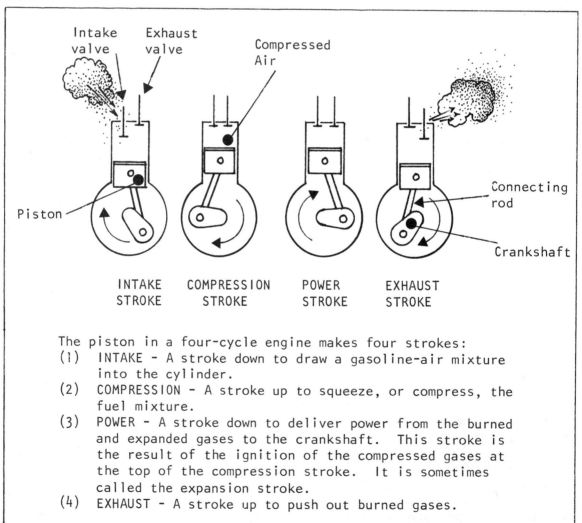

The piston in a four-cycle engine makes four strokes:
(1)   INTAKE - A stroke down to draw a gasoline-air mixture into the cylinder.
(2)   COMPRESSION - A stroke up to squeeze, or compress, the fuel mixture.
(3)   POWER - A stroke down to deliver power from the burned and expanded gases to the crankshaft. This stroke is the result of the ignition of the compressed gases at the top of the compression stroke. It is sometimes called the expansion stroke.
(4)   EXHAUST - A stroke up to push out burned gases.

Figure 12-4. This diagram shows what happens inside a gasoline engine.

The intake and exhaust valves in the top of a cylinder must open and close at the precise instants at which the piston makes its intake stroke and its exhaust stroke. Here's how they operate.

The typical valve operating system is called the valve train. It consists of four principal parts: a *camshaft, valve lifters (or cam followers), push rods*, and *rocker arm assembly*. You can see these parts in Figure 12-1. The camshaft is Number 10. A push rod is shown as Number 6. Number 5 is a rocker arm.

● *The Camshaft*

The camshaft is a long, straight shaft, studded with elliptical knobs, called *cams*. The cams are spaced along the shaft's length.

● *The Valve Lifters and Push Rods*

Resting on the cams are the valve lifters, one for each cam. These are sometimes called cam followers. On top of the valve lifters are the push rods.

As the camshaft rotates, the cams, of course, rotate with it. A cam bumps and lifts the intake valve's push rod, the long rod that sits in a small hole in the top of the valve lifter. (See Figure 12-5.)

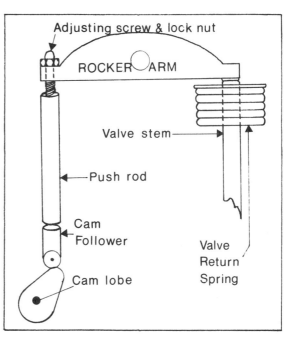

Figure 12-5. The valve train.

● *The Rocker Arm Assembly*

The rocker arm operates like a teeter-totter (or seesaw). As the push rod is pushed up by the cam, the valve stem pushes the valve down into the cylinder. Now that there is an opening at the top of the cylinder, fuel-air mixture can enter. This same teeter-totter action opens the exhaust valve to allow the burned gases to be exhausted from the cylinder.

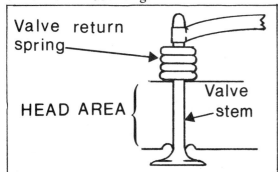

Figure 12-6. Valve, stem and head area.

● *The Valves Themselves*

The intake and exhaust valves are poppet-type valves. (See Figure 12-6.) These form a good seal to the combustion chamber of the cylinder.

A coil spring holds the valve face against the top of the combustion chamber until the rocker arm movement forces the valve down into the cylinder, opening the

209

HOW THE VALVES OPERATE   (cont.)

valve. The valve stays open only for a fraction of a second. Then, it closes securely.

To close the valve, the coil spring forces the valve face back up against the *valve seat*. The closing of the valve seals the cylinder again. It also pushes the push rod and valve lifter back onto the cam to begin the start of another engine cycle as the cam revolves.

SIX IMPORTANT SYSTEMS

The gasoline engine is made up of several interdependent operating systems. We will discuss the six basic systems here: the air intake system, the cooling system, the lubricating system, the fuel system, the electrical system, and the ignition system. You will see how each system helps the gasoline engine to operate properly, smoothly, and continually. Each system must operate if all systems are to function and the engine is to deliver its power.

● The Air Intake System

The purpose of the air intake system is to provide gasoline to the engine in a combustible vapor. Gasoline is pumped from the gas tank by and through the *fuel pump* and into the *carburetor*. (See Figure 12-1, Number 2.) Gasoline burns best when it is mixed with air. Therefore, the carburetor mixes 15 parts of air to one part of gasoline. This forms the combustible vapor.

The vacuum created by the intake stroke of the piston draws this vapor from the carburetor, through the intake manifold, and into the cylinder, filling it. The compression stroke compresses the vapor up into the combustion chamber, and the vapor is ignited by the spark that leaps between the electrodes of the spark plug.

● The Cooling System

The continuous exploding action of the vaporized gases and the terrific speed of the metal pistons and other moving engine parts produces great heat. Some of the engine's parts would melt if it were not for the cooling system.

All of today's large trucks have water-cooled engines. The heat generated in the engine is transferred through the walls of the water jacket into the water that flows to the radiator. The heat is then dissipated by the air flowing through the radiator core.

The cooling system consists of the radiator, a water pump, a fan, a thermostat, and the necessary water hoses. The *water hoses* carry the water from the top of the engine block to the radiator where the water is cooled and pumped back into the engine. The *fan* pulls air through the radiator to cool the water while the truck is standing still and the engine is operating. Belts from the engine run the fan and water pump. The *water pump* pumps the water through the engine, from the bottom of the radiator (where it is cool), through the engine block, cylinder head, and back (now hot) to the top of the radiator.

Figure 12-7. A heavy-duty conventional gasoline truck. Chains have been properly used to secure the cargo. *Courtesy of American Trucking Associations, Inc.*

SIX IMPORTANT SYSTEMS (cont.)

The heated water flows down through the radiator core, and the heat dissipates into the air that is flowing through the radiator. The *thermostat* regulates and controls the operating temperature of the engine.

● *The Lubricating System*

The lubricating system supplies oil to the moving metal parts in the engine. As we mentioned in Chapter 5, oil has other jobs besides keeping the engine lubricated. Oil also reduces heat and cleans away dirt and contamination, and carbon particles. Oil prevents excessive friction of the engine's moving parts.

Oil is pumped through the *oil pump* from the oil intake that is located in the oil pan. The oil enters the *oil filter* which strains out the contaminants and carbon particles. The clean oil travels through the drilled oil galleries of the engine's moving parts. Excess oil drains down through the drainholes to the oil pan to be recirculated through the lubricating system.

SIX IMPORTANT SYSTEMS (cont.)

⬤ *The Fuel System*

There are two fuel systems in general use. These are the gravity-feed and the pressure-feed systems. In the *gravity system*, gravity moves the fuel from the tank to the engine. In the *pressure system*, a pump is used to move the fuel to the engine.

The basic fuel system for both the gravity and pressure systems include these parts:

1. A *storage tank* for gasoline

2. *Fuel lines* to carry the gasoline to the carburetor

3. A *carburetor* to mix air with gasoline

4. An *intake manifold* to distribute the fuel mixture to the cylinders

5. An *exhaust manifold* to carry away the burned gases

6. *Fuel gauges* to tell how much gasoline is in the storage tank

7. A *gasoline filter* to clean dirt out of the fuel

8. An *air cleaner* to take dirt out of the air that is mixed with the gasoline

9. A *muffler* to reduce the pressure of the exhaust gases so they make less noise when they are released into the air

10. An *exhaust pipe* to carry off the poisonous exhaust gases

⬤ *The Electrical System*

The electrical system consists of the battery, alternator (or generator), regulator, and wire needed to connect them. The job of this system is to produce the electrical energy to power the starter motor. The starter motor starts the truck engine and supplies energy for

- the ignition,

- the lighting system, and

- other electrical needs and accessories such as the radio, CB, etc.

The *alternator* (or *generator*) converts the mechanical energy it receives from the crankshaft into electrical energy.

The *regulator* controls the produced electrical energy so that just the right amount is available to meet the needs of the electrical system.

SIX IMPORTANT SYSTEMS   (cont.)

The *battery* stores electrical energy to start the engine and operate the electrical equipment when the alternator's output is not enough to handle the needs of the truck's electrical system.

● *The Ignition System*

The ignition system is the electrical circuit necessary to set fire to, or ignite, the fuel mixture in the various cylinders at different times. The high-voltage current is carried through a distributor. (See Figure 12-1, Number 3.) The *distributor* delivers the electricity to each cylinder at the exact moment when the piston reaches the top of the compression stroke. The electric current jumps a gap between two terminals (or electrodes) and sets fire to the gasoline-air mixture. The two terminals are incased in insulating material. The insulating materials plus the two terminals is called a spark plug.

Figure 12-8. 350 V-8 gasoline engine for a Chevrolet truck.
Courtesy of Chevrolet Motor Division, General Motors Corporation

SIX IMPORTANT SYSTEMS (cont.)

The ignition system is made up of two complete electrical circuits: a 12-volt primary circuit and a 20,000-volt secondary circuit.

The primary circuit has a 12-volt battery, an ignition switch, a coil, a distributor, breakerpoints, and a condenser. To have a complete circuit, the electrical impulse that goes to every piece of electrical equipment must return to its source: the battery. That's why one post of the battery and each piece of electrical equipment is connected to the frame of the truck. The frame of the truck is the "ground." That is, the truck frame is the return path of the electrical impulse, and it is grounded within itself. The electric impulse flows *from* the positive post of the battery, *through* the ignition switch, coil, breakerpoints, and condenser, *to* the "ground." Then, it flows *back* to the negative pole of the battery.

The *battery* is the original source of the electricity. The *ignition switch* is a means of breaking or opening the circuit to stop or start the engine. The *coil* is the pulse transformer that changes the low voltage of the primary circuit (12-volts) into the high voltage of the secondary circuit (20,000 volts). The breakerpoints and condenser control the timing of the secondary impulses. The *breakerpoints* (or *"points"*) are timed by a cam lobe to open every time a piston reaches the top of its compression stroke. The *condenser* holds excess electricity in the primary flow to assist the breakerpoints in making a clean break without sparking.

The secondary circuit starts at the coil. Each time the breakerpoints open, high voltage is produced by the coil and travels from the coil through the secondary part of the distributor (the cap and rotor) to the spark plug. The spark plug, with its two electrodes that protrude into the combustion chamber, ignites the compressed vapor in that chamber. The voltage at one side of the spark plug is now 20,000 volts. The voltage at the other side is only 12 volts. The voltage of the two sides tries to equalize itself, so a spark jumps across the spark plug gap - from one electrode to the other. When it jumps across the gap, the spark ignites the compressed gas and air.

This brings us back to where we started in this section.

FOUR
WAYS
TO CLASSIFY
ENGINES
|
Gasoline engines are classified according to the number of piston strokes, the arrangement of their valves, the arrangement of their cylinders or their type of compression.

● *Number of Piston Strokes*

All truck gasoline engines are either two-cycle or four-cycle engines. To review, the cycle refers to the number of strokes, up-and-down movements, that the piston makes each time it turns the crankshaft. The piston in a four-cycle engine makes four strokes. Nearly all gasoline engines used in motor vehicles are four-cycle. A two-cycle engine draws in a fresh fuel mixture as it ends its power stroke. It exhausts the hot gases as it begins its return stroke. (We'll talk more about this in the next chapter.)

A two-cycle engine is less efficient than a four-cycle engine. Here's why. Some of the incoming fuel mixes with the exhaust gases and goes out with them. This wastes fuel. It also loses some of the engine's power. However, both types of engines have their place. Two-cycle engines are used when speed and efficiency can be sacrificed to make the weight lighter, as in a power lawn mower.

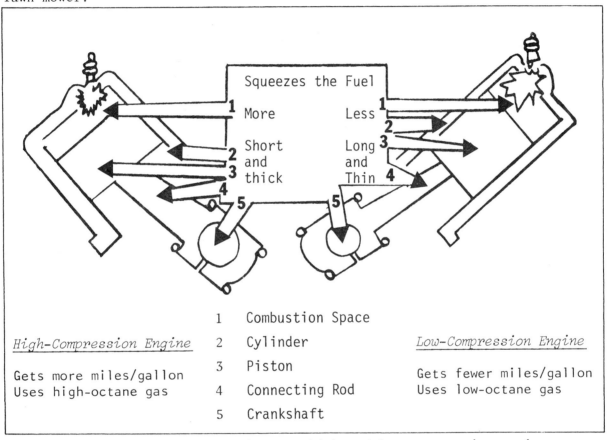

	1	Combustion Space	
High-Compression Engine	2	Cylinder	*Low-Compression Engine*
	3	Piston	
Gets more miles/gallon	4	Connecting Rod	Gets fewer miles/gallon
Uses high-octane gas	5	Crankshaft	Uses low-octane gas

Figure 12-9. Differences between high and low-compression engines.

● *Compression*

The first gasoline engines were low-compression engines. This meant that they did not squeeze the fuel mixture very tightly in the cylinders. The reason was this: they used low-octane gasoline. Low-octane gas knocked, or did not burn properly, when it was highly compressed.

The development of high-octane gasoline permitted the building of high-compression engines. These squeeze the fuel mixture tightly. As the fuel mixture burns, it expands more violently and generates more power. (See Figure 12-9.)

The compression ratio of a truck engine is a comparison of two things:

1. the amount of space inside a cylinder above a piston at the bottom of the piston stroke, and

2. the amount of space inside a cylinder above the piston when that piston is at the top of its stroke.

When the piston is at the top of its stroke, the space left inside of the cylinder is much smaller. This smaller space is the combustion chamber.

Engines vary according to their compression ratios. Let's look, for example, at an engine with a ten-to-one compression ratio. If the cylinder, with its piston at the bottom would contain 100 cubic inches of fuel-air mixture, that cylinder would contain only ten cubic inches of fuel-air mixture when the piston is at the top. The fuel-air mixture would be one-tenth of its former volume. Thus, the engine would have a ten-to-one compression ratio.

● *Valve Arrangement*

Engines are sometimes classified according to valve arrangement. An *L-head engine* has both the intake valve and exhaust valve side by side on the same side of the cylinder. In a *T-head engine*, the two valves are mounted side by side in the cylinder head, directly over the cylinder. (A T-head engine is sometimes called an over-head valve engine.)

● *Cylinder Arrangement*

Finally, engines are classified according to the way the cylinders are arranged in the engine block and according to the number of cylinders. The most common arrangements are *in-line*, *V-type*, *horizontal-opposed*, and *radial*. (See Figure 12-10.) Most gasoline engines have an even number of cylinders: four, six, eight, sixteen, or more.

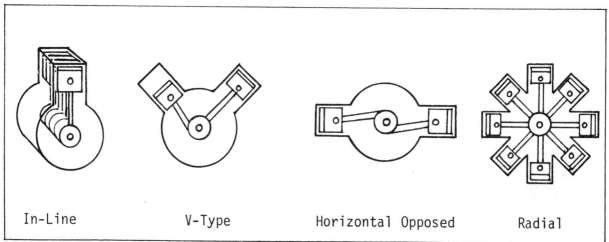

| In-Line | V-Type | Horizontal Opposed | Radial |

Figure 12-10.   The four most common cylinder arrangements.

SUMMARY | There were three main things we talked about in this chapter. The first was how the internal combustion engine operates. The second was how six systems in the truck help to keep the gasoline engine operating smoothly. The third was the four ways in which gasoline engines can be classified.

To explain how the gasoline engine works, we began by defining major components of it: the block and crankcase, the cylinders, the pistons, and the crankshaft. It is the crankshaft that delivers the power formed in the cylinders to the driving wheels to move the truck.

Then, we went through the four strokes of the "Otto Cycle" or four-cycle engine. On the intake stroke, the piston moves down in the cylinder, creating a vacuum which draws a gasoline-air mixture into the combustion chamber. On the compression stroke, the piston moves up, compresses the air, and a spark from the spark plug ignites the mixture. On the power stroke, the explosion caused by the spark plug pushes the piston back down again. Finally, on the exhaust stroke, the piston moves back up, forces the burned gases out the exhaust valve, and the cycle is ready to begin again.

Next, we explained how the valve train operates. The camshaft turns, and as it turns, elliptical knobs on it, called cams, push up the push rods. The push rods push up one side of the rocker arm, and that automatically pushes down the valve stem on the other end of the rocker arm. The valve stem, coming down, opens a valve. Some rocker arms cause intake valves to open; others cause exhaust valves to open. The valves are closed again by a coil spring.

All six systems of the gasoline engine have to operate continually if the engine is going to work right. The air intake system sees to it that gasoline and air are mixed in the correct proportions in the carburetor. The fuel pump pumps gasoline to the carburetor. Then, a vacuum pulls the combustible vapor into the combustion chamber. The cooling system uses a radiator, water pump, fan and thermostat to reduce the terrible heat created by the internal combustion engine's moving parts. Water runs through the engine and heats up. Then, it is cooled by running through the radiator. The cool water is sent back through the engine, continuing the cycle. The lubricating system helps to cool the engine by cutting down friction between the metal parts. It also keeps the engine clean by picking up dirt, contaminants, and carbon particles, then filtering them out in the oil filter and washing them out at oil changes. The fuel system carries the gasoline to the carburetor where air mixes with it. Then, it distributes the fuel-air mixture into the cylinders and carries away burned gases after combustion. Other key parts of the fuel system clean dirt out of the fuel, clean the air, muffle the noise, store the gasoline and tell the driver how much fuel is left in the tank. The electrical system produces electrical energy to start the starter motor and keep the electrical parts of the truck operating. Finally, the ignition system provides a way for the spark plug to work. The distributor delivers electricity to each cylinder at just the right time. Since the voltage on one side of the spark plug (on one electrode) is 20,000 volts, and the voltage on the other side is only 12 volts, a spark jumps across the gap. This spark ignites the compressed gases and drives the piston down during the compression stroke.

217

Finally, we talked about four ways of classifying engines. First, they may be either two-stroke or four-stroke. Most engines are four-stroke - the kind we described in this chapter. Second, they may be either high or low compression. Most engines today are high compression because this provides better mileage and more power. Third, the valves may be arranged either on one side of the cylinder or over the cylinder. And fourth, the cylinders may be placed in an in-line, V-type, horizontal-opposed, or radial arrangement.

Chances are, this has not been an easy chapter to understand. It is literally packed full of terminology and concepts about how the gasoline engine works. Therefore, you may wish to read it again to be sure you understand this important information. Or, you may wish to go onto the next chapter, "Diesel Engines," to see if it helps to clarify things. Chapter 13 goes over some of these ideas and terms again because the diesel engine has many, but not all, of the same working parts. Even so, a little review of this chapter first may help you to keep the two engines straight.

GLOSSARY

It is impossible to discuss how the gasoline engine works without using a lot of names for major and minor parts of the truck engine. The more of these you can become familiar with, the better. However, we are including here only the most important ones - the ones you will probably hear most often. If you can learn the minor parts of the engine as well, great.

block: The engine's strong, metal housing which contains all of the engine's principal parts, either in it or attached to it. Sometimes called the cylinder block.

cams: Egg-shaped knobs on the camshaft which push the push rods. They are considered a part of the valve train.

camshaft: A long, straight shaft, covered with elliptical knobs, called cams. As the camshaft turns, the cams push the push rods, helping to open the cylinder valves. In the four-cycle engine, the camshaft turns at one-half the speed of the crankshaft.

carburetor: A device which mixes air with gasoline spray to form a mixture. This mixture is distributed to the cylinders by the intake manifold so that it can be exploded by a spark from the spark plug.

combustible: This word can describe something that catches fire easily or it can refer to something that is flammable. In other words, something can *be* combustible or it can be *a* combustible; the word can be used as an adjective or noun.

combustion chamber: The chamber formed at the top of the cylinder by the cylinder head. Here, compressed gases are ignited by the spark plug.

GLOSSARY (cont.)

compress: To squeeze; to press together; to condense.

connecting rod: A straight shaft which connects the piston to the crankshaft, making the crankshaft turn as the piston comes down. (It also pushes the piston up as the crankshaft turns.) (See Figure 13-3.)

crankshaft: A strong, metal shaft inside the crankcase, covered with "offsets" (because they are "set off" from the shaft) or "cranks." These offsets transmit the power of the pistons to the crankshaft. This causes the crankshaft to turn or revolve. As the crankshaft revolves, it sends power to the differential gears, and they change the direction of the turning so that the driving wheels turn and the truck moves. (See Figure 13-4.)

cylinders: Hollow, metal compartments which are shaped like a bunch of disks stacked on top of each other. The pistons move up and down in them. Above the pistons is the combustion chamber; below the piston is the connecting rod. (See Figure 13-3.)

dissipate: To drive away; to scatter; to disperse.

four-cycle engine: An internal combustion engine in which the piston makes four different strokes before it begins repeating the strokes again, two up and two down. The four cycles or strokes are intake, compression, power, and exhaust.

piston: A solid, metal object which is cylinder-shaped, but closed off at the top. There is one piston in each of the engine's cylinders, and they move up and down. When a piston moves up, it either compresses the fuel mixture or drives exploded gases away. When it moves down, it causes a connecting rod to turn the crankshaft. (See Figure 13-3.)

push rods: Little, metal arms which are placed between the cams and the rocker arms. They are part of the valve train.

rocker arm assembly: A device which operates like a seesaw. The push rod pushes up one end so that the opposite end pushes down, opening a valve into the combustion chamber. Part of the valve train.

spark plug: An encasement for two electrodes. It protrudes into the combustion chamber of a gasoline engine, sparks, and sets off an explosion.

valve train: The entire assembly which causes the valves into the combustion chamber to open at just the right time.

► CHECKING THE FACTS

Each sentence below has two words or groups of words in it in *italics*. The two words or word groups are divided by a slash mark (/). You can make the sentences true by <u>crossing out</u> one of the two words or word groups.

Example: This chapter was about how the *gasoline*/~~diesel~~ engine works.

1. The *block/crankcase* is the strong, metal housing for the engine's many moving parts.

2. The *camshaft/crankshaft* delivers the power formed in the cylinders to the driving wheels.

3. Compression of the fuel-air mixture takes place in the *piston/combustion chamber*.

4. The *push rods/connecting rods* move up and down as the camshaft revolves and cams hit them.

5. The *push rods/connecting rods* are part of the valve train.

6. The *push rods/connecting rods* cause the crankshaft to move.

7. Gasoline and air are mixed 15 parts air to one part gasoline in the *carburetor/distributor*.

8. The *cooling system/lubricating system* keeps the engine cool and cleans away dirt, contaminants and carbon particles.

9. The original source of electricity in the truck engine is the *battery/condenser*.

10. Gasoline engines can operate on either a four-stroke or a *six-stroke/two-stroke* cycle.

11. A gasoline engine is often called an *explosive combustion/internal combustion* engine.

12. A *low compression/high compression* engine squeezes the fuel very tightly in the cylinders.

13. The *exhaust pipe/muffler* carries off poisonous gases from the engine.

14. The two types of fuel systems in general use are the pressure-feed and the *gravity-feed/pump-feed*.

15. During compression, the piston moves up *exhausting the exploded gases/squeezing the gasoline-air mixture*.

16. The expanding gas mixture pushes the piston down, turning the crankshaft, during the *intake/power* stroke.

■ GETTING THE MAIN IDEAS

1. Diagram the four-stroke principle.

2. Explain how the valve train functions. You may use an outline, a chart, a drawing, or paragraph form to make your explanation. Use whichever way works best for you.

3. How does the cooling system in a water-cooled engine work? Explain, mentioning the function of the radiator, water hoses, water pump, and thermostat.

4. Explain what would happen if the spark plug didn't spark.

★ GOING BEYOND THE FACTS AND IDEAS

1. If you were going to select a gasoline engine to drive in San Francisco on your pure bottled water delivery route, which type would you select and why?
    A. two-cycle or four-cycle?
    B. high-compression or low-compression?
    C. in-line, V-type, horizontal-opposed or radial?

2. Explain how a malfunction in <u>each</u> of the following components would affect the engine. Assume that only one thing went wrong on one trip, not that all of these things malfunctioned simultaneously.
    A. distributor
    B. carburetor
    C. cams worn down
    D. cylinder head cracked
    E. spark plugs
    F. water hose cracked
    G. water pump
    H. oil filter filled with contaminants and dirt
    I. generator
    J. air cleaner dirty
    K. coil
    L. breakerpoints

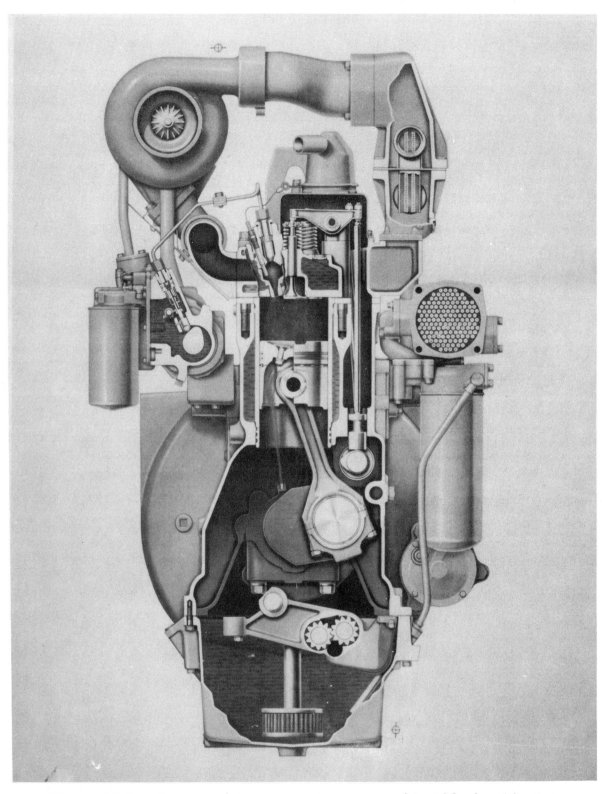

Figure 13-1. How many key components can you identify in this Cat
Model 3306 diesel engine? It's a four-cycle, turbocharged, after-
cooled model. It is particularly suited to weight-limited uses,
such as in construction and bulk transport vehicles because of its
low weight. It can deliver up to 270 hp (horsepower) and delivers
full power at altitudes up to 5,000 feet. *Courtesy of Caterpillar
Tractor Company, Engine Division*

222

Figure 13-2. Cat engine, Model 3306. Same as engine shown in Figure 13-1. *Courtesy of Caterpillar Tractor Company, Engine Division*

Chapter Thirteen

DIESEL ENGINES

BEFORE
YOU
READ

The diesel engine is the engine commonly used to power heavy-duty trucks. Therefore, it is important for you to understand its basic operation. So, first, we'll take a look at how it resembles and differs from the gasoline engine. And, next, we'll examine the way both four-cycle and two-cycle diesel engines work.

After our explanation of how the diesel engine operates, we'll go into other things about the diesel engine. We'll discuss three components which are frequently added to diesel truck engines - turbochargers, aftercoolers, and retarders (or engine brakes).

Once again, we're suggesting that you use the SQ3R method to study this chapter. Maybe you've already found it so helpful that you've been using it to study *each* chapter. It helps, doesn't it? Especially when there are a lot of new terms to learn and a lot of technical information to understand and remember. You probably know the system by now. Can you fill in the key words of the SQ3R in the following blanks?

_____ the chapter. Turn each heading or sub-heading

into a _____ . Then, _____ each section to

answer your question. _____ what you have just

read. Finally, answer your questions from memory; that is _____ .

Now you're ready to begin tackling this chapter. The SQ3R approach will help you learn the information so you have it when you need it on the job.

A COMPARISON OF DIESEL AND GASOLINE ENGINES

A diesel engine is a high-compression, internal combustion engine which depends upon the heat of compression for ignition. Basically, both kinds of internal combustion engines (gasoline and diesel) are alike. But there are important differences between them.

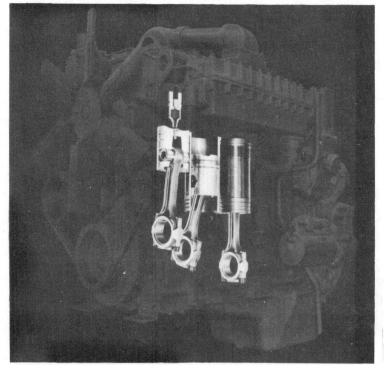

Figure 13-3. Cutaway of a Cat engine, showing the cylinder liners, pistons, and connecting rods in different stages. *Courtesy of Caterpillar Tractor Co., Engine Division*

● *Similarities*

Both gasoline and diesel engines need three elements: air, fuel, and ignition. A diesel engine's functions and parts are similar to those in a gas engine. Like the gas engine, the diesel gets its power from the explosive burning of a fuel-air combination inside the cylinder area, driving the pistons downward to turn the crankshaft.

Like the gas engine, the diesel has a block and crankcase with a head (or heads) and an oil pan. It has a crankshaft and camshaft with their offsets and cams. It has pistons and connecting rods, and it has valve lifters, push rods, and rocker arm assemblies.

A COMPARISON (cont.)

Diesels come in either V-type or in-line cylinder arrangements.

These are some of the similarities between a diesel and gasoline engine.

● *Differences*

Although the functions are alike, diesel engines, and their parts, are structurally heavier and stronger than their counterpart, the gasoline engines. They have to be stronger and heavier because they have *higher compression* and *greater intensity of generated heat within the cylinders*.

Unlike the gas engine, the diesel engine has *no spark plugs* to ignite an already mixed combination of air and fuel, and there is *no carburetor* to mix liquid fuel with air into a combustible vapor. Instead, ultra-high compression heats air so high that the hot air ignites the diesel fuel which has been injected into the engine's combustion chamber.

Here's how it works. Air heats up when it is compressed. Air is squeezed in a diesel engine's combustion chamber at a 16 to one compression ratio. This compression heats the air from a starting temperature of 200° F (94° C) to over 1000° F (538° C). At the end of the compression stroke, the diesel fuel is injected into this ultra-heated combustion chamber in a mist.

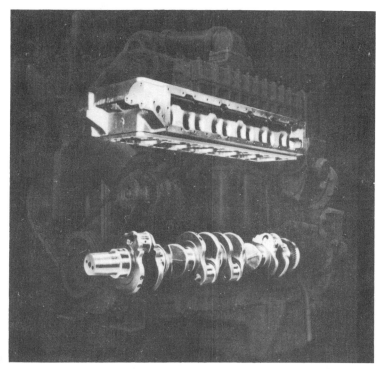

Figure 13-4. Cutaway of a Cat engine, showing the cylinder head (top) and crankshaft journal (bottom). *Courtesy of Caterpillar Tractor Co., Engine Division*

Figure 13-5. Cutaway of same Cat engine, showing valve train, camshaft, valves, oil filters and oil cooler. *Courtesy of Caterpillar Tractor Co., Engine Division*

A COMPARISON (cont.)

Both gasoline and diesel oil come from petroleum which is a flammable liquid. Gasoline is highly volatile; that is, it evaporates easily. Mixed with air, gasoline easily makes a combustible vapor.

Diesel fuel is a heavier liquid. Unlike gasoline, diesel fuel does not vaporize easily and it is less volatile, meaning it doesn't evaporate or turn into a mist easily. So, a fuel injector has to be used to break the diesel fuel into a mist and spray this mist into the combustion chamber.

As soon as the injector sprays the fuel into the chamber, ultra-hot compressed air ignites the mist, and a terrific explosion occurs. The explosion expands the mixture of misted diesel fuel and air and drives the piston down with terrific pressure.

Figure 13-6 illustrates one type of fuel injector. Figure 13-7 illustrates the fuel injection cycle of a PT injector.

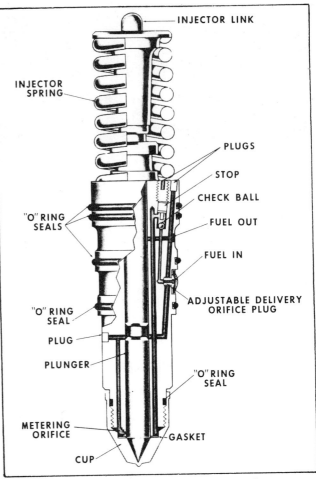

Figure 13-6. Cross section of a cylindrical PT (type B) fuel injector. A series of small holes in the tip breaks diesel fuel into a mist and injects it into the combustion chamber. *Courtesy of Cummins Engine Company*

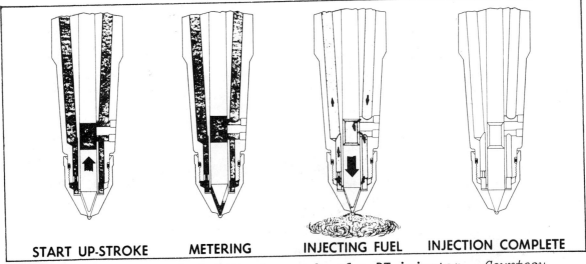

START UP-STROKE   **METERING**   **INJECTING FUEL**   **INJECTION COMPLETE**

Figure 13-7. The fuel injection cycle of a PT injector. *Courtesy of Cummins Engine Company*

Gasoline engines almost always operate on the four-stroke cycle (the "Otto Cycle"). In trucks, gasoline engines are always four-stroke. However, diesel truck engines can be either four-stroke or two-stroke. Therefore, we'll discuss both in this chapter. Since there are differences between the gasoline four-stroke and the diesel four-stroke, we'll go through the complete four-cycle diesel engine operation on the next couple of pages.

INTAKE STROKE	COMPRESSION STROKE	POWER STROKE	EXHAUST STROKE
Air intake valve open	Air about to be compressed	Oil intake valve open, diesel fuel injected	Exhaust valve open

| (Intake valve closes at bottom of stroke.) | (At top of stroke, fuel injector sprays in diesel fuel.) | (As piston reaches bottom, exhaust valve opens.) | (At top of stroke, waste gases get pushed out, intake valve opens, cycle begins again.) |

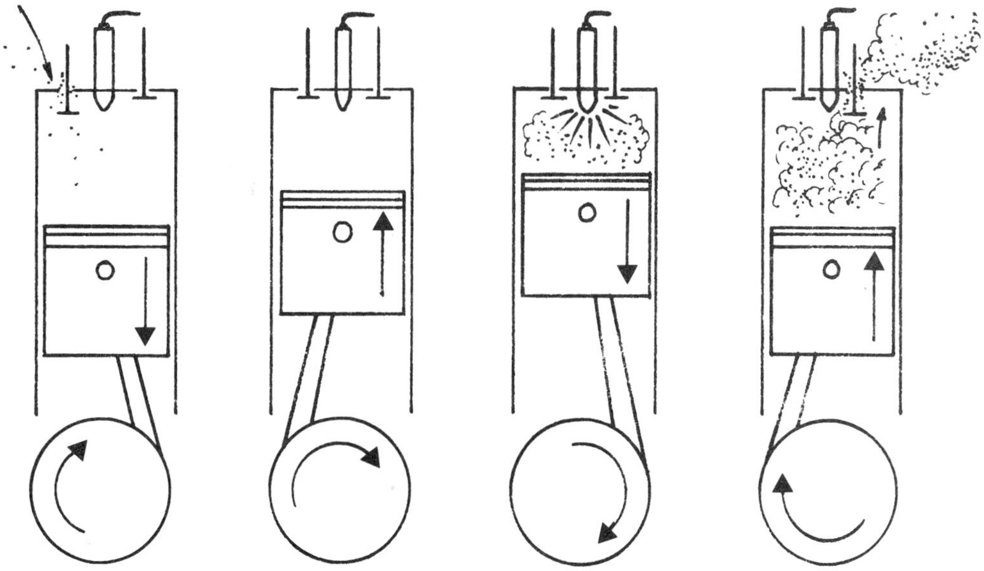

Figure 13-8. This diagram shows how a single cylinder in a four-cycle engine operates. On stroke one, the piston moves down, drawing air into the cylinder. On stroke two, the rising piston compresses the air in the cylinder, raising the temperature to about 1000° F (538° C) or more. When misted diesel fuel is sprayed into the cylinder, the heat causes it to burn explosively, forcing the piston down in stroke 3, the power stroke. On stroke 4, the piston rises again, emptying the cylinder.

THE FOUR-STROKE ENGINE (cont.)

The diesel engine has the same four strokes as a gasoline engine: intake, compression, power, and exhaust. However, slightly different things happen during them. As in the gasoline engine, all four of them take place in a matter of microseconds.

● *Intake Stroke*

On the downward intake stroke of the piston, air (*not* fuel-air mixture) is drawn through the intake valve into the cylinder.

● *Compression Stroke*

At the bottom of the intake stroke, the intake valve closes, and the piston moves upward for the compression stroke.

Now, when something is compressed (or squeezed in on itself) to a high degree, it becomes very hot. This is especially true of air. It is this physical fact that makes it possible for the air to ignite the diesel fuel inside the engine's cylinders. As the piston moves up in the cylinder, it compresses the air 16 to one. This means that the air inside the combustion chamber becomes one-sixteenth of its normal volume after being compressed. At this point, the air is hot enough to ignite diesel fuel. So, at the top of the compression stroke, the fuel injector sprays diesel fuel into the superheated air of the combustion chamber. This causes an explosive burning of the fuel.

● *Power Stroke*

This explosion drives the piston downward in its power stroke. This downstroke is called the power stroke because it does the work of the engine. It delivers energy to the crankshaft.

● *Exhaust Stroke*

As the piston reaches the bottom of its power stroke, the exhaust valve opens. The upward movement of the exhaust stroke pushes the burned gas through the exhaust valve and into the exhaust system.

THE TWO-STROKE ENGINE | Another type of diesel-power engine is used today: the two-stroke diesel engine. There are both similarities and differences between the two and four-stroke engine.

● *Similarities to the Four-Stroke Engine*

The two-stroke engine also needs air, fuel and ignition. The four-stroke engine follows a specific pattern. The two-stroke engine also follows a set pattern (or sequence) of actions in its firing order. In both engines, the cylinder must be filled with air, the air must be compressed in the combustion chamber, and fuel must be injected into it, bringing about ignition. The expanding force must be used and the burned gases must be exhausted from the cylinder.

THE TWO-STROKE ENGINE   (cont.)

● *Differences from the Four-Stroke Engine*

The two-stroke engine accomplishes all of the actions mentioned above. However, it makes them happen in only two strokes of the piston. It eliminates the exhaust and intake strokes and it uses only the *compression* and *power* strokes. In the two-stroke, an *air blower* fills the cylinders with air and expels the burned gases. As in the four-cycle, the valves still open into the cylinders, but now both valves are exhaust valves. *Ports* in the lower part of the cylinder admit air into the cylinder. The air blower keeps an air pressure on these ports at all times. When the piston moves upward in the cylinder, the piston acts like a valve, covering the ports and closing off the air supply. When the piston moves down below these ports, air enters the cylinder.

● *Power*

The two-stroke cycle begins with the piston at the bottom of its power stroke. The ports are uncovered. Air is blown through the ports and up toward the open exhaust valves.

● *Compression*

As the piston moves upward, the valves close, and the piston covers the intake ports. The compression stroke has begun. Air is compressed in the combustion chamber.

When the piston reaches the top of its compression stroke, fuel is ignited and ignition takes place. This starts the power stroke again.

Figure 13-9. A two-stroke diesel engine. Notice that there are no intake valves in this engine. There are only the four exhaust valves. You can see several key components in this illustration, including the crankshaft, a connecting rod and piston, cylinder liner, push rod and rocker arm, and, on the left, the turbocharger. *Courtesy of Detroit Diesel Allison, Division General Motors Corporation*

● *Power (Again)*

The exhaust valves open and the burned gases begin to escape. As the piston completes its power stroke, the ports are uncovered, and the incoming air moves up. The incoming air pushes the exhausted gases out of the cylinder and fills the cylinder with fresh air to begin a new cycle.

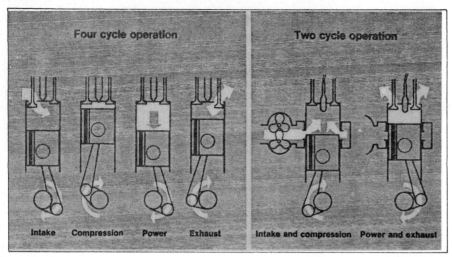

Four cycle operation

Two cycle operation

Intake Compression Power Exhaust

Intake and compression Power and exhaust

Figure 13-10 (opposite). Diagrams of four-cycle and two-cycle operations. In a four-cycle engine, there is one full piston stroke for each of the four parts of the cycle: intake, compression, power, and exhaust. A two-cycle engine combines these into two strokes, one upward and one downward. *Courtesy of Cummins Engine Co.*

TURBOCHARGERS

A *turbocharger* allows you to obtain additional power from your engine. Here's how it works. The turbocharger pumps additional air into your engine's combustion chamber. Because there is more air in the chamber, the engine can burn a larger fuel charge in its cylinder. This gives you more power from the same basic engine.

The turbocharger, itself, gets its energy from the engine's exhaust gases. The hot exhaust gases actually drive the turbocharger's turbine. Figure 13-11 shows how the hot exhaust gases pass through the turbine chamber. (See the arrows on the left.) These hot gases cause the blades in the turbine to rotate. As the blades rotate, they turn the turbine's wheel and shaft. The rotating shaft, in turn, rotates a fan-like device, called an impeller. The

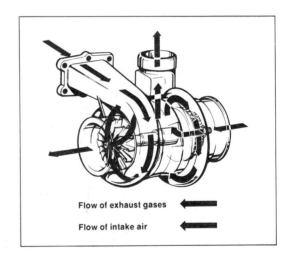

Flow of exhaust gases

Flow of intake air

Figure 13-11. How a turbocharger works. The arrows at left show exhaust gases turning the turbine. The arrows on the right show the impeller pulling air into the turbocharger. The air goes out the top, into the intake manifold. *Courtesy of Cummins Engine Co.*

impeller draws air into the turbocharger. This air is then compressed and forced into the engine's intake manifold and cylinders.

The ends of the turbo shaft, where the blades are, are called the turbine end. This is the side the exhaust flows out of. (Left side of diagram above) The other side of the turbocharger that forces air into the engine is called the impeller side. (Right side of diagram above)

TURBOCHARGERS   (cont.)

Besides adding to the engine's power, a turbocharger can help an engine to operate smoothly. At high altitudes, air is thinner. Thinner air causes a truck without a turbocharger to drop in horsepower. A turbocharger, installed in an engine, delivers enough air at high altitudes for the normal fuel charge to be burned. Thus, the turbocharger makes for even horsepower at high and low altitudes.

A *supercharger* has the same function as a turbocharger. However, it is driven by the engine's gear train, not by exhaust gases.

Figure 13-12.   Cutaway Cat engine, showing turbocharger, aftercooler, and engine block. *Courtesy of Caterpillar Tractor Co., Engine Division*

AFTERCOOLERS

An *aftercooler* may be called an aftercooler, an intercooler, or a thermal cooler. But whatever it is called, it serves the same purpose: to cool the intake air from a turbocharger. An aftercooler is a miniature radiator enclosed in an aluminum housing. It is usually placed along the side of the engine head area. (See Figure 13-14.)

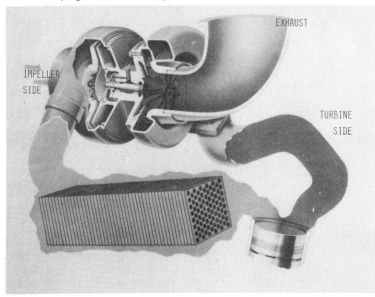

Figure 13-13.   Drawing to illustrate passage of air from turbo to aftercooler to cylinder. *Courtesy of Caterpillar Tractor Co., Engine Division.*

As the intake air passes through the turbocharger, the temperature of the air is increased to a dangerous level. To offset the high temperature of the compressed air, the air passes through a small radiator. Engine water circulates through the core of this small radiator. As the air passes over and around the tubes, the heat is dissipated because it transfers to the water cooling system. The air temperature from the impeller side of the turbo will be around 220°F (104°C). The aftercooler cools it to about 168°F (76°C).

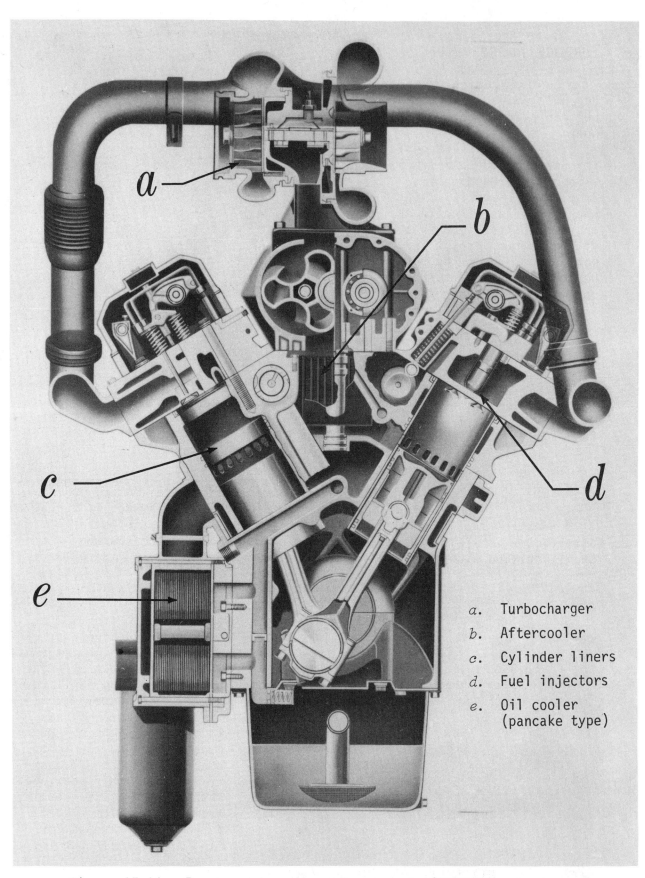

a. Turbocharger

b. Aftercooler

c. Cylinder liners

d. Fuel injectors

e. Oil cooler
   (pancake type)

Figure 13-14. Front cutaway view of two-cycle 8V92T Detroit Diesel Allison engine. *Courtesy of Detroit Diesel Allison, Division General Motors Corporation*

RETARDERS | A great many diesel engines are equipped with *retarders*. Some retarders are also called *engine brakes*. Retarders give your truck braking power which is independent of the air brake system. They slow the rig by retarding the engine itself.

There are two main advantages of retarders. *First*, they shorten stopping distances and tend to slow the vehicle more smoothly. A smooth slowdown is especially important on slick surfaces (such as ice or rain-covered roadways). On these surfaces, a rig might skid or even jackknife if it slows too abruptly. Thus, many people will tell you that retarders improve safety. *Second*, they extend the life of your brakes. One manufacturer claims that the life of the brake shoes is often increased three or more times when you add a retarder. They can also increase tire life.

Three common retarders are the Caterpillar BrakeSaver, the Williams Exhaust Brake, and the Jake Brake (by Jacobs Mfg. Co.). Each retards the engine and helps to slow the vehicle, but each operates in a different way. We will discuss each separately.

Figure 13-15. The Williams Blue Ox Exhaust Brake is one type of retarder. It is illustrated here as it would normally be positioned on one type of diesel engine. *Courtesy of Dana Corporation, Williams Air Controls*

233

HOUSING   ROTOR STATOR

Figure 13-16. The Caterpillar BrakeSaver retarder. The three basic internal elements are illustrated: housing, rotor, and stator. *Courtesy of Caterpillar Tractor Co., Engine Division*

RETARDERS (cont.)

● *The Caterpillar BrakeSaver*

The BrakeSaver is illustrated above. Some models are activated manually by the driver. Others go on automatically when you remove your foot from the throttle.

Once it has been put into operation, here's how it works. Oil from your engine flows through a valve into the retarder. The rotor in the retarder directs the engine oil against the stator. The pressure of the oil between the rotor and stator converts the energy into heat, slowing the engine. The more the volume of oil increases, the more retarding effect you get. When the retarder is turned off, the valve shuts off the oil and the rotor pumps out the remaining oil. This allows the engine to run free again with no retarding effect. Basically, then, the BrakeSaver works by building up oil pressure between two opposing parts, therefore restricting movement.

Any unit like this must have a cooler of some sort to cool the oil because the frictional build-up inside the unit is very high. Therefore, an oil cooler is used. It is usually placed on the side of the engine. Oil flows through the unit and heat is dissipated.

RETARDERS   (cont.)

The Williams Exhaust Brake

The Williams engine brake is an exhaust brake (or compression brake). An *exhaust brake* operates similarly to the way a dampener works in a stovepipe. As you can see from Figure 13-17, the Williams brake is basically an exhaust pipe. Inside of it is a baffleplate (a sliding gate). When the brake comes on, an air chamber moves the baffleplate so that it closes off the exhaust pipe. When the exhaust pipe is closed off, the engine must work against the pressure to force the exhaust out of the stack. This retards the engine.

The purpose of the exhaust brake is to slow (or partially stop) the exhaust from leaving the engine. This stoppage creates back pressure inside the engine, and the back pressure slows down or "brakes" the engine itself. Let's explain it a different way. On the engine's exhaust stroke, the exhaust valve is open, but the exhaust brake keeps the exhaust air from escaping into the manifold. This back pressure exerts a retarding or braking effect on the pistons throughout their entire exhaust stroke. The effort needed to turn the engine against this back pressure, plus normal friction, slows the vehicle. When the retarding effect is no longer needed, the baffleplate is moved to the open position, and the engine functions normally.

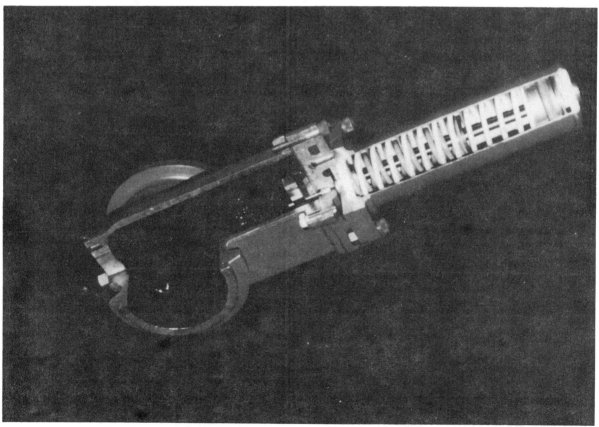

Figure 13-17. The Williams Blue Ox Exhaust Brake. When the driver activates the retarder, a baffleplate cuts off exhaust so that it can't leave the engine. Since the engine has to work harder to fight the pressure which has built up, it slows down, slowing the vehicle with it. *Courtesy of Dana Corporation, Williams Air Controls*

235

Figure 13-18. Jacobs most popular Jake Brake. *Courtesy of THE JACOBS MANUFACTURING COMPANY, VEHICLE EQUIPMENT DIVISION, EAST DUDLEY TOWN ROAD, BLOOMFIELD, CONNECTICUT 06002*

RETARDERS (cont.)

● *The Jake Brake*

Perhaps the best known of all retarders is the Jacobs or "Jake" Brake. (See Figure 13-18.) Simply explained, the Jake Brake operates by converting the engine into a power-absorbing air compressor. When the Jake Brake is switched on, the engine cycle itself is affected. Near the top of the normal compression stroke, compressed air and its energy is released throughout the exhaust system. With the compressed air gone, the energy needed to return the piston to its bottom position has to come from someplace else. Thus, the energy is drawn from the vehicle's momentum. This drains away some of the truck's energy and slows it down. The driver controls the operation of the Jake Brake manually, and in some rigs, the driver can control the amount of retarding effect.

● *A Word of Caution about Retarders*

Retarders should *never* be used to do all the work of stopping a big rig. They should be used in coordination with the air brakes. By using *both the air brakes and a retarder* to slow the vehicle, the driver has more control, and both safety and brake life are increased.

SUMMARY | In this chapter, we explained the operation of the diesel engine and three components often added to it: turbochargers, aftercoolers and retarders.

First, we noted similarities and differences between gasoline and diesel engines. In both engines, power comes from explosions in the combustion chambers of the cylinders. The explosion forces the piston down, and the piston, coming down, rotates the crankshaft. Differential gears change the direction of the rotating force, and the drive axle turns the wheels, moving the truck.

The main difference between a gasoline and diesel truck is in the way the explosion in the cylinder takes place. In a gasoline engine, the compression stroke squeezes a fuel-air mixture. Then, a spark plug ignites the mixture. In a diesel engine, the compression stroke squeezes only air in the combustion chamber. This compression makes the air extremely hot. Then, fuel injectors spray diesel fuel into the hot air in a mist. The air is so hot that it ignites the diesel fuel.

Diesel engines operate on either a four-stroke or two-stroke cycle. The four-stroke cycle is intake, compression, power and exhaust. During intake, air enters the cylinder through the intake valve. During compression, the intake valve closes, and the piston moves up, compressing the air. Then, injectors spray diesel fuel into the combustion chamber in a mist, and the explosion occurs. During the power stroke, the piston moves down, delivering power to the crankshaft. Finally, during exhaust, the exhaust valve opens and the piston moves up, pushing out the burned gases. Immediately, the process is ready to begin again with the intake stroke.

A two-stroke engine doesn't have intake valves. Exhaust valves let the burned gases out, but air comes into the cylinders through ports in the sides of the cylinders. The ports are open all the time, but when the piston moves up in the cylinder, it covers them, closing them off. When the piston moves below the ports, an air blower blows air into the cylinder through the open ports. The exhaust valves open. The incoming air pushes the exhaust gases from the last explosion out through the exhaust valves at the top of the combustion chamber. During compression, the exhaust valves are closed and the piston moves up, compressing the air. Diesel fuel is injected into the compressed air and the explosion takes place, driving the piston downward again. The two strokes are called power and compression.

A turbocharger pumps more air into the engine's combustion chamber than it would have without a turbocharger. It gives your engine more power and helps it operate more smoothly at high altitudes. None of the power of the engine has to be used to run the turbocharger. Instead, it puts the escaping exhaust gases to work. These gases would have been wasted. Instead, they turn blades in the turbocharger. These blades are attached to one end of a shaft. An impeller is attached to the other end of the shaft. As the blades turn, the impeller turns, drawing air into the turbocharger. The turbocharger compresses the air and sends it into the intake manifold which carries air to the cylinders. Turbochargers increase the amount of air going into the combustion chamber, so they give the engine more power.

SUMMARY (cont.)

An aftercooler cools the air from a turbocharger before the air goes into the engine's cylinders. It works like a miniature radiator.

Retarders (or "engine brakes") work with the air brake system to stop the truck. They draw energy away from the engine, retarding it. The Caterpillar BrakeSaver restricts movement in the engine by building up pressure between two moving parts. The Williams Exhaust Brake closes off the exhaust pipe. Since the burned gases can't escape out the exhaust pipe, the engine has trouble making a new exhaust stroke. It can't work efficiently, so the engine slows down. The Jake Brake stops the compression stroke from operating. It opens the exhaust valve during compression which means that air can't be properly compressed and heated. Since the air doesn't get hot enough to ignite the diesel fuel, no explosion takes place. The crankshaft has to move the piston up and down, instead of the piston moving the crankshaft around. In other words, the engine draws energy away from the crankshaft, instead of sending energy to it. Retarders are useful because they help a vehicle stop quickly and smoothly and because they help you to get longer wear out of your air brake system and tires. You always want to use them *with* your air brakes to stop your vehicle. Don't expect a retarder to stop a heavy-duty diesel without help from the air brake system.

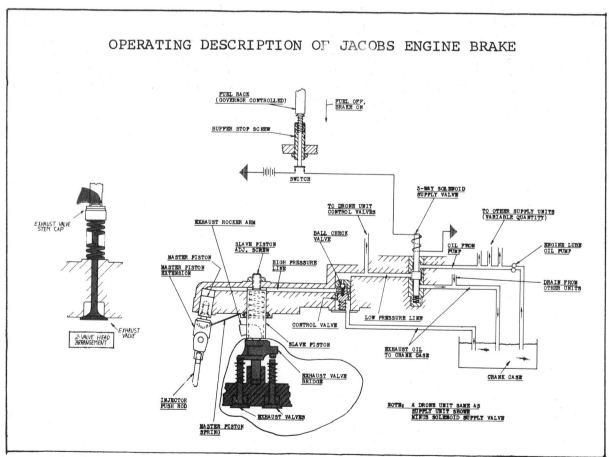

Figure 13-19. Diagram illustrating the operation of the Jake Brake.
Courtesy of THE JACOBS MANUFACTURING COMPANY, VEHICLE EQUIPMENT DIVISION, EAST DUDLEY TOWN ROAD, BLOOMFIELD, CONNECTICUT 06002

238

GLOSSARY

aftercooler: A device which cools air after the air has gone through a turbocharger.

flammable (inflammable): Refers to something that readily catches fire. You can say you are carrying flammables in your tanker, or you can say you're carrying flammable liquids or gases in it. Both mean the same thing.

fuel injector: A device which breaks diesel fuel into a mist and shoots this diesel mist into the engine's combustion chamber. (See Figures 13-6 and 13-7.)

impeller: In a diesel engine, the impeller is part of the turbocharger. It draws air into the turbocharger.

momentum: The force with which an object moves. Usually, it means a vehicle's forward movement. If you break a vehicle's momentum, you slow it or stop it.

supercharger: A device which increases the amount of air sent into the combustion chamber of a diesel engine. It differs from a turbocharger because it is driven by the engine's gear train, not exhaust gases.

turbine: An engine which works because air, water, steam, or gas pushes against blades or vanes. In a diesel engine, a turbine in the turbocharger rotates a shaft which makes the impeller work.

turbocharger: A device which increases the amount of air sent into the combustion chamber of a diesel engine. It is driven by hot exhaust gases, and it increases the power of the engine to which it has been added.

two-cycle engine: An internal combustion engine in which the piston makes two different strokes before it repeats the strokes. The two cycles are compression and power.

vapor: A steamlike mist; an evaporated liquid.

volatile: Something which evaporates or turns into a mist easily is volatile.

▶ CHECKING THE FACTS

Each of the following questions needs a short answer. Use a separate sheet of paper to answer the questions on.

1. How is a diesel engine like a gasoline engine? You might answer this question by listing several parts or operations they have in common.

2. What ignites the diesel fuel in a diesel engine?

3. Which is more volatile - gasoline or diesel fuel?

4. How does diesel fuel enter the combustion chamber?

5. How does air enter a combustion chamber in a four-stroke diesel engine? How does air enter a combustion chamber in a two-stroke diesel engine?

6. What heats the air in the cylinder of a diesel engine?

7. How is a two-stroke diesel engine like a four-stroke diesel engine?

8. What are the two strokes of a two-stroke diesel engine?

9. Where does a turbocharger get its energy? How about a supercharger?

10. What is the purpose of an aftercooler?

11. What is the purpose of a retarder?

12. Name three kinds of retarders.

■ GETTING THE MAIN IDEAS

Circle the letter of the phrase that best completes each sentence or best answers each question below.

1. Both gasoline and diesel engines need three elements:
    A. turbochargers, aftercoolers and retarders.
    B. turbochargers, superchargers and aftercoolers.
    C. air, fuel and ignition.
    D. energy, power and momentum.

2. Three components of both gasoline and diesel engines are
    A. cylinder, valve train and crankshaft.
    B. combustion chamber, piston and fuel injector.
    C. cylinder, crankshaft and spark plug.
    D. cylinder, crankshaft and carburetor.

3. The main purpose of a fuel injector is
   A. to turn diesel fuel into a mist and inject it into the combustion chamber.
   B. to inject diesel fuel into the intake manifold.
   C. to turn misted diesel fuel into a liquid and inject it into the combustion chamber.
   D. to increase the amount of fuel injected into the cylinder so that a diesel engine produces more power.

4. One component a two-stroke engine <u>does</u> <u>not</u> <u>have</u> is
   A. an exhaust valve.
   B. a port.
   C. an intake manifold.
   D. an intake valve.

5. What forces exhaust gases out of the combustion chamber of a two-stroke engine?
   A. an air blower
   B. air entering through the intake ports
   C. an impeller
   D. the piston rising upward

In the space before each statement, place a plus (+) if the statement is true. Place a zero (0) if the statement is false.

_____ 6. All diesel engines need spark plugs for ignition.

_____ 7. The compression ratio of a gas engine is the same as a diesel.

_____ 8. A two-cycle diesel engine needs a carburetor.

_____ 9. Two-cycle diesel engines have air blowers and intake ports.

_____ 10. The compression of the air in the diesel cylinder creates the heat to ignite the fuel.

_____ 11. The two cycles of a two-stroke engine are compression and power.

_____ 12. All diesel engines have turbochargers and aftercoolers.

_____ 13. Only some diesel engines have retarders.

_____ 14. The purpose of an turbocharger is to add to the engine's power and help it operate smoothly at high altitudes.

_____ 15. You should never use a retarder (engine brake) and the truck's regular brakes at the same time.

_____ 16. Two advantages of retarders are (1) they prolong the life of your brakes, and (2) they help you stop more smoothly.

241

1. If you had to choose between a turbocharger and a supercharger for your engine, which one would you choose and why?

2. Which engine would be more affected by a breakdown in the cooling system - a gasoline or diesel engine? Why?

3. Outline the typical four-stroke diesel engine cycle.

4. Explain why a turbocharger or supercharger helps an engine operate more smoothly at high altitudes.

5. Explain briefly how all three retarders discussed in this chapter operate - in your own words. Then, assume that your boss asks you which kind you want installed in your engine. Which one would you choose and why? Are there some arguments you would use to convince the boss that your choice is the best one?

Figure 14-1. *Courtesy of The Goodyear Tire and Rubber Co.*

Chapter Fourteen

THE ELECTRICAL SYSTEM

WEATHER CONDITIONS What can one say about the weather? At times, it's great, and at times, it's rotten! Snow is beautiful. But ask a truck driver about snow, and she or he will say, "What rotten weather!" What is beautiful may also be dangerous. Weather has many woes to visit on the driver. However, weather usually gives us warnings. So, unless you are too stubborn or too dumb to heed these warnings, you can handle the weather.

● *Snow*

Snow varies from very dry to very wet, depending on the geographical area you are in. Among other things, snow makes you lose traction. This especially affects your *steering* and *directional control*. Furthermore, this loss of traction makes it *hard to get started from a dead stop* and *very difficult to stop* once you're in motion. If you let your wheels spin, the tire surfaces get warm from the frictional spin. The warm tires melt the snow and make traction even more difficult. Then, as the melted snow cools again, it freezes into ice.

I remember seeing a driver park a rig in the snow one time. The wheels were on plowed snow, but the snow beneath the center of the rig was banked about a foot and a half high. During the night, the heat of the gear boxes and rear end melted the snow around them. Then, later, the snow froze again, forming an ice barrier around the wheel housings. In the morning, you couldn't budge the rig with a fifty-ton wrecker.

Common sense is an absolute essential when you drive in snow. You aren't driving a snow plow, so don't try hitting the open road during heavy snows unless you want to spend a couple of days in the cab of your rig - marooned. That can be mighty dangerous. Be smart. Park and wait for the plow to clear the road.

Figure 14-2. This scene is beautiful, but full of hidden dangers for the trucker. Snow and cold weather make it hard to start the engine, steer, and stop, among other things. *Reprinted with permission of Fruehauf Division, Fruehauf Corporation*

There's an odd thing about the snow in Alaska that you learn if you're driving up there. It's so dry that most of the time, you don't need chains, except for pulling (driving up) steep hills. It's in the spring, when the snow begins to melt, that you need chains. The mud is so bad that, most of the time, you need chains to pull any hill where the road bed is dirt.

As if the problems mentioned above weren't enough, another serious problem concerning snow is the way it comes at you and your windshield. Especially at night, it has a tendency to hypnotize you until you can't see, or until you miss a turn. Remember too, that after a snowstorm, the temperature usually drops. This makes the road surface slicker, and it may also mean that ice is just underneath the surface.

● *Rain*

Let's not overlook rain. It may be only a few rain drops, or it may be many rain drops, but both create dangerous conditions for driving. Unfortunately, many drivers don't realize this. They think that only heavy rains are a problem.

A few rain drops can be very hazardous. A few drops of rain bring the oil and rubber particles left by other vehicles up to the surface wherever there has been a lot of traffic. This leaves a slick film for you to slide on. It happens mainly at intersections where vehicles have stopped and dripped oil over and over.

Here's a second situation where just a little rain is hazardous. It occurs on roadways where there's a film of water that can't drain off. As your road speed increases, or as the volume of water increases, your tires can't push through the water to reach the road surface. Therefore, your tires ride up on the film of water. You are hydroplaning. Hydroplaning means you have water between your tire surface and the road surface. The only solution is to *slow down* until you can feel the rig respond to the brakes or the steering wheel.

Your brakes can hydroplane too. As you run in the rain, the water boils around your brakes. It soaks the linings and creates a film of water between the brake shoe and the brake drum. The brake shoes can't contact the drums because of the water. As the water is driven away, the shoe meets the drum. But since the shoe is soaked with water, it allows the drum to slide by. Finally, when the frictional heat dries the moisture out of the shoe, the brake grabs. But by this time, you have traveled 300 or 400 feet. The danger is doubled. First, you take too long to stop to be safe. Second, not all the brakes grab at the same time or with the same resistance. Maybe the left, rear wheel grabs. Then, the right, front wheel grabs. Then, a trailer wheel grabs on one side. By this time, you are skidding all over the road with your rig acting like a wet noodle.

● *Using Your Head*

Using your head in inclement weather is a must. Sometimes the only solution to a problem brought on by poor weather is one you come up with yourself. I remember one driver who used his head with an interesting result.

There was about a foot of snow on the ground. The driver had a semi load of carpeting, rolled up in heavy plastic. The carpet had to be delivered down a steep alley to the warehouse. The driver knew if he backed all the way down the alley, he would never be able to pull back up to the street, especially with an empty rig and no traction. First, he contacted the warehouse. Then, he backed down the alley as far as he dared, opened the rear doors, and pushed the carpets out. As they hit the snow, they slid down the hill, right to the warehouse door.

The three major dangers from weather are *snow*, *rain* and *fog*. "Hold on just a minute," you say. "What about tornados, hurricanes and things like that?" Good question. Why don't we list them as major driving dangers? Because you shouldn't be driving in those conditions. If there appears to be a danger of tornado, hurricane, heavy dust, heavy sandstorm, or some similar condition, *don't attempt to drive*. The dangers aren't worth the risk. Snow, rain and fog occur fairly often, and you will be driving in them - more in some areas, less in others. Their frequency and their effect on you and your truck makes them major dangers. You should treat them as such. In all three, the byword is *caution*, and *reduction of speed* is essential. Watch ruts on curves and freezing surfaces on bridges and in hollows. Even without snow, in the fall of the year, wet leaves in a shaded area can be very slippery.

Don't drive if there are blizzard conditions. You're human. You're not a wizard. And, if you do try to go out in a blizzard, you'll find yourself marooned, and may end up buried or frozen. You can run out of fuel, or run into a snowdrift, and you won't be able to walk back.

I remember a friend who almost lost his life because he insisted on pulling out during a heavy snowstorm. He wasn't even adequately dressed for the weather. The only thing that saved his life when the snow finally stopped was this. He had a furniture van, and he was able to climb up in back. He got down between the loading pads for warmth. When he was found, he was about 15 pounds lighter in weight.

Figure 14-3. *Reprinted from "Winter Survival," Department of Energy, Office of Consumer Affairs, Washington, DC*

WEATHER CONDITIONS   (cont.)

● *Bad Weather's Effect on the Electrical System*

So far, we have spoken about running in inclement weather. Now, we need to consider the effect that bad weather will have on the truck's electrical system. The prime culprit is usually *rainy weather*. It isn't just the driver that gets soaked. As we've already mentioned, the brakes can get soaked. But so does the underpart of the vehicle, and this is where all the wiring is located.

One of the most annoying situations is a short in the wiring system. It can happen in the trailer. It can happen in the tractor. But, it always seems to happen late at night, when you're dead tired and it is pouring rain. If anything can get to a wiring system to create shorts, believe me, it's water. Most drivers don't realize that the speed of their truck creates terrific pressure on the water being sprayed up from the wheels on the underside of the rig.

Sometimes, like when you're running through a deep puddle, the force of the water has enough of an impact to tear a wire loose. And, if rain isn't enough of a headache, how about weather so cold that snow and ice buildup hangs on wires. Ever noticed this on a telephone cable? The same thing may occur on the underside of your rig. The weight of the ice is enough to tear a wire out of a light socket.

A further discouragement is met when you come out of a nice, warm hotel or sleeper berth, and find the cold weather has pulled your batteries down to zero. This is a great way to start your day as a driver!

There's no way a trucker can avoid all the troubles that bad weather conditions can create. But you can lessen their effect on you and your rig by getting to know how your truck's electrical system works. That is what the rest of this chapter is designed to help you do. Before you can determine what Old Man Winter's done to your battery or wires, you need to know how the electrical system works. So, if you're interested in finding the smoothest way of handling some of the hassles we talked about above, read on.

AN
OVERALL
PICTURE

Diesel trucks have a basic 12-volt electrical system. The electrical system includes an alternator (or generator in some older rigs), and all lights and gauges. It is made up of many wires, circuit breakers, fuses and terminals, all interconnected. The basic wires that run throughout the dashboard are usually enclosed in what we call a loom, or often refer to as a wiring harness or body harness. This harness is the carrier for the wires as they leave the terminal block. (Review Figure 5-12.) Wires in all trucks are color coded for trouble shooting. Color coding makes a particular wire easier to trace from one point to another for most people.

The electricity travels through the wires from the batteries to the instruments in the dashboard, as well as from the alternator to the junction or terminal block. From the terminal block, the wiring harness will travel

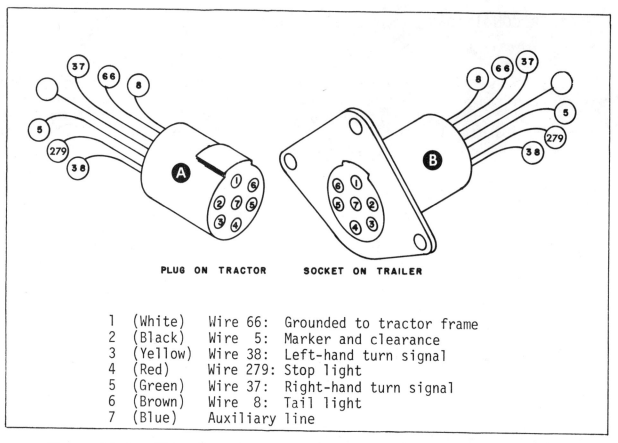

PLUG ON TRACTOR   SOCKET ON TRAILER

1	(White)	Wire 66:	Grounded to tractor frame
2	(Black)	Wire 5:	Marker and clearance
3	(Yellow)	Wire 38:	Left-hand turn signal
4	(Red)	Wire 279:	Stop light
5	(Green)	Wire 37:	Right-hand turn signal
6	(Brown)	Wire 8:	Tail light
7	(Blue)	Auxiliary line	

Figure 14-4. This diagram shows the tractor plug, marked (A), and the trailer socket, marked (B). These two make the electrical connection between the tractor and trailer. (In this case, it is a cab-over trac- tor and semi-trailer.) This seven-wire electrical connection is nick- named the "pigtail." Notice the color coding of the wires. *Courtesy of Peterbilt Motors Company*

AN OVERALL PICTURE (cont.)

through the frame of the truck to the rear of the cab, winding up at the seven- wire plug that goes to the trailer connector (or socket). (See Figure 14-4.) These wires carry the necessary electricity to the trailer for such things as the clearance lights, turn signals and stoplights.

The electrical system of a large diesel truck is complex. You can get an idea of just how complex it is by taking a look at one electrical system dia- gram in Figure 14-5. This early system is still in use in many trucks on the road today.

THE
STARTER | The electrical system only deviates from the basic 12-volt system in one place: the starting system. The *starter* on the largest diesels are normally 24 volts because of the enormous power needed to turn the engine over fast enough to start the ignition pattern.

THE STARTER   (cont.)

Most heavy-duty diesel starters are electrical. However, many rigs are equipped with air starters. An air starter is like an electric starter. The only exception is that an air starter uses compressed air pressure from the truck air tank to activate the starter instead of electrical current. Which kind your truck has will probably depend upon your employer's personal preference. Air starters are as good as electric starters, and in some situations may even be a better choice. For instance, a battery operating in extreme cold may be pulled down overnight. An electrical starter will lose effectiveness in this situation, but an air starter won't.

THE BATTERIES

Our explanation of how the electrical system works will start with the source of power: the *batteries*. Many of the largest diesels will have four, large, six-volt batteries. That's what it takes to start the largest engine.

● *Arrangement of the Batteries in the Engine*

Usually, batteries will be group four type, heavy-duty batteries. In some cases, a truck will have two of the six-volt batteries in a carrier on one side of the chassis and two others on the opposite side of the chassis. However, in most trucks that use 24-volt starters, all four will be combined into what we call a *series parallel circuit*. To form this circuit, the batteries are first connected, side by side, into two pairs. Then, the two pairs are connected to provide the 24 volts needed to turn the starter. The two pairs of batteries work together to start the engine, whether they are mounted together or mounted on separate sides of the chassis. When you hit the starter button, the two groups combine to provide the starter with 24 volts.

● *Maintenance of the Batteries*

Periodically, you will want to check out the batteries. You'll look to see that there is no dirt or corrosion, that there are no loose connections, that they have enough water, etc. If you inspect only one set of two, you had better look for another two somewhere else - like under the cab or step, because these are common locations for the second set. Remember, many diesels will have four batteries, so look for them.

Be very careful when you're putting a jumper cable or charger on the system. Hook the positive and negative cables correctly so you don't endanger yourself. You don't want to create a dead ground or short between the four batteries. If you do, the extreme heat will melt the terminals or buckle the plates in the battery. You may even get an explosion as the gases escaping from the caps over the filler holes are of an explosive nature. The National Society for the Blind and the National Safety Council at Long Beach, California, announced that over 800 people were blinded in 1978 due to battery explosions of one sort or another. So, before you ever try to jump a truck, you should be sure that someone has taught you to do it correctly. Then, if you find yourself in this predicament, that is, if you have to jump a battery, wear a pair of safety glasses or a face shield. That is the best thing you can do for your own safety.

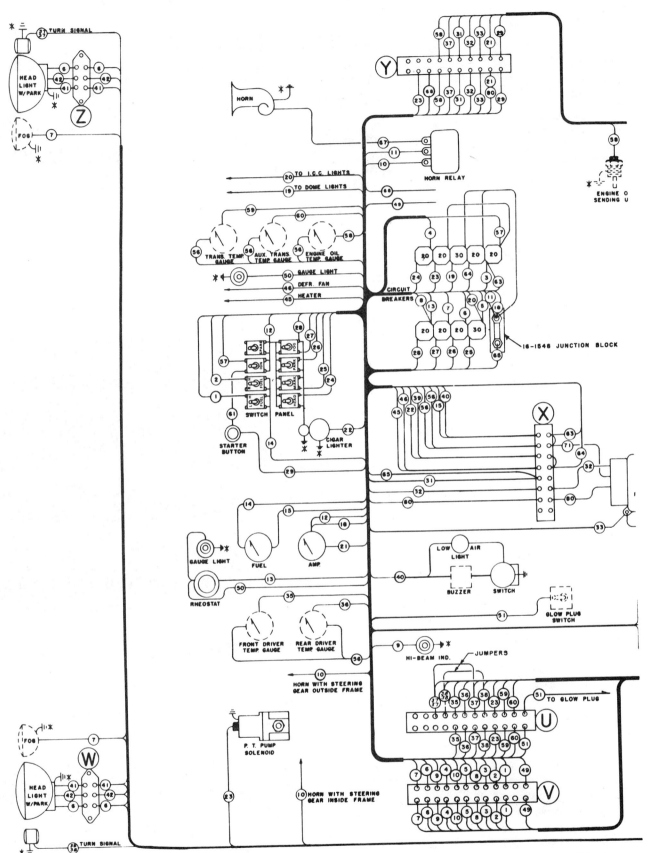

Figure 14-5. Wiring diagram for an older conventional tractor. Diagram shows an arrangement common in diesel rigs: four six-volt batteries. The number of batteries needed to start a heavy-duty rig will vary from two to four. *Courtesy of Peterbilt Motors Company*

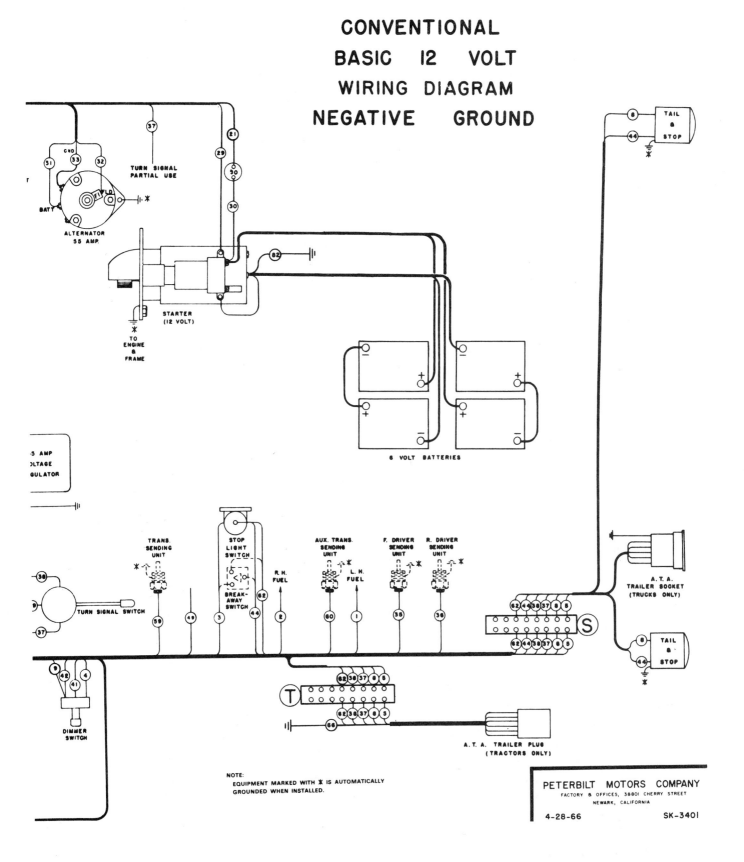

CONVENTIONAL
BASIC 12 VOLT
WIRING DIAGRAM
NEGATIVE GROUND

6 VOLT BATTERIES

ALTERNATOR 55 AMP.

STARTER (12 VOLT)

TO ENGINE & FRAME

TURN SIGNAL PARTIAL USE

5 AMP VOLTAGE REGULATOR

TRANS. SENDING UNIT

STOP LIGHT SWITCH

BREAK-AWAY SWITCH

R.H. FUEL

AUX. TRANS. SENDING UNIT

L.H. FUEL

F. DRIVER SENDING UNIT

R. DRIVER SENDING UNIT

TURN SIGNAL SWITCH

DIMMER SWITCH

A.T.A. TRAILER SOCKET (TRUCKS ONLY)

A.T.A. TRAILER PLUG (TRACTORS ONLY)

TAIL & STOP

TAIL & STOP

NOTE:
EQUIPMENT MARKED WITH ✗ IS AUTOMATICALLY GROUNDED WHEN INSTALLED.

PETERBILT MOTORS COMPANY
FACTORY & OFFICES, 38801 CHERRY STREET
NEWARK, CALIFORNIA

4-28-66   SK-3401

251

THE BATTERIES (cont.)

Most basic problems encountered with any truck electrical system are caused by either a bad ground or a short. A bad ground is the most common. If you encounter one of these two problems, start looking for the cause at the source: the batteries. Check all terminals and cables leading out from the batteries. They should be tight and clean. A film of dirt across the top of the batteries will drain the current overnight as the batteries sweat. There are enough mineral particles in the dirt to act as a conductor. Dirt has the same effect on the batteries as if you laid a piece of steel across the terminals, except at a much slower rate. So, *keep the batteries clean.*

Batteries are very often neglected by the average driver until they fail to perform. Once a battery fails, the driver cleans it up, tightens the cables, or adds water. In other words, the driver does the maintenance that should have been done long ago. Then, in goes a fast charge which causes internal heat, and the life of the batteries is shortened. *Don't fast-charge the batteries if you can avoid it.* Use a slow charge. If the water level is down to the top of the plates, replace it with *distilled water* only. Don't use tap water because the minerals in the tap water will end up as sediment on the plates and bottom of the battery cell, shortening its service life.

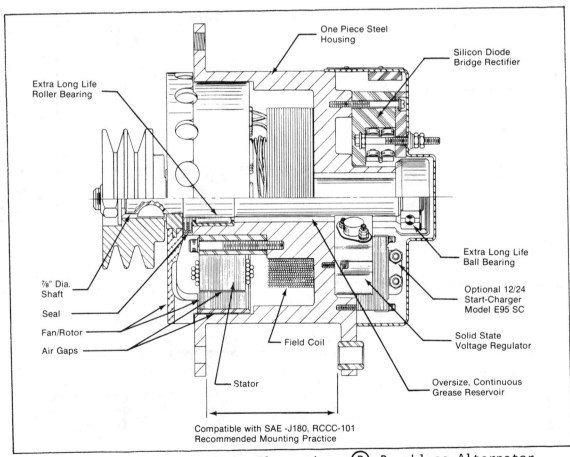

Figure 14-6. Diagram of the Electrodyne ®️ Brushless Alternator. This alternator is belt-driven. *Reprinted with permission of Electrodyne ®️ Systems, Inc.*

THE VOLTAGE REGULATOR

The rate of charge of the battery is controlled by the *voltage regulator*. As the batteries reach full charge, the regulator tapers the charging rate off so you don't overcharge the battery and boil the water out.

THE ALTERNATOR OR GENERATOR

The truck *alternator* or *generator* is the charging unit that replaces the power taken from the batteries. An alternator is preferred over a generator because the alternator will put out 40 amps at a very low rpm, but a generator has to run at a high rpm for maximum performance. Under most conditions, you don't need delivery of 40 amps all the time. But for those times when you do (such as right after a long starting period when the starter has been cranking a long time to start the engine), it's good to have the more powerful charging unit: the alternator.

THE WIRES

Wiring for a semi-trailer is usually not visible to the naked eye. In a van, the wires will be inside the wall and roof panels. They will also run beneath the frame on the underside of the trailer. They run from the rear lights and accessories on the trailer, up to the nose of the trailer, to the electrical plug which is illustrated in Figure 14-4. The only way a driver can follow the wires is to use a wiring diagram like the one shown in Figure 14-7. Otherwise, the wires will have to be traced from each, individual light or accessory, foot by foot, to find where each wire winds up. Basically, the wires are color coded from each light so that they can be traced.

A driver doesn't necessarily need to know the wiring diagram of a trailer. The shop usually keeps the diagrams. The extent of the repairs a driver will make are usually nothing but a broken wire close to a defective light or a poor ground at the base of the light. A driver wouldn't delve into making major repairs. In fact, when an inexperienced driver attempts to cut and relocate wires, he or she usually ends up with a catastrophe and a source of future problems. Therefore, you shouldn't attempt to fix anything other than a simple, broken wire or simple short. That's what the shop is for.

THE CIRCUIT BREAKERS

The electrical system is protected from overload by *circuit breakers*. If a short occurs, or a voltage regulator malfunctions, too much power can begin to pour into the system. As soon as the circuit breaker detects this overload, it disconnects (or "breaks"), and the part of the system which is affected by the malfunction stops operating. In other words, the circuit breakers in a truck operate in much the same way as they do in a house.

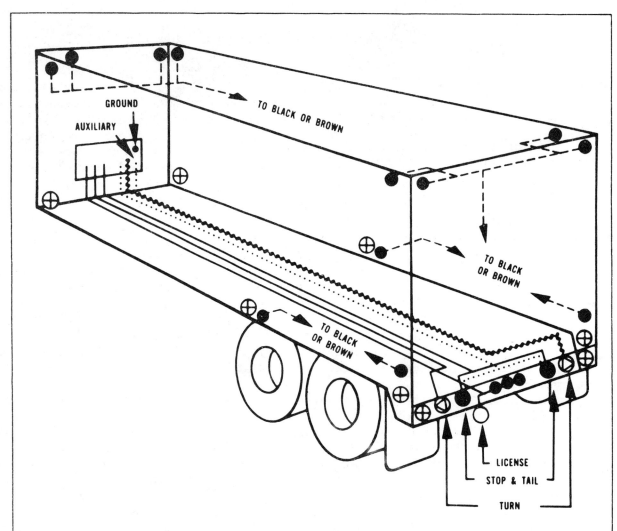

ATA WIRE COLORS & CODE

ATA WIRE COLOR	SHOWN ABOVE AS	FUNCTION
White	Location Only	Ground
Black	————————	Identification & License
Yellow	————————	Left Turn
Green	∿∿∿∿∿∿∿∿∿	Right Turn
Red	————————	Stop
Brown	··················	Tail
Black	— — — — — —	Clearance & Marker
Blue	··················	Auxiliary

Figure 14-7. The above diagram shows a typical wiring pattern for a van. Where might the wires run in a jeep, jo-dog or when there are multiple units connected together? There may be times when there are as many as five seven-wire plug connections. *Courtesy of Phillips Manufacturing Company*

IN CLOSING | As we said in the beginning of this chapter, the truck's electrical system is a complicated one. It is important for you to understand how it operates and how to maintain it. For example, check the batteries frequently to see that they have enough distilled water. There are a few problems caused by simple shorts that you can handle on your own. But if it's anything more complicated than that, get an electrician.

SUMMARY | Bad weather has an effect on many of the truck's systems. But if there's one system it affects more than the others, it's the electrical system. That's why we began this chapter with some stories and cautions about what to do if you're driving in snow or rain. Snow makes it hard for you to steer and control your vehicle because you don't have much traction. It's hard to get started and it's hard to stop. And if you aren't careful, you'll find that the warmth of your rig when it stops in snow will melt the snow and leave you frozen in ice the next morning. Too much snow makes driving impossible, so don't drive in blizzards or on roads that haven't been plowed. Heavy rains and light rains are both dangerous. Light rains, especially after a period of dryness, bring oil and rubber particles to the top of a road surface and make it extremely slippery. Heavy rains can create a lot of problems, including flooding. They can cause your tires or brakes to hydroplane, and both of these are very dangerous. Snow, rain and fog all create hazardous driving conditions. They require you to be even more cautious than usual and to reduce your speed.

Bad weather affects the electrical system in a number of ways. It can create shorts in the wiring system. It can tear wires loose. It can pull your batteries down to zero.

The diesel truck has a 12-volt electrical system. The only exception may be the starter motor which may be 24 volts. The alternator or generator creates power when the engine is running to replenish the energy taken from the battery. To keep operating properly, the batteries have to be clean and free of corrosion. They also have to be filled with distilled water to the proper level, and the cables should be secured tightly. The voltage regulator sees that the battery gets the right amount of charge - not too much and not too little.

Wires carry the electrical current to all of the parts that need electricity to operate: clearance lamps, turn signals, tail lights, etc., including the CB and radio. The unit that takes electrical power from the truck to the trailer is nicknamed the "pigtail." Actually, it is a plug and socket device. The wires in a trailer are usually hidden inside the walls, floor and roof. They are color coded so that you can follow their paths.

If something shorts out or if the voltage regulator overcharges, a circuit breaker will disconnect. This keeps damage from spreading.

SUMMARY   (cont.)

The electrical system of a heavy-duty diesel is very complicated, very complex, and tampering with it, if you don't know exactly what you're doing, will only bring you trouble. The best thing to do is this. Know enough about how your truck's system works to do three things:

(1) Be able to handle simple things. For example, be able to handle a simple short; be able to reconnect a wire simply torn loose by wind or water pressure, and be able to reset circuit breakers.

(2) Be able to explain to an electrician at the shop what malfunction is occurring.

(3) Maintain the battery.

GLOSSARY

alternator: A device in the truck engine which turns mechanical energy into electrical energy. The energy it produces is in the form of an alternating current which is then converted to direct current for the truck system.

circuit breaker: A device which automatically shuts off electricity in a circuit. It is a safety device to prevent damage because it breaks (or shuts off the current) when overloaded.

generator: A device which turns mechanical energy into electrical energy for recharging the battery.

hydroplane: A hydroplane is a boat that skims along the top of water. So, in trucking, if something is hydroplaning, it means it is running on top of water. Brakes hydroplane when water gets between the shoe and the drum. Tires hydroplane when there is a lot of water on the roadway and the rig is moving very fast. In both cases, hydroplaning is very dangerous.

inclement: Rough, stormy, harsh or cruel.

pigtail: The cable used to transmit electrical power to the truck trailer.

terminal: The connector at either end of an electric cable.

voltage regulator: A device which regulates or controls the amount of charge which enters the battery.

Put a plus (+) before the statement if it is true. Put a zero (0) before the statement if it is false.

_____ 1. Snow is dangerous because it makes you lose traction.

_____ 2. The three most difficult conditions for driving are heavy sand-storms, snow, and fog.

_____ 3. After a snowstorm, the temperature usually drops. This is dangerous because ice can form under the surface and make the road very slippery.

_____ 4. Heavy rains are usually a hazard, but light ones usually not.

_____ 5. There are two dangers caused when your brakes hydroplane. First, it takes longer to stop. Second, brakes on each wheel can grab at different times.

_____ 6. The basic electrical system in a diesel truck is 12-volt.

_____ 7. The largest diesels usually have two, 12-volt car batteries to start the 24-volt starter.

_____ 8. The charging rate does not affect battery life.

_____ 9. Dirt piled on top of batteries doesn't affect their performance.

_____ 10. Truck wires are color coded, meaning they are one color in the engine, one color in the cab, one color for the tractor lights and signals, and a different color throughout the trailer.

_____ 11. Most problems in a truck electrical system are caused by either a bad ground or a short.

_____ 12. If water gets down to the top of the plates, you should add distilled water to the battery.

_____ 13. Truck drivers should only fix simple, broken wires, simple shorts and reset circuit breakers. They shouldn't try to fix other electrical system problems.

_____ 14. The truck pigtail is the grounding wire hanging down at the rear of the trailer.

■ GETTING THE MAIN IDEAS

Each sentence below needs one or more words to be complete. By filling in the blanks, you will be reviewing some of the key ideas from the chapter.

1. The _____ replaces the power taken from the battery in a modern, heavy-duty diesel.

2. You wouldn't have anywhere to store electrical energy in a truck if you didn't have a _____.

3. Two protective devices in the truck's electrical system are the _____ and the _____.

4. When you are driving a semi, you want to be sure the _____ is connected. If it isn't, you'll have electricity in the tractor, but not in the trailer.

5. Don't drive if the weather forecast predicts _____

_____.

If you answer the following questions, you'll be applying the teachings of this chapter to your own truck driving career.

6. What precautions will you take if you are driving in a heavy snow?

7. Have you ever driven a car or truck in rain, snow, or fog? What safe driving tips could you give other drivers based on your experience?

8. Using a colored pencil or marker, trace the path of the wires that bring power to the turn signals in Figure 14-7.

9. What precautions should you take if you are asked by a fellow trucker to "jump" a rig.

10. Why should you have a basic understanding of the truck's electrical system? How much should you know to do your own job well? (That is, the driving job you already have or hope to begin with.)

★ GOING BEYOND THE FACTS AND IDEAS

1. Several parts of the rig in Figure 14-1 are operating off the electrical system. (1) What are they? List the obvious and not-so-obvious. (2) Which alternator is probably creating more electrical energy - the one in the rig in Figure 14-1 or in 14-2. Why?

2. You're driving down a busy, but old highway. It's a rainy night, and there are other rigs and cars, some within 250 feet. Your brakes begin to hydroplane. What do you do?

3. Study Figure 14-7. Now, design a rewiring diagram for the required electrical parts on a gooseneck trailer.

4. You've been driving down a road in northern Wyoming. The road is filled with pot holes. You stop for a cup of "hundred mile coffee," and another trucker tells you you've got no stop lights. You figure a pot hole made a circuit breaker "break," so you reset it. Still no stop lights. What do you do?

Figure 15-1. You never know what you'll wind up carrying when you begin a career in trucking. But you can bet it isn't a novice who got the job of driving this huge Kenworth truck and its massive cargo. It takes a great many people to plan and execute a trip like this KW is setting out on. *Photo courtesy of Jim Felt*

Chapter Fifteen

HEAVY DUTY DIESEL HEADACHES

THE
STORY OF
MARGUERITE

A heavy-duty diesel is a huge piece of equipment. Because it is so massive, a driver often thinks it is built like a tank and can be treated like a tank. Not so. Here's a personal example of what can happen to any driver, any time, if that driver doesn't know the equipment being used and its capabilities.

THE STORY OF MARGUERITE (cont.)

● *Running Late*

This time, the true story is of a heavy hauler. To avoid using her real name, we'll call her Marguerite. Marguerite's truck breaks down on the road which means she is running late. It also means she's getting pretty tense. When you're running late with heavy equipment, a tension always starts to build up. Why? Because, due to the size of the equipment, you have to be off the road before the heavy traffic begins.

When her rig broke down, Marguerite was quite close to her delivery point. So, the dealership that was waiting for the machine sent a mechanic out to get the truck running. That was faster than having the carrier's mechanic drive out to her.

While the mechanic was repairing the truck, he noticed that the clearance underneath the low-bed was very slight. In fact, there were only about *six inches* of ground clearance. Not much. The mechanic fixed the trouble; then, he gave Marguerite instructions on how to get to the shop. He further instructed her to be sure to go to the *third driveway* before trying to turn in.

● *The Wrong Driveway*

Evidently, Marguerite misunderstood or wasn't paying attention to the instructions, because she turned into the *first driveway* instead, and this one had a high sidewalk. The belly of the trailer would not clear the sidewalk, and Marguerite high-centered it. (This is what we call being high and dry, in a pickle.) Can you picture the tractor sitting in the driveway with the trailer belly sitting on the sidewalk and 40 feet of trailer still out in the street, blocking traffic?

The load on the low-bed was a D-9 Caterpillar weighing roughly 50 tons. So it wasn't hard for the shop to notice the driver hung up on their driveway. At Marguerite's request, they sent another D-9 down to pull her truck off the sidewalk. (By this time, Marguerite was really ruffled.) The mechanic backed the D-9 up to the front of her tractor, and Marguerite placed the chains on the back of the Cat. She wrapped the other ends of the chains around the front axle of her tractor. This way, they were going to tow tractor, trailer and cargo all into the driveway.

While this was going on, I walked down to take a look at the situation. I told the mechanic not to try to pull the truck at anything over a dead idle. I asked the driver if she was sure she knew what she was doing. I won't quote her remarks, but they were to this effect: "Get me off the ... sidewalk, and quick!"

● *The Wrong Solution*

At a dead idle, the machine wasn't moving the truck at all. It was stuck fairly solid. Just then, I was called back to the shop. I returned to check out the situation just in time to hear Marguerite screaming to the mechanic on the Cat, "Give it some throttle and go!" Wrong advice. The mechanic couldn't hear me shout because he was too far away, and my voice didn't carry over the roar. When he put the Cat in gear, it promptly moved off, pulling the front axle, springs, wheels and fender right out from under the truck. Needless to say, this is not the way to solve a bad situation. The Cat in the trailer was still hung up on the sidewalk.

Now it was too late. The damage had been done. But what would you do in a similar situation? You have a choice. The Cat driver could have put his dozer blade up against the front corner of the trailer and pushed the trailer back out into the street. That would have been the easy way of doing it. Or, the driver of the low-bed could have moved the Cat backwards on the trailer to relieve some of the weight and then backed out into the street. (Just another one of the everyday situations truckers find themselves in.)

DRIVING A RIG IS A THINKING JOB

The workday for a truck driver may begin very nicely, just as for any other person starting the day, but one thing is sure in the trucking business. It's this: If your thinking cap isn't on and you're not aware of *everything going on around you*, you are about to develop a series of your own problems or headaches. These problems are not necessarily confined to a novice, or beginning driver. They happen each and every day to any driver who doesn't have his or her wits intact. In trucking, you have to have your whole mind on the job. You have to think out every move, and anticipate every other driver's move, if you want to keep from getting involved in these so-called headaches.

In the rest of this chapter, we'll take a look at some of the heavy duty diesel headaches and see how they might be avoided. We can't cover them all. Probably, you can add to the list. But, at least, we can investigate some of the types of things you can expect and suggest ways of handling them.

LIGHT WEIGHT RIGS

The majority of components in today's rigs are aluminum and fiberglass to save weight and, therefore, fuel. But it also makes driving them dangerous unless you know what you are doing.

For example, consider a cab-over weighing about 13,700 pounds with a 375 hp engine. The weight on the front axle is about 9,500 pounds, but there isn't much weight on the tractor's drive axles

Figure 15-2. Both tractors and trailers are lightweight today. Safe drivers consider the rig's weight as they drive. *Courtesy of Pullman Trailmobile*

Figure 15-3. Two Kenworth sleeper cabs, sporting vista cruiser windows. Top-of-the-line tractors like this are not just owned by owner-operators. Some fleet owners feel they can attract better drivers if they offer them the comfort of luxuries like full-sized closets and beds, TVs and separate stereo speakers in the sleeper. *Courtesy of Jim Felt Photography*

until you add a loaded trailer.

● *Bob Tailing*

If you are running a light rig or bob tailing, and you have to stop fast, you may be in trouble unless you brake very gently. It's easy for the rear axle of a tandem to lift up and cause both axles to hop. The rig will lose braking power and may even spin around.

Remember, the weight of the tractor is all in front. When you're towing a loaded trailer, the heavy engine weight over the front axle is balanced by the weight of the trailer on the rear axles. When you're bob tailing or towing a light trailer, you don't have the counterbalance of the trailer weight. If you hit the air brakes hard, the axles will hop and bounce because there is no weight to hold them down.

Don't overestimate your stopping ability. Air brakes will feel real good and slow the rig down with only a few pounds of air. But if you apply full pressure, you may have overreacted enough to put yourself in trouble. The only way to avoid the hopping action of the brake is to touch the brake pedal *very lightly*. Apply the minimal amount of pressure for a fast, easy stop. It's a driver necessity to avoid hopping action if you're bob tailing or pulling a light (or empty) trailer.

● *High Cube Vans*

But say you add a high cube van to your tractor. This puts the load up high over the tractor wheels. If you hit a curve at too fast a speed, centrifugal force will make the trailer lean hard. You won't realize it because the engine weight will make the front axle stay down on the road. However, the curve and speed will increase the outboard lean. Amazing as it seems, the tractor frame will actually twist. This allows the inside drive axles to lift off the pavement without your knowledge. Over you go, due to a little too much speed! This is a common occurrence on freeway ramps.

LIGHT WEIGHT RIGS   (cont.)

How do you prevent danger caused by bob tailing and light weight rigs? You develop an awareness of your truck's performance. You get to know its characteristics. And you watch the road.

JAKE
BRAKE
USE

Good drivers get comfortable, but never relax their eyes or minds. They keep the cab slightly cool to stay awake and sit up straight, always anticipating the other driver's move. They know how to use the rig's equipment at the right time - equipment such as a Jake Brake. (See Chapter 13.)

The truck's gear ratio has an effect on the performance of any retarder, such as the Jake Brake. Don't fly off a hill at 80 mph in overdrive and expect the brake to slow you to a stop. The lower you go in the gears, the more effective the brake is.

OVERHANG
AND
SWAY

Long overhang (a load that extends beyond the bed of the truck) will cause the rig to sway and, again, possibly jackknife. If there is weight along with the overhang, it will cause a driver to steer into and out of a curve. Watch the swing at the front and rear overhang so you don't tag another vehicle on swinging a corner.

Here's another time you need to be very careful. Sometimes the design of the trailer makes the tractor kingpin sit way back under the nose of the trailer. If your kingpin is sitting in this position, watch the trailer nose very carefully. When you're backing in a jackknifed position, the swing of the trailer nose may stretch the air hoses or hit another trailer. (See Figure 17-7.)

TIRES

● *Tires in Foul Weather*

Caution! If you are empty in wet weather or on slick ground, beware of a sudden jackknife. Many rigs use a large, cross-rib design on the driver tires. If your tires are like this, be wary. You won't have any traction on wet ground. Watch out for skids. A large, cross-rib design can give you ulcers in wet weather, especially if you are bob tailing between picking up trailers. Wait and see for yourself. You'll have your turn at using your head; then you'll remember reading this.

High flotation type tires are especially dangerous, even more so than the large, cross-rib, due to the lack of a tread that will bite into the pavement. Water on the road surface will cause them to hydroplane. What is your protection? Reduce your speed.

Figure 15-4. Special tire treads of today's rigs help a driver keep moving, but they cannot perform beyond what they were designed for. A driver must use common sense to offset poor driving conditions. *Courtesy of The Goodyear Tire and Rubber Company*

TIRES (cont.)

● *Running a Flat Tire*

Dual tires are a safety that the car driver doesn't have. If a tire blows out, at least the truck driver still has the other. So she or he won't usually skid and twist like the car driver with a blow out. However, all this safety is lost if you keep running once you've had a flat.

Shallow dish wheels give a slight concave effect to the rim. They have some advantages, but they can also create problems. Dual tires mounted on shallow dish wheels will contact each other at times - particularly when you're carrying a heavy load. The contact occurs because the clearance between the wheels is slight, sometimes as little as one inch. If one tire becomes soft or flat, it will contact the other tire, create excessive heat and then blow out.

TIRES   (cont.)

Don't run a flat tire if possible. Due to the excessive heat, it will
eventually catch fire. If you want a tough fire to squelch, this is it. When
you see a rig with two flats on an axle, you can be sure the driver had run a
flat. When the first tire went flat, the good tire had to carry the whole load.
Instead of stopping for repair, the driver kept going. Finally, the good tire
blew from overload and the rims hit the ground.

● *Tires and Desert Heat*

When you're running the desert, don't check the air pressure when the
tires are hot. And keep a slightly *higher pressure in a tube-type tire* to cut
the flexing and heat. Don't lower the pressure in hot country. Many unin-
formed drivers do this. But lowering the pressure only creates more heat.
Slow down to 50 mph if you're loaded heavy at midday and you won't have tire
problems. Keep rolling at 60 mph, and I'll guarantee you, tire loss will occur.

REFLECTIONS
AND
SHADOWS | When you're running into the sun, watch the flashes that
will momentarily blind you or hide the application of
stop lights on a vehicle up ahead. You can get a good
deal of reflection from the rear windows of an automobile,
and if it keeps up, you can lose your cool. Another annoyance can come from
your own rear view mirrors. They will cause a reflection if you set them to
take in the sides of your trailer. After you put up with this two or three
times, you'll realize why we suggest setting them differently. Set them so
your normal view is out about four feet from the side of the rig at the rear.
Whether it's day or night, sun or car light reflections from the side of your
trailer will bug you to no end. If the mirrors are out a little, it helps you
on cornering and lessens the trouble-causing blind spots along the sides.

BLIND
SPOTS | All kinds of trailers will have blind spots along both
of their sides. Be aware of these blind spots as you
drive, when you park, and when you're stopped or backing.

But blind spots don't happen only alongside both sides of your trailer.
You have them up front too. Have you ever thought about the corner posts next
to the windshield? How about the posts at the back corners of the cab? Or
how about behind the mirrors? These are all danger zones. How do you avoid
them? Well, let's take the blind spots one by one.

(1)   When you enter an intersection, sit up straight in the seat. Move
      your head forward and back so you can see a car which might be hidden
      behind the windshield strip. A vehicle may be approaching you off to
      one side - back about 200 or 300 feet. As you move out, the path of
      the vehicle could follow right in line with the corner blind spots
      until the two of you have an unplanned meeting.

(2)   Don't take your eyes off the area in front of the hood if you're
      waiting at a stop light in a large, conventional, like a Pete or KW.

BLIND SPOTS (cont.)

The height of the hood will hide anyone, especially a little child. If someone steps off the curb in front of you while your eyes are off the area, you may not see the person. You can hide a subcompact under the nose of a large conventional tractor very easily. So watch this area!

Figure 15-5. There are a number of blind spots and danger spots on this rig. That's why extra spotters ride along. But you won't usually have this type of help. You need to watch the blind spots yourself, including the area hidden by the conventional's hood. *Courtesy of White Motor Corp.*

(3) Cars or bicycles may come down a side street. These may also be hidden behind your mirrors as in #1 above. If you aren't moving forward and back, you may be moving in a collision course with a bike or other vehicle without knowing it.

(4) Your trailer's rear corners, of course, are blind. But it is the little, unnoticed corners that are the bad ones. Again, move forward and back to overcome the hazard. Watch the rear of your trailer while backing. Someone may step out behind the rig at the last minute. *Never back when in doubt. Get out and look first and have someone guide you.* This is the safest way.

(5) Watch low overhead coverings on docks when you're backing. It's often the small nuisance or petty accident that causes a driver to lose a job.

(6) Be wary turning corners. An auto or child on a bike may be trying to sneak beside your trailer as you swing out to clear the corner.

Have you ever expected to have a car coming toward you when you take off a freeway off-ramp? Well, from now on, you'd better expect this and much more.

NIGHT DRIVING

At night, you will have a lot of questions about where the cars are alongside your rig. Rainy weather is especially bad because you get pavement reflections from car lights. The best way to protect yourself is to add the convex-type, paste-on mirrors to your rear view mirrors. (See Figure 15-6.) Another good way to protect yourself is to buy a combination, West Coast type mirror. This kind has a diminishing-type mirror in a separate, lower frame. It is slightly more expensive than a standard mirror, but the advantages are tremendous.

Remember one thing. These bull's eye mirrors, or whatever you want to call them, are a diminishing type. When you see a car in view, it may seem to be 100 feet behind you when it's actually right at your tail end. Use these mirrors to offset your blind spots in lane changing and backing up. They will pick up anything along your sides and rear, but they won't tell you how far the vehicle is from you. Once you've seen it in the bull's eye, you can locate the vehicle in the large mirror and make your move, if clear.

It takes a little practice to use bull's eye mirrors rapidly. Even for a veteran, it takes a moment to tell which lane a car is in when you look into the mirror. You have to identify the traffic lanes. In the moment or so it takes to do this, you can't see what's going on in front of you. That's why a driver has to keep checking the rear view every few minutes. You need to know what's going on all around you, especially in heavy, fast-moving traffic.

It isn't easy to estimate the speed and distances of oncoming traffic at night. This makes passing another vehicle harder at night than during the day. If a car is in front of an oncoming rig, you have double trouble. Here's what can happen. You spot the cab lights that belong to the rig in the distance and think the car's headlights belong to the truck. You don't realize that there's an automobile too. You may not be aware of this until there's a break in the terrain, allowing you to tell that there are two vehicles instead of one. If you try to pass, the closer vehicle, hidden in the headlight pattern, is the one you will run off the road or wipe out.

STAYING AWAKE | Long hours seem to be habitual with good drivers. If you want to stay awake, chew gum when you're tired. Move your eyes and move in the seat often. Keep the cab cool and ventilated. Crunch on peanut brittle, hard candy or raw vegetables. Get out at least once every three hours for coffee and exercise. That's about all you can do. It's just a matter of conditioning yourself.

FOREIGN OBJECTS AND OTHER UNEXPECTED TROUBLES | Have you ever considered that a small bee or wasp can wreck a 35-ton truck? Well, don't forget such things as Mother Nature and her insects. Many a driver has lost control of a rig as a result of being stung on the face or neck while driving, or just by trying to smack one with a pad or glove.

Figure 15-6. Convex-type, paste-on rear view mirror. *From the author's own collection*

FOREIGN OBJECTS AND OTHER UNEXPECTED TROUBLES (cont.)

There are other things, too, that seem small until they cause the wreck of a 35-ton rig. There is dirt carried by a gust of wind that hits you in the side of the face as another rig passes. A rock or bug can bounce off the mirror and hit you in the face. You can hit a fog bank, black ice or frost in a hollow during cold weather. Or, you can be driving along a road and start over a bridge only to find that while the road was clear of frost, the bridge is frozen, and over you go. *You must expect all of these things and more to happen while you're driving.* A truck driver's job is not a scenic tour, so work at it if you expect to be the best. Always expect the unexpected, and you'll stay alive.

EXPECT THE UNEXPECTED | Have you ever watched the rigs coming at you to judge if they are steady or weaving over the center of the road? Have you ever wondered if the drivers might have distorted vision because they're high on pep pills or just tired? Do you expect yourself or another rig near you to blow a steering tire? Well, as we've said before, you'd better. From now on, you take nothing for granted. Trust nothing to luck. Remember, on a two-lane road, the rigs whistle by each other only a foot or so apart when they're passing. Even a strong gust of wind can cause one to stray into the oncoming traffic, causing a head-on collision.

This is a law for truckers: *In a situation where there are quite a few cars or trucks stacked up behind you on a hill, you do not signal the autos around if it appears clear to you.* Here's the reason why. *You* know the signal, but the motorist doesn't. He or she may sit back there wondering what you are doing. Then, all of a sudden, it may dawn on the car driver, "The trucker wants me to pass!" By this time, you may be in a curve or to the crest of a hill, and here they come, along with another vehicle, head-on. It doesn't take much imagination to guess the outcome.

Here is another dandy. You are running downhill, loaded. You are holding her back to a safe speed, and the cars behind come flying down behind you. They are expecting to pass, even though this is a very narrow road. They are traveling about 65 mph, and you are doing about 20 mph. If they don't run into your rear end, you'll be lucky. They may try to go around you when there isn't room and run you off the road, unless you had anticipated the problem.

Or how about rounding a curve to find a car trying to pass a string of vehicles. It's in your lane and here you come. Again, always expect the unexpected. Stay alert and stay alive!

SUMMARY | The story of Marguerite's blunder drove home this point: Know your equipment and its capabilities. There were a couple of secondary points it made too. First, pay attention to instructions. Second, if you're in a pickle, calm down, and take a couple of minutes to consider all the possible solutions. Then, get the help you need, and proceed cautiously.

Light weight rigs can create dangerous situations. Bob tailing can be hazardous because there's no weight on the rear axles. If you brake too fast, the rear axles can lift up, or "hop," and you may lose your braking power. And, if you have a light trailer in tow, you might jackknife. It isn't just modern trailers that are light weight. Tractors are lighter than in the past too. If your trailer is tall and short, it can upset the rig if you go around a curve too fast. You have to get to know your rig and watch the road to avoid danger.

We talked about a lot of problem situations in this chapter. Three of them were proper use of retarders, overhang and sway, and reflections. Remember that your retarder can't do the whole job of stopping a huge diesel. To slow the rig, use your gears and air brake system too. If your load extends beyond your trailer bed, or if your trailer has a long nose, be careful. You don't want it to jackknife or hit another vehicle as you turn a corner. Reflections from lights on a rainy night are especially annoying, but all kinds of reflections cause trouble. You can even get them from the side of your own rig. Set your mirrors so they miss the side of the rig and you'll solve the problem.

There are many kinds of tires, and some are better than others. Get to know the characteristics of your tires. Take their drawbacks into account as you plan your driving techniques. If you get a flat, change it right away. Otherwise, you'll lose the one beside it and you may end up in an accident or with a nasty fire on your hands - or both. In hot climates, cut your speed so your tires don't get so hot that they blow.

We talked a lot about blind spots. Large trucks have many of them. One special caution is this: if you're stopped at an intersection in a conventional cab, keep your eyes on the area around the hood. A person, small car, or bike would be invisible to you if it moved in front of the hood when you were not watching the area. Also, watch the area behind you by moving forward and back in your seat. You don't want to collide with something approaching in a blind spot. Finally, never back if you are not sure it is safe. Have a doubt? Get out. Look. And have someone guide you if needed for absolute safety.

Day or night, use your bull's eye mirror to check your side blind spots, but don't forget: They distort distances. Be very careful when you're passing vehicles. Things are distorted in all kinds of ways at night. Stay awake by keeping the cab cool and full of fresh air. Crunch on something hard, move around, and stop for a break at least every three hours if you're sleepy.

We ended the chapter by saying, "Expect the unexpected." Almost anything can happen. Stay alert and stay alive.

GLOSSARY

intact: Undamaged, in one piece.

overhang: Something that juts out, or projects beyond the trailer bed. An overhang is usually marked with a red flag. If the overhang projects over a specified limit, you have to use a flag to mark it.

▶ CHECKING THE FACTS

Circle the letter of the phrase that best completes each sentence or best answers each question.

1. What did Marguerite do wrong?
    A. She didn't know her equipment's capabilities.
    B. She didn't listen to instructions.
    C. She didn't think before acting.
    D. All of the above.

2. What makes today's rigs dangerous?
    A. They are light weight and comfortable.
    B. The air brake systems don't work if you're bob tailing.
    C. The vans are too high for their length.
    D. The trailers are heavier than the tractors.

3. Your engine retarder works best
    A. if you have tires with a cross-rib design.
    B. if you go lower in your gears while going down a hill.
    C. if you let it work alone and don't let your air brake system interfere.
    D. at high road speeds.

4. An overhang on a trailer may
    A. pull the kingpin out of the fifth wheel.
    B. make the tandem axles "hop" on braking.
    C. affect your steering. It can make the rig sway or even cause a jackknife.
    D. lift the front tractor axle off the roadway.

5. If your tires lose traction on wet or slick ground, you should
    A. drop into a lower gear and increase your road speed.
    B. reduce your road speed.
    C. record the condition on your post-trip inspection sheet.
    D. tell the shop or your boss to buy new tires.

6. What will happen if you run on a flat tire?
    A. Nothing. That's why trucks have dual tires. It reduces the number of breakdowns on the road.
    B. You'll hit the ground.
    C. The flat can contact the tire next to it and cause that one to blow too or catch fire.
    D. You'll bend the tire rim.

7. Say you're driving through the desert on a hot, summer day. To reduce the chance of a blowout, how fast should you travel when loaded heavy?
    A. 50 mph
    B. 55 mph
    C. 60 mph
    D. none of the above

8. Things like the setting sun or car headlights can reflect off the side of a van. To avoid this, set your rear view mirrors so your normal view at the rear corner is about
   A. 8 feet out from rear of trailer
   B. 4 feet out from rear of trailer
   C. 2 feet out from rear of trailer
   D. 6 inches out from rear of trailer

9. Which of the following statements is true?
   A. Rear view and bull's eye mirrors get rid of all blind spots on an interstate rig.
   B. Conventional cabs have blind spots under the hood, but cab-overs don't have any blind spots anywhere if they use bull's eye mirrors.
   C. If your mirrors are set correctly, the only place you'll have blind spots is directly behind the trailer.
   D. Heavy duty diesels have many blind spots. You need to be aware of all of them.

■ GETTING THE MAIN IDEAS

Circle the letter of the phrase that best completes each sentence or best answers each question.

1. Marguerite could have solved her problem by
   A. letting the Cat driver tow her rig into the dock with chains.
   B. moving the Cat to the rear of the trailer to relieve weight at the gooseneck, then backing into the street.
   C. using the dozer blade of the second Cat to push the rig into the dock.
   D. unloading her cargo with a forklift, then pushing the trailer into the dock with the Cat.

2. What makes bob tailing dangerous?
   A. Drivers are used to the weight of a full trailer. It's hard for them to adjust throttle pressure to the lighter weight vehicle.
   B. The air brake system is inefficient without the trailer hooked up.
   C. Drivers tend to hit the brakes too gently. They overcompensate for the loss of weight.
   D. Most of the weight is on the front axle. There's no balancing weight on the rear axles to hold them down.

3. What was the purpose of this chapter?
   A. To point out driving conditions and situations that you should avoid.
   B. To point out situations that arise all the time and help you find ways of dealing with them.
   C. To explain what you should not do in hazardous situations.
   D. To help you select equipment which will help you avoid danger.

4. Which of the following things can cause a jackknife?
   A. Applying the brakes hard while towing an empty, light weight van
   B. Running with an empty tanker combination in wet weather
   C. A long overhang
   D. All of the above

271

5. A bull's eye or diminishing type mirror was designed so you could
   A. get a better idea of how far vehicles are from your rig.
   B. spot vehicles in your blind spots.
   C. reduce the glare of headlights at night.
   D. none of the above.

The last three questions require a short answer each.

6. You're stopped at an intersection in a huge conventional tractor. How can you be sure that you will not run over a child on a tricycle or a person in a wheel chair as you pull out?

_____

_____

7. As you approach an intersection, how do you eliminate blind spots?

_____

8. Why don't you signal motorists to pass you if you are traveling very slowly up a hill and there is a line of vehicles behind you?

_____

_____

★ GOING BEYOND THE FACTS AND IDEAS

1. Here are three major points made in this chapter. Which one do you think is the most important and why?
   A. Always expect the unexpected.
   B. Never back a rig when in doubt.
   C. Know your rig's capabilities.

2. Pulling the information from this chapter, compile your own list of truckers' laws. You may want to make these a trucker's ten commandments, a list of 12 do's and don'ts, whatever. You may even put them on a poster. (It's okay to use laws already stated in the chapter They don't all have to be original.)

3. This chapter lists a number of "unexpected things" that can cause an accident or problem situation. For example, it lists hitting a fog bank, dirt carried by a gust of wind, and bridges that are frozen before the rest of the roadway. What additional "unexpected things" can you list? These should be things drivers should be alert for, but things not listed in this chapter.

Figure 16-1. "Doubles" (a tractor and two semi-trailers) are in common use in states that allow them. The front of the second trailer mounts on a converter dolly. *Courtesy of Utility Trailer Mfg. Co.*

Chapter Sixteen

ENGAGING AND DISENGAGING TRAILERS

IT
HAPPENS
ALL
THE
TIME

Remember back in Chapter 8, "Inspection of Equipment," when we talked about Brenda? You may recall that she performed a beautiful inspection on the entire rig before she took off. She was really going to impress the other drivers who were looking on. The problem was, when she got to her first stop, she found that she'd hooked up to the wrong trailer. So the inspection, good as it was, was on the right tractor, but the wrong trailer. Well, the same thing happened to me one time, but in reverse.

IT HAPPENS ALL THE TIME (cont.)

One Saturday morning, while working in the San Diego area, another driver and I went into town to pick up some tires. It was a hot load for a tire distributor. (That doesn't mean stolen. It means rush cargo.) When we pulled into the yard, we checked the trailer that was supposed to have a partial load of tires in it and couldn't find any tires in that or any of the other vans.

We jumped on the phone and called Bud, our dispatcher. We thought possibly some other driver had already delivered the load and we hadn't been notified.

Bud told us, "No the load is still there waiting. It's gotta be." But, it wasn't.

Then, we asked if anyone else had gone out that morning. Bud said, "Yes, Don has run up to LA to pick up another load with an empty van."

Now we knew where our tires were. There had been a partial load of tires in the van and Don hadn't checked. We had to make a flying run to LA to transfer them and bring them back down to San Diego.

The pickup we had scheduled was supposed to be an easy one. Just go around town, pick up a small load and deliver it. But, thanks to Don, it got complicated.

What we're talking about in this chapter is a complicated subject in itself. It may not seem that way after you've performed the task many times. But when you are first learning how to hook and unhook (engage and disengage) the trailers, there's a lot to consider. The first thing you want to consider, however, is this: Are you hooking up to the correct trailer?

BEFORE YOU READ ON | Something happens as you begin reading a chapter of a book. If you know a lot about the chapter's topic, you may approach it with a small chip on your shoulder. You may be saying to the author, "You can't tell me anything new about that," so you read without picking up much information. On the other hand, you may have a more pleasant feeling. For example, you may feel relieved because the chapter will be easier for you than some of the other chapters have been. Each person's reactions are different. Even your own reactions are different from day to day, depending on your mood.

If you know little or nothing about the subject of the chapter, different feelings surface. You may wonder if you'll be able to understand the chapter, or if it will confuse you. Or, you may approach the chapter with interest because it is going to teach you something and make you better qualified as a driver.

The thing is, each reader approaches a chapter with a different set of background facts, knowledge, experience and attitudes. As we've said before, what's important is that you use the chapter to get what *you need* out of it.

Otherwise, there really isn't much sense reading it. Therefore, we're going to suggest that before you read this chapter, you do two things.

First, write down how you feel about the subject of the chapter. If it's, "This is going to be boring because I've been hooking up trailers for a year without a mishap," write that down. If it's, "I'll never be able to do this until someone shows me how anyway," write that down. If it's, "I've got to get this information into my head," write that down. After all, it's good to identify your feelings.

Second, perhaps even more important, do <u>one</u> of the following things:

1. Make a list of *your* expectations for the chapter. For example, list what it will stress as the key points in making hook-ups. Or, write down the trailer and truck components you think will be used to make hook-ups. Then, read to see if you're right.

2. Write down a few questions *you have* about making hook-ups or unhooking trailers. What problems are you seeking an answer to? Is there something that keeps going wrong when you engage trailers. Maybe your questions are more basic, more like, "Do you need any tools to make a hook-up?" or "What are the major mistakes to avoid?" Whatever you hope this chapter will answer for you - that's the question to ask. Try to write down about five questions. Then, read to answer the questions.

Do one of these two things before reading any further.

Figure 16-2. A single hopper 10-yard-capacity bottom dump pull trailer. It would be used in a set of bottom dumps for both on- and off-highway hauling of dirt, gravel, sand or other bulk materials. *Courtesy of Timpte-Beall, Inc.*

TWIN TRAILERS The use of twin trailers, or doubles, developed in the Western United States. It is now becoming more common in other areas too. Various states still restrict rigs to one trailer, however, and many Eastern states still don't allow twin trailers to be pulled over their highways. Expressways, beltways, motorways, freeways, thruways - whatever you call them, they are becoming more common. As they do, doubles and even triples (the hooking up of three 26 to 30-foot trailers) are becoming widespread. Therefore, we'll be going through the steps for engaging and disengaging the first trailer *and* any additional trailers.

There are two basic reasons for doubles. First, you have an increased cargo area. Second, your load can be split, and you can head toward two destinations at the same time.

But doubles do present a problem in handling to any driver, especially on wet or slick road surfaces. The length of the trailers will vary. They may be 20, 30 or 40 feet long, or somewhere in between. Twin 40-footers are actually safer to handle than two shorts, even though the overall length is greater. The longer length of the boxes has a tendency to stabilize the unit.

Figure 16-3. The DC-5 transspring counterbalanced converter dolly. These are used extensively in doubles operations. Prior to development of this type of dolly, the old dollies were called "man killers" because of their habit of snapping back with the drawbar when weight was placed on their fifth wheel area. *Courtesy of Utility Trailer Mfg. Co.*

THE DRIVER'S RESPONSIBILITY

Many yards and terminals employ persons to handle the hook-ups. Nevertheless, it remains the driver's responsibility to check out the coupled set of doubles before taking it out on the road. Don't take our word for it. Check section 391.31 (c) of the MCSR. Ability to couple and uncouple trailers is included in the driver's road test.

The DOT regs state that a driver who will be driving combos must show skill and competence in, "Coupling and uncoupling of combination units." That is, a driver must be able to hook up the tractor and first trailer. Plus, if he or she drives doubles or triples, the driver has to know how to add additional trailers by using a *dolly*. (See Figure 16-3.) These dollies may also be called *converters* or *auxiliary gears*. When the operation is complete, the result must be a *multi-unit rig* which can be fully controlled from the driver's position in the cab.

A BY THE NUMBERS PROCEDURE	Some companies or trucking terminals have their own procedures for the coupling and uncoupling of trailers. But, we'll study the procedures most often followed by professional truckers - the basic procedures. The object is to make certain that no key point is overlooked.

It is extremely difficult to make hook-ups for a set of twin trailers. How would you like to be driving a triple combination and look in your rear view mirror just in time to see the last trailer heading into oncoming traffic? Or over an embankment? You skip a few steps, obviously, in connecting only one trailer, but the proper and safe connection of it is just as important. One key concept for all drivers to remember is this: *Hook-ups must be properly made.* This fact seems almost too obvious, but it is so important, that it must be stressed.

Because making proper hook-ups is so important, it is wise to follow a step-by-step method. We call it, doing it by the numbers. Here, on the following pages, is the by-the-numbers procedure for make-up and break-up of trailers. We'll start with removing, or disengaging, the last trailer of a set of doubles by separating it from the converter dolly. Next, we disengage the lead trailer from the dolly. Then, we disengage the lead trailer from the tractor. That's sections A - C. Sections D - F are the same process in reverse, that is, making the connections. If the rig you are driving has only a single trailer, you follow the numbers in sections C and D only.

Figure 16-4. Two views of the same accident involving doubles.
When you're driving doubles, don't make any sudden moves or else!
Courtesy of the California Highway Patrol

BREAK-UP AND MAKE-UP OF TWIN TRAILERS

A. Break *Rear* Trailer/Dolly

1. Chock rear trailer wheels.

2. Crank landing gear down.

3. Close air line valves on rear of *lead* trailer.

4. Disconnect air lines between *rear* trailer and dolly and stow them on the dolly.

5. Disconnect electrical pigtail between the rear trailer and dolly and stow on dolly.

6. Disengage fifth wheel/kingpin lock on *dolly* (converter gear).

7. Bleed off dolly air tank.

8. Slowly drive away from rear trailer.

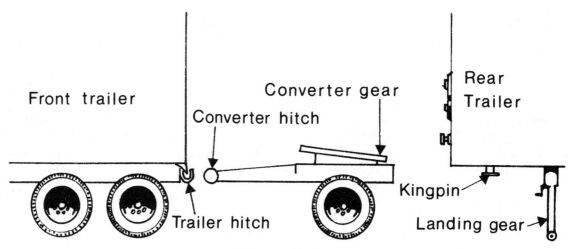

Figure 16-5.

B. Break *Lead* Trailer/Dolly

9. Chock dolly wheels.

10. Disconnect air lines between *front* trailer and dolly (from rear of front trailer) and stow on dolly.

11. Disconnect electrical pigtail between front trailer and dolly (from rear of front trailer) and stow on dolly.

12. Lower *dolly* landing gear or stand; release pintle hook (trailer hitch) lock.

13. Unhook safety chain and separate dolly from trailer.

C. Break *Tractor/Trailer*

14. Release tractor protection valve (breakaway valve).

15. Chock trailer wheels.

16. Crank landing gear down.

17. Disengage fifth wheel/kingpin lock on trailer.

18. Disconnect air lines from trailer and stow on *tractor*.

19. Disconnect electrical pigtail from trailer and stow on *tractor*.

20. Slowly drive away from trailer.

D. Make *Tractor/Trailer*

21. Align and back tractor towards trailer - fifth wheel against trailer. (See Figure 6-7.)

22. Insure that trailer wheels are properly chocked.

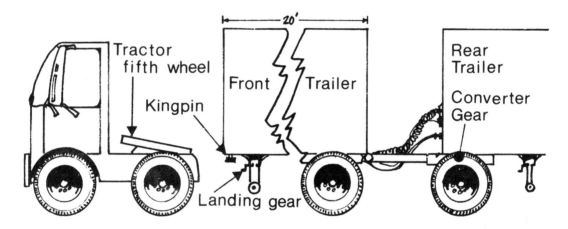

Figure 16-6.

23. Connect tractor air lines to trailer.

24. Connect tractor electrical pigtail to trailer.

25. Activate tractor protection valve (breakaway valve), supplying air to trailer.

26. Apply trailer brake (trailer hand valve). Approximately two inches travel on lever of hand valve should be sufficient.

27. Back tractor under trailer to engage and lock fifth wheel/kingpin. (See Figure 6-7.)

28. Make forward gear tug against pin to insure locking.

29. Make visual check of fifth wheel/kingpin lock. Crank up landing gear.

30. Remove chocks from trailer wheels.

BREAK-UP AND MAKE-UP OF TWIN TRAILERS (cont.)

E. Make *Lead* Trailer/Dolly

31. Position *dolly eye* (converter hitch) to engage in pintle (trailer hitch) on rear of lead trailer. (See Figure 16-5.)

32. Raise *dolly* landing gear or stand. Engage and secure pintle lock.

33. Hook safety chain. The hook opening should be towards the lead trailer. Make a forward motion with the open end of the hook.

34. Connect dolly air lines to <u>rear</u> of *lead* trailer.

35. Connect dolly electrical pigtail to <u>rear</u> of *lead* trailer.

F. Make *Rear* Trailer/Dolly

36. Close dolly air tank petcock (drain valve).

37. Connect dolly emergency air line to *rear* trailer.

38. Open emergency air line valve on *lead* trailer to charge *rear* trailer.

39. Close emergency air line valve on *lead* trailer.

40. Disconnect dolly emergency air line from *rear* trailer.

41. Bleed off dolly air tank.

42. Back dolly under rear trailer to engage and lock fifth wheel/kingpin. (See Figure 16-5.)

43. Make forward gear tug against pin to insure locking.

44. Make visual check of fifth wheel/kingpin lock.

45. Connect dolly air lines to *rear* trailer.

46. Connect electrical pigtail to *rear* trailer.

47. Open air line valves on *lead* trailer.

48. Crank *rear* trailer landing gear up.

49. Check out air brake slack adjuster action on lead trailer. ☆

50. Check out air brake slack adjuster action on dolly. ☆

51. Check out air brake slack adjuster action on rear trailer. ☆

☆ The slack adjusters are your best indicator of whether your brakes are on or off. If you can move the slack adjusters by hand, the brakes are off. If you can't budge the slack adjusters at all, the brakes are applied.

▷ Remember: As equipment changes, it is your responsibility as a driver to keep up with the latest changes.

▷ *NOTE: After you have made the various connections, you will want to check out the air brake system. If all air lines are hooked up okay and not crossed, the brakes on the trailer and converter dolly wheels will be in the off position (retracted) when the tractor protection valve is in the normal run position.*

Go to the cab and apply the foot valve. All the brakes should come on if you have made your connections properly. If the brakes stay on, after you've lifted your foot off the foot valve, start looking for a problem.

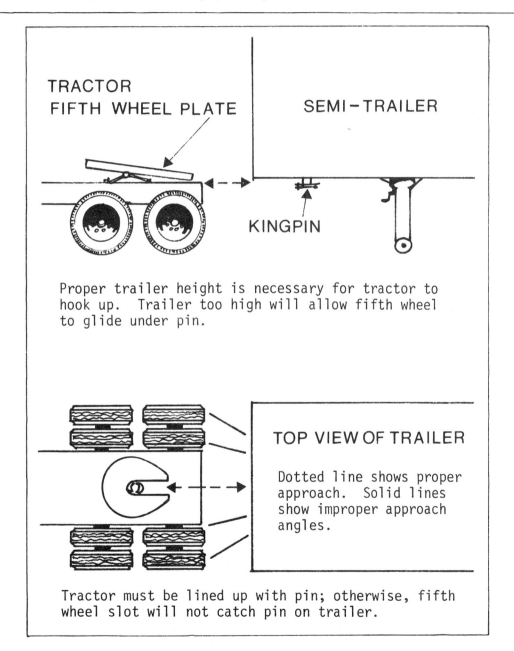

TRACTOR
FIFTH WHEEL PLATE

SEMI-TRAILER

KINGPIN

Proper trailer height is necessary for tractor to hook up. Trailer too high will allow fifth wheel to glide under pin.

TOP VIEW OF TRAILER

Dotted line shows proper approach. Solid lines show improper approach angles.

Tractor must be lined up with pin; otherwise, fifth wheel slot will not catch pin on trailer.

Figure 16-7. Side and top views of tractor-trailer approaches. If the trailer is too high as you approach, or if you approach from an angle, the fifth wheel and kingpin won't meet and no connection will be made.

IN CLOSING In making tractor-trailer hook-ups, keep the following points in mind:

- Procedures will vary from company to company. Follow the company or terminal regulations where you are working.

- Always examine all aspects of any trucking operation from a safety first standpoint.

- Safety of your unit and the motoring public is of prime importance as well as your fast, efficient performance behind the wheel and while loading or unloading freight.

- If you don't understand how your rig functions, you will have doubt and anxiety which may cause you to lose attention to traffic and have an accident. Therefore, learn well the method of hook-up and drop to eliminate any error.

Figure 16-8. One has to ask what happened in this accident involving doubles and what happened to the driver. *Courtesy of the California Highway Patrol*

When you have taken care of all of the above points, your hook-up operation is complete. Remember, if you did not couple the vehicles yourself, you will want to test the hook-up before you head out from the terminal. (Review Chapter 6, "Testing the Hook-up." If you have followed the method above by the numbers, you've tested the hook-up as a part of your procedure.) When you have completed your coupling procedure and it has been tested, you are ready to roll and make your scheduled deliveries.

SUMMARY It is difficult to summarize the key points in this chapter. You may have found this out for yourself if you tried to write down the key points as you read. Each and every action you take in disengaging trailers is a key action. You can't leave any of them out. And the importance of each action is even greater when you're engaging trailers because you don't want the units to become uncoupled on the road.

Figure 16-9. Examine all aspects of trucking from a safety first angle. *Courtesy California Highway Patrol*

Therefore, the best thing you can do right now is to reread the charts, titled, "Break-up and Make-up of Twin Trailers." Let that take the place of your summary. As you read, try to see the importance of each action. And try to come up with some way of your own for remembering the order in which you should take each action.

GLOSSARY |

dolly eye (converter hitch): A circular catch (shaped like a donut), made of heavy metal. It is used to secure the converter dolly to the trailer in front of it. Also known as converter ring, tongue ring, or eye.

disengage (break): Detach or uncouple; unhook.

hot load: Rush cargo; an emergency shipment of cargo needed in a hurry. Also, an illegal shipment.

lead trailer: The front trailer in a set of doubles or triples. The trailer secured directly to the tractor or truck.

pintle (trailer hitch): A hook used to connect one thing with another. The trailer hitch secures the trailer to the converter dolly, working with the dolly eye like a hook and eye.

pull trailer: A trailer with axles and wheels at the front and back; a full trailer.

slack adjuster: A lever device for mechanically adjusting the S cam shaft between floating ends of brake shoes to remove slack generated by worn shoes.

stabilize: To make steady or secure.

triple: A combination (or multi-unit rig) with three trailers.

▶ CHECKING THE FACTS

Put a plus (+) before the statement if it is true. Put a zero (0) before the statement if it is false.

_____ 1. There are only two times when a driver doesn't need to know how to engage and disengage trailers: (1) if the driver never drives them, and (2) if the company has someone hired to do it.

_____ 2. You can add a second trailer to a combination by using a dolly.

_____ 3. Converter dollies have landing gear and an air tank.

_____ 4. After you break rear trailer and dolly, you bleed the dolly air tank. Then, you break the lead trailer and dolly.

_____ 5. You crank down the lead trailer's landing gear before you unhook the lead trailer and tractor at the fifth wheel/kingpin.

_____ 6. You make the fifth wheel/kingpin connection between tractor and trailer. <u>Then</u>, you attach the glad hands and electrical pigtail.

_____ 7. You secure the dolly to the rear trailer. <u>Then</u>, you attach the converter gear to the lead trailer.

_____ 8. Here's the next thing you do after making the tractor-trailer coupling: Test the connection. To do this, drive forward against the pin to tug on it and be sure it is locked tight.

■ GETTING THE MAIN IDEAS

Put a plus (+) before the statement if it is true. Put a zero (0) before the statement if it is false.

_____ 1. All US states allow doubles on interstate highways.

_____ 2. If your rig has a trailer hand valve, you don't need to chock the trailer wheels when breaking them.

_____ 3. The air lines and electrical pigtail for both the <u>back</u> of the lead trailer and the front of the rear trailer are stowed on the converter gear.

_____ 4. The connection between the dolly and the <u>rear</u> of the <u>lead</u> trailer is made with an auxiliary fifth wheel <u>and</u> kingpin.

_____ 5. To disengage the pintle hook and dolly eye, you <u>manually</u> lift the eye off the pintle.

_____ 6. If you're driving a triple, you probably have <u>two</u> converter dollies (except where you have one or more <u>pull</u> trailers).

_____ 7. Some of the steps for engaging trailers which are listed in this chapter are "double checks." That is, beginning drivers should follow them to be sure they haven't missed anything, but experienced drivers will often skip them.

_____ 8. All aspects of trucking should be looked at from the angle of safety first.

★ GOING BEYOND THE FACTS AND IDEAS

1. Have you ever made tractor-lead trailer connections? Was the system you followed different, in any part, from the by-the-numbers method in this chapter? If so, discuss the differences; then tell which method seems better, safer, more efficient to you.

2. List <u>each</u> action you take when you make-up twin trailers to get the <u>brakes</u> to work on both trailers. Tell why each action is important for the brakes to work properly. Then, list each thing you do when you disengage twin trailers to disconnect the braking system and why each action is important. (List only those actions you do that relate to the braking system operation.)

Figure 17-1. Typical truck terminal showing tractor leaving dock
with trailer. *Courtesy of American Trucking Associations, Inc.*

Chapter Seventeen

YARD MANEUVERING

BEFORE
YOU
READ

Back in Chapter 4, we introduced you to the things all
drivers are tested on during the road test. There are
seven skills which every driver must be able to perform
competently. These are minimums which means this: You
may know how to do more, but you must know *at least how to do these things.*
We'll list them on the following page and see how well we're doing at covering
these areas. A chart might be useful.

	Skill Required	Chapter Covering the Skill
1	Performing a pre-trip inspection	.Chapter 8
2	Placing the vehicle in operation	.Chapter 6
	Smoothness of handling the vehicle	.Chapters 6, 9, 11
3	Coupling and uncoupling combination units	.Chapter 16
4	Backing the vehicle	.Chapter 11
	Parking the vehicle	
5	Braking	.Chapter 9
	Slowing the vehicle by means other than braking	.Chapter 6 (gearing down) Chapter 13 (using retarders)
6	Operating the vehicle in traffic	.Chapter 7 (DOT regulations) Chapter 15 (blind spots, etc.)
	Passing other vehicles	.Chapter 7 (DOT regulations) Chapter 15 (night driving)
7	General driving ability	.Throughout the book
	Knowledge of rules and regs	.Chapers 3, 4, 7
	Handling freight	

We'll be going over some of these categories again from a different angle in future chapters. For example, there will be more rules and regs in Chapters 19, 20, 22, 24, and 25, and more on smoothness of handling the vehicle and general driving ability in Chapter 23.

But where are the gaps in the above chart? What have we neglected altogether? Write the two areas in the space below:

_____

_____

BEFORE YOU READ   (cont.)

Well, we aren't going to neglect them for much longer. In this chapter,
our subject is parking the vehicle, and in the next chapter, it's handling
freight. Let's take a moment to preview the chapter.

Before your future employer gives you a test in traffic, you'll probably
be tested in the yard. It makes sense because this gives your examiner a
chance to see how you do with a minimum of risk to you, company personnel, the
equipment and other highway users. If you don't do well enough on your yard
test, you may never get out on the highway. But, while it makes sense, it also
means that you have to handle some of the most difficult things first. You may
have to maneuver the rig around docks, barricades, holes, and barrels.

We'll begin the chapter by giving you some key ideas to keep in mind whenever you approach a dock and park (or spot) your trailer. We'll list the most
common types of docks and provide you with illustrations of many of them.
Then, we'll focus on two special kinds of yard maneuvering: spotting trailers
on railroad flat cars and parallel parking. Next, just to be sure you feel
secure about passing your yard test, we'll explain just what is expected of you
during the test. We'll cover the four most common sub-tests of the yard test:
the alley dock problem, the offset alley problem, the serpentine problem, and
the parallel parking problem.

ANALYZE
THE
SITUATION
This may sound like an odd way to begin a chapter on
yard maneuvering, but it's the only logical place to
start. Before you can proceed into any yard or dock
area, you must stop and *analyze the situation*. Every
time you approach a dock, you have a different set of circumstances. Even if
you park your trailer in the same terminal every day, circumstances can vary.
Trucks, trailers, autos, equipment, etc. in the yard all form obstacles. You
will have to vary your driving technique to get around these obstacles and up
to the dock.

Everything depends on being set up right from the beginning. In other
words, stop, analyze the situation (check out the dock or hole and all obstacles), and decide how you should make your approach. Get yourself set up right
before you take a shot at maneuvering toward that hole.

I have seen good road drivers literally fall apart in a cab when they are
required to back into a tight spot. A simple thing like going out into a dirt
field to turn around may cause you more grief than you can imagine, especially
if there has been a recent rain or if the ground was plowed not too long ago.
You drive onto the field and, before you know it, you get that sinking sensation. The weight of your rig causes it to sink deeper and deeper into the dirt,
and the next thing you know, you have a nice towing bill. So remember this:
Before you go into an open field, look it over. If necessary walk it before
you drive it.

It isn't just dirt that a heavy rig can sink into either. Truck yards are
built to handle heavy rigs, but many supermarket and shopping centers are not
paved to handle your weight. *Watch for signs in these areas*. If there's a

sign saying, "No trucks," "No heavy trucks," or something like that, don't drive or park in the area. If you do, you may wind up paying for a new paving job. Remember, shopping centers and supermarket parking lots are not truck terminals. There may be a good reason why heavy-duty trucks are not allowed.

SPOTTERS AND YARD MULES

Normally, running a rig coast to coast involves very little backing, if any at all. As incredible as it may seem, a driver can drive from New York to California and never back a truck. Ever heard a driver say, "I don't get paid for going backward"? You will. Some drivers seem to pride themselves on the fact that they never back a rig. That's not such a good idea. Eventually, every driver is going to have to park a rig at a dock. In fact, 90% of the time, you'll be doing your own spotting, so it's best to learn how from the beginning.

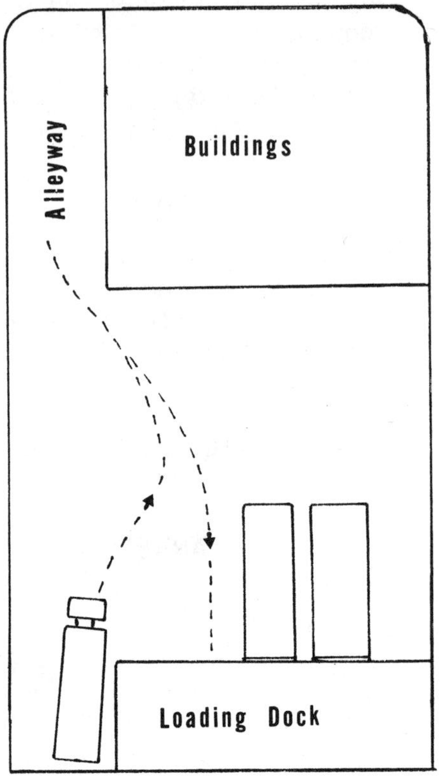

Some yards or terminals will have spotters. These persons have the job of picking up trailers that drivers have dropped and parking, or spotting, them at the dock. If you arrive at a dock with a spotter, you're on Easy Street.

Usually a spotter will have a special tractor, designed to shuttle trailers around the yard. Truckers have a lot of names for these tractors: *shuttle tractors, jockey tractors, yard mules and Gotes* are four of their names. Yard mules make the job of spotting quicker and easier because they have hydraulic-lift fifth wheels. The spotter runs the fifth wheel under the kingpin, then uses the hydraulic fifth wheel to lift the trailer up. The landing gear never has to be drawn up because the mule has lifted it off the ground. Using a yard mule, a spotter can move trailers around a yard in half the time it would take a driver without a mule to do it.

Figure 17-2. Limited access straight dock beside an alleyway.

The spotter, or trailer jockey, will break up the line rigs and spot the trailers where they are needed. The jockey also makes up the units for the road and sets them at the ready line for the road driver.

SPOTTING THE RIG YOURSELF

Only the large truck terminals have spotters. The rest of the time (90% of the time), you'll have to park your own trailer. Therefore, you will have to know the basic approaches and how to set yourself up. If not, you are

SPOTTING THE RIG YOURSELF   (cont.)

going to do a lot of unnecessary work. You may end up losing your cool a number of times before you get smart and realize there must be an easier way to do it. Here are the basic steps to follow:

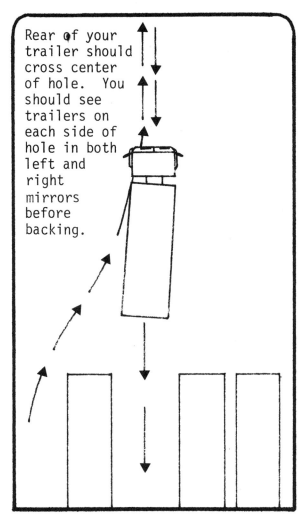

Rear of your trailer should cross center of hole. You should see trailers on each side of hole in both left and right mirrors before backing.

Figure 17-3. A straight platform with no obstacles but with very little clearance on either side of the hole.

1. Look the situation over.

2. Plan your moves.

3. Make your move. Use your mirrors properly if you are backing.

4. If you realize you've started off wrong, stop, pull away and try again.

It will help to keep a couple of points in mind. First, don't let the nose of your tractor get boxed in. Leave yourself room to maneuver in. Second, make sure you're clear of people and obstacles. Watch out for autos, forklifts, and other trucks and for obstacles such as fire plugs, drain pipes protruding out of building walls, etc. Above all, look out for people who might be in the area - pedestrians and other workers. Remember, you have *six sides* to your rig. Don't forget about the front and rear top sections of your trailer. Don't start into a dock and wind up taking the roof off your trailer or off the building.

KINDS OF DOCKS

As we said above, there are many different types of docks. Here are the major kinds:

1. Straight platforms   (See Figures 17-2 and 17-3.)

2. Dog leg or angle docks   (See Figure 17-4.)

3. Recessed docks   (See Figure 17-6.)

4. Dead end yards with corner docks   (See Figure 17-7.)

5. Docks inside warehouses

6. Step docks

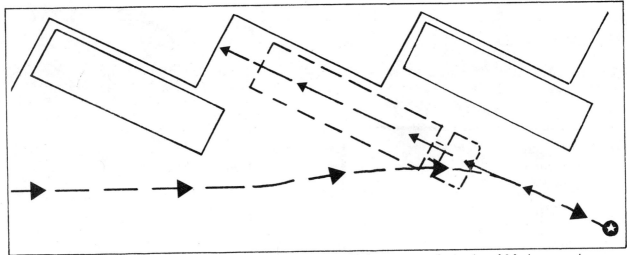

Figure 17-4. Dog leg or angle dock. This type of dock will be used where there is a lack of parking area or cramped quarters. Notice that the tractor is angled slightly to the left. The driver used the left-hand mirror the majority of the time.

KINDS OF DOCKS (cont.)

7. Parallel docks (See Figure 17-9.)

8. Flush street doors on the side of a building

9. Underground docking complexes or subway docks (See Figure 17-5.)

10. Piers

11. Railroad box car doors

12. Railroad flat cars (See Figure 17-8.)

Each type of dock requires specific maneuvering techniques which are best learned on the rig. However, there are some general pointers which will help you spot your rig in a variety of places.

- If you're backing into a straight hole, you should be able to see the hole with both side mirrors.

- If the hole is on the left side of your vehicle, you should be able to see the hole in your left-hand mirror.

- If the hole is on the right side of your vehicle, you should be able to see the hole in your right-hand mirror.

If you can see the hole as described above, you know you're set up right to begin with. In addition, two abilities will help you approach many different docks: *backing* and *parallel parking*. We discussed backing in Chapter 11 and we'll discuss parallel parking later in this chapter.

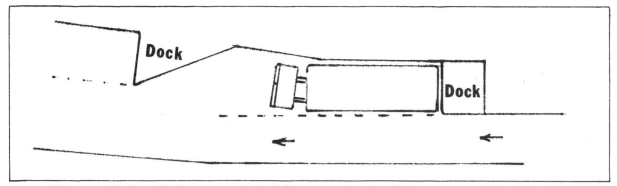

Figure 17-5. Underground docking complex. This type of docking requires heavy attention to both your mirrors. The dotted line indicates a guideline which is normally painted on the pavement. You must stay inside of this guideline to stay clear of flowing traffic. Some underground docks use curbing instead of guidelines.

KINDS OF DOCKS (cont.)

Each dock has its own problems. You may have to drive down an alley, under an overhang or overhead pipe, or down a narrow street to get to the dock. Learning how to maneuver your rig in these docks is all a matter of practice, nothing more. Look at the dock. Figure out what you should do to approach it. Then, proceed cautiously. Most important, don't be afraid to stop and check your position if you need to after you've moved a few feet. If you need to have another worker call out directions to you as you maneuver, do it. The idea is not to look like a flashy driver. The idea is to spot your trailer at the dock without damage to your rig, the cargo, the dock, or anything in the yard.

Figure 17-6. Recessed dock. This type of dock simply requires straight docking down into a hole.

Careful examination of the illustrations in this chapter will help you approach various kinds of docks. Pay special attention to the arrows in the illustrations. As you examine the drawings, ask yourself how you should turn your tractor and trailer to wind up safely in the hole.

When you approach a new type of dock, don't think of it as a headache. Think of it as a way to improve your skills at maneuvering. Once you have successfully handled all the kinds of docks listed above, you will be quite proficient at yard maneuvering. The more of these docks you encounter as a new driver the better you'll drive.

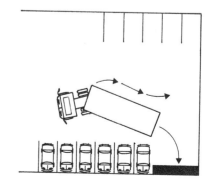

Figure 17-7. Dead end yard with corner dock.

A TOUGH
TYPE OF
BACKING

Under "Kinds of Docks," above, we mentioned railroad
flat cars. What you're trying to do here is spot your
trailer on a railroad flat car. The idea is to back
the rig onto a flat car, disengage the tractor from the
trailer, and secure the trailer to the flat car. Then, your trailer will ride
piggy-back to its destination. (See Figure 17-8. Truckers call trailers on
railroad cars "pigs.") Although this involves only straight backing, it is
probably the most difficult type of backing you'll ever encounter. So a few
words of caution seem appropriate.

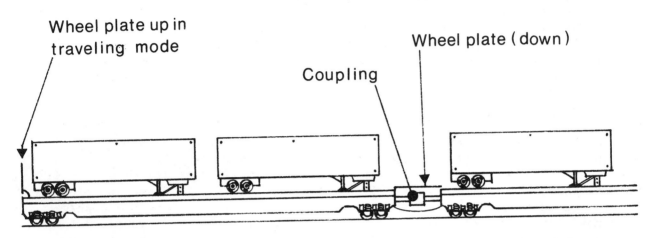

Figure 17-8. Trailers riding piggy-back. Before you begin driving
(backing) from one flat car to another, be sure the wheel plates are
down.

You'll usually load more than one trailer (or pig) at a time when you're
doing this type of loading. In fact, you'll usually see two or three flat cars
shoved into a dock, and you'll have to load them all full of trailers, one
right after the other. This can be a hair-raising experience if you don't know
what you're doing. For one thing, if you don't back perfectly straight, you
and your rig can fall right off the side of the flat car.

Between each car, you'll find wheel plates or coupling plates. (See Figure 17-8.) The purpose of the wheel plates is to cover the couplings between
the railroad cars so you can drive from one car to another. So, the first
thing you do before driving onto the cars is this: Put down the wheel plates
between railroad cars. Then, begin by backing the first semi-trailer clear out
to the furthest end car. Drop the trailer there; then go get another one. Taking one trailer out at a time, gradually work your way back to the car nearest
the dock. (Warning: Be sure to chock the flat cars to keep them from rolling.)

You have to drop the trailer in exactly the right spot on the railroad
car. A fifth wheel plate on the flat car secures the trailer during transit.
This fifth wheel plate is cranked up mechanically from the floor of the car
and mates with the trailer pin to support and stabilize the trailer. If you
aren't in the right spot, you won't be able to make the connection between the
trailer kingpin and the fifth wheel, and you won't be able to stabilize the
nose of the trailer for transit.

SEALED
TRAILERS │ Many trailers involved in piggy-back operations are
sealed. This means that a thin metal strip, approximately 8 inches by ¼ inch wide, is inserted through the
door lock where the padlock would ordinarily be. One end of the seal inserts
into a locking device on the other end of the seal strip. Seals are one-time
units. Once they are locked, you can't separate the ends. They must be cut
off. All seals are coded and numbered to keep cargo safe.

The obvious reason for sealing trailers is security of the cargo. This is
especially important on trailers traveling by rail because during stops some
flat cars may be out of view of security agents and railroad workers.

Trailers being hauled over the road are also sealed sometimes, especially
when the cargo is very expensive or very appealing. Typically, frozen meats,
beer and alcohol and extremely valuable commodities like jewelry would travel
in sealed trailers. No matter whose seal is on a trailer, make sure it stays
intact. Don't let anyone pull the seal off until you're sure the person who
is to receive the cargo has accepted the load.

Also, when you're loading cargo that is to be sealed, don't pull away
from the dock until you're told to do so. At the dock, you or a dock worker
can keep an eye on the cargo. If you pull away, someone might steal something
before the seal has been put in place. You never know when someone has a key
for a padlock, but a seal can't be broken without you noticing it. So don't
pull away until you're told to do so and only when the authorized person is
ready to place the seal on the door.

PARALLEL
PARKING │ Parallel parking is difficult to learn without actually
being in the rig and practicing. Each vehicle will back
and turn differently. When and how fast do you turn a
wheel? When do you reverse the steering wheel direction? It's hard to say.
It depends upon the truck's wheel base and other considerations. Therefore,
we have kept our comments about how to parallel park straight trucks and semis
to a minimum. There are a few basics that you ought to learn before you get
into the cab and here they are.

● *Parallel Parking a Straight Truck*

When you approach a parking space, make the front of the unit weave slightly into the hole. Continue forward, bringing the nose of the vehicle back out
of the hole and traveling slightly beyond the obstacle in the way. This leaves
the back of your unit facing into the hole. As you back in, turn the unit so
the right rear wheels head toward the curb. When the unit is approximately
two-thirds of the way into the hole and the right front corner of the truck has
cleared the obstacle, turn the steering wheel to the left as quickly as possible, while backing the truck very slowly. This will allow the front of the
truck to come into the curbing, placing you in a position parallel to the curb.

To be legally parked at a curb, the truck should be within 12 inches of
the curb at the side of the front and rear tires. But, in many cases, considering the width of the truck, you may need to place the wheels within *an inch
or two* of the curb to keep the left side from protruding into the traffic lane.

293

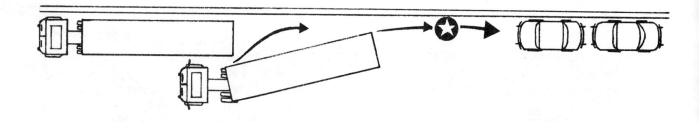

Parallel Parking

1. Pull trailer halfway up side of parked rig.
2. Right mirror should see curbing where ✪ is shown.
3. Rear wheels should be three foot from curb at ✪ .
4. With rear wheels at ✪ your tractor should be at rear of parked rig.
5. Turn your tractor rear sharply to curb. When wheels are four foot
    from curb, quickly turn tractor nose to curb.

Figure 17-9.

PARALLEL PARKING   (cont.)

● *Parallel Parking a Semi-Trailer*

Let's say you have a 40-foot trailer and a 15-foot tractor, for a total length of 55 feet. To parallel park at a curb, you must have at least 60 or 65 feet of space to allow you to maneuver into the hole.

As you approach the hole, weave the tractor slowly into the parking hole, coming back out again with the tractor to the left to clear any obstacle in front. This maneuver should not take the right front corner of the tractor any closer than about four feet from the curb. As you come out of the hole with the tractor heading slightly to the left (back into the traffic lane) immediately start turning toward the right. This should put your tractor about parallel with a vehicle (if one is parked there), and about five feet away from it. You should be able to look into your rear view mirror and see down the right side of your trailer and into the hole.

As you back up, because of the angle of your truck at this point, the rear of the trailer should start into the hole. When the rear trailer wheels are approximately two-thirds of the distance back into the hole, approximately three feet from the curbing, you should start turning the back of the tractor into the hole. When the back of the tractor is at about the 45° angle, your tractor wheels should be approximately four feet from the curbing. As soon as the front of the tractor clears whatever is on the right side, immediately and quickly turn the steering wheel as far as you can to bring the nose of the tractor into the hole, headed for the curbing. If you didn't break the tractor too sharply backing in for the curb, this should put your whole rig within inches of the curb line.

Figure 17-10. Driver pulls a dry freight van away from the receiving dock. *Courtesy of American Trucking Associations, Inc.*

As you are backing the tractor towards the curbing, you needn't worry too much about the trailer wheels climbing the curb if you are positioned properly. The rear of the trailer will have a tendency to come back out of the hole as the tractor backs in. If you do find the rear wheels of the trailer hitting the curb too soon, however, pull forward about six or eight feet and break the rear of the tractor into the curbing a little sooner. This will cause the trailer wheels to track away from the curb sooner.

YARD TESTS | Most yard tests consist of backing into holes at a loading dock to check the applicant's ability to handle a truck or semi. Points are deducted for an excessive amount of corrections or pullups when backing into a hole.

You start with 50 points, and for each correction, you lose five points during the test. Any hard bumping into a dock when backing or getting too close to another vehicle will cause you to lose points. Getting too close to another rig will cause you to lose points because you'll have to pull forward and correct. If you misalign a unit at a dock, you will also lose points.

● *The Alley Dock Problem*

To test a driver's docking ability, a driver must maneuver the vehicle between other units or barricades and stop within a specified distance from the loading platform. (See Figure 17-11.) The idea is to see how well a driver can perform under conditions a driver meets daily in pickup and delivery.

YARD TESTS (cont.)

This type of maneuvering may also be required when a driver encounters detours, traffic accidents, etc. (In fact, the type of driving required in all four problems might be required in clearing a roadway after an accident or other problem.) Demerits, or loss of points, are usually for stricking a barricade, running over a curb, making too many maneuvers or corrections when backing, or endangering nearby equipment.

● *Offset Alley Problem*

In the Offset Alley Problem, drivers must maneuver their vehicles between offset barricades by moving forward. (See Figure 17-12.) The movement must be continuous. Any stops or re-positioning of a vehicle is penalized by loss of points. The objective is to have the driver watch on four corners of the unit so the vehicle is not bumped or scraped while traveling through tight spots. A typical test starts with 50 points and five points are subtracted for each infraction. These maneuvers may also be timed.

● *The Serpentine Problem*

The Serpentine Problem requires a driver to drive between barricades, weaving in and out, without stopping and without touching any of the obstacles. After driving through, the driver has to back through, using the same maneuvers. Again, the idea is to create a situation similar to everyday driving problems, and scoring is usually the same as in other tests.

● *Parallel Parking Problem*

As you might imagine, in the Parallel Parking Problem, you have to park your unit parallel to a curb or something made to look like a curb. Your skill at this task will show whether or not your are ready to do things like make curbside deliveries and park at truck stops for that much needed hot breakfast and cup of hundred mile coffee. You will have a

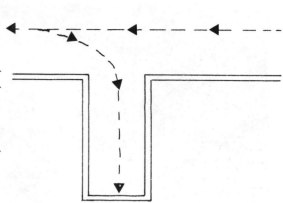

Figure 17-11. The Alley Dock Problem.

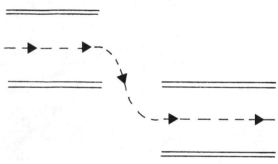

Figure 17-12. The Offset Alley Problem.

Figure 17-13. The Serpentine Problem.

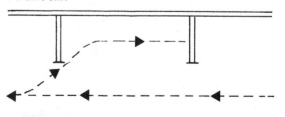

Figure 17-14. The Parallel Parking Problem.

limited area to do this in and will be required to come within a specified number of inches of the curb. You may be timed, and a lot of maneuvering back and forth or hitting a barrier or curb will make you lose points.

SUMMARY | In this chapter, we focused on parking the vehicle. Each yard, terminal and dock is different, so you will need to vary your maneuvering techniques to suit each situation. However, there are some rules that apply to all docking situations. First, analyze the situation; look it over. Second, plan your moves. Third, make your move toward the dock, proceeding cautiously. Fourth, if you find you aren't approaching as you need to be, stop, pull away and try again. Finally, don't rely on your mirrors alone. If you aren't sure you won't hit anything, get out and check before backing in.

Some large terminals employ spotters. Their job is to shuttle trailers around the yard, spotting them where they are needed. Spotters may also make up the units for the road drivers. Many spotters use yard mules for moving trailers around.

After looking at various kinds of docks, we focused on two types of maneuvering: spotting trailers on railroad flat cars and parallel parking. Three things to remember in spotting pigs are (1) put down the wheel plates, (2) begin by loading the pig on the furthest car out and working up toward the dock, and (3) back absolutely straight. Parallel parking is different for a straight truck and semi-trailer, as is all backing. However, in any parallel parking maneuver, weave slightly into the hole as you drive forward. This will set your back up toward the space you're moving into. After you've completed your maneuver, check to see that your distance from the curb is legal, not more than one foot away from the curb.

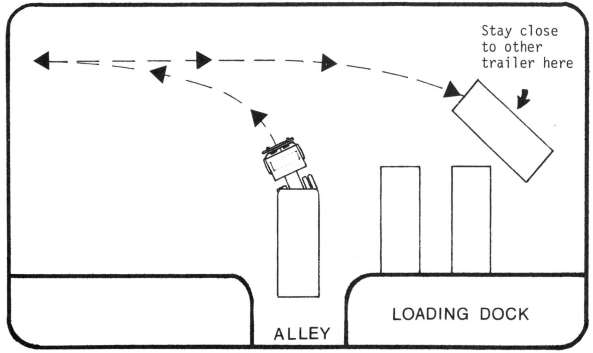

Figure 17-15.

SUMMARY (cont.)

Many trucking companies will begin your road test with a yard test, consisting of four problems: The Alley Dock Problem, the Offset Alley Problem, the Serpentine Problem, and the Parallel Parking Problem. The idea of these tests is to simulate actual driving problems without endangering the company equipment, the examiner or other personnel, the applicant or other motorists on the open road. Each driver begins with a given number of points, usually 50 for each "problem." Points are deducted for things like striking a barricade; running over a curb; too many maneuvers, pullups or corrections; and for other indications that the driver is having trouble maneuvering the vehicle or vehicles.

GLOSSARY

dock: A platform where trucks are loaded and unloaded.

hole: An area between parked rigs; a dock or space at a dock.

misalign: To line up poorly; to fail to bring into a straight line.

misjudgment: A poor choice; an error in judgment.

piggy-back operation: Railroad flat cars loaded with truck trailers. Trailers, often called pigs, are secured to the flat car by fifth wheels which crank up mechanically from the car floor. Chains help to secure the trailers.

spot: To park, or to position and then park.

spotter: An employee whose job it is to park vehicles brought in by line drivers. The word is also used to refer to workers who ride along on an oversized haul to see that no obstacles are encountered and to point out obstacles if they appear.

sealed trailer: A trailer locked with a thin metal strip instead of a padlock. Sealing a trailer is a security measure. Usually, a sealed trailer must be signed for before it is opened.

wheel plate: A metal plate which, when lowered, covers the coupling between two railroad cars. Also called coupling plate.

yard mule: A truck tractor specially designed to move trailers around in a terminal. A hydraulic fifth wheel lifts the trailer's landing gear off the ground, speeding the process of pickup and drop-off of trailers.

Circle the letter of the phrase that <u>best</u> completes each sentence or
<u>best</u> answers each question.

1. Before you can proceed into any yard or dock area, you must
   A. perform your post-trip inspection.
   B. break the seal on your trailer if you're driving a sealed trailer.
   C. stop and analyze the situation.
   D. turn your rig around and back in.

2. In the trucking industry, a spotter
   A. paints worn spots on trucks.
   B. takes stains out of clothing, rugs, etc., being hauled.
   C. is an insurance agent who reports poor driving techniques to a
      driver's employer.
   D. has the job of moving trailers from one location to another within
      a terminal.

3. Parking a rig
   A. is a part of your road test.
   B. is best done by the dispatcher.
   C. is 90% of your job as a coast-to-coast driver.
   D. None of the above.

4. A dog leg or angle dock is usually found where
   A. they have poor drivers.
   B. there are cramped quarters.
   C. only in terminals for short trailers.
   D. a large percentage of the trailers are 40-foot trailers.

5. Which of the following docks requires straight backing?
   A. a recessed dock
   B. an underground docking complex
   C. a dog leg dock
   D. a dead end yard with a corner dock

6. If the hole is on the left side of your vehicle, you should
   A. be able to see the hole in your right-hand mirror.
   B. be able to see the hole in your left-hand mirror.
   C. be able to see the hole in both mirrors.
   D. ask a dock worker to guide you in.

7. When loading pigs on flat cars
   A. be sure the wheel plates are in the up position before driving
      onto the rail cars.
   B. be sure to separate the bulls from the sows.
   C. back the trailer onto the furthest car out first.
   D. the coupling plates will keep you from falling off the side.

8. As you approach a hole to parallel park a semi-trailer
   A. check to see if you can pull straight in without backing.
   B. use the trailer hand brake to slow the trailer before the tractor.
   C. continually check your rear view mirror for vehicles.
   D. weave slowly into the parking hole and come back out again.

■ GETTING THE MAIN IDEAS

1. You arrive at the dock shown in Figure 17-1. What steps will you follow to arrive safely at the dock? What type of maneuvering will you use? What special cautions, if any, should you keep in mind?

2. Choose one of the types of docks illustrated in this chapter: the dog leg, dead end yard or underground docking complex. Explain what the diagram means. That is, explain how you would maneuver your semi-trailer to arrive safely at the dock.

3. In your own words, explain how to parallel park a single-axle tractor pulling a 22-foot trailer. You may use chart, paragraph, or diagram. Assume that the space to park in is 50-foot long. There is a low-bed in front of the space and a dry freight van behind it.

4. What types of things make you lose points during a yard test?

5. What is the most important factor in fast, efficient spotting? (Choose A, B, C, or D.)
   A. how fast you can back up
   B. how straight you can back up
   C. how well you judge relationships and sizes of spaces
   D. how you set yourself up

★ GOING BEYOND THE FACTS AND IDEAS

1. Diagram a dock that you would call a "headache dock." It may be one you've encountered or heard of. Give your diagram to another driver and ask him or her to diagram or explain how a rig should be spotted in the problem dock. (Then, have that person draw you a problem dock and you spot the rig by diagram or explanation.)

2. You arrive at a terminal you've never been at before. How do you know whether there is a spotter or whether you should spot your rig yourself? How do you know where to spot your rig?

3. List the characteristics you would look for if you were an employer and wanted to hire a spotter. What skills and personal qualities would a good spotter have?

Figure 18-1. *Courtesy of Bekins Van Lines Company*

Chapter Eighteen

LOADING AND UNLOADING VEHICLES

BEFORE
YOU
READ

As we've said before, there are many tasks, besides driving, that a professional trucker handles. And it's important to know how to handle these tasks efficiently and smoothly.

At times, perhaps often in your career, you will be involved in loading and unloading freight. If you work as a local driver, loading and unloading will be a part of your everyday job. Some truckers break into the industry by working as a dock worker for a while, then begin driving once they have shown themselves to be responsible. Even if you begin driving right away, there will be times when you will need to help at the dock. Therefore, it is extremely important for you to know how to handle dock (or terminal) operations. This includes loading and unloading vehicles which we'll talk about in this chapter, and securing cargo which we'll talk about in Chapter 20.

In this chapter, we'll be using a number of terms which may be new to you. Therefore, to help you understand the chapter, we have defined them here, at the beginning. Other words in the chapter may be new to you, but since their meanings are fairly clear when they are used in the chapter, we have put them at the end, in the normal glossary. So, before you begin the chapter itself, we suggest that you read through the meanings of the words below and take the short quiz on their meanings. If you do so, you should find the chapter easier to read.

bill of lading: An itemized list of goods contained in a shipment.

central checking: Where a number of trailers are spotted close together so that one person can check many trailers being unloaded at the same time.

checker: A person who checks off pieces of cargo as others (dock workers or drivers) unload them from a truck.

consignee: One to whom goods are shipped.

discrepancy: An error; a difference between one thing (such as a freight bill) and another (such as the amount or type of cargo included in a shipment).

drag line: A method of moving freight car around a terminal. The drag line is a moving cable. Carts are attached to the line which provides power for them to move around. The cable may be sunk into a ot in the floor or it may hang overhead like a trolley car setup.

freight bill: A document which gives a description of the freight, its weight, amount of charges, taxes, and tells whether the shipment is prepaid or collect. Charges paid in advance are called prepaid freight bills. Charges collected at the destination are called collect or destination freight bills.

freight manifest: Same as a bill of lading.

inbound freight: Freight coming into the terminal.

line driver: A driver who usually runs from terminal to terminal over a fairly long distance. The haul is rarely interrupted to pick up freight.

line haul: Movement of freight between cities and/or states, provinces, countries, etc., not including pickup and delivery.

line-haul unit: A rig that is assigned to an over-the-road freight movement, not a local city delivery type of pickup unit. Line-haul units are usually the best mechanical units in the fleet.

overage: Excess freight over the quantity believed to have been shipped, or more than the quantity shown on the shipping document.

shortage: Less freight than is shown on the shipping document. The word is also used in everyday language to mean an insufficiency, having less than needed for something.

steel loading plate: A thin sheet of steel, usually ¼ inch thick and about three feet wide and four feet long. Steel loading plates are laid on the dock surface between the rear of the trailer and the dock so you can run your hand truck in and out of the trailer on them.

● *Terminology Quiz*

One of the definitions on the right goes with each of the terms on the left. You can match them correctly by putting the letter of the definition before the term it defines on the left. Use each definition only one time.

_____ 1. steel loading plate

_____ 2. drag line

_____ 3. central checking

_____ 4. line driver

_____ 5. bill of lading

_____ 6. checker

_____ 7. freight bill

_____ 8. overage

_____ 9. discrepancy

_____ 10. line haul

_____ 11. consignee

_____ 12. shortage

A. having more freight than the freight manifest says you should

B. having less freight than the freight manifest says you should

C. an over-the-road hauler

D. a difference

E. a cable for moving carts around a dock

F. long distance cargo movement

G. a form listing the shipped goods

H. something used to cover up any gap between a trailer deck and the loading dock

I. the person goods are sent to

J. a person who marks off things as they are unloaded

K. a place where a lot of trailers are docked together for unloading

L. a form describing the cargo and all related charges

Here's how the chapter will be organized. First, we will talk about the need for different types of trailers. Then, we will give an illustration of how time is wasted when you don't carefully plan your loading and unloading. Next, we'll describe kinds of delivery equipment, hand trucks, forklifts, etc. Since there are specific procedures to follow when you unload at a terminal, we'll talk about them next. Then, we'll give some tips on how to handle cargo without damaging it and how to stow it (that is, load or pack it in an orderly manner). Finally, we'll talk briefly about three things: completing the loading operation, sealed cargoes, and safety inspections. And we'll close with a few tips to help make your job run a little more smoothly.

DIFFERENT LOADS REQUIRE DIFFERENT TRAILERS

Freight hauling today is complex. Different types of trailers are needed to haul the many different types of loads. If you need refrigeration for a load, you need a reefer. If you're handling a lot of dry freight, made up of boxes and cartons, you can load it either in a van or on a flat-bed, depending on which is available. Special types of trailers are needed to haul some of the bulky items, such as factory machinery.

You read about many different types of trailers in Chapter 10, but there are many specialized trailers too. It seems that every time we turn around there is a need for a special type of trailer or another challenging load to carry. Just think. How do we get the big propellers to the navy yard? How do we get the aircraft to the airports? How are trucks transported to the markets and subway cars to rapid transit districts? The list goes on and on.

For each type of load, there is usually a trailer style that will handle it. That's why we have so many specialized carriers. Some companies, for example, handle only industrial and construction equipment loads. You'll find everything from flat-bed trailers to seven and nine-axle low-bed trailers in one of these company yards.

Figure 18-2. The Hallco-Glide Live Floor can unload a 40-foot trailer in less than 12 minutes. Hydraulic power moves the floor toward the rear to unload or toward the front to load. *Courtesy of Hallco Manufacturing Company, Inc.*

There is a special method of loading and unloading for each type of trail-er. Remember one thing. If you load something onto a trailer, at some point it has to be unloaded. Therefore, you must consider how the load is going to be removed from a trailer while you're still loading it.

| HOW NOT TO DO IT | Here's a typical example of how *not* to handle the loading and unloading operation. A driver was loading a number of small cartons onto a flat-bed trailer. We'll call him Sonny. |

Sonny didn't want to let the consignee have the pallets, so he off-loaded each box and stacked it on his trailer. When he arrived at the customer's yard, Sonny found a forklift, but there were no empty pallets, so he had to unload each carton and carry it into the warehouse individually.

If he had left the freight on the pallets at his pickup point, Sonny could have unloaded the pallets in the warehouse and stacked the cartons on the floor. Then, he could have stacked the empty pallets back on his trailer and returned them to his yard. He wouldn't have had to carry each carton into the warehouse and stack it.

By not thinking ahead, Sonny lost about four hours time. If you use your head while loading or unloading a trailer, you can speed your load. If you don't, you can lose as much as a full day. What's the cause? Lack of planning.

| DELIVERY EQUIPMENT | Special equipment makes the handling of cargo more effi-cient. Here is a short run-down on the main items. |

● *Pry Bars and Hand Trucks*

First, you have a long pry bar, known as a *Johnson Bar*. It is a huge, flat, wooden bar with a small set of wheels on one end and a small, steel lip on the other end of the handle. The lip reaches under the edge of a crate, giving you the leverage needed to lift the crate.

A *dolly* or *hand truck* is a cousin to the original Johnson bar, except that a two-wheel dolly is really a hand truck for carrying a number of cartons. An-other name for the hand truck is a *two-wheeler*. (Should you walk into a freight company office and be asked by the dispatcher if you can handle a two-wheeler, don't reply, "Yes, I've ridden a bicycle since I was seven." The dispatcher is referring to a hand truck for moving freight around the dock areas and into the trucks.)

● *Pallet Jacks*

A pallet jack is a hydraulic jack assembly on wheels. It is capable of lifting a two or three-thousand pound, loaded pallet from the floor to be *pulled around, re-spotted* and *put down again*. A pallet jack lifts loads only *two or three inches off the floor*, giving just enough clearance beneath to move it.

DELIVERY EQUIPMENT
(cont.)

A pallet jack is also very handy for pulling pallets out of the nose of a 40-foot trailer when there is no forklift available. (See Figures 18-3 and 18-4.)

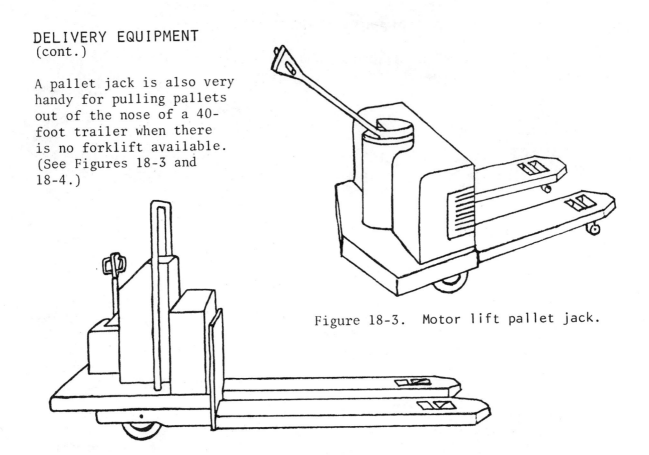

Figure 18-3. Motor lift pallet jack.

Figure 18-4. Motorized pallet jack.

● *Forklifts*

A *forklift* differs slightly from a pallet jack. A forklift can *lift loaded pallets to a great height for stacking*. A pallet jack can only lift loads a few inches off the ground.

The length of the forks will vary. For example, a small 4000-pound capacity forklift will have forks that are approximately 40 inches long. A 6000-pound machine may have forks that are 54 inches long.

The height to which a forklift can lift things also varies. Notice the differences between the forklifts shown in Figures 18-5 through 18-9.

Figure 18-5. Forklift. High lift truck.

306

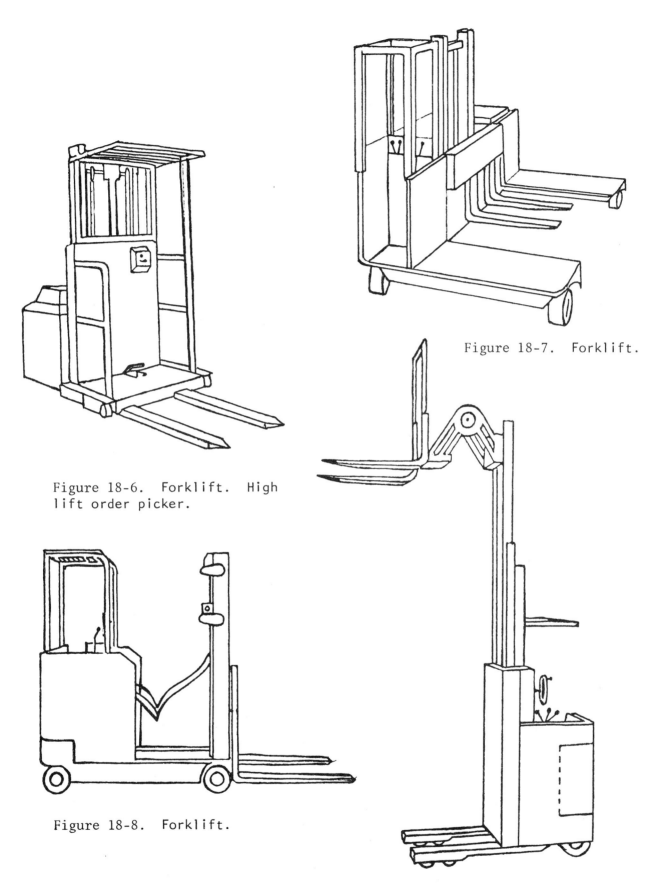

Figure 18-7. Forklift.

Figure 18-6. Forklift. High
lift order picker.

Figure 18-8. Forklift.

Figure 18-9. Forklift. Reach
rider high lift.

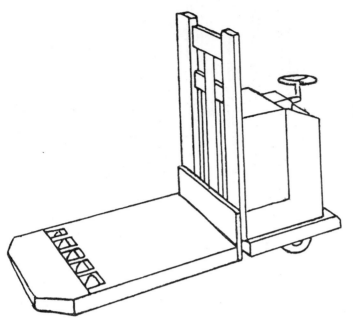

Figure 18-10. High lift
platform truck.

DELIVERY EQUIPMENT (cont.)

● *Platform Trucks*

A *platform truck* differs from a forklift because it has a *platform to hold and lift the load, instead of forks.*

● *Characteristics of All 3*

Pallet jacks, forklifts and platform trucks are the basic three kinds of materials handling equipment usually found in the industry. They are found, primarily, in warehouses that handle high volumes or huge amounts of freight.

They can be powered by a gasoline engine or by electrical motors, and each handles a variety of objects.

CHECKING INBOUND FREIGHT AS IT IS UNLOADED	It is customary for city drivers, or local drivers, to handle the breakout and loading of freight in the dock area. A line driver very rarely becomes involved in the actual handling of the freight at a terminal. Instead, all freight to and from a line-haul unit is handled by

the dock workers. *"Lumpers"* (a name commonly used for dock workers) are often assisted by the local city drivers. (Dock workers are also called *breakout persons* because they break out, or unload, the freight.)

● *Checking Loads Against the Freight Bill*

When a long-line trucker drives a load into the shipping terminal, the dock worker checks the *freight bill* against the corresponding inbound freight as it is unloaded. If the dock worker notices any discrepancies between what was supposed to be included in the shipment and what has been, she or he notes these discrepancies on the freight bill. That is, she or he jots down any overage, shortage, or changes in the shipment.

Often, one checker will be assigned to two loads, parked side by side. Each load will have one breakout person or lumper. This helps the task of checking the accuracy of shipment to move quickly and efficiently. The checker checks the two loads simultaneously as the two breakout persons unload the freight. In terminals where central checking is used, one checker may check anywhere from three to eight units at the same time. Where a drag line is used, one person may handle both jobs, checking and unloading the unit, as a simultaneous operation.

CHECKING FREIGHT AS IT IS UNLOADED (cont.)

● *Unloading Exception Reports*

Besides noting any discrepancies on the freight bill, the checker prepares an *unloading exception report*. This report covers the discrepancies in the shipment, and is filled out according to the supervisor's directions. It lists such things as damage, missing pieces, etc.

● *Docked Freight*

Sometimes, freight will be docked. That is, it will be stored at the shipping terminal for a while. If this is the case, you will want to be careful to keep the docked shipment separate from other shipments. Check the freight bill carefully to see that all items to be docked are properly stored.

● *Freight in Transit*

Sometimes freight in transit moves direct from one unit to another. If you are responsible for moving freight from one rig to another, combine shipments only if all shipments being combined have the same destination and the same carrier.

HANDLING CARGO

● *Causes of Damage*

Over one-fourth of the money paid out on insurance claims is for damage caused by improper handling, loading and stowing. These claims can be prevented by handling, stacking and loading all freight with care, and observing all precautionary markings, such as "Fragile," "This End Up," etc. We've listed the principal causes of damage to freight below. Each cause is actually the result of carelessness and inefficiency. Remember them, and most important, never be guilty of them.

● Rough handling of fragile merchandise

● Stowing cartons containing cans, glass jars, or bottles on edge

● Stowing cases containing liquids in cans with pry-off lids upside-down

● Stowing cases or drums containing liquids that might leak on top of, or near, expensive dry freight

● Stowing any merchandise in such a manner that motion of the truck will cause it to shift or to fall and break or damage other freight by the fall

● Loading cylinders or reels without proper blocking (nailed, if needed) to stop them from rolling

HANDLING CARGO   (cont.)

- Loading cases, cartons, etc., upside-down or on edge when clearly marked, "This Side Up"

- Loading cartons, rugs, etc., on top of castings, iron, machinery or other rough freight without protection

- Loading dry freight on bodies with holes in roof, floor, sides, or doors with leaks

- Loading freight in bodies without proper rear doors or curtains

- Storing fragile freight on floor and heavy freight on top

- Improperly securing with ropes, top covers or curtains - or insecure fastening of doors

- Stowing full or empty drums with bungs (that is, openings) down

- Receiving freight not properly loaded

- Dropping freight from tailgate to street (Use skids.)

- Allowing freight to drop on its ends

- Using hand trucks improperly

- Excessive and rough handling of materials in bags and bundles

- Failure to level off remainder of load after delivery of partial load

- Failure to remove nails from floor of truck or trailer

- Stowing freight likely to absorb odors next to freight giving off odors

Rough handling of freight is never tolerated in the trucking industry, so don't throw packages or cartons. It's bad enough when the end misses a forward pass on which a touchdown depends, but when an employee is on the receiving end of a package of freight, and misses, somebody's money is tossed away. Don't handle packages by the twine or cord either. Handle them in the same way you would handle a sealed carton.

As we've said above, damages to freight all come from carelessness and inefficiency. We might sum up this subject with one rule. It will probably go further than anything else in reducing damage to freight. *"Handle the freight as if it belonged to you."* Get rid of a careless attitude. After all, a job worth doing is worth doing well.

HANDLING CARGO   (cont.)

● *Using Hand Trucks*

A hand truck makes it easier
to move freight from one place to
another. It is *not* to be used to
push or shove freight into place.
The nose or lip of a hand truck is
sharp and if it is used to push or
nudge freight, it will cause damage.
There are other ways you can cause
damage with a hand truck too. One
is dumping the load by lifting the
truck handles and allowing the load
to slide off. Another is toppling
the load. This is where you lose
some of the cartons or load off the
top because you've overloaded or
improperly loaded the hand truck.

How can you avoid damage?
Here are four things you can do.

1. Keep the hand truck in
    good repair to eliminate
    the possibility of injur-
    ing people and damaging
    freight.

Figure 18-11. Rear view into freight
box, showing dock cart loaded with
freight. *Courtesy of American Trucking
Associations, Inc.*

2. Breakover the pile of
    freight to be loaded be-
    fore running the blade of the hand truck under boxes and cartons.

3. Place a packing pad between the article and the hand truck if you
    are loading something that might be marred or chafed easily.

4. Keep the dock and vehicles clear of loose pipes, wood, and other
    hazards. Use steel loading plates when they are available. They
    make hand trucking easier, prevent toppling of packages, prevent the
    possibility of personal injury and protect the equipment.

● *Using Mechanical Handling Equipment*

Space for maneuvering is limited on a dock. So operating mechanized
equipment is a job calling for considerable skill and planning. Other employe-
ees are constantly moving about. Equipment and freight are being moved. To
avoid injury to yourself and others, you have to give your full attention to
the job you are doing. Inattention, even for a brief moment, can easily result in disaster.

If you operate mechanical handling equipment, try to work at a steady
pace. Sudden bursts of speed are harder on you. They're also harder on your
equipment and can be a hazard to others around you.

HANDLING CARGO (cont.)

The purpose of forklifts and other mechanical equipment is similar to that of a hand truck: to move freight from one place to another. Of course, you will want to operate the equipment in such a manner that the freight being moved and other freight on the dock and in vehicles is not damaged. Chances are, your company will give you some simple rules to help guard against damage when you use this type of equipment. But here are a few basic safety points to remember when you're operating a forklift. The first two have to do with the protruding forks in front of the forklift that go underneath the pallet.

1. When you're running the forks through a pallet, be sure you are clear so that you don't shove the rear pallet off the far side, hitting a worker or rig.

2. Whenever you approach a load, be careful that you don't run the forks too far under the load. You don't want them to come out the other side and possibly knock a hole in a wall or the side of a trailer.

3. Watch the tilt movement of the forks. If you try to unload two pallets high at the same time, it may lead to trouble. The top one may shake off. Always take one at a time.

4. Whenever you stack a load on a trailer, be sure that the *lower* part of the load won't shift out from under the *upper* tier due to road vibration.

5. Check the trailer for chocks before you run a forklift into a trailer that has been dropped at a dock. It's fairly common for the dropped trailer to have a leak in the air system. If the trailer brakes release and there aren't any chocks under the wheels, the trailer may roll away from the dock as the forklift runs toward the trailer's nose. The weight of the forklift running toward the nose may be just enough to make it roll away, and you may not like where you wind up when you come back out of the trailer with the load on the forklift.

Figure 18-12. Forklift loading pallets of rock dust into a van. This van is equipped with the Hallco-Glide Live Floor. *Courtesy of Hallco Mfg. Co., Inc.*

● *Hauling Forklifts*

Most drivers, in the business for some time, have had to haul large forklifts at one time or another. Often, the front forks and mast are removed before it is hauled. Otherwise, it would be too tall to clear legal height limits. However, this creates a very dangerous situation unless you know what you're doing.

If you have to haul a forklift with the front forks and mast removed, remember this: The traction and weight are gone on the drive wheels. All the weight is on the rear steering

axle.   If you try to climb a ramp, no matter how slight, *you won't make it.*
You have no traction.   If you try to drive off a ramp, *you will sail down the*
ramp and keep right on going.   The wheels will lock up and slide without stopping you because you have *no traction* without the weight of the mast on the
front.   So, if you're going to haul a forklift, remember this: You must drive
the forklift off a dock when loading it, and onto a dock when unloading it if
the mast has been removed.

STOWING FREIGHT	Loading a truck or trailer is not an easy job. You have to use your common sense to do it right, but you need more than that. You have to be able to picture how the load will stand movement over the route it is to take.

Some people have a knack for loading.   Others never learn.   Household
goods movers know that loading the vehicle is the most important part of the
job, and they employ people who have the knack for the job.   But, in hauling
general commodities, *loading is just as important.*   In fact, it is often harder
to safely load a trailer with miscellaneous general freight than to load a furniture van where pads can be used for protection.

● *Begin with a Clean Space*

Before you start to load equipment, see that the loading space is thoroughly clean.   Good housekeeping is essential to safe loading.   Remove all projecting objects that might injure freight, and clean out all siftings of dry
paint, carbon black, and any other foreign matter.

● *Load Freight Carefully*

Unpackaged items such as pipes, cans, freight in bundles, batteries, car-
boys, automobile parts, farm implements, motors, machinery, etc., present special problems.   Rugs, linoleum and other long, bulky freight also cause difficulty.   It is impossible to give anything except general rules for loading
because each commodity usually has some characteristic which you need to consider when you load it.   But there are a few general rules which you can follow.
Those listed below will, if observed, go a long way toward keeping damage to a
minimum.

1.   Load freight so that precautionary marks indicating how the freight
     should be loaded are observed.

2.   Load freight so that it won't shift.

3.   Use dunnage, blocking, paperboard, etc., when necessary, to protect
     the load.

4.   Load commodities in pails, tubs, buckets and friction top cans *tops*
     up to prevent leakage.   Don't stack them too high.   Separate layers
     with corrugated or solid fibreboard.

STOWING FREIGHT   (cont.)

5. Avoid using hooks. Hooks may occasionally be safely used, but more often, they damage the cargo. Therefore, don't use them unless your employer has okayed their use in handling specific commodities.

6. Don't stack freight so high that it will topple when other freight is stacked close to it or removed from its vicinity.

7. In stacking freight, make every effort to have the destination marking visible, if possible. But, under no circumstances, stack a container in disregard of instructions such as "This Side Up."

● *Reporting Discrepancies*

When you are loading a truck, you will be given some type of shipping document to work from, just as you are given one when you are unloading. The actual count (or pieces of cargo) as you load must tally with the count on the shipping document. Make a report to the appropriate supervisor if a shipment loads out short or over.

Whenever possible, it's a good idea to check docked freight on the dock before loading it. Then, if a shipment checks short, it can be held on the dock, with less handling, until the shipper can be contacted and asked for a re-check of the original shipping records. Of course, if a shipment is too large to check on the dock, you can check it as it is loaded. Then, if it checks out short or over, you can leave it on the line-haul unit and report the discrepancy to the proper supervisor.

COMPLETING THE LOADING OPERATION | When you've finished loading the cargo, close and lock or seal the doors or gates on the unit. If the unit has a curtain, pull the curtain down and fasten it. Remember that no loading operation is complete, however, until it has been properly secured, or tied down, if it needs it. (We will discuss this in Chapter 20.)

SEALED CARGO | As we mentioned briefly in Chapter 17, some cargo is *sealed*. Again, this means that instead of using a padlock to lock the doors of the trailer, a thin metal strip secures the doors. These seals are used only once. They see to it that the trailer doors are kept closed from point of pickup (or point of loading) to point of delivery. The following are examples of cargo which may be sealed: shipments of liquor, cigarettes, canned food products, food such as hams, fresh produce, and any valuable commodity. As you may've guessed, cargo is usually sealed so that it will be secure against vandalism and theft.

Each seal will have a *seal number* on the seal itself. This seal number must be recorded on a *seal record* by either the shipper or dispatcher. Then, the seal record is kept by the shipper and a copy is mailed to the consignee so it can be checked at the other end against the seal itself.

Figure 18-13. Both trailers and containers can travel as sealed cargo. *Courtesy of Pettibone Corporation*

SEALED CARGO   (cont.)

When a driver reaches the delivery point with a sealed cargo, the seal numbers must be checked to see that they agree with those on the seal record. Sometimes a driver will do this checking, but at other times, there will be a person designated at the delivery terminal to do this check. If there is a discrepancy between the two numbers, the driver or other person doing the checking will usually call the station that applied for the seal. (This station may be the shipper.) However, some companies have different steps which are to be followed when a discrepancy is found. You should always follow your company policies.

Some sealed cargoes require a *signature* at the delivery point to show that the seal was checked against the seal record, found to match, and that the trailer was still sealed when the shipment was received. If a signature is required on a load you carry, you will want to be sure to get the signature *before* the seal is broken and the trailer doors opened.

SEALED CARGO   (cont.)

Occasionally, something will happen to break the seal before the delivery point is reached. For example, you could be involved in an accident or a fire. Or, inspection might be required by the Department of Agriculture if you're carrying produce. Here's what you should do if the seals are broken enroute:

- *If the seal is broken by the Agriculture Inspector,* she or he will insert the government's own seal with an inspection report stating that they have broken the original seal and resealed the trailer.

- *In any other event,* contact your dispatcher for instructions. Then, make a written report of how the seal was broken. You can make this report on your trip report or on the freight manifest, or wherever your dispatcher says to write it.

But say a seal has been broken enroute and you suspect the cargo unit may have been entered. What do you do? Inspect the cargo to see whether or not it is intact, that is, undamaged and untouched. If something appears damaged or missing, notify your dispatcher and the local police department immediately. The cardinal rule in any broken seal situation is to *immediately notify your dispatcher* for advice as to what procedure to follow.

SAFETY
INSPECTIONS | Periodically, a *"Dock Safety Inspection"* form or *"Shop Safety Inspection"* form may be used to satisfy management that the working area is safe. This means it is to be clean and free from hazards. Many times, dock areas become strewn with old boxes of rope, cable, strapping from boxes, broken pallets and other dunnage. Human nature seems to dictate that most workers will climb over bales of strapping before trying to pick them up. It seems to be a matter of "let the other person do it."

So, usually once a month, a transportation supervisor or dock supervisor will pull out a form and go through the terminal and surrounding areas using a check-off sheet. These check-off sheets include everything from observing employees working to the availability of fire extinguishers, from oil spots on the floor to grease leaks from forklifts in the warehouse, to the condition of the restrooms. Completing the inspection form is usually the responsibility of the supervisor or designated safety representative. However, each driver should participate in keeping his or her area clean and safe. Congestion and activity at the loading docks makes them get cluttered very quickly.

Only the very largest companies would use a shop safety inspection form like the one shown in Figure 18-14. Others would not have the time to do so. They'd simply use a shorter dock safety inspection form. Dock and shop safety forms are not quite the same, but both cover all the basic areas. The shop safety form has some extra items on it, but the main objectives of both forms are housekeeping and fire control.

Shop Safety Inspection

ATA Form C0660
Reorder From:
American Trucking Assns., Inc.
1616 P Street, N.W.
Washington, D. C. 20036

TERMINAL _____

INSPECTED BY _____ DATE _____

SAFE WORK PRACTICES

CHECK ONE:
YES NO

Note locations, nature of violations & recommendations for improvement

☐ ☐ **1.** Employees in good health, dressed properly for job
☐ ☐ **2.** Smoking rules obeyed
☐ ☐ **3.** Use of proper equipment handling techniques (lifting & moving)
☐ ☐ **4.** Use of equipment guards as needed
☐ ☐ **5.** Use of personal protective equipment as needed
☐ ☐ **6.** Air pressure for cleaning reduced to 30 psi
☐ ☐ **7.** No evidence of horseplay, improper climbing, jumping, running or other unsafe acts
☐ ☐ **8.** Employee work places clean and orderly (free of spills, oil, grease, trash, etc)
☐ ☐ **9.** Tools and machines used properly
☐ ☐ **10.** Tools and machines properly maintained
☐ ☐ **11.** Flame or spark producing operations isolated from flammable liquids and materials
☐ ☐ **12.** Flammables in proper containers and stored properly
☐ ☐ **13.** Welding operations accomplished safely (employee properly dressed, has he inspected hoses, provided ventilation, cylinders secure, valves turned off when job completed, caps in place, acetylene cylinders chained)
☐ ☐ **14.** Containers bonded when transferring flammable liquids
☐ ☐ **15.** Dip tanks closed when not in use
☐ ☐ **16.** Flammable liquid spills cleaned up immediately
☐ ☐ **17.** Proper use of stands to support vehicle (not jacks)
☐ ☐ **18.** Safe procedure followed when moving vehicles
☐ ☐ **19.** Ventilating devices used when engines running

HOUSEKEEPING

☐ ☐ **1.** Floors clean, free of defects, no grease & oil spills
☐ ☐ **2.** Signs show maximum floor loading
☐ ☐ **3.** Trash containers sufficient in number and no overflow
☐ ☐ **4.** Permanent aisle marked and clear of objects
☐ ☐ **5.** Stairs clear and in good repair
☐ ☐ **6.** Permanent ladders firmly attached and in good condition
☐ ☐ **7.** Cleaning supplies readily available
☐ ☐ **8.** Storage areas neatly kept
☐ ☐ **9.** Ladders stored properly and free of defects

FIRE CONTROL

☐ ☐ **1.** Fire doors closed, free of obstructions
☐ ☐ **2.** Exits properly marked. "No Exits" marked
☐ ☐ **3.** Fire instructions posted
☐ ☐ **4.** No smoking areas designated, and signs posted
☐ ☐ **5.** Fire extinguishers in good condition, at proper height, visible, accessible, securely mounted, marked & tagged

(continued on back)

Figure 18-14 (Front Side). Large trucking companies may use a form like this one to inspect working areas for safety.

317

Note locations, nature of violations & recommendations for improvement

☐ ☐ 6. Hazardous materials located away from heat, flame, water and damage

☐ ☐ 7. Flammable liquids stored properly, provision for bonding & materials available to clean up spills

☐ ☐ 8. Are hazardous operations isolated (welding, grinding, cutting, etc.)

☐ ☐ 9. Are combustible materials safety stored away from flames and sparks

ELECTRICAL

☐ ☐ 1. Permanent wiring, boxes, switches, outlets and lights secure and free of defects

☐ ☐ 2. Breaker and fuse boxes clean and proper

☐ ☐ 3. Machines, tools, vending and water machines grounded and working properly

☐ ☐ 4. Wiring for extension cords, portable lights and tools free of cuts, kinks, wear, used properly and plugs tight

☐ ☐ 5. Protective devices for equipment in use

☐ ☐ 6. Lighting sufficient, free from glare

HEALTH AND SANITATION

☐ ☐ 1. Food areas clean and maintained

☐ ☐ 2. Bathroom areas clean and equipped

☐ ☐ 3. Noise level OK—noise protectors and controls in use

☐ ☐ 4. Lighting systems adequate for general and special needs

☐ ☐ 5. Ventilation good—includes special venting as needed

☐ ☐ 6. Hazardous processes separated

☐ ☐ 7. First aid kit available and maintained, 1st aider on duty

☐ ☐ 8. Water for quick wash off in battery rooms

☐ ☐ 9. Protective equipment adequate, stored neatly, accessible and used

MACHINES, EQUIPMENT, TOOLS

☐ ☐ 1. Electrical equipment and tools protected by ground or double insulation

☐ ☐ 2. Moving parts within 7 feet of floor enclosed (fans, pulley, etc)

☐ ☐ 3. Machines guarded at point of operation (grinders, etc)

☐ ☐ 4. Hoists, cranes & jacks marked for rating

☐ ☐ 5. Hoists, ropes, slings and hooks in good condition

☐ ☐ 6. Spray booth has "No Smoking" sign, filters clear, fire extinguisher near, explosion proof wiring, sprinkler system OK, trash containers adequate, flammables in booth limited

☐ ☐ 7. Dip tanks: fire extinguishers nearby, "No Smoking" sign, ventilation good, tanks have automatic and manual closures, tanks isolated from sparks, heat, flame

☐ ☐ 8. Hand tools in good repair—no burrs, loose handles, etc.

Figure 18-14 (Back Side)

A FEW FINAL NOTES We cannot possibly cover all of the loading techniques in this book. There are guidelines for handling nearly every commodity from candy to burial caskets, from window frames to butter, from corrugated iron to bananas, from marble to fireworks. Once you know what you'll be hauling and the type of rig you'll be driving, you can develop efficient techniques for loading your cargo on your rig. Each commodity and each trailer has its own loading characteristics. Obviously you're not going to load an open top van full of tomatoes in the same way you load a Caterpillar onto a low-bed. Nevertheless, one thing remains the same. In loading both commodities, you treat the freight as if it belonged to you, with the utmost care to avoid damage. (One way to learn more about loading a specific type of trailer is to write to the manufacturer for information.)

There are many things we didn't have time to mention in this chapter. Here's one we didn't get into: towing a forklift. Many rigs have been tangled up due to towing one. Forklifts are very hard to stop unless they have a surge brake. Here's what you want to keep in mind: The weight of the towing unit must be heavier than the weight of the forklift. Forklifts weigh a lot more than their small size makes them appear to weigh, so be careful. If you break this rule, don't expect to stop when you apply the brakes, especially in wet weather. Even if you're traveling only 10 mph in the yard, you may keep right on going. Again, you have to keep learning in this business.

Finally, remember while you're loading that you will also have to tie-down and unload. Keep this in mind while you're loading and plan your method of tie-down and unloading then. Also, while you're driving down the road, there will be a lot of pressure on the load. This pressure will make the load try to surge forward and move sideways. Keep this pressure in mind when you decide how to secure the load.

SUMMARY We began and ended this chapter by saying that different types of loads require different types of trailers and each load has its own loading and unloading characteristics. The best time to plan how you're going to unload is during the loading operation. Lack of planning wastes time and effort.

Drivers and dock workers use many types of handling equipment. Two non-mechanized tools are the Johnson Bar, a lever for lifting crates, and the hand truck (also called a two-wheeler or a dolly). The hand truck allows you to carry a number of cartons at once and to do so without straining your back. It is not to be used for shoving packages into place. The mechanical handling equipment most commonly used are the pallet jack, forklift and platform truck. A pallet jack has wide forks and lifts pallets just a few inches above the floor so they can be moved around. A forklift has forks, usually less wide, but very strong, and it is used for lifting pallets to a great height for stacking and loading. A platform truck can also lift a load, but it has a platform instead of forks.

Figure 18-15.   Driver moving a skid with a pallet jack. *Courtesy of The Service Recorder Company*

SUMMARY   (cont.)

Whenever you load or unload, you mark off pieces of freight against a shipping document, either a freight bill or a bill of lading (also called a freight manifest). Any shortage, overage or difference in type or condition of the freight needs to be recorded. Often, a checker will do the checking against the document while a driver or dock worker loads or unloads. But sometimes the dock worker or driver checks the document against the load. Whoever does the checking records any discrepancies. The method of recording these differences depends upon company policy.

There are many causes of damage to cargo, but they are all the result of carelessness and inefficiency. So, if you remember the rule, "Treat the freight as if it belonged to you," damages will be reduced. One key guideline, however, is to always obey precautionary markings on packages, such as, "This Side Up."

When you're using mechanical handling equipment work steadily and smoothly. Sudden bursts of speed are hard on you, your equipment and others working nearby. Also, be careful not to run the forks through the pallet and out the other side. Carry only one pallet at a time, and chock the trailer wheels before you enter it on a forklift.

If you're hauling sealed cargo, be sure the seal number is checked against the seal record before the seal is broken. If a signature is required, be sure to get it. Then, if a discrepancy is found between the two numbers, follow your employer's wishes in recording the difference and taking needed action. If the seal is broken in transit, follow company policy in reporting how it was broken. If the load appears to have been tampered with, check it out for missing or damaged items.

For safety and efficiency, all loading materials and areas should be kept clean and free from hazards. This includes the hand trucks, forklifts, etc.; the truck's cargo area, and the dock. Everything should be kept in good, working order.

GLOSSARY

docked freight: Cargo which is stored at the terminal before being sent on.

dunnage: The primary meaning of dunnage is packing. It refers, particularly to loose wood, and it is used to keep cargo from shifting in transit and being damaged. Dunnage is used as a brace or cradle around some forms of cargo to hold it in place where lines or chains wouldn't be sufficient. The word is also used to mean personal belongings, such as materials left around a dock, miscellaneous articles.

forklift: A machine used to move and stack goods which are loaded on pallets or skids. It has forks and can lift things to a great height.

fragile: Easily broken; delicate.

hand truck (dolly or two-wheeler): A non-motorized device with two wheels. A driver places cartons on the lip of the unit, tips it back slightly and wheels the unit to where he or she wants to unload it.

Johnson bar: A lever with wheels for lifting crates or cartons.

lumper: A dock worker; one who unloads trucks at the dock. Also called a breakout person.

mast: A vertical pole, as at the front of a forklift.

pallet jack: A hydraulic jack assembly on wheels for moving freight around in a warehouse or terminal.

platform truck: A machine used to move a load around. It has a platform and can lift things higher than a pallet jack can.

skid: A wood or steel platform similar to a pallet and used with a pallet jack or forklift.

unloading exception report: A form on which to report discrepancies in a shipment - damage, missing pieces, overage, etc.

► CHECKING THE FACTS

Answer each question briefly in the space provided. Use your own paper for Number 10.

1. What should Sonny have done to make unloading more efficient? _____

_____

_____

2. Who does more loading and unloading - a lumper, a checker, or a line-haul driver? _____

3. If a supervisor asks you to help breakout a load, what does he or she mean? _____

_____

4. Before you dock freight, you should check the freight bill. What for?

_____

5. What three things cause one fourth of all freight damage? _____

_____

_____

6. How many pallets should you carry at a time with a forklift? _____

_____

7. Give the purpose of each of the following pieces of equipment.

a. steel loading plate _____

_____

b. two-wheeler _____

_____

c. pallet jack _____

_____

d. drag line _____

_____

8. When do you check a load against a shipping document? _____

_____

9. When do you break a seal on a sealed trailer? _____

_____

_____

10. Many causes of damage were listed in this chapter. List five or more of them.

Match the materials handling equipment on the left with the uses on the right. The letter of the use may be placed in the blank before the type of equipment. Use each letter only one time, and fill in all blanks.

_____ 1. Johnson bar

_____ 2. hand truck

_____ 3. dock cart

_____ 4. pallet jack

_____ 5. forklift

_____ 6. platform truck

_____ 7. hook

A. moving three cartons of books from the dock into a van

B. moving 12 one-foot square cartons of balloon freight from the front of the warehouse to the dock

C. moving a pallet of bags of fertilizer from a trailer to a balcony shelf for storing

D. lifting bales of unrefined cotton from a field to a trailer deck which is four feet off the ground

E. raising the bottom of a heavy chest of drawers so that movers can carry it by hand into a furniture van

F. moving a pallet of bottled beverages to a different area of the warehouse

G. moving a four-legged drill press from the dock into an open van

8. _____ 9. _____

Accurately label the two pieces of equipment shown above.

Choose <u>any</u> <u>four</u> of the questions below and answer them on a separate sheet.

10. Why should a trailer be chocked before you ride a forklift into it to pick up freight?

11. When should you plan your unloading technique?

12. What are the two main objectives of safety inspections?

13. What are some differences between a line haul driver and a local delivery driver?

14. What special cautions should you take after off-loading a partial shipment and preparing to drive on to your next stop?

15. What danger is involved in removing the front forks and mast from a forklift?

16. What is an unloading exception report?

★ GOING BEYOND THE FACTS AND IDEAS

1. What types of shippers and receivers might use central checking? How about drag lines?

2. Outline the steps involved in handling the entire process of loading a van? (Specify the type of commodity you're loading if you like.)

3. Imagine being the supervisor of a dock. You've been asked by your employer to make up a list of 10-12 do's and don'ts for dock workers. What items would you list and why? (Again, you may specify the type or types of commodities being handled at your dock if you like.)

Figure 19-1. The Departments of Transportation of US states set rules for loads that are too high, too wide, too long, and too heavy. Before driving oversized loads over state roads, the driver must obtain a permit. Sometimes, as with this extremely long load, the state will provide an escort. *Courtesy of California Highway Patrol*

Chapter Nineteen

PERMIT HAULING

ILLEGAL PRACTICES | One of the first things we covered in this book was rules and regulations. That's because we want to stress the importance of running legally. Remember, when we talk about rules and regulations, we're referring not only to the DOT regs, but to city, county and state laws as well. Obeying the rules and regulations includes obeying speed laws, weight laws, and individual traffic laws. Nevertheless, regardless of what he or she learns in training, it doesn't take the novice long to find out that there are many ways to get around most of these rules.

When a driver starts running cross country, the driver expects to have the log book checked almost daily. That's, after all, what he or she learned in training. But, sadly, this isn't the case. Why? Because most law enforcement personnel are spread so thin that it's impossible for them to cover the

Figure 19-2. **Weigh stations are clearly** marked along highways. Drivers are required to stop when they are open. *Photo by H. Haase*

ILLEGAL PRACTICES (cont.)

multitude of violations that go on each day. This includes the state patrol and Interstate Commerce Commission inspectors. A driver may not have anyone ask for the log book or question his or her hours for weeks or months at a time. Unfortunately, this is a common situation today.

Let's say we have a driver who has to pick up a load in a small Arizona town. There are weigh stations at the main highway entrances, both in and out of the state. But a sharp driver can usually find a back road that will bypass scales and ports of entry.

Say our driver, Ramona, is going to haul a piece of heavy machinery that requires special permits. She *should* apply for the permit before picking up the load. The problem is this: the city where she has to obtain the permit may be 75 miles away. So, rather than go through the hassle, Ramona goes ahead and loads the equipment, then runs with it as hard as she can to her destination. She hopes to get the load there without getting caught. This is what we call *"bootlegging a load."*

Try to picture this situation. It actually happened. A driver (we'll call him Al) was hauling a heavy Cat on a low-bed, late at night. The weight exceeded 40 tons. Al was to meet the owner of the machine at a truck stop in a small town so the owner could lead him out to the spot where he was to drop the machine. Al waited until very late for the owner to show up. In fact, it was close to midnight when he finally showed. The owner told Al to warm up, and he'd lead over a back road to his ranch without waiting for daylight and having to go through all the formalities of entering another state.

As Al followed the owner's pickup, they came to a very small, rickety-looking bridge. Al stopped before crossing, to see if the bridge would hold the weight of the combined truck and machine. The owner assured him, "Sure, we run trucks over here all the time. It's just a short cut." So, Al proceeded very slowly out onto the wooden bridge.

Figure 19-3. **The driver must check the** weight on each axle at a scale. *Photo by H. Haase*

326

ILLEGAL PRACTICES   (cont.)

When he was about halfway over, Al felt the sensation of the bridge sway-
ing. Keeping a cool head, he didn't change his speed, but just gently moved
ahead and reached the other side with a large sigh of relief. You can imagine
Al's feelings on a pitch black evening, with nothing but his headlights showing a section of the bridge up ahead, not knowing what the bridge underneath
is like, nor how high he is in the air.

To continue, Al raced over the back roads, unloaded the Cat and headed
back the same way he'd come. But this time, as he came to the river crossing,
it was just cracking dawn. As he pulled up the dirt approach to the bridge,
he noticed a small sign someone had just tacked onto the bridge. It said,
"Load Limit 5 Tons." Even with the empty truck, Al was scared. This is a matter to give a driver a good case of ulcers, and it happens too many times in a
driver's experience.

You've heard enough times about illegal practices which drivers have engaged in to avoid weigh stations and suchlike. Why do drivers go to so much
trouble to skirt the law? In this chapter, we'll talk about what the law
really says about permit hauling and why the laws are there.

PERMIT
LOADS | Any load that has dimensions exceeding your state's legal
height, weight and length limits will require special
hauling permits. This includes machinery, buildings, and
a variety of other objects. These loads are referred to as *permit loads*.
Most areas place restrictions on when permit loads may travel. In some areas,
they may not travel during peak traffic hours. In some areas, they aren't allowed on roadways after sundown. In other areas, they can't travel after sunup.

ROAD AND
TIRE WEIGHT
LIMITS

● *Road Limits*

Many government agencies have road maps on the walls of their permit offices. To quickly identify particular load limit ratings for these roads,
these maps are color coded, green, yellow, blue and so on. For instance, if
the limit for Highway #17 is 34,000 pounds per axle, there may be a green cray-
on line drawn along the highway route for the restricted area. This restric-
tion might be due to a bridge in that section that will not carry the weight.
The various states use their own coding methods as a convenience, and color
coding is used only on road maps.

As a driver, you could take your own map of the areas you drive, and with
various color crayons, follow the routes with specific colors. How you mark
your map will depend on the weight limits and the colors you choose to use in
your own coding.

ROAD AND TIRE WEIGHT LIMITS (cont.)

Figure 19-4. This county road in a midwestern state is very clearly marked for weight by a coding system known to truck drivers. *Photo by M. McFadden*

Most states publish the weight limits for various regions on a map sheet. These sheets are available at the government office involved. If you need a map sheet for a state road, you get it at the State Division of Highways (or the name used for your state's highway department). If it is a county highway, you get it at the County Road Office. For city streets, most permits are acquired at the City Engineer's Office.

● *Tire Limits*

The next thing to consider is tire limits. All tire weight limits are specified by the tire manufacturer, depending on the size, structure and air pressure maintained in each particular tire. There is no specific tire limit set for all tires of the same size because the limit will vary with the structure of the tires. The structure dictates the load capacity as set forth by government standards.

The *"bridge law"* is used by most western states. It means that the weight carried on a rig must be supported by a specified number of tires. In other words, the more tires you have to carry the load, the more weight you may carry, up to a given maximum. Legal load weights vary from state to state, but the Department of Transportation is trying to standardize axle weights over the interstate system. At the time of print, many states have legal single-axle weight limits of 20,000 pounds. Steering axle weight limits vary, but are usually around 12,500 pounds. In most states, the tandem-axle (8 tires) limit is 32,000 to 34,000 pounds.

● *Tire Limits and Road Limits Work Together*

To determine the number of pounds you may carry over a road, you have to consider three things:

1. The color code on the road map

2. The number of axles on your rig

3. The length of your rig

You have to know all three things before you can tell how heavy a load your rig is allowed to carry over a road.

While the colors may differ from state to state, or county to county, here is an example of how the color designations would be used.

ROAD AND TIRE WEIGHT LIMITS   (cont.)

- *"Green load limit"* roads might allow a maximum tandem-axle weight of 40,000 pounds and a maximum single-axle weight of 24,000 pounds.

- A *"purple route"* or *"purple road"* classification might allow 48,000 pounds on tandem axles and 28,000 pounds on single axles.

The colors used for various weight limits may change from state to state. Purple, green or red may be used, depending upon what system applies.

Remember that not only are there state limits, but each city and county sets its own standards for roads too. The public works department or road department of each city, county, and state sets maximum allowable weights for areas within its jurisdiction. Each time you carry a permit load on these roads, you must have a permit from the agency involved. You don't need a permit to cross a road. However, if you travel on it, your load must be registered with the department. Any police officer can stop you and ask to see your "overload permit" for a heavy, long, high or wide load. *Any load that is over the normal size allowed is considered a permit load.* Thus, if your load is oversized or extra heavy, be sure you have obtained the proper permit.

| DEPT. OF TRANSPORTATION | **TRANSPORTATION PERMIT** | STATE OF CALIFORNIA |

IN COMPLIANCE WITH YOUR REQUEST AND SUBJECT TO ALL OF THE TERMS, CONDITIONS AND RESTRICTIONS WRITTEN BELOW AND THE PRINTED REGULATIONS ATTACHED PERMISSION IS HEREBY GRANTED TO:

NAME | PERMITTEE
A.B.C. Trucking Co.
ADDRESS
123 Third St., San Diego, CA

K.H. Goodman   1 /14/
AUTHORIZED AGENT   DATE

☒ HAUL
☐ DRIVE
☐ TOW

LOAD OR EQUIPMENT
D8 Cat - Dozer
- Ripper

TYPE VEHICLE: 7-axle combination

FROM: San Diego, CA   TO: National City, CA

VIA ROUTES: State - 163 - 5 - and return

EFFECTIVE: 1-15 (AM/PM) 1 /15/
EXPIRES: SUNSET   1/16/

MOVING AUTHORIZED
YES / NO
☒ ☐ SUNRISE TO SUNSET
☐ ☒ SAT.
☐ ☒ SUN.
☐ ☒ HOLIDAY
☐ ☒ SUNSET TO SUNRISE
☐ ☒ INCLEMENT WEATHER

STATE USE ONLY

AUTHORIZED STATE REPRESENTATIVE
PILOT CAR ☒ YES ☐ NO

☐ TRP
☐ DLR
LIC.

ATTACHMENTS
REGULATIONS

NOT TO EXCEED DIMENSIONS SHOWN BELOW

		AXLE NUMBER	1	2	3	4	5	6	7	8	9	
HEIGHT	15'	NUMBER TIRES	2	4	4	8	8	8	8			☐ CASH
WIDTH	14' 6"	AXLE SPACING	Legal									☐ CREDIT
LENGTH	90'											☐ EXEMPT
OVERHANG	None	AXLE WIDTH	10'									1 TRIPS
WEIGHT - - - - - - - ALLOWABLE LOAD			160,000#									

ORIG - - ACCTG.
YELLOW - - PERMITTEE
PINK - - - FILE

FEE
15.00
$

DMO-M-P-16 (REV. 1-6-75)   EST. 0411. 30609-500 1-75 120M TRIP W OSP

Figure 19-5. This permit is used for transporting oversize permit loads over state highways. Similar forms may be obtained from city and county road offices for travel on city and county roads.

BUYING PERMITS | Cities and counties may require a deposit or permit fee. This fee is to cover the cost of issuance. The fee is **not** refundable. If **you** have to get three permits (**one** each for city, county and state), you may be paying as much as $60.00 for your load.

The reason for the permits is basically to keep you off structures that will not carry the load. How would you like to have a bridge collapse with you on it or a hidden culvert give way beneath you as you are rolling down the road?

Some towns may not require that you buy a permit to carry your oversized load on their streets. This applies especially to small towns which are right next to larger ones. To travel through these towns, you may only need to call the police department and tell them of the load. They may even provide you with an escort so you won't get lost or encounter a low bridge.

Figure 19-6. When the State Historical Society of Wisconsin wanted to move the first Catholic cathedral in the state to their developing multicultural museum in Eagle, Wisconsin, they called on truckers to do the job. *Courtesy of the State Historical Society of Wisconsin in Old World Wisconsin Outdoor Museum*

ROUTING |

Usually, the various state or county departments will route you. Then again, you may be required to select the route yourself. Then, all they'll do is type it up on the permit form they are giving you. If this is the case, you had better be well prepared, with a pre-planned route. A good city map is a necessity to keep out of trouble.

Don't ever assume you have nothing to worry about; that's a mistake.

A detour, due to road work, may put you a mile or more off your original route and right into a bad turn or low-hanging obstacle. Instead, whenever there is a change of route, call the permit office for approval to proceed. Don't assume the responsibility of changing your route yourself. If you are caught off your permit route you may be fined anywhere from $200.00 to $1,000.00 or more. The sum can vary, but it can be very expensive. Plus, you may have trouble getting future permits.

330

Figure 19-7. The 35-mile route from Milwaukee to Eagle had to be intricately worked out. Bridges had to be crossed, and roads wide enough for the church had to be found. After months of planning, roads were closed, and the truckers set out - at night. *Coutesy of the State Historical Society of Wisconsin in Old World Wisconsin Outdoor Museum*

Figure 19-8 (Below). Thanks to truckers, St. Peter's Church, built in about 1839, now rests with other buildings in Old World Wisconsin. From every corner of the state, actual structures, typical of the many different ethnic groups which settled Wisconsin, have been moved to the 565-acre site. They have been restored on land similar to the land the settlers cleared to establish their farms. Without truckers who were extremely careful in their handling of these historic buildings, this ethnic museum could not have been possible. *Courtesy of the State Historical Society of Wisconsin in Old World Wisconsin Outdoor Museum*

DON'T TAKE CHANCES — Don't take chances and assume you can sneak a load through. It's not worth the risk. It isn't only the law you have to look out for. Persons in the machinery business may turn you in the minute you're spotted. This is their way of stopping illegal competition. It's a small world, and everyone knows what the other person is up to. There isn't a machine moved that isn't noticed by other companies in the area, or by their employees, within the first hour you are on the road.

You don't want to forget that the company that owns the equipment may have shopped around for the lowest rate, and this alerted everyone! So they are all watching to see who gets the haul. When you roll down the road, they know you underbid them and they don't take it too kindly.

A situation that usually costs a driver a job goes like this. You are out on the job. On the way back, another contractor stops you and asks if you can move his or her machine down the road a couple of miles. It isn't taking you out of your way, and you can make a quick 20 or 30 bucks, so you do it. You may get away with it the first time or two, but you'll eventually be spotted and lose your job. It's not worth it. But too many drivers can't resist that easy money. The first time you take it, you're hooked.

Here's why you should avoid this practice: (1) Your own company is not being paid for hauling the machine; you are bootlegging it. (2) Even more important, *you do not have a permit* to move the machine over any distance. Lack of a permit, as we have already noted, can carry severe penalties.

SUMMARY — Rules and regulations include federal, state, county and city laws, as well as your own company's policies. You are expected to follow all of these rules and regs, even if months go by without anyone checking up on you. Running illegally is a complete no no and will get you into serious trouble eventually.

Permit loads are loads which are too high, too wide, too long or too heavy to be legal in the city, county or state you want to haul them in. So, before you can haul them, you have to apply for a permit. The government body which provides your permit will okay a route for you to follow, tell you what hours you may travel with the load, and sometimes provide an escort.

Many road departments will color code their roads. Each color designates a different weight limit per axle. These weight limits are the maximum amounts that can be carried on the roads. Maps showing limits on each road in a vicinity are usually available at the government office involved.

Besides road limits, there are tire limits. The limit that can be carried by a given tire depends on many different things. Number of tires, as well as axles, is also very important in figuring out how heavy a load you can carry on a road. The "bridge law" sets requirements for the number of tires needed to carry different weights. The three things which go together to determine how many pounds you can carry over a road are road weight limit, number of axles on the rig, and rig length.

SUMMARY (cont.)

The reason for permits is to keep you off structures, such as bridges and roadbeds, that won't carry the load. So, if you've been routed one way and run into some type of trouble or detour, don't reroute yourself. First, your new way may not work. Second, you can be fined.

GLOSSARY

bootleg: To carry illegally.

bridge law: The more tires you have to carry the load, the more weight you can carry up to a given maximum. Specific weight limits are given for each number of tires.

Figure 19-9. Mooney Brothers Corp., of New Castle, PA, won the "Out-standing Hauling Job of the Year" award with this load. The award is made by the Heavy-Specialized Carriers Conference. They transported a total of 1,480 *tons* of nuclear reactor components in 14 intricately controlled moves. The moves were each 51 miles long from a Chester, PA dock to the power plant near Limerick. The loads averaged from 85 to 150 tons each and were supported on a specially built Talbert Trans-porter, riding on 80 wheels. The transporter is steerable from the rear and can extend its load-bearing axles through a range of five feet to spread the weight of the load while crossing bridges. The moves required nearly two years of pre-planning and close coordination with local highway and police authorities. The route wound through narrow congested city streets, over 37 bridges and under 11 over-passes. *Courtesy of the White Motor Corporation*

333

GLOSSARY   (cont.)

culvert: A passage under either a road or railroad which is covered with an arch so that water can flow underneath.

exceed: To be or go beyond or over. For example, to exceed the speed limit or weight limit.

permit load: An oversized load; a load which is heavier, taller, wider, or longer than legally allowed without a permit.

weigh station: A government-run place with scales for weighing each axle of a truck or combination unit to see that it complies with regulations.

▶ CHECKING THE FACTS

Answer each question briefly in the space provided.

1. What four things can make a load a permit load? _____

_____

_____

2. What made the load in Figure 19-1 a permit load? _____

_____   _____

3. Why was the load in Figure 19-9 probably a permit load? _____

_____

_____

4. What is bootlegging a load? _____

_____

5. How many axles does the rig mentioned in Figure 19-5 have? _____

What is the load? _____ How many tires

does the rig have? _____ How much does it weigh? _____

How many trips will it make? _____

When can the trips be made? _____

Why do you think it is a permit load? _____

_____

_____

6. How much over the bridge's weight limit was Al's rig and load? _____

_____

7. If you're going to carry a permit load, when do you apply for the permit? _____

■ GETTING THE MAIN IDEAS

Put a plus (+) before the statement if it is true. Put a zero (0) before the statement if it is false.

_____ 1. The driver is responsible for checking his route before driving a heavy load over it.

_____ 2. When the photo in Figure 19-2 was taken, all commercial trucks were required to stop to be weighed.

_____ 3. When there is any doubt as to clearing or crossing a bridge, the driver should always double check for errors and call his or her dispatcher before proceeding.

_____ 4. Permit loads are restricted to certain routes.

_____ 5. There is no charge for a permit. The application process is just supposed to keep you from winding up on a structure that can't carry your load.

_____ 6. A permit load is subject to inspection anywhere along your route by government officials.

_____ 7. State permits are issued by the state. City permits are issued by the county you're traveling in.

_____ 8. If you are caught violating your permit route, you will be fined and may lose your right to haul in the future.

_____ 9. The law requires carriers to work out routes for hauling permit loads within 14 working days after first asking the government agency for help in planning the route.

_____ 10. When a carrier selects a rig to carry a permit load, it considers the number of tires, but not the type of tires.

_____ 11. The bridge law used by many states says this: You must have a government escort to cross a bridge when carrying a permit load.

_____ 12. Permit loads may not normally move after dark. However, some governing bodies make exceptions.

★ GOING BEYOND THE FACTS AND IDEAS

1. Al, the driver of the 40-ton load, found himself in a pretty poor situation when he arrived at dawn at the wooden bridge. What questionable actions had he taken to get himself into the predicament? What might he have done to avoid it?

2. Explain why a state highway commission might schedule a permit load to be carried only between 8 PM and 6 AM.

3. Select a rig you're familiar with. How many axles (load-carrying axles) does it have? Find out how much weight each axle is capable of carrying. If it was loaded to its maximum weight on all axles, could you drive it over the bridge pictured in Figure 23-2?

4. Assume that your state has a tandem-axle weight limit of 34,000 pounds. However, on state roads marked as "purple routes," 48,000 pounds are allowed. Do you need a permit to haul a load weighing 47,500 pounds on a tandem-axle trailer over a purple route?

Chapter Twenty

SECURING THE CARGO

BEFORE YOU READ | Before you begin reading this chapter, ask yourself a few questions to get yourself thinking about securing cargo. It may help to write your answers down or tell them to someone else. (Doesn't that always seem to make us think harder?) Answering these questions will help you realize what you already know about tie-downs and will help you recognize your own views of their importance. Here are the questions:

1. What does tie-down or securing a load really mean?

2. Why is proper securing of a load important?

3. How important is it?

4. Who sets the standards for tie-downs?

5. How do you decide how to tie-down a load?

6. Who is to blame if a tie-down doesn't hold?

7. Have you ever seen a poorly secured load moving down the roadway? How did you feel about the individuals who loaded and secured the cargo? Describe the problems and how they could have been corrected.

Figure 20-1. The highway patrol officer who photographed this incident described it as a "spilled load." What things contributed to the accident? *Courtesy of the California Highway Patrol*

WHAT CAN ONE TEACH ABOUT TIE-DOWNS? As you can tell from the length of this chapter, we aren't spending much time on securing the cargo. Why is that? It isn't because of its lack of importance. The reason is this: Each load is different. Each load must be individually examined to determine the type of tie-down needed to secure the load.

There are really only two types of things you can say about tie-downs. First, you can mention *very basic things* because they fit every case. Second, you can list the *DOT regulations on securing cargo* because we're all responsible for knowing these rules. That's what this chapter will do. Beyond that, it's a matter of keeping your eyes open, using your head, and learning effective tie-down procedures on the job.

THE BASICS

● *Why You Want To Do It Right*

The reason for securing cargo is to see that it doesn't shift and damage the freight or, worse than that, wind up on the side of the highway or in a busy city intersection. This happens all too often. So often, that truckers and law enforcement officials have a name for it, "a spilled load." Over the years, probably every kind of load you can imagine has spilled on a roadway: bottled beverages as in Figure 20-1, heavy construction equipment, frozen turkeys, loose grains, tomatoes, huge plates of glass, sand, gravel, dry cement, live cattle. You name it, our highway departments have cleaned it up.

Every spilled load results in massive damage to the cargo, often destruction of it. More than that, it creates a very hazardous condition, affecting the motoring public. This hazard is increased when it occurs at night or during inclement weather when visibility is poor or roads are slick. And, it doesn't exactly lend prestige to the truck driving profession. None of the effects of a spilled load are very positive. So, the question becomes, "How do you prevent a spilled or damaged load?"

● *What You Want to Watch Out For*

When a driver ties down a load, or secures a load, she or he uses *ropes*, *chains*, *straps* or *cables*. The main purpose is to keep whatever she or he is hauling from moving. The driver must secure the load from up and down movement and keep it from shifting from front to back or one side to the other.

When you're loading, use your eyes and study the cargo area or floor to see how you should load it. Once it has been loaded, ask yourself these questions:

● Will it move or swing or roll? If so, which way will it go?

● What will happen if I stop short, turn a corner fast or pull up a steep grade? Will the cargo move or shift? If so, which way will it go?

THE BASICS (cont.)

The answers to these questions will tell you how to secure the load to prohibit any movement.

Here's one more thing to consider. Tie-downs do not just apply to open trailers like low-beds and flat-beds. Damage to cargo can happen inside a closed van too. Just because your load doesn't end up on the side of the free-way, it doesn't mean you don't have to worry about proper securing of the load against movement or shifting. The same questions apply. "Will the cargo move, shift or roll in the trailer?" "If so, which way will it go?" Plan your tie-downs just as you would for an open deck.

Figure 20-2. A Model 977 Cat track loader. *Courtesy of Caterpillar Tractor Company*

Let's talk about heavy equipment hauling for a moment too. What will happen to a large piece of equipment, like the one shown in Figure 20-2 or larger, if you hit the brakes hard? You won't lose it off the rear, so where will it go? You guessed it, off the front or side. What will happen to that same piece of equipment if you hit something? Same thing. Or how about going into a sharp curve too fast? You will literally throw the machine off the trailer deck. When you're completing a flat, long curve, a high tensile, steel trailer or low-bed will spring up and down. This can cause a machine to walk off the side, especially if there is mud or grease beneath the tracks. (So keep the deck clean and dry if you want to stay healthy.)

● *No Simple Solution*

Many states have set basic rules for tying down such items as loads of steel (things like bars, coils, or flat-plate steel), and the DOT has also set some very basic guidelines as to how to tie-down loads. These are put forth in the MCSR (Motor Carrier Safety Regulations), that little book that you have to carry and just about have memorized. However, there is no way any state or government can come up with a uniform tie-down because every truck is loaded differently and, with such a variety of products and equipment, it is the responsibility of the driver to secure the load. To do this, she or he uses whatever means she or he has available to make sure the load doesn't come off the rig.

One more point, and then we'll go on to the rules and regulations given in the MSCR. No matter how you tie-down your load, the way you drive your truck is the most important factor involved in the safety of your load. Your driving technique will determine whether or not you lose the load.

Figure 20-3. Typical five-axle lumber rig with legal number of cable tie-downs. *Courtesy of American Trucking Associations, Inc.*

The regulations listed below are all taken from the MCSR, Section 393.100. The letters in parentheses, (a), (b), etc., are called *paragraphs* by the DOT. The sections under the paragraphs are called *subparagraphs*, and they are shown by numbers in parentheses: (1), (2), etc. If you understand this way of speaking, that the DOT uses, it will help you understand the MCSR a little better.

MCSR 393.100 (a) This section applies to trucks, truck tractors, semi-trailers, full trailers and pole trailers. Each of those motor vehicles must, when transporting cargo, *be loaded and equipped to prevent the shifting or falling of the cargo* in the manner prescribed by the rules of this section, as follows:

(b) Each cargo-carrying motor vehicle must be equipped with devices providing protection against shifting or falling cargo that meet the requirements of either subparagraph (1), (2), (3) or (4) of this paragraph. *(That is Option A, B, C, or D.)*

(1) Option A. The vehicle must have *sides, sideboards, or stakes, and a rear endgate, endboard, or stakes.* These devices must be *strong enough* and *high enough* to assure that the cargo will not shift upon, or fall from the vehicle. These devices must have *no aperture large enough to permit cargo in contact with one or more of the devices to pass through.*

(2) Option B. The vehicle must have *at least one tie-down assembly that has the strength to secure an article against movement in any direction,* and this strength must be *at least 1½ times the weight of that article.* There must be such a tie-down assembly *for each 10 linear feet of lading or fraction thereof. (This is a basic requirement. The DOT goes into more detail about specifications for the tie-down assemblies and hooks, etc., that attach the cables, etc., to the vehicle.)*

MCSR 393.100 (b) (cont.)

A pole trailer or an expandable trailer transporting metal articles under the special rules of paragraph (c) of this section is required only to have two or more of these tie-down assemblies at each end of the trailer. (See paragraph (c) below.)

In addition, the vehicle must have *as many tie-down assemblies* meeting the above requirements *as are necessary to secure all cargo* being transported, either *by direct contact* between the cargo and the tie-down assemblies <u>*or by dunnage*</u> which is in contact with the cargo and is secured by tie-down assemblies.

(3) <u>Option C</u>. (This option applies to vehicles transporting metal articles only.) A vehicle transporting cargo which consists of metal articles must conform to either the rules in subparagraph (1), (2), or (4) of this paragraph or the special rules for transportation of metal articles set forth in paragraph (c) of this section. (See below.)

(4) <u>Option D</u>. The vehicle must have *other means of protecting against shifting or falling cargo* which are similar to, and *at least as effective as*, those specified in subparagraphs (1), (2), or (3) of this paragraph.

(c) Special rules for metal articles. The rules of this paragraph apply to motor vehicles transporting cargo consisting of metal articles if that vehicle does not conform to the rules listed in MCSR 393.100 (b).

(NOTE: This paragraph sets special rules for both loading and securing metal articles such as coils, ingots, rods, tin mill products, etc. There are different rules for different types of metal products. If you are hauling one of these articles, be sure your loading and tie-down method meets these specifications.)

SUMMARY | The reason you secure or tie-down a load is this: You want to keep it from moving or shifting its position in any way. Pressure will exert itself on the load as you drive. It will try to get it to move toward the rear while you're accelerating. It will make it lean to one side as you round a corner. And, it will send it surging forward when you brake, unless it is securely tied down. If you don't use strong enough cable or rope, or if you don't secure the pressure points, you may have a lot of breakage in a trailer or spill your load off a flat-bed or low-bed.

SUMMARY   (cont.)

Every load is different and needs to be secured differently. So, although securing a load is very important, there isn't too much one can say about how to do it. Much has to be learned through experience, but the best thing you can do before securing a load is this: Ask yourself which way a load will tend to lean or move while your driving, turning and braking. That will tell you where the pressure points are and how to secure it. Your tie-down should prohibit any movement.

The DOT has set a few guidelines in the MCSR for securing cargo. Each driver is required to see that the load is secured to protect against shifting or falling cargo. This can be done by things like stakes, sides, and endboards if these are strong enough to keep the load from moving. They also have to keep any part of the cargo from falling through a hole. Or, the load may be secured by tie-down assemblies. These assemblies, like cables, must be one and a half times stronger than the weight of the thing you've tied down. Or, the load may be secured in some other way like these ways if that way is just as effective. The DOT also sets specific rules for tying down metal products and even for how to load them.

As a driver, you are responsible for knowing exactly what the DOT requires, so you might want to read Section 393.100 through 393.106 in the MCSR book. We have listed the key points in this chapter, but not all of the points. Finally, remember that no tie-down in the world, no matter how good, will protect your cargo if you drive recklessly. Your excellent tie-down techniques must be used with a good driving technique if you want your cargo to arrive undamaged.

GLOSSARY

aperture: An opening; a gap; a hole.

high tensile: Able to be extended or stretched. A high tensile trailer can bend with the weight of a heavy piece of equipment without breaking.

lading: Freight. This is another word for cargo and is where we get the term "bill of lading," meaning a list of items of freight.

tracks: The steel rollers used by many bulldozers, loaders, cranes, etc., to move the machine; a means for moving a heavy piece of equipment which is sometimes used in place of tires. (See Figure 20-2.)

▶ CHECKING THE FACTS

Circle the letter of the phrase that <u>best</u> completes each sentence or <u>best</u> answers each question.

1. Figure 20-1 is of
    A. an accurate tie-down.
    B. a legal, but not effective tie-down.
    C. a spilled load.
    D. a load that should have been in a van.

342

2. What does the MCSR say about tie-down procedures?
   A. It lists specific tie-down procedures for over 100 different loads.
   B. It explains a uniform tie-down procedure which can be used on all loads except construction equipment, permit loads and metal products.
   C. It gives no rules on tie-downs because it says each load is different.
   D. It sets forth very basic guidelines about tie-down procedures.

3. Why do loads in vans have to be tied down sometimes?
   A. so the load doesn't shift or roll and damage the cargo
   B. to prevent a spilled load
   C. to separate cargo going to different consignees
   D. to keep balloon freight from rising

4. What can happen when you're driving a trailer that springs up and down on curves?
   A. The hooks on the end of the cable may open, freeing the tie-down.
   B. A bulldozer or loader may walk off the side of the trailer.
   C. The trailer deck may crack and spill your load.
   D. The combination may jackknife.

5. What question do you ask yourself before you secure a load?
   A. "What type of cable, strap, rope or chain should I use?"
   B. "What will look most professional to the motoring public?"
   C. "Will the load move or swing or roll? If so, which way will it go?"
   D. "What is my route like? Will I need special chains or other tie-downs for hills, long curves, etc.?"

6. A good tie-down protects your load against any movement. What is the other thing which will decide whether you lose your load or not?
   A. your driving technique
   B. your braking technique
   C. your loading technique
   D. the type of commodity you are carrying

7. The MCSR says your load must be protected against
   A. extreme heat and extreme cold
   B. vandalism
   C. shifting or falling
   D. leaning or spilling

8. Under subparagraph (2) (Option B) the DOT says that tie-down assemblies have to touch one of two things. What are the two things?
   A. the load or the rear trailer door.
   B. the load or the rear trailer curtain.
   C. the cargo or the trailer deck
   D. the cargo or dunnage secured to the deck

■ GETTING THE MAIN IDEAS

Now that you have read the chapter, go back and answer the questions which were asked on the first page of the chapter. If you wrote out the answers before you read the chapter, you might do this: Reread your original answers. See what changes you would make in your answers, if any. Add your changes or modifications to your original answers or rewrite your answers.

★ GOING BEYOND THE FACTS AND IDEAS

1. Examine the accident in Figure 20-1. What do you think happened? What are all of the factors which may have contributed to the incident? Who was at fault? Do you think the driver was given a traffic citation? Finally, was the driver of this vehicle in compliance with DOT regulations as listed in MCSR 393.100?

2. Describe the type of tie-down used in Figure 20-3. Which subparagraph of paragraph 393.100 (b) does the tie-down meet the requirements of? Explain how it meets the requirements. Then, decide whether you feel the tie-down will hold the load or not. What would have to happen for this load to spill?

Figure 21-1. This International truck, with a van body, is designed for city and suburban delivery operations. It has a 9.0 liter diesel engine. *Courtesy of International Harvester*

Chapter Twenty-One

LOCAL DELIVERY AND COMPANY IMAGE

BEFORE
YOU
READ

In this book, we have spent most of our time talking about heavy-duty diesel driving - the type of driving typical of a line-haul driver. However, when you enter a career in trucking, you may choose to become a local, or small delivery truck, operator. So, in this chapter, we're going to take a look at some of the special concerns of the local driver. In the first half of the chapter, we'll look at some special characteristics of local delivery. In the second half, we'll look at customer relations. That is, we'll see how your actions and appearance affect your company's image.

The first half of the chapter will be especially interesting to the person considering local delivery as a career. If you haven't considered driving a small delivery truck, you might find yourself thinking about it after reading the chapter. On the other hand, you might decide it's not for you. The second half of the chapter, on company image, is important for all drivers. This includes local *and* over-the-road drivers. We're including company image in this chapter because the local driver has more contact with the public than

BEFORE YOU READ (cont.)

the line-haul driver does. Even so, all drivers are representatives of their companys. So, all drivers should be concerned with how their actions affect the company image.

Before you read on, how about finding out what you already know? Your own common sense will tell you a lot. This time, don't preview the chapter. If you're used to using the SQ3R study method, terrific, but don't use it right now. Instead, without looking ahead, ask yourself these two questions and then answer them.

1. What are some of the important differences between local delivery and long-line hauling?

_____

_____

_____

_____

2. What are the four most important things you should do to help develop a good company image for yourself and/or for your employer?

_____

_____

_____

_____

Spend a few moments answering the above questions. Think about them. After you have answered the questions, you may use the SQ3R approach to study the chapter if you like.

CHARACTERISTICS OF LOCAL DELIVERY

When you are involved in local delivery of any type, you are still a truck driver. However, your duties will vary quite a bit from driving a tractor-trailer combination. Your responsibilities will remain the same to *your company, the general motoring public*, and *most laws*. Local delivery drivers are not subject to DOT rules and regulations regarding hours of service. Thus, they may work many hours of overtime, depending upon the work load.

There are some advantages of this type of job. The work is fairly steady because it is not usually affected by seasonal manufacturing. And, you are home every night.

Problems with fender-bender types of accidents are greatly increased because you are often exposed to heavy traffic. You have a heavy schedule, narrow streets, and a great number of stops. On the other hand, the long-line driver doesn't usually make a delivery until he or she reaches the final destination, perhaps hundreds of miles away.

What are some of the other differences from line-haul driving? Usually, you have a load of boxes to carry or a hand truck full of boxes to handle, up and down, at nearly every stop. Often, there are many flights of stairs to climb. Furthermore, there may be no parking areas available and the street may be congested, so you may have to double-park. Let's take a look at some of the hazards that you'll want to avoid in the local delivery business.

> THREE
> HAZARDS
> TO AVOID

● *Moving Without Looking First*

The local driver is stopping and then going all day long. Because of this, the driver tends to move the vehicle (or him or herself) first - before looking to see if the path is clear. This can become almost a routine. But it's a very bad habit, whether you're driving a bakery truck, a milk truck or a UPS van. Therefore, you must use extreme caution, not only in driving, but in entering and leaving your vehicle.

Here's an example of why a look-before-you-leap attitude is important. You have parked along the curb in the garment district in New York City. Right alongside your truck is a sidewalk elevator with steel doors covering it. While you're in the back of your truck, picking up an armful of boxes, the elevator rises from beneath the sidewalk, coming up from the basement of the building. You don't hear the bell ringing because of the traffic noise. As you step out your side door, that first step is a very, very long one.

Sidewalk elevators aren't the only things that can cause accidents. You have to watch out for open manholes, passing vehicles, and many other dangers.

● *Leaving Doors Unlocked*

Another hazard has to do with theft from the delivery truck. If you're old enough, perhaps you remember the old steal-the-pies-from-the-bakery-wagon trick. Unfortunately, to the driver, the situation isn't as funny as the old cartoons made it. So, whether you're driving a pastry wagon or something with less tempting cargo, lock your truck doors.

Always check your company regulations regarding locked doors on your truck. Your employer has been in the business for a while, and knows what is likely to happen. You don't want to lose cargo. Most companies are very strict with this regulation, and they require an accurate count of the pieces. Be sure that there are no shortages to mar your day.

THREE HAZARDS TO AVOID   (cont.)

● *Runaway Trucks*

Many drivers have lost delivery trucks on hills. Here's what happens. The driver quickly sets the hand brake and jumps out of the truck, leaving the engine running for a so-called quick delivery. When the driver returns, she or he finds that the hand brake didn't hold the truck. The truck is still there. The only problem is, now it's in someone's front yard.

Once again, most companies have definite regulations on how to secure your vehicle when you make a stop. These include the following:

● turning the wheels into the curb

● setting the hand brake

● leaving the truck in gear

● turning the ignition off

● placing chocks at the rear wheels

YOUR RESPONSIBILITY

We've talked a lot about the huge responsibility of the heavy-duty truck driver. After all, the line-haul driver's equipment costs thousands and thousands of dollars. But, if you choose local delivery, don't forget: Your responsiblities are just as great, if not greater than the driver of a 30-ton semi. Why? Because you are exposed to denser traffic every hour of your working day.

Now let's get down to specifics which govern your work with small delivery trucks.

Figure 21-2. A small, local delivery truck, ready for loading. *Courtesy of Pullman Trailmobile*

BEGINNING YOUR DAY

All small delivery trucks, often called *retail delivery trucks*, are loaded out at the warehouse each morning, very early. If you work for a milk company, or a bread company, it is not unusual to start your day at 3:00 AM so you can make the necessary early morning deliveries. If you work for a company such as United Parcel Service, a florist, or a department store which has its own trucks, the customary procedure is to start your day at 7:00 or even 8:00 AM.

Normally, each driver is responsible for loading his or her own truck. Most small parcel companies have a general routine. If you work for a small parcel company, your day may progress something like this.

Most of your packages are at a given point on the loading dock. Your truck is there, backed in, ready for you to load. (Occasionally, the truck will not be spotted before you arrive. There may be times when you have to fuel your truck and back it into the dock area or up to the door.) As you load your parcels or packages, you check each piece against the delivery receipt to make sure everything is correct. You check address, weight, type of packages, number of packages, etc. Thus, you also make sure you don't have a package that belongs on another truck. This procedure usually takes from one to one and one-half hours. Then, you're ready to hit the street. If you arrive at 8:00 o'clock, you are usually on the road by 9:30. From that point on, you follow your route.

YOUR ROUTE

Normally, your route is all established with a given number of stops. Most drivers are assigned a particular route or area. If you are given a set route, you will become familiar with your individual stops so that you don't always have to refer to a map to find the addresses. By keeping you on a fixed route, your company will know approximately how long it will take you to make 30 or 40 deliveries and return on a normal working day. Often, the only variation from day to day will be the number of stops you make. An average route may cover a central area in the center of a city with as many as 40 to 60 stops a day. So you can see you don't have time to sit and daydream.

Larger companies will often transfer you to another route while you are breaking in, or learning a route. They may keep doing this until you have covered all the routes in their territory. In this way, if a driver is off work or on vacation, you can easily sub for him or her.

WORKING HOURS AND BONUSES

During the winter holiday season, you should plan on quite a few overtime hours. You may spend from 10 to 14 hours on the job each day although during the rest of the year you will probably cover the same route within an eight-hour period. A few parcel delivery companies have a bonus system. The more freight you handle, the more money you earn above your hourly wage. In other words, from start to finish, it's a matter of go, go, go, as fast as possible, but not at the expense of safety or courtesy to your customers.

WORKING HOURS AND BONUSES   (cont.)

Competition is always around the corner, waiting to step in and grab your account should you fail to do a good job. You are your company's best sales-person. You are the one in personal contact with each customer, and your company will often be judged by your actions. Many times, how you conduct yourself makes the difference between getting and keeping the business or losing it.

BENEFITS

A good percentage of the companies furnish uniforms for all of their drivers. Many will also have the typical benefits: a pension, hospitalization, paid holidays, etc. These are some of the things you'll want to consider when you choose a company to work for.

PROMOTION

Most local delivery companies will assign jobs on a seniority basis. As you build seniority, you may want to drive one of the larger, semi-trailers that run between cities. Ever wonder how a company selects the drivers to drive their sets of doubles between cities? Local drivers bid on these jobs. Naturally, the driver who has five or more years experience and bids for the job will have a better chance of getting the tractor-trailer run than someone who has just started with the company.

Normally, the line jobs are placed on the company bulletin board on a *"bid list."* If you are interested in a job, you place your name on the bid list for consideration. It may be that the drivers with seniority are not interested in long-line driving. If so, you may stand a good chance of being chosen.

But switching to long-line driving isn't the only type of advancement for a driver. Many drivers tire of fighting traffic daily and request an inside warehouse job. Inside, they'll be sorting freight and handling bills. They may go from that to handling freight or a dispatch job. It is also possible to go from there to a warehouse supervisor's position. You may have a good personality and want to get into the sales end of the work. So, you may end up as a regional salesperson, soliciting freight for your company or picking up new accounts.

Local delivery is not a blind alley job. There is considerable potential for advancement. In many cases, the opportunity for advancement is greater when you're working for a local delivery company than when you're sitting behind the wheel of an over-the-road rig.

CUSTOMER RELATIONS

A good rapport with customers is all part of your day's work - whatever your goal in trucking is. I have known a number of drivers who have quit one company because of a better offer from a rival company, and they have taken most of their accounts with them! So the personal contacts you make count for a lot. Don't underestimate the potential. The opportunities are there. How you handle them is

CUSTOMER RELATIONS (cont.)

the deciding factor. It boils down to how dedicated you are in performing your duties. We have a saying in trucking: "A lazy driver never gets ahead. He just gets down the road."

COMPANY IMAGE

How important a part does a driver play in building good customer relations? Some companies feel a driver can represent the industry to a greater extent than salespeople. A good driver averages more stops per day than the average salesperson,

Figure 21-3. Good customer relations can make the difference between staying in business and going out of business. The Bekins Company sported this fleet in San Francisco in 1912. Not all the vans were motor trucks in those days. Shown here are a number of different units. *Courtesy of Bekins Van Lines Company*

and every pickup or delivery can be classified as a "call" on a customer. The driver is the company's direct representative. Most shipping and receiving clerks see the driver more often than any salesperson or other company representatives.

A good driver, then, is always selling. The driver may not be selling a product, but she or he is selling the only thing a trucking company can sell: *service*. Service includes many things. Four of these things are promptness, cooperation, appearance and courtesy.

PROMPTNESS

How can you help your company and customer by being prompt? By getting to the customer early enough to allow the items being delivered to go into production. A customer shouldn't have to call to trace a shipment. That's an annoyance. Tracing a shipment takes time from the customer's other work. Of course, it also means there has been a delay in shipment. And even a five or ten minute delay can be very costly. Production schedules often depend on receiving raw materials or parts on time; they can also depend on shipping finished products on time.

COOPERATION

Cooperation with shipping and receiving clerks is a large part of the selling job. You should work hard to obey all rules of the plant: speed within the plant, smoking, etc. Some concerns use separate doors for shipping and receiving. If you're delivering a shipment, use the receiving doors. If you're making a pickup, use the shipping doors.

351

COOPERATION   (cont.)

Don't wait until the receiving clerk is ready to receive your freight to start searching through the load for it. Know *what* you are going to deliver when you are ready to deliver it.

Is it always necessary to wait in line to be loaded or unloaded? No. If all shipping or receiving doors are filled, don't wait to back into the dock if you only have a small package. A receiving or shipping clerk will respect a driver who carries a small package instead of causing congestion by backing the truck in. Industry has production problems too. Cooperate by doing your best to cut down on congestion and speed the load.

Another way you can show cooperation is to know all about the services your company can render. A customer may ask you whether or not your company can handle a shipment. If you have a point list or route guide available, you may be able to answer the question. If you're in doubt, call your route or rate clerk. This shows the customer that your company is eager to serve. If your schedule is too tight for you to make the call, you can still show the same eagerness to serve. Tell the customer that you are not sure whether or not your trucking company can handle the load, but that you know the office can give that information. Then, give the customer the *correct phone number* (including area code and extension) and the *name of the person to talk to*. Whichever plan you use, be cooperative, helpful and polite. Your company can grow and prosper only by increasing its business. Increased tonnage is increased business. Knowing that your company can handle a certain shipment will help the shipping clerk move freight and add another shipment to your company's business.

If your company can handle a load, the customer may wish to ship it immediately. So keep some bills of lading in your truck at all times.

Figure 21-4. Bastanchury Bottled Water Company drivers own their own gasoline trucks. Driver, Howard Lauck, is proud of his rig and keeps it shining. *Photo by M. McFadden*

PERSONAL APPEARANCE

Appearance is very important in local delivery trucking. Cleanliness isn't expensive. It's important that you begin your day by taking time to do things like wash, shave, and comb your hair before going to work.

Your choice of clothes can make either a good or a bad impression too. Uniforms are ideal, but they mean nothing unless you keep them clean and in good repair. A driver who takes pride in her or himself and in her or his

PERSONAL APPEARANCE
(cont.)

appearance usually takes pride in the equipment and work too. Customers (and employers) know this. You may find that they judge your work by your appearance. If they do, how will they judge it?

COURTESY ON AND OFF THE ROAD

Shippers take pride in the commodities their companies manufacture and ship. They believe they manufacture first-class merchandise, so they expect it to be sold in first-class condition. Take care in loading their products onto your truck and unloading it onto their dock. If you throw it, you'll probably find you're throwing away a customer too.

Figure 21-5. Customers often develop an image of a company after one look at and a few moments conversation with a driver. Howard Lauck has a smile and a polite word for every customer. He even goes that extra mile of emptying the water bottle into the customer's water cooler if she or he needs his help. *Photo by M. McFadden*

Shipping and receiving clerks have work to do, just as you have. Don't take up their time solving all the world's problems. Don't hang around the plant or get into someone's way. When you've unloaded or loaded the freight, and the bills have been properly signed, thank the clerk, checker or lumper; then, be on your way. They have other trucks to load and unload. Don't spend time talking with other employees or drivers either.

We'd better mention three other things too. They, too, are a part of on and off the road courtesy:

- Be careful of your talk. Abusive language and profanity do not impress people.

- Alcohol and work don't mix. Therefore, the use of intoxicants is strictly forbidden.

- Be courteous and polite at all times.

We've mentioned a number of things that will help lead to good relations between the company and the shipper or consignee. But a large part of your work will deal with people who never directly ship or receive even a pound of freight. These people are the *general public*. And these are the people responsible for making most of the trucker's laws.

COURTESY ON AND OFF THE ROAD (cont.)

Your driving habits will definitely influence the thinking of the general public. Are trucks a menace on the streets of our cities and the highways of our states? Proper driving habits will greatly influence the thinking of the driving public. We truckers never know who might be driving ahead of us or in back of us. We never know if it's someone we might want to impress. Someone once said that one rotten apple can spoil a bushel full of good ones. Well, one bad driver can cause a lot of harmful legislation.

SUMMARY | Local delivery drivers are not subject to the DOT laws; however, most other laws relating to truck driving affect them too. Some of the advantages of local delivery are that the work is fairly steady, you are home every night, there is room for advancement, and most companies offer benefits such as paid holidays and medical insurance.

Local delivery has its hazards however. The driver usually drives in heavy traffic for at least a good portion of the day. This can increase the possibility of minor accidents. Drivers of local trucks learn to avoid three other hazards too. They learn to look before moving - either their body or their truck. They learn to lock their truck doors. And they learn to secure their vehicle properly when stopped for a pickup or delivery.

Most drivers will load their own trucks at the beginning of their workday. Typically, they will make 30 to 60 stops per day, usually following a set route. During the holiday season, they may have to work overtime to complete their delivery schedules.

As a small delivery truck driver, you are your company's main public relations representative. You see more customers than a salesperson or company representative ever has time to see. Therefore, the company image depends on you. You need to be prompt in making your deliveries and pickups. You will want to cooperate with customers in any way you can because this often increases business for the carrier. Since your appearance is a sign of your attitude toward your job, you will want to be neat, clean, and wear appropriate clothing. Finally, as a company representative, you should show courtesy to your customers and to the motoring public. Remember, the man or woman driving behind you might be on his or her way to vote on a law regarding trucking.

GLOSSARY |

account: A person or company that uses the services of a carrier on a continuing basis. The person or company is called an account because some type of payment arrangement has been set up. That is, the company or person has an account with the trucking firm.

bid list: A seniority list. Drivers place their names on it to bid for a desirable route or run.

GLOSSARY (cont.)

rapport: Harmony; a good relationship. The word is pronounced ra·pore'.

route guide (point list): A list or map of the pickups and deliveries a driver must make.

tonnage: The total amount of a shipment, calculated in tons. The word also has another meaning. Sometimes it refers to a charge per ton on cargo. This charge can be made at a port, canal or dock, or it can be a tax based on the amount of cargo a ship carries.

trace: In trucking, to trace usually means to put a tracer on. A tracer is a request that a carrier locate a shipment. A customer may trace something to speed its movement, to establish proof of delivery, or to request an answer to a previously filed claim.

▶ CHECKING THE FACTS

Put a plus (+) before the statement if it is true. Put a zero (0) before the statement if it is false.

_____ 1. Local drivers are subject to the same hours of service laws as over-the-road drivers are.

_____ 2. A local driver can expect to have extra time off around the Christmas holiday season.

_____ 3. A local driver does more loading and unloading of vehicles than an over-the-road driver normally does.

_____ 4. A local driver usually has more contact with customers than a line-haul driver does.

_____ 5. It is a danger to leave your truck doors unlocked.

_____ 6. One hazard for a local driver is runaway trucks.

_____ 7. A local driver often has to get to the warehouse each morning to plan his or her route.

_____ 8. It usually takes a local driver 3 hours to load the delivery truck if a lumper didn't do it for the driver.

_____ 9. Some drivers have been known to take their accounts with them when they take a job with a different carrier.

_____ 10. A good driver will see to it that his or her accounts trace all shipments.

_____ 11. If you're making a delivery, you should use the shipping doors.

_____ 12. One way to show cooperation is to answer questions from a customer about whether or not your company can handle a shipment.

■ GETTING THE MAIN IDEAS

1. Why do we say that the local driver is the carrier's public relations representative?

2. What can a driver do to improve the carrier's company image?

3. What are some of the hazards of driving in the city?

4. Say you're making 50 deliveries a day in a hilly city like San Francisco or Quebec City. How should you secure your vehicle at each stop?

5. What are the main differences between local delivery truck driving and over-the-road driving?

★ GOING BEYOND THE FACTS AND IDEAS

1. How can you be cooperative and courteous if you have to make 60 stops each day?

2. What can a driver do (either a local or a line-haul driver) to show courtesy to the motoring public as he or she drives?

3. Explain how a delay in delivering raw materials or parts might affect a consignee.

4. What qualities do you have that would make you a good local driver?

5. Would you rather drive a line-haul unit or a small delivery truck? What are your reasons?

Chapter
Twenty-Two

ACCIDENTS
AND
FIRE
PREVENTION

ACCIDENT ON A FOGGY NIGHT

In the last chapter, we talked about road courtesy. Every commercial driver has a responsibility to help create a good image of truck drivers as a whole. That's true. But use your head about how you show road courtesy. Otherwise, you may cause an accident or make a small accident into a larger one. Remember this: Your first responsiblity is to protect your rig. Let's take a look at how one helpful driver created a monstrous situation. We'll call the driver Emmett.

Figure 22-1. Two serious truck accidents are pictured here. The driver of one of these rigs was killed. *Courtesy of the California Highway Patrol*

Emmett is driving a tank truck, loaded with fuel, on a foggy evening. He spots a fender-bender accident in the center lane of the highway. Emmett decides to be helpful, so he pulls his rig over to the shoulder. He leaves the rear end of his tanker only a foot off the paved portion of the highway. Mind you, this is in dense fog. Assuming the four-way blinkers will protect the back of the rig, Emmett dashes across the highway to lend a helping hand.

While Emmett is lending a hand, a bus comes through the fog and collides with the rear end of the tanker. In the next few minutes about 30 more vehicles plow into the back of the bus or each other. The highway now looks like a junkyard. There is a monstrous bonfire and people and automobiles are scattered over an area of 400 feet or more.

ACCIDENT ON A FOGGY NIGHT (cont.)

Emmett was in a hurry to help someone out. But, in so doing, he created another accident which was much, much worse. This kind of situation has happened many times over the years. And it will happen again and again on our interstate highways unless all drivers learn not to expose themselves, or their equipment, to this kind of peril.

BEFORE YOU READ ON | In this chapter, we will talk about how to prevent accidents and fires and what to do in case of fire or accident. To help you pick up the key ideas, we have provided you with a study sheet, below. You will find the answers in order as you read the chapter.

1. What are the <u>three</u> <u>main</u> <u>rules</u> a driver must follow after an accident?

   _____

   _____

   _____

2. How do you protect the scene of an accident? _____

   _____

3. How do you contact the police and your terminal of an accident if there is no phone nearby?

   _____

4. Ideally, who should fill out the preliminary accident report? _____

   _____ Who fills it out if that person

   can't? _____

5. According to the DOT, what kinds of accidents must be reported? _____

   _____

6. What is the best prevention for fires? _____

   _____

7. Give one specific thing you can do for protection if there is an electrical fire in your rig?

   _____

8. What should you do before you open a manhole cover on a tank truck? _____

   _____

9. What two things do you tell the fire department if you call them about a fire on your rig?

    _____

10. How often should you check your fire extinguisher to see that it is in working order?

    _____

11. What human failure seems to cause more truck accidents than any other human failing? (According to the DOT study)

    _____

12. What two mechanical failures seem to cause more truck accidents than any other component breakdown? (According to the DOT study)

    _____

    _____

| DRIVER'S RESPONSIBILITY AT THE SCENE OF AN ACCIDENT | A truck driver today has to be a Philadelphia lawyer. Whenever a rig is involved in an accident, the driver must follow a strict set of rules. You need to know what to do, and what *not* to do. So, first we'll give three essential rules to follow anytime you have an accident. We'll talk briefly about first aid. Then, we'll give the steps you should follow after having an accident. |

● *Three Essential Rules*

1. Get down every possible bit of information about the accident. Do this while it is fresh in your mind. Get down all the facts on paper. Use diagrams. (Later, you will give this information to your employer and its insurance company.)

2. Get all the information you can from witnesses. Write down the witnesses' names, license plate numbers and any other information you can.

3. Be unfailingly courteous to those involved in the accident, to the police and other authorities at the scene, and to any witnesses or bystanders you come in contact with. But *never admit guilt,* even if you were at fault.

● *First Aid*

These are three hard and fast rules you must abide by. Have we forgotten anything? Yes, one very important duty: If there is no one better qualified around, take care of the injured parties first. If you don't know what you're doing, try to make them as comfortable as possible. Don't try to play doctor because you may make someone's injury worse. And playing doctor can result in a lawsuit. There's a big difference between giving first aid and providing the services of a doctor.

According to the American National Red Cross, *first aid* is "the immediate and temporary care given the victim of an accident or sudden illness until the service of a physician can be obtained." The wording of this definition is very important. Notice the key words: *"immediate," "temporary,"* and *"until the services of a physician can be obtained."* If you ever give first aid, keep those words in mind.

If you plan to be driving a lot, there's a good chance that sometime in your life you may be the first person to arrive at the scene of an accident, even if you weren't involved in the accident. To be well-prepared, you might want to enroll in a first aid course sometime.

● *Steps to Take*

When a truck is involved in an accident, the driver and his or her company almost always have two strikes against them. There just seems to be a general attitude that big trucks and big companies might be careless. So, as a driver, you will want to protect yourself and your company. You can do this by getting all the important information down on paper, and later, reporting it accurately. Most important, do nothing to arouse additional antagonism. The following steps are aimed at achieving these objectives.

1. STOP. Failure to stop at the scene of an accident in which you are involved is a criminal offense. It will subject you to the penalty of the law, in addition to disciplinary action by your company.

2. PROTECT THE SCENE. Turn on your truck's four-way flashers. Then, *immediately* set out your warning devices. Remember, the DOT requires one warning device approximately 100 feet in each direction from the scene and one near the scene. If the accident occurs near a curve or crest of a hill, set the signals further out, but don't put them over 500 feet from the accident. In most cases, you will probably use three emergency reflectors. (Refer back to Figure 7-3.) However, some vehicles will be equipped with a different type of warning device. Some may have three electric emergency lanterns. Some may have three liquid-burning emergency flares, also called pot torches. And some may have three red emergency reflectors. Whichever kind you have, you must have three and they must be placed at the distances from the accident that we just gave. MCSR 393.95(g) says, however, that you can't carry pot torches on specified types of vehicles. For example, you can't carry them on tank trucks which are hauling flammable liquids. (Refer back to Chapter 7 for exact placement.)

Use *extreme caution* with flame-producing emergency signals if there is spilled fuel present. Also, post reliable bystanders to help conrol traffic if necessary. Be sure to warn them of dangers, what to watch out for, etc.

3. Assist any injured persons. But *don't* move an injured person unless it's absolutely necessary. Keep any injured person as warm as possible (not hot) while you wait for an ambulance, doctor or other competent person to handle their removal. If you are trained in first aid, give it.

4. Notify the police. If you can't get to a nearby phone, write a carefully worded note. On the note, give the location and apparent seriousness of the accident. Give the note to a motorist who appears reliable and ask her or him to notify the police for you. *Don't leave your equipment and cargo unguarded unless there is an extreme emergency.*

5. Notify your nearest company terminal. There are two times when you *must* notify your nearest company terminal. First, in case of serious accident. Second, in *every* case where a fatality or injury occurs. Your company must notify its insurance company without delay. If you can't reach a company official, notify the nearest office of the insurance company. This phone number should be listed in your accident report kit. Ask someone at the insurance office to contact the proper official in your company. What happens if you can't handle this task yourself? Again, give the information to a bystander who appears reliable, and ask that person to make the notification for you.

6. Be specific. Be specific when you report an accident to anyone. Whether it's by phone or messenger, give the following information: (1) exact location, (2) exact time, (3) extent of injury or damage, (4) condition of cargo, and (5) where you can be reached.

In calling a company terminal, be sure you're talking to someone who can act on your report. Make a note of the person's name for future reference.

Figure 22-2. One frequent cause of truck accidents is running off the road. In the photo at left, the driver ran off a freeway offramp. At right, the driver ran off into an open trench. *Courtesy of the California Highway Patrol*

7. Be sure a preliminary accident report form is filled out. If a company traffic safety official arrives at the scene, she or he will normally fill out the form. But, if that person is not around, you will have to complete the form yourself. (A sample preliminary accident report form is shown in Figure 22-3. It has been properly completed.)

    The company you work for will have someone investigate the accident. That person will need the information on the preliminary accident form when she or he does the investigation. So be sure you have accurately recorded all information on the form. Later, the investigator will complete another form, called the "Supervisor's Investigation Report." (A sample investigation report is shown, properly completed, in Figure 22-4.)

8. Get the names and addresses of all witnesses, both for and against you. If a witness refuses to give a name, note the license number of his or her automobile or truck. But what do you do if there are no witnesses of your accident? Write down the name and address of the first person to arrive at the scene.

9. Be polite. Give your name and your company's name. Offer to show your Class One or Chauffeur's license (or whatever truck driver's license you have). But don't discuss the accident with anyone except the police or representatives of your company or your insurance company. Any statements you make may be used against you later. It doesn't matter what the circumstances are - *admit nothing; promise nothing,* and *don't argue!*

10. Have pictures taken if possible. Don't move and don't allow anyone else to move any of the vehicles until someone arrives who can verify or witness the position of the vehicles. They should also witness the length and position of skid marks. (See Figure 22-2, right.) And, if the accident was at night, they should witness the lights on the truck. If the accident was serious, try to hire a commercial photographer. Then, instruct the photographer to lock the plates in a safe place. Later, the plates should be surrendered only to a company official.

11. Record the following information. You'll need these things to make a complete accident report.

    1. Exact location, time and date.

    2. Make, model, type and license number of every vehicle involved.

    3. Names and addresses of all persons involved: drivers, owners and passengers of all vehicles, *and* owners of other property involved. (For example, the names of the owners of the land shown in Figure 22-1 should be obtained.)

    4. Names and addresses of insurance companies which cover the vehicles or other property involved.

PRELIMINARY REPORT OF ACCIDENT OR LOSS

Form C0820, Reorder from
American Trucking Associations, Inc
1616 P Street, N.W.
Washington, D.C. 20036

Exact Date of Accident _Feb. 6_ Time _8_ ☒ A.M. ☐ P.M. Day of Week _Wednesday_

HOW MANY VEHICLES WERE INVOLVED IN ACCIDENT?

Company Employee _M. Peachy_ Truck # 13 Tractor No. _# 13_ Trailer No. _____

Can you be reached by phone, if necessary to call back?

Area Code _714_ Phone No. _239-7707_ City _San Diego_

Accident Within City or Village Limits	Accident Occurred	In _San Diego_ (City or Village) _San Diego_ (County)

On _10th St. Terminal_ (Street) At or Near _Safe. Co. Loading Dock_ Door #10 (Cross Street)

Accident Outside City Or Village Limits

Accident Occurred On _____ (Route Number and road name) Near _____ (Town) In _____ (County)

At _____ (Name intersection or state distance and direction from nearest community, highway junction, crossroad, railroad crossing or bridge) Width _____ of Road (2-3-4 or more lanes) Were Lanes Marked? Yes ☐ No ☐

Were Opposing Lanes Separated by a Curb or Mall? _____ Yes ☐ No ☐

TYPE OF TRAFFIC CONTROL AT PLACE OF ACCIDENT

1—Police Officer ☐ 2—Signal Light ☐ 3—Stop Sign ☐ 4—Caution Sign ☐ 5—Other Control ☐ 6—No Control ☐

Cause of Accident or Loss

Weather _Clear_ Condition of Road _Good_

Description of accident: _Truck was parked at dock. It rolled away from dock with brake set and hit car rear fender that was not supposed to be in the area. Brakes didn't hold. Parking brake was set._

Driver of Other Vehicle

Name _A. Vasquez_ Make of Vehicle _Chev._
Address _210 Main St. S.D._ (Street or R.D.) (City & State) Model _1970_
Operator's License No. _DOC1001 CA_ (No.) (State) Registration _WPA81C CA_ (No.) (State)

Was Anyone Injured? _____ Yes ☐ No ☒
Company Employee _____ ☐ ☒
Occupants other vehicles _parked_ ☐ ☒
Pedestrians _____ ☐ ☒
Have you called Police? _____ ☐ ☒
Have you secured witnesses—names & addresses? _____ ☐ ☒
Have you called doctor and/or ambulance? _____ ☐ ☒
Where have injured persons been taken?
Hospital _____
City _____
Did accident involve fire or explosion? _____ ☐ ☒
Can your unit proceed safely under own power? _____ ☒ ☐
Do you need mechanic or wrecker or another unit? _____ ☒ ☐
Have you properly set emergency warning devices? _____ ☐ ☒

Notes on instructions to Company Employee: *(Use other side of this form for additional information)*

Person Notified _Dispatcher_ Time _9:00_ A.M. / P.M.

Date _2-6_ Signature _M Peachy_

Figure 22-3. A properly completed preliminary accident form.

SUPERVISOR'S INVESTIGATION REPORT
MOTOR VEHICLE

The unsafe acts of drivers and the unsafe conditions that cause accidents can be corrected only when they are known specifically. It is your responsibility to **find** them and **name** them and to **state** the **remedy** for them in this report.

COMPANY	TERMINAL OR DIVISION
Safe Company Trucking	Tenth Street Terminal
DRIVER	TYPE OF VEHICLE AND/OR IDENTIFYING NO.
M. Peachy	Single Truck

LOCATION OF ACCIDENT (Street, town, state)	DATE AND TIME OF ACCIDENT
Tenth Street Terminal Yard	February 6 8 AM

NO. OF **PERSONS INJURED** AND EXTENT OF PROPERTY **DAMAGE** (Company and other)

No injuries.

Left rear fender (apx. $50.00 damage)

No damage to truck, bumper contacted car.

DESCRIPTION OF **ACCIDENT** (State in detail what occurred just before, and at the time of the accident)

Truck rolled away from loading dock, no chocks were placed at rear wheels. Truck was not in gear, parking brake was not securely set. (Truck brakes were out of adjustment.) Truck rolled apx. 10 feet and struck rear fender of parked car in yard. Car was parked illegally in yard.

DESCRIBE UNSAFE **CONDITIONS** of vehicle and/or road, contributing to accident (Faulty brakes, lights—icy, wet clay, etc.)

No chock blocks on truck.

Brakes out of adjustment.

UNSAFE ACT (Describe the unsafe action of driver as turning from wrong lane, speeding, failing to signal, etc.)

Brakes not secured when parked. Truck not in gear.

Car parked in truck area.

REMEDY (As a supervisor, what action have you taken or do you propose taking to prevent a repeat accident?)

Check truck dock for chocks. Require chocks at loading dock and stops.

Driver issued warning. Keep private vehicles out of loading area.

SUPERVISOR R. Ray	REVIEWED AND APPROVED BY	DATE REPORT PREPARED February 8

C-5062 REV. 2-67   PRINTED IN U.S.A.   (Use reverse side for sketch and additional detail)

Figure 22-4. A properly completed accident investigation report.

364

As you might expect, the MCSR has something to say about accidents. In MCSR sections 392.40 and 392.41 it lists the duties of a driver who has been in an accident.

MCSR 392.40   Every driver of a motor vehicle involved in an accident from which there results injury to or death of any person or persons, or property damage of any kind, regardless of the amount, shall:

A.   Stop immediately.

B.   Take all precautions to prevent further accident at the scene.

C.   Render all reasonable assistance to injured persons. Drivers are not required to know first aid, but should take all possible steps to assist the injured. (Movement of injured persons by a driver should not be undertaken if likely to cause further injury.)

D.   To any person demanding it, the driver should give his or her name and address, the name and address of the motor carrier for whom he or she is employed, the state tag registration number of the vehicle involved and, if requested, exhibit his or her Chauffeur's or Operator's license.

E.   Report all details of the accident as soon as practical after its occurrence to the motor carrier by whom she or he is then employed.

MCSR 392.41   Striking Unattended Vehicle. If the vehicle your rig strikes is unattended, stop and try to locate the owner. If you cannot find the owner, leave a note on the unattended vehicle. On the note, give your name, address and the name of the carrier for whom you are driving.

Figure 22-5. What happened in this accident? Was it a tie-down problem? Did the driver try to take the curve too fast? *Courtesy of the California Highway Patrol*

FIRE PREVENTION

Fire prevention is a very serious subject. Fire may affect you personally by burning, crippling or killing you. It may destroy your vehicle. It may take your job if your vehicle and terminals are burned. America suffers a severe fire *every fifty minutes* and suffers a loss of over a billion dollars annually from fires.

Figure 22-6. A tanker upside down is one of the worst fire hazards there is. *From the author's own collection*

PREVENTING FIRES

The best prevention for fires is good housekeeping. By good housekeeping, we mean keeping the cab clean and free from debris. Things like oily rags, oil or grease on the floor can cause fires to erupt and help them spread. It's also important to keep the engine clean and free of unnecessary oil and dirt.

The truck driver must always know what she or he is hauling on each trip. This way, she or he will know the precautions to follow in case of fire and exactly what to do to fight the fire and avoid tragedy.

● *Common Fire Hazards*

One of the most frequent causes of fire is *low tire pressure*. There is an obvious way to correct this: Make sure your tires are correctly inflated. (When your tires are checked, have your brake drums checked at the same time for overheating.) Remember, flat or low tires can cause tough fires. Fires caused by tires are very hard to control.

Electrical fires are hot and may get a good start before the driver knows about the fire. Then, they'll keep burning. The only way to keep out of this kind of trouble is this: See that all wiring and electrical equipment is ship-shape. If an electrical fire does begin, *pull the battery cables off the terminals.*

Loose exhaust piping is a fire hazard. So is piping that has holes or leaks or is too close to fuel lines, wood or truck body parts.

Be careful if you smoke as you drive. See that the cigarette, pipe or cigar ashes are completely out before you throw them away. This will help to prevent fire within the vehicle and along the road. In fact, don't "throw" them away at all. Use the ash tray. The DOT has specific rules about smoking. You may *not* smoke when transporting explosives, dangerous articles, flammable liquids, or liquefied petroleum gas.

366

PREVENTING FIRES   (cont.)

● *Flammable and Combustible Liquids*

Under DOT regulations, a *flammable liquid* is one which has a flash point of <u>less than</u> 80° F (27° C). Gasoline is an example of a flammable liquid. (See Figure 22-7.) If you are hauling flammable liquids, what do you suppose one of your primary duties is? To protect your rig against any type of static or frictional sparks. Static lines, or grounding lines, hang beneath a truck for this purpose.

A *combustible liquid* is a liquid which will burn, but its flash point may be <u>over</u> 80° F (27° C). Kerosene, fuel oil and diesel fuel are combustible liquids under the DOT definition.

Liquefied petroleum gas is heavier than air and flows just like water. Occasionally, during an accident the tank will rupture or leak and the fuel will catch fire. If this happens, allow it to burn at the point of rupture. This may keep it from spreading over a wider area and creating a more serious fire and explosion hazard. It is advisable to spray water on the fuel tank shell to keep it cool and prevent further rupture. But this type of fire is very dangerous and very hot. Don't try to be a hero.

● *Flat Tires*

If you have a flat tire, remove it immediately after stopping. It may have been running hot and may flame up soon after you stop or even *an hour or more afterwards*. What should you do if a tire does catch fire? If possible, locate a water supply to drench and cool the tire fire. Tire fires will burn fiercely and flare up when "out" unless they are drenched and cooled. Always try to remove the tire first. Sand and dirt will help smother and cool a tire if water is not available. Remember this: All fires are fought by either drenching or smothering. Fire cannot burn without air.

● *Park Away From Danger*

Never fail to stop to help another driver whose rig is on fire. But, first be sure that your own rig is parked at a safe distance from the fire. Preferably, you should park it upgrade from the burning vehicle.

Figure 22-7. A three-axle cab-over tractor with a gasoline trailer of approximately 8000 gallons capacity. *Courtesy of American Trucking Associations, Inc.*

367

PREVENTING FIRES   (cont.)

● *Grounding Wires and Static Lines*

It is very important to ground a tanker before loading or unloading it. So, when you're loading or unloading a tank truck, attach grounding lines or static lines *as soon as you stop* and *before you open the manhole covers* to the tank compartment or attach loading or unloading lines. Liquid flowing through the lines creates static charges. When you attach grounding lines or static lines, you ground the vehicle.

Figure 22-8. Model 424, 5 lb fire extinguisher. The ABC symbols show that the fire extinguisher can be used on three types of fires: (A) wood, paper, cloth, trash and other ordinary materials; (B) gasoline, grease, oil, paint and other flammable liquids, and (C) for live electrical equipment. *Courtesy of Amerex Corporation*

WHAT TO DO IN CASE OF FIRE | If you become stalled, wrecked, or turned over, there are some things you can do to lessen the dangers to yourself and others. Here are the first two things you can do to reduce fire danger:

1. Check to see that the ignition is turned off. If it isn't, turn it off.

2. Check to see if fuel is leaking from the tank or a broken fuel line. Fumes may accumulate. If they do, they could be ignited either by a careless smoker or a short in the electrical system.

Then, stay with the vehicle. Be ready to take all precautions against fire. If a fire does occur, be prepared to fight it. Also, be ready to direct traffic around the vehicle to avoid accidents. Leave the scene *only* under one of these two conditions:

● if your personal safety is at stake, or

● if there is no other way of getting help.

● *Fires in Town*

If you are in town and your rig catches fire, immediately call the fire department. Park near a large, open area, away from congestion if possible.

● *Fires on the Highway*

If your rig catches fire out on the highway, you should do two things. (1) Start your fire fighting immediately with the fire fighting equipment you have. (2) Ask the first available person to call the fire department.

WHAT TO DO IN CASE OF FIRE (cont.)

● *What to Tell the Fire Department*

The fire department needs specific information. First, tell them of the exact location of the fire. Second, tell them what type of fire it is. This way, they'll know what equipment to bring to fight the fire properly.

> ▷ *NOTE: Some fire fighting techniques use water sprays and foam. These methods are very effective in putting out large fires involving gasoline tankers. Basically, water is not used to extinguish the flame, but to cool down the surrounding areas and the vehicle. It becomes a heat shield. The fire fighter has to be very careful that the water does not carry the burning fluid.*
>
> *Most fire departments know these techniques. Most drivers don't. Besides, drivers don't have the special equipment needed. A person should never use a stream of water around a flammable liquid fire unless that person has the proper equipment and has been trained to use it.*

● *Types of Fire Extinguishers*

The DOT has authorized three types of fire extinguishers for use on trucks. Here are the ones they have authorized:

1. The dry power type (4 pounds minimum)

2. The vaporizing liquid type (1½ quarts minimum)

3. The carbon dioxide type (4 pounds minimum)

These extinquishers are authorized because they work on oil, gasoline and electrical fires. These are the types of fires likely to occur on trucks. Plus, they are not subject to freezing under normal operating conditions.

You should check and recharge fire extinguishers after each use. If you don't need to use an extinguisher, you should check it at least once a year. Use the procedure recommended for checking the type of extinguisher you have. Most fire extinguishers have plates attached to them with operating instructions on them. Read the instructions plate, and know how to use your extinguisher before you need to use it.

● *Fires on Tankers*

A manhole fire is a fire in the tank compartment of a tanker. The quickest way to put out a manhole fire is to *close the manhole cover*. This will snuff out the fire. In fact, that's what the manhole is for.

HOW TO USE

To familiarize users with the proper steps in operating fire extinguishers Amerex furnishes a detailed owners manual with every extinguisher including the how to use illustrations shown below.

1. HOLD UPRIGHT— PULL PIN
(TO SNAP WIRE SEAL)

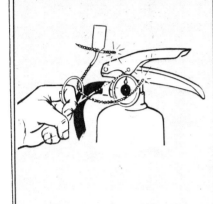

2. SQUEEZE LEVER

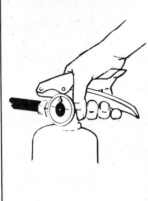

3. AIM AT BASE OF FIRE
(SWEEP QUICKLY USING SIDE TO SIDE MOTION)

8-10 Ft.

WHERE TO USE

Use your extinguisher only on the types of fires designated by the letter symbols and picture symbols shown below and on the nameplate.

TYPES OF FIRES

LETTER SYMBOL		PICTURE SYMBOL
	For wood, paper, cloth, trash and other ordinary materials.	
	For gasoline, grease, oil, paint and other flammable liquids.	
	For live electrical equipment.	

TYPES OF EXTINGUISHERS
CLASS A

CLASS BC

CLASS ABC

Figure 22-9. Chart showing how and where to use various kinds of fire extinguishers. Letter symbols show the types of fires on which a unit may be used. *Courtesy of Amerex Corporation*

If the load is leaking, a fire may start in the pool of leaked fluid. If you can't control the fire, use shovels to dam the pool. This will help prevent the spread of leaking flammable liquids.

There is great danger in allowing overflow or spillage to run into a sewer or stream. The flammable liquid will float on the surface, and flammable materials can be carried to areas far from the actual spillage. In addition, overflow into sewers can cause explosive mixtures by evaporation.

A good rule to use in fighting a small spill fire is this: *Attack from the edge of the fire toward the source of spillage*. Keep trying to push the fire back toward the source of leakage. Don't let that leakage get around you.

The greatest fire hazard is a tank truck upside down. The reason is this: The relief valves and vents may be inoperative because they've been buried in dirt. Thus, there is no way to relieve the internal pressure built up by the fire. In case of fire on a compressed gas tank, there is no entirely safe place within a half mile. So you should keep spectators as far away as possible. If you have to remain in the vicinity, stay away from the area lying along the line toward which the tank is headed. Experience has shown this to be the greatest danger area. The head (or the top of the tank where the valve is) is the weakest point. If it blows, the tank may take off like a rocket.

● *Placement of Emergency Equipment*

As we mentioned above, most vehicles will carry reflective types of warning devices. However, some rigs will use flame-producing devices instead. These cannot be used near rigs carrying flammable liquids. However, they can still be dangerous, even when used near small gasoline trucks. Therefore, if your rig uses flame-producing warning devices, be very careful in placing them out. They may burn your vehicle under the following conditions:

- if they are accidentally struck by other traffic and knocked under the vehicle

- if they are lighted and placed too close when the disabled vehicle has gasoline leaking from it

- if, when it is raining, they are placed where leaking gasoline may run over the wet road surface to the flame

- if the flare is placed too close to the vehicle

● *After the Fire is Out*

After any fire is out, make sure all affected parts are cool. Don't leave the vehicle too soon. Fire may flare up again. Recheck frequently. Don't turn on the ignition, lights or other electrical circuits until the wiring and electrical system have been checked for short circuits. Any embers should be thoroughly doused with water.

| FIVE IMPORTANT STEPS TO TAKE | If the fire is large and fire fighting equipment is not immediately available, here are the five steps you should take in case of a truck fire: |

1. Ask someone to call the fire department for you.

2. Keep spectators at a safe distance.

3. If the fire involves leaking gasoline, dam up the spillage. Keep the burning fuel as far from the vehicle as possible.

4. Salvage cargo, if possible, by

   a. Unhitching tractor or truck from the trailer.

   b. Piling cargo at a safe distance from the burning vehicle or leaking gasoline. Naturally, it is not always possible to unload a burning vehicle. It depends on where the fire is.

5. Protect yourself and all other persons at all times.

Remember, all fires must be reported to your supervisor, terminal manager or other authorized person. Small and large fires must both be reported.

| WHAT CAUSES ACCIDENTS? | We've talked about your responsibilities at the scene of an accident. We've talked about fires and how to prevent them. And, we've talked about what to do in case of an accident involving a fire. But what causes accidents? Let's take a look at some of the common causes. |

The DOT continually evaluates accidents involving commercial trucks. DOT officials want to find out what the specific problem areas are. Between 1973 and 1976, they studied 497 accidents of unusual severity. These 497 accidents killed 783 persons, injured 1,651 persons and cost $23,405,075 in property damage. Perhaps some of the results of this four-year study will help us find out what some of the problems are.

Two of the causes of accidents are human failure and equipment failure. The DOT's report includes a chart for each of these causes. They list all of the accidents caused by human factors on one chart, and all of the accidents caused by mechanical defects on another. (See Figures 22-10 and 22-11.)

Look at the chart on human failures. (Don't let the word "ambience" throw you. It's just a term borrowed from psychology. It means "things that distract you or take your mind off what you're doing.") Do you see any causes of accidents that we've talked about before? Which one caused more accidents than any other single factor?

Human Factor Accidents — Ambience

	Day	Dawn/Dusk	Night	Total
Human Factors:				
Inattentive	65	6	41	112
Dozed	21	5	41	67
Asleep	4	1	14	19
Fatigued	19	3	19	41
Excess Hours	18	2	11	31
Drinking	9	5	9	23
Intoxicated	6	4	17	27
Drugs	5	0	6	11
Ill	1	0	2	3
Excessive Speed	43	7	18	68
Too Fast for Conditions	27	6	25	58
Total	218	39	203	460
Poor Driving Skills:				
Following Too Closely	10	1	9	20
Not Driving Defensively	2	0	2	4
Failure to Downshift	10	3	8	21
Unsafe Passing	6	0	2	8
Unsafe Entry onto Highway	3	1	3	7
Inexperienced	24	2	16	42
Careless/Reckless	10	2	4	16
Poor Judgment	5	0	5	10
Momentarily Distracted	10	0	4	14
Underaged	6	1	3	10
Failure to Yield	1	0	2	3
Overdriving Headlamps	1	0	2	3
Total	88	10	60	158
Grand Total	306	49	263	618

Figure 22-10. This chart summarizes the driver-related causes of unusually severe accidents investigated by the DOT's Bureau of Motor Carrier Safety. One of the recurring causes of accidents was speed - excessive speed or speed too fast for conditions. What other causes happened over and over? *Reprinted from Analysis and Summary of Accident Investigations 1973-1976, US DOT publication*

WHAT CAUSES ACCIDENTS?   (cont.)

What's the answer? *Inattention*. Sound familiar? You bet. In fact, we ended Chapter 15, "Heavy Duty Diesel Driving Headaches," with these words, "Expect the unexpected." Add to the number one cause - *dozing, sleeping, fatigue* and *excess hours* - and the theme repeats itself: "Stay alert and stay alive."

Now let's look at the mechanical failures. What were the two main causes of fatalities and injuries? Tires and brakes. We've talked about the importance of proper brake maintenance before. As we said in Chapter 9, it's more important to be able to stop your rig than to get it going. Therefore, keeping your air brake system in good condition is even more important than proper engine care. We also talked about tires, both in this chapter and in Chapter 15.

Now let's take a look at a few of the actual accident investigation reports made by DOT officials. These are not the full investigation reports. They are summaries of the reports, but they point out the main causes of the accidents.

● *Summaries of DOT Accident Investigations*

● Jan. 17, (Saturday) 7:45 AM, US 50, Sacramento, California. Bus (31 passengers) collided with rear of car; a tractor-trailer (salvage crates) struck rear of a pickup, a tractor cargo-tank trailer (gasoline) collided and overran a car. Fire engulfed car struck by tanker, its occupants were trapped in wreckage. Chain-type collision involved three commercial vehicles and 17 non-commercial vehicles. Heavy fog. 4 fatalities, 5 injuries, $11,700 PD.☆

Speed too fast for conditions.

● Jan. 26, (Monday) 5:20 AM, I-89, Enfield, New Hampshire. Tractor cargo-tank trailer (gasoline) drifted off right side of road, climbed a snowbank, overturned. Cargo spilled. Rain-wet pavement. No casualties, $10,000 PD.

Underaged, inexperienced truck driver (19) dozed at the wheel; fatigued. License under suspension.

● Feb. 13, (Friday) 12:25 PM, I-8, near Gila Bend, Arizona. Tractor-trailer (Class B Explosives) ran off road, struck two autos, three motorcycles, four pedestrians. Fuel tank on first auto struck ruptured, fire ensued. 1 fatality, 7 injuries, $50,000 PD.

Truck driver dozed at the wheel, fatigued.

☆ The "PD" at the end of the reports stands for "Property Damage." Accident insurance policies refer to PL and PD limits, meaning Public Liability and Property Damage.

Mechanical Defect Accidents

	Collision With Motor Vehicles				Single Vehicle				Total	Casualties		Property Damage
	Head-On	Rear-End	Side	Other	Ran Off Road/Overturned	Fixed Object	Other	Loading/Unloading		Fatalities	Injuries	
Tires	5	0	1	0	12	0	1	0	19	20	15	$ 580,300
Brakes	0	9	4	0	15	1	1	0	30	29	79	1,344,800
Coupling Devices	2	0	1	2	2	0	1	0	8	6	4	83,700
Electrical System	0	3	0	0	0	0	0	0	3	3	2	165,000
Steering	2	0	1	0	0	0	0	0	3	3	6	149,000
Suspension	0	0	0	0	1	0	0	0	1	0	1	50,000
Other	2	1	0	1	4	0	7	3	18	11	57	995,100
Total	11	13	7	3	34	1	10	3	82	72	164	$3,367,900

Figure 22-11.

This chart summarizes the equipment-related causes of unusually severe accidents investigated by the DOT's Bureau of Motor Carrier Safety. *Reprinted from Analysis and Summary of Accident Investigations 1973-1976, US DOT publication*

WHAT CAUSES ACCIDENTS? (cont.)

- Feb. 18, (Wednesday) 6:15 PM, city streets, intersection, Washington, DC. Tractor-trailer (rolls of roofing paper) descending steep downgrade, struck rear of car stopped at intersection, knocked down traffic signal support, ran off pavement, struck and penetrated apartment building. Truck driver, passenger and three occupants of apartment building killed. Five fatalities, three injuries, $90,000 PD.

  Truck driver inattentive; deficient brakes. Vehicle improperly inspected and maintained. Poor driving record.

- Mar. 14, (Sunday) 8 PM, I-40, near Arlington, Tennessee. Tractor-trailer (general freight) veered off right side of road, ran down an embankment, came to rest in an upright position. Driver injured. 1 injury, $5,000 PD.

  Right front tire blew out. Seatbelts in use - beneficial.

- Apr. 6, (Tuesday) 7:30 AM, National Park Service Route 4, near Beatty, Nevada. Runaway tractor-trailer (chemicals and various hazardous materials) failed to negotiate downgrade curve, ran off road, down embankment, overturned. Truck driver ejected, killed. 1 fatality, $61,000 PD.

  Truck driver (21) inexperienced, failed to downshift. Brake fade. No physical certificate. Additional signing recommended for area.

- Apr. 15, (Thursday) 9 AM, Kansas Turnpike, near Emporia, Kansas. Tractor cargo-tank trailer (resin) ran off road, overturned down an embankment. Dome covers damaged, portion of cargo released. Truck driver injured. One injury, $34,000 PD.

  Truck driver dozed at the wheel.

- Apr. 27, (Thursday) 10 PM, I-40, near Brisco, Arkansas. Tractor cargo-tank trailer (hydrogen peroxide) ran off right side of road, overturned down an embankment. Combination separated. Leak developed while tanker was being uprighted. During transfer of product to another vehicle, fire ensued. Traffic rerouted. Driver injured. One injury, $34,400 PD.

  Right front tire blew out. Possibility - lock ring on wheel defective.

You should be able to read between the lines of these reports to find out an important fact. Accidents can happen anywhere, any time. They can happen on busy, city streets, on the open highway, even on special park routes in unpopulated areas. They can happen in the East, Midwest, West, North or South. They occur in the early hours of the morning, late at night, or any time during the day. The point is this: You can't just pay attention part of the time. You can't watch your speed just part of the time. You can't be sure your rig is properly maintained sometimes. Driving is a full-time job.

WHAT CAUSES ACCIDENTS? (cont.)

We've just talked about the major factors contributing to an accident. But keep this in mind: Many different conditions can cause accidents. You may be awake and attentive. Your brakes may be in excellent condition and your tires properly inflated. But you can still have an accident. We'll be talking about some of these causes more in the next chapter, "Mousetrapping Yourself."

SUMMARY | A driver's first responsibility is to protect his or her rig from accidents, theft, and fire. Therefore, in this chapter, we talked about how to prevent accidents and fires. We also gave specific instructions for what to do in case of accident or fire.

The first thing a driver should do when involved in an accident is give first aid to any injured persons. Then, the driver should follow three key rules. First, record important information while it is fresh in the mind. Second, record names and addresses of all witnesses. Third, show courtesy to all people, but don't admit guilt. These are the three major rules regarding accidents.

Another way of looking at your behavior at the scene of an accident is to examine the steps you should take, in order. Here are the steps:

1. Stop.

2. Protect the scene by properly setting out your warning devices.

3. Help any injured persons. (Over-the-road truckers should take a course in first aid since they are often first on the scene of an accident.)

4. Notify the police by phone or note carried by a reliable motorist.

5. Notify your nearest company terminal by phone or note carried by a reliable motorist.

6. Be specific in reporting the accident.

7. Fill out a preliminary accident report or see that a company traffic safety official fills one out.

8. Record the names and addresses of all witnesses. If there are no witnesses, get the name and address of the first person to arrive at the scene.

9. Be polite and give your name and company's name. Don't admit guilt. Don't promise anything. Don't argue.

10. Have pictures taken.

11. Record important information about time and place, vehicles involved, and insurance companies.

SUMMARY   (cont.)

The MCSR rules cover the same guidelines for conduct after an accident. In addition, they add that you should try to locate the owner of any vehicle if you hit it when no one is in it. Leave a note if you can't find the owner.

The best fire prevention is good housekeeping. But there are other things you can do to avoid fire and to keep a fire from spreading. Make sure your tires are properly inflated. See that all wiring and electrical equipment is in good condition. If you do have an electrical fire, pull the battery cables off their terminals. See that your piping is free from holes or leaks and that it is properly secured. If you smoke as you drive, use your ash tray. Protect against sparks if you are hauling flammable liquids. Remove a flat tire as soon as you stop so it doesn't flare up. Park away from any burning object.

If your rig is involved in a fire, take precautions to see that it doesn't spread. Turn your ignition off. Watch for accumulating fumes and warn others of their presence. If you are in town, phone the fire department immediately. If you are on the open road, begin fire fighting with your equipment. If the fire involves leaking fluid, allow the fire to burn at the point of rupture, but try to dam it up. Attack from the edge of the fire toward the source of the spill. Ask the first person you see to phone the fire department. Whenever you call the fire department, tell them exactly where the fire is and what kind of fire it is.

Allow all affected parts to cool after a fire before you try to start up the rig again. Don't start up until you've had your wiring and electrical system checked out.

We ended the chapter by looking at the results of a DOT study of 497 severe accidents. Many accidents are caused by human failures. The most common human failure is inattention. The next two most common human causes of accidents are speed and tiredness. Other accidents are caused by failures of the truck equipment. And the most common of these failures are problems related to tires and problems related to brakes. Nevertheless, these are only a few of the many causes of accidents. We'll talk about other causes in the next chapter.

GLOSSARY

combustible liquid: A liquid which can catch fire if its vapors reach a temperature of over 80° F (27° C). Diesel fuel is a combustible liquid.

first aid: The immediate and temporary care given the victim of an accident or sudden illness until the services of a physician can be obtained.

flammable liquid: A liquid which will catch fire if its vapors reach a high enough temperature. Temperatures under 80° F (27° C) are enough to let it catch fire from a spark, flash, etc. Gasoline is a flammable liquid.

GLOSSARY   (cont.)

flash point: The lowest temperature at which a liquid's vapor will catch fire from a flash, spark, etc.

grounding lines (static lines): Straps or chains that ground a unit. They prevent an atmospheric or frictional spark that would ignite fuel in the tank.

manhole cover: Filler caps on top of a fuel tanker. They are large enough for a person to enter to clean the inside of the tank.

pot torch: An older type of emergency warning device. It burns liquid and gives off a flare. Pot torches are no longer allowed to be used with vehicles hauling gasoline or other hazardous cargo.

preliminary accident report: A report filled out at the scene of an accident. It records things like number of vehicles involved in the accident, road and weather conditions, how the accident occurred, driver's name, etc. Usually the company traffic safety official will complete the form, but if she or he is not available, the driver completes the form.

rupture: A break or tear; or, as a verb, to tear or break apart.

state tag registration: License tag.

unattended vehicle: A vehicle with no driver in it or around it.

▶ CHECKING THE FACTS

By filling in the blanks in the sentences below, you will be reviewing some of the key facts in this chapter. You might see how you do without looking back at the chapter; then, check the chapter for the facts you can't recall from memory. The numbers in parentheses are just there to number the blanks. They don't mean anything else.

If your rig catches fire in town, you should park near a large, (1) _____

_____ area, away from (2) _____ if

possible. Call the (3) _____ immediately.

If you're out on the open highway and it happens, start your (4) _____

_____ immediately with the equipment you

have. Then, ask the (5) _____ to

call the fire department.

379

First aid is the (6) _____ and (7) _____

care given an accident victim until (8) _____

_____ .

If you have an accident, stop, turn on your (9) _____

_____ and, immediately, set out your (10) _____

_____ .

If you can't get to a phone after an accident, write a carefully worded

(11) _____ . Give it to a (12) _____

_____ . Don't leave your cargo (13) _____

_____ .

When you report your accident, be specific. Give your exact (14) _____

_____ , the exact (15) _____ , the

extent of (16) _____ , the

condition of the (17) _____ , and where you can

(18) _____ . Make a note of the

(19) _____ for future reference.

Above all, be polite to everyone at the scene of an accident. Admit

(20) _____ ; promise (21) _____

_____ , and

don't (22) _____ .

If you have an electrical fire, pull the (23) _____

off the (24) _____ . If the fire in-

volves a tire, remove the (25) _____ and

cool it with (26) _____ , (27) _____ or

(28) _____ . If the fire is in a tanker's tank

compartment, close the (29) _____

The chart in Figure 22-10 shows the number of accidents caused by human errors. A total of 112 accidents were caused by inattention. 65 of them were during the (30) _____ and 41 were during the (31) _____. A total of 68 accidents were caused by (32) _____. A total of 67 were caused by (33) _____. 58 were caused by (34) _____. Only 3 accidents were caused by (35) _____

■ GETTING THE MAIN IDEAS

Put a plus (+) before the statement if it is true. Put a zero (0) before the statement if it is false.

_____ 1. The three <u>main</u> rules to follow after having an accident are (1) contact your employer immediately (2) get witnesses names and addresses and (3) be courteous.

_____ 2. You and a co-driver have an accident. Neither is injured. There is no phone nearby. One of you should guard the cargo and one should handle safety precautions. You should have a reliable-appearing motorist contact the police and your company.

_____ 3. If you are unloading a gasoline tanker, attach grounding lines before opening the manhole covers.

_____ 4. The best prevention for fires is good housekeeping in the cab, under the hood, everywhere.

_____ 5. The fire department needs to know two things when you call them about a truck fire: (1) what kind of rig you're driving and (2) what kind of cargo you're carrying.

_____ 6. According to the DOT study, more fires are caused by brake and tire defects than any other kind of mechanical breakdown.

_____ 7. According to Figure 22-10, inattention and tiredness cause more accidents than speeding (including speeds too fast for conditions).

_____ 8. According to Figure 22-10, more drivers fall asleep or doze off at night than during the day.

_____ 9. According to Figure 22-10, inexperience causes more accidents than misuse of amphetamines and alcohol.

_____ 10. According to Figure 22-11, almost half of the accidents from mechanical failures involved vehicles which ran off the road or overturned.

_____ 11. Emmett should probably not have stopped to help the driver who had an accident.

_____ 12. At the scene of the accident it is more important to properly record facts than to decide who was at fault.

_____ 13. Regardless of who fills the preliminary accident report out, its purpose is this: to describe the accident and record a judgment of what the unsafe actions and unsafe conditions were. (If there were any.)

_____ 14. You should not remove a flat tire until it has cooled. Flat tires may be extremely hot and can burn your hands badly.

_____ 15. Combustible liquids are far more dangerous, on the whole, than flammable liquids.

_____ 16. If you must park near a rig which is on fire, park upgrade from it if possible. (However, don't park in the direction in which a burning tanker is headed.)

_____ 17. A fire extinguisher with the symbols ABC on it can be used to fight just about any kind of fire.

_____ 18. If a pool of flammable liquid is aflame, try to dam it. Work from the source of spillage toward the outside of the spill.

_____ 19. One of your main responsibilities at an accident is to avoid further accident, fire, damage or injury.

_____ 20. Truckers should not administer first aid because their companies could be sued if they were to do something wrong.

★ GOING BEYOND THE FACTS AND IDEAS

1. You drive a dry freight van filled with general freight. You notice a flat tire and stop to change it at a rest stop. Before you have removed the tire, a large motor home runs into your rear end at 15 mph. Outline the steps you take to properly handle the entire situation.

2. You drive the rig shown in Figure 22-6. List as many things as you can think of that you can do to reduce the danger of fire.

3. Assume that you work for the Bureau of Motor Carrier Safety. Now that you have the information in Figure 22-10, what changes would you make in trucking laws, training or licensing to reduce the number of severe accidents.

Figure 23-1. *Reprinted from Balance Magazine through the courtesy of Hendrickson Manufacturing Company, Tandem Division*

Chapter Twenty-Three

MOUSETRAPPING YOURSELF

BEFORE YOU READ | Mousetrapping yourself. What do you suppose that means? You might say this: Getting yourself into a situation that's hard or impossible to get out of. There are a lot of things truckers do to mousetrap themselves. This chapter will look at several of these mousetrap situations. It will be up to you to figure out how to avoid the mousetraps. Why not begin by taking time to think up answers to the following four questions? You might discuss your answers with another person or write your answers down.

1. What does this sentence mean? "Don't make any assumptions about what another driver is going to do."

2. Can a route become too familiar for your own good?

3. Euphoria is a strong feeling of well-being. If you're euphoric, you feel on top of the world. Might euphoria ever cause an accident?

4. Think about all the new things a new driver has to remember about driving a diesel truck - things like proper use of the air brake system and proper steering behavior. What mistakes do you think new drivers make more often than any other mistakes?

GETTING
STARTED
IN
TRUCKING

The trucking industry now employs both men and women. At first, women were accepted into the industry with reluctance. Even today there is some reluctance on the part of some companies and male drivers. But, as time goes by, the resistance to women behind the wheel gradually disappears. This is primarily because women are good truck drivers, and they are often much more assertive in proving their worth than most men. In other words, they're making it on their own through their involvement and their efficiency. In fact, some male drivers prefer a woman as a co-driver, not because she may be an attractive woman, but because she tries harder.

Just how do women enter the field of truck driving? All kinds of ways, just like men. But some get started because their husbands drive. A woman who is married to a trucker probably shouldn't expect her husband to teach her to drive, however. Sometimes it works beautifully, but sometimes it's the wrong approach. The husband, as an experienced driver, may take a dominant position and harass his wife about every little mistake. (For the same reason, many accomplished musicians refuse to teach their children to play a musical instrument. They'll pay someone else to teach their children before they will teach them themselves. It just seems to be human nature to be less patient with someone close to us than to someone else.)

So, in general, it is not advisable for a woman to expect her husband to teach her to drive a truck. (In the same way, it wouldn't be a good idea for a man to expect his wife to teach him to drive. It goes both ways.) A person is better off going to a good driving school or taking a course at a public school, if available.

● *Be Careful About Who You Go To Work For*

Both men and women face the same problems in getting started. As a new truck driving course graduate, with the heavy-duty license in hand, each student considers him or herself a truck driver. Unfortunately, the student still doesn't have the experience to back up the motivation. This being true, any new driver should be very cautious in choosing who she or he goes to work for, especially in an over-the-road operation. Once employed, new drivers should keep *their eyes and ears open* and *their mouths shut* while they get to know the operation.

Let's tag along with Ginger on her first job. She considered herself fortunate in landing a job on a cross country haul. The run was Los Angeles to New York. On the way back, they'd be hitting 30 other states, zigzagging wherever the loads fell, gypsying around. Ginger's senior driver treated her well. He was extremely polite. (So polite that she should have been suspicious.)

One of the first things Ginger noticed was this: They were constantly running illegal. They were violating weight laws and bypassing the truck scales. Then too, she noticed that her senior driver handled a lot of his dealings in a bar or parking lot. She kept her eyes open and took note of the freight being loaded. She compared it with the bills of lading, and things didn't always check out. They were loading different commodities than they listed.

GETTING STARTED (cont.)

Now, hauling unlisted commodities may mean you're hauling hot (or stolen) freight. Or, it could mean the driver is loading inter-state-controlled cargo without the proper hauling rights. But, in either case, it's something to be concerned about.

Chances are, when Ginger was hired, her employer thought she was too inexperienced to know what was going on.

Her senior driver had asked her to carry a small hand gun in her shoulder bag. It was too obvious in his pocket, he said. To explain why she should carry a gun, he said, "It's for your own protection

Figure 23-2. Most bridges have signs that clearly list the regulations for bridge usage. If you don't want to mousetrap yourself, you don't want to disregard the signs. *From the author's own collection*

against hijackers." (What Ginger didn't know was that her co-driver had a past prison record, and it would have been a real hazard for him to be caught with a gun.) Quite innocently, she was put in the position of carrying a concealed weapon without a license.

So here's Ginger, her first driving experience, and already she's headed down the wrong road. She is innocent. Nevertheless, she is involved. And her involvement could get her into real trouble with the authorities.

Fortunately, after a few months of running, Ginger returned to her home base. She unwound some of her experiences with friends, one of whom was an experienced driver.

He confirmed Ginger's worst fears. "Something's wrong there," he said. "You were right to pay attention to what was going on. I've worked for some good gypsy operations and some bad ones, and the only clue you have about which is which is the driver's actions." He finally said if it was him, he'd quit.

She did quit, and also took her friend's other advice to quit next time as soon as she found herself in a bad situation - before she got in trouble. Ginger learned, and she went on to a good career in trucking.

This is the point. You have to be careful in accepting a job - either your first job or any other one. If the company looks legitimate, sounds good, and you want the job, take it. But, if things begin to look fishy, and you investigate and find they are, you better do the same thing Ginger did. Quit.

THE THREE LEADING CAUSES OF DRIVER-RELATED ACCIDENTS	It isn't only new drivers who find themselves in potentially dangerous situations. There are many experienced drivers, with a good number of years experience, who find themselves in very shaky situations. Usually, the cause is one of three leading causes:

1. Lack of attention, better known as "doping off behind the wheel." (As you already know, this is the most frequent cause of accidents.)

2. Any assumption regarding the movement of other vehicles.

3. Too much speed.

You might refer back to Figure 22-10 and see if these aren't the most common causes of accidents. Put these three factors *together*, and any driver will be in trouble. Let's look at some examples of how inattention, making assumptions, and speed can get a driver into trouble.

● *Lack of Attention*

Example Number One: Boredom. The driver is on a familiar route with a number of stops. He gets used to running the same streets over and over. At times, he thinks the truck can negotiate the route by itself, like the old horse on the milk wagon. One day, he ends up crashing broadside into a car in an intersection. He just didn't notice that a new stop sign had been installed.

Example Number Two: Short Trips. The driver works for a lumber yard. She is only going down the street to her other yard, so she doesn't bother to chain down her load. After all, the street is lightly traveled, it's only two blocks, and she does this every day. One day, a man drives around the corner too fast, and our driver has to swerve to avoid hitting him. *Or maybe* one day, she just happens to turn the wheel too fast when she turns into the yard. In either case, off goes her load.

These are just two examples of how inattention can contribute to accidents, death and injury in the big rigs running on our streets and open highways. You can probably think of many more.

● *Making an Assumption*

Example Number Three: Indecision. It is very dangerous to assume the vehicle in front of you is going to *complete* a movement. Let's say you are following a car, and you are approaching a freeway offramp. The automobile in front of you starts to veer off to the right, heading toward the offramp. But, at the last minute, the driver decides to come back over. Apparently, the driver decided not to take the exit. This puts the car right in front of your truck. You have to swerve or hit your brakes hard. In either case, you are the one who's in trouble. Indecision on the part of drivers often causes accidents. (And often, the driver who created the situation isn't even involved in the accident.)

THREE LEADING CAUSES (cont.)

Example Number Four: Euphoria. Take the driver with a good truck who has just finished eating a good lunch on a beautiful, sunny day. Nine times out of ten, the driver will start running too fast for the road condition. This driver tends to become very relaxed and euphoric.

Let's say our driver is rolling across the desert, approaching a small town. It's easy to lose all sense of speed when you're traveling the open road, and that's what happens to our driver. He doesn't notice he's reached the town limits and doesn't slow down. Another rig, however, did notice the speed limit and town limit signs and slowed down. This second rig is up in front of our driver.

Let's get an aerial view of the situation - a view our driver doesn't have. Meanwhile, up ahead of both trucks, are two truck stops. One is on each side of the two-lane highway. A station wagon is coming out of the truck stop on the right, and it's about to make a left turn across the highway. (Now back to our driver.)

All of a sudden, our driver notices the slow-moving rig in front of him. His mind isn't moving as fast as his rig is, so he doesn't think to slow down. Traffic seems clear, however, so our driver decides quickly to pass the other truck and keep going. He approaches the left rear of the other truck, to pass. He can't see the station wagon leaving the truck stop on the right.

Now, the driver of the station wagon sees the front truck, but she isn't aware of the truck passing from behind, so she makes her left turn. Here comes our driver, barreling down the highway.

The results are clear. The driver in the front truck was also unaware of the truck passing from behind. Had he noticed, he might have been able to warn the driver of the station wagon. (Maybe, and maybe not. Signals can be easily misunderstood.) This is a case of double negligence. Neither driver was paying attention. And the negligence on the part of both drivers contributed to the accident.

We're back to the rule against making assumptions. In this case, the driver assumed the road was clear. He didn't stop to think that a vehicle might be coming out of the truck stop. Remember, you can't just consider what *your* vehicle is doing. You have to watch out for everyone else around.

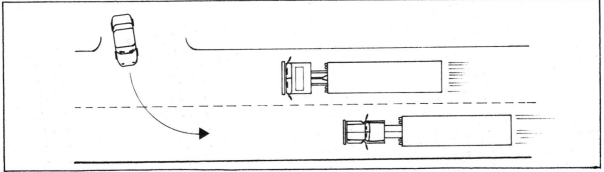

Figure 23-3. Truck passing on a two-lane highway. The driver can't see the car which is making a left turn up ahead.

THREE LEADING CAUSES   (cont.)

Example Number Five: Tailgating.

Here's another mousetrap situation. This one is caused by tailgating.
One truck is tailgating another truck on a freeway. There are entry ramps on
the right-hand side. A car driver enters the freeway. He tries to break into
the fast-moving truck traffic lane without realizing how fast the traffic is
going. He pulls right in front of the front truck. What's the trucker to do?
If she applies her brakes quickly, the truck behind her will probably plow into her rig, even if her brakes *do* stop her rig properly.

However you look at it, this is a bad situation. The only thing the
front driver could do is to pull into the lane on her left - if it's empty.
If she was monitoring all lanes like she should have been, she'd know if it
was empty or not. If it's not empty, she's definitely mousetrapped.

Example Number Six: Tailgating Again. Let's take another example. You
are tailgating the truck ahead. You're both going fast. All of a sudden, the
truck ahead of you moves over to the left to avoid a vehicle in front. Again,
by the time you see what's happening, you're in real trouble. The cause? You
were doping off, assuming something, or trusting to luck. The odds are against
the driver who doesn't give driving full attention. Sooner or later, a situation like this will occur, and an accident will happen. And sometimes it just
takes one.

● *How Much Is Too Much Speed?*

All the above examples can be classified under our Number One Problem,
"Lack of Attention," or Number Two, "Making Assumptions." Now let's look at
too much speed.

Most of the time when we talk about speed, we refer to a high rate of
speed. But speed itself can be a very dangerous thing, even at 25 mph. You
might be in a situation where you should only be going 15 mph. Let's look at
an example.

Example Number Seven: Going Too Fast for Conditions. Suppose you are a
construction driver, and you're traveling down a haul road, running about 35
mph. Just as you break over the crest of a hill, the road turns into a snake
trail. You see a water wagon approaching, spraying the road to keep the dust
down. You don't know it, but just around the next turn is a bunch of equipment, parked alongside the road. Now, water makes dirt very slick. If you
don't slow down, you're vehicle will start acting like it's wearing roller
skates, and you'll wind up either going off the road or slamming into the
parked construction equipment. So you see, you don't have to be traveling
fast to be speeding.

To sum up, every vehicle is capable of handling almost all road situations. So, again, it falls squarely on a driver's shoulders to keep the rig
operating safely. A driver's vigilance and ability to operate the equipment
can offset any bad conditions that may be encountered.

COMMON MISTAKES OF THE NOVICE DRIVER

Most novice drivers make the common mistakes. In fact, it almost seems fair to say that every novice driver will make them. These mistakes begin the moment the driver fires off the engine for the first time.

Unless you are an unusually careful new driver, you will make many of these mistakes. Notice that we said, "Unless you are an *unusually careful* new driver." Maybe you have less experience than Jill or Joe Truck Driver, studying in the seat next to you. But that doesn't always mean that Jill or Joe is going to be a better driver. Most of the mistakes listed in this chapter are due to carelessness. The know-it-all who gets in the cab and starts speeding down the roadway is probably the most likely driver to make these mistakes.

We wrote this book to help you avoid the pitfalls that most novice drivers fall into. Take your time when you're learning. Figure there's always more to be learned, and you might be one of the few new drivers to avoid these mistakes. As you read on, decide what you will do to avoid these pitfalls when you get behind the wheel.

● *Mistake Number One - Trying to Start the Engine with the Key Alone*

As we said above, the mistakes the novice driver makes begin the moment she or he fires off the engine for the first time. For instance, you get into the cab, and you see a starter on the ignition key. There may be a push button starter in a different place, but, as a new driver, you haven't thought to look for it. That's it - Mistake Number One: *Trying to start the engine with the key alone.*

It doesn't look stupid to take a good, long look at the instrument panel before starting up the engine. It looks stupid not to - unless, of course, you know the truck because you've been driving it every day.

Get into the cab. Look over the dashboard, at the instruments and switches. Find out where everything is located. In short, get to know the truck's instrument panel. *Then*, try to start her up.

● *Mistake Number Two - Pumping the Throttle*

Pumping the throttle in a diesel, as you would in an automobile, doesn't help. In fact, it creates trouble. When the engine does start, the throttle will be three-quarters open, causing the engine to completely wind up to maximum rpm. This is hard on a cold engine.

● *Mistake Number Three - Putting the Truck in Gear Too Soon*

The new driver will put the truck in gear and attempt to move up to a higher gear without allowing enough air pressure to build. It takes time to build enough air pressure for safe stopping. The engine needs to warm up slowly. This also takes time. Typically, the new driver doesn't wait long enough for air pressure to build. The result is this: The truck won't move because the spring brakes stay locked up. The reason? Insufficient or unsafe operating air pressure.

Figure 23-4. Each truck dashboard or instrument panel is slightly different. This one is in a cab-over Transtar II. Always take time to look over a new instrument panel before you start up the engine. *Courtesy of International Harvester*

COMMON MISTAKES OF THE NOVICE DRIVER (cont.)

● *Mistake Number Four - Revving the Engine*

Revving the engine before letting the clutch engage is probably the hardest habit you, as a novice driver, will have to break. Revving causes unnecessary clutch slipping and heat build-up from friction.

● *Mistake Number Five - Not Knowing the Gear Positions*

This is a beaut! Think about it. What do you think is going to happen when you start moving a truck out if you don't know where the **gear positions** are? There's going to be a lot of confusion and a lot of clashing and grinding of gears. The reason? You didn't take time to check the **gear shift** pattern. Following this mistake, we come to a related one ---

● *Mistake Number Six - Not Knowing How to Double-Clutch*

Reading the instructions for double-clutching is one thing, but remembering and putting the rules into practice is something else. Without the proper rhythm, it's mass confusion.

COMMON MISTAKES OF THE NOVICE DRIVER   (cont.)

You can practice the double-clutch action in a car or pickup with a manual transmission. This will help you develop the rhythm of the two-shift movements. Although the diesel rig is larger and heavier, the principle is the same.

Remember, you depress the clutch two times for each shift when you're double-clutching. As you pick up speed in first gear, you depress the clutch to move the gearshift knob into neutral. Release the clutch, then quickly depress the clutch again as you place the gearshift knob into second gear. This is double-clutching.

The idea is to time your shift to eliminate gear clashing. The proper rhythm will do this. A diesel has a very heavy gear box, and the double-clutch action is necessary to allow time for the gears to mesh and engage with each other quietly.

● *Mistake Number Seven - Moving Too Fast, Overconfidence*

Let's say you are finally becoming proficient with gear shifting. Your confidence soars. You begin to move too fast for your ability to handle the truck and gears. That's when the fun starts. You can well imagine.

You're a beginner, running in a 35-mile-an-hour zone, right at the speed limit. You know that you have to make a right turn two blocks ahead. Invariably, as a new driver, you'll wait until you are within a rig-length of the corner before you realize the need to slow down. Here's the situation that develops.

You try to slow down abruptly because you're running too fast to negotiate the turn. At the same time, the engine is turning too slowly. You should be gearing down. But, while all this is going on, you have other things to watch. You should be watching the right hand mirror to be sure no vehicles will be crushed between the right side of your trailer and the curb, as you make your turn. At the same time, you are trying to turn the steering wheel, watch the street you are entering, slow down, downshift and watch the tail end of your trailer - all at once. You are not an octopus with six eyes, yet at that point, you need at least three legs, four arms, and several eyes.

● *Mistake Number Eight - Tailgating*

We talked about this beauty above. You have mastered mistakes one through seven and you're feeling your oats. You think speed makes a truck driver. Thus, you tend to run right up onto the vehicle in front of you. *Tailgating is probably the worst mistake of all.*

Besides tailgating, you are over-driving your vision. That is, you're failing to drive ahead of yourself. You can't be watching out for other drivers because you can't even see what they're doing. You can't drive ahead of yourself when you're tailgating because you're right on the back of another vehicle. Thus, you don't have an unobstructed view of the road ahead. You fail to consider vehicles on either side early enough to make proper lane changes without getting into trouble. Dangerous in a car any time, *tailgating becomes disastrous in a truck because of the differences in the braking system.*

COMMON MISTAKES OF THE NOVICE DRIVER   (cont.)

Most new drivers figure that if air brakes on a rig are great when you're empty, they'll also be great when you're loaded. They have forgotten to consider one fact. You don't dare step down hard on a brake because of the load you're carrying. The load may break loose and come right through the cab.

● *Don't Charge Into a Situation. Look First.*

The list could go on, but these eight mistakes are the ones drivers make most often. These are the ones you must school yourself to avoid. On top of them, you want to keep yourself out of the mousetrap situations we discussed at the beginning of the chapter. You'll keep yourself out of a lot of trouble just by keeping away from all of the problems we've discussed in this chapter.

Even so, there are a great many other things to watch out for. In the last chapter, we saw that the two most common mechanical causes of bad accidents are tire problems and brake problems. You could blow a front tire. Or a brake hose or brake diaphragm could blow. But, in addition, your wheels could lock up or a trailer might break loose because a pin wasn't hooked properly. On the road, you must be constantly aware of these possibilities.

We might learn something from the man who visits a zoo. A cage door is open, and he walks in, slamming the door behind him. All of a sudden, he finds out he's in with a gorilla. He should have learned the same thing all truck drivers need to learn, especially when they're approaching any kind of turn or traffic situation: *Look first; don't charge into something.*

Many experienced drivers have a motto: "What you see one-half or one-quarter mile ahead of your rig determines what you do right now." Don't wait until you're on top of a situation and then go through confusion and panic. Look! Think! Decide what to do ahead of time. Plan your moves early.

SUMMARY | As a new driver, you have a lot of things to watch out for. First, you have to select your employer carefully. Then, you want to keep out of mousetraps.

There are three leading causes of driver-error accidents. The first is inattention. The second is making assumptions. The third is speed too fast for conditions. Inattention and making assumptions often work together. For example, if you're tailgating, you're not paying attention to the road around you and you're assuming that the vehicle in front of you won't blow a tire, have a wheel lock-up, slam on its brakes, etc. Add speeds of 55 mph to a tailgating situation, and you've really mousetrapped yourself. Remember, a speed of even 25 mph can be excessive under certain road, weather, or traffic conditions.

Most novice drivers make some or all of the eight common mistakes when they begin driving. First, they'll try to start the engine before taking a good look at the dashboard. The result? They may try to start the engine with the key alone, forgetting that there may be another important button to be used with the key. Second, they'll pump the throttle. This lets the engine wind up to maximum rpm and can damage the engine. Third, they put the truck in gear before it has built up safe operating air pressure levels. Fourth, they rev the engine. Fifth, they don't know the gear positions. Sixth, they don't remember how to double-clutch, or never learned how to do it smoothly. Seventh, they move too fast. They don't have time to watch out for other vehicles, people or structures, and they can't handle their vehicle safely. Finally, they tailgate. Tailgating is much more dangerous in a diesel truck than in a car because of the way the air brake system operates. It's also more dangerous because you may be carrying a heavy load. A heavy load can break loose and come right on through the cab if you slam on your brakes.

A truck driver has to plan moves early. The trucker has to expect the worst out of every other driver on the road. Expect someone to pull right in front of you. Expect that pickup in front of you to blow a tire. This will make you ready for emergency situations. You'll be checking the lanes beside you to see if you can pull over in case of emergency. You'll make sure your brakes are in good condition. Drive far enough back from other vehicles so you can see the whole road, intersections, even what's going on in service stations off to the side. Keep your eyes open. If you know what's going on around you, you won't charge into a situation. You'll be able to look first.

GLOSSARY

aerial: Belonging to the air; from the air.

assumption: Something taken for granted; something you expect.

euphoria: A strong feeling of well-being; feeling that everything is wonderful. The poet, Robert Browning, expressed this feeling when he said, "God's in his heaven--All's right with the world!"

gypsy: An independent truck operator. A gypsy drives his or her own truck and picks up freight wherever possible. Or, the gypsy leases his or her rig to an authorized carrier for one or more trips.

indecision: Not being able to make a decision or changing one's mind a lot.

mousetrap: A very dangerous situation; something that leads to an accident; a bad situation that's hard to get out of.

negligence: Carelessness; failing to do something that is required or important.

negotiate: To handle successfully; to do skillfully.

► CHECKING THE FACTS

Answer the following questions (or do as the instructions say) on a separate sheet of paper.

1. What were three things that made Ginger wonder if her company was legitimate?

2. Driver failures cause many accidents. What three driver errors cause more accidents than other driver errors?

3. What is tailgating?

4. List the eight common mistakes of the novice driver.

5. List the steps for double-clutching.

■ GETTING THE MAIN IDEAS

Circle the letter of the phrase that best completes each sentence or best answers each question. More than one answer may be true, so be sure you select the best answer.

1. You're following a car down the freeway. The car driver veers off to the right towards an offramp. What should you do? (You've been going five miles under the speed limit.)
   A. Speed up and fill the gap left by the car.
   B. Drop back in case the car driver decides not to take the offramp.
   C. Stay where you are in case the car driver decides not to take the offramp.
   D. Gradually speed up, but watch the car and everything around you, in case something changes the situation.

2. In Example Number Two (Short Trips), what did the driver do wrong?
   A. She was inattentive. In one case, she had to swerve. In the other, she turned the wheel too fast.
   B. She moved too fast. She shouldn't have swerved in one case. In the other, she turned into the yard too sharply.
   C. She was tailgating.
   D. She didn't tie down her load properly.

3. Here are four statements about euphoria. Which is the most true?
   A. The trucker should never feel euphoric on the road because it can cause inattention.
   B. It's okay to feel euphoric on a beautiful day, but keep your attention on your driving.
   C. Euphoria is something that usually happens after eating a good meal.
   D. Euphoria is a leading cause of accidents.

4. The main problem with tailgating is
   A. you don't have room to stop in an emergency.
   B. it encourages speeding.
   C. it makes the driver in front of you nervous.
   D. it's liable to get you a traffic citation.

5. Speed is a danger
   A. whenever you can't safely negotiate the road at the speed ·you're traveling.
   B. whenever the road, traffic or weather conditions are bad.
   C. whenever you're exceeding the speed limits for a road.
   D. whenever you're tailgating, turning corners or descending a grade.

6. Who is most likely to get in an accident?
   A. the vigilant driver
   B. the negligent driver
   C. the young driver
   D. the inexperienced driver

7. Why do you take a good look at the dashboard before driving a truck for the first time?
   A. to find the starter button
   B. to find out what kind of gear box and shifting pattern it has
   C. to get to know the rig and its various controls
   D. to make sure everything is in good, operating condition

8. You should practice double-clutching before you go to work for a carrier
   A. only in a diesel if that's what you'll be driving.
   B. only in a truck with the same kind of gear box you'll drive.
   C. in a car or pickup with a manual transmission.
   D. Don't practice double-clutching. Learn it on the job. Otherwise, you can build bad habits that your employer will have to break before teaching you on company equipment.

9. When you're about to make a right turn,
   A. begin slowing down when you're a rig-length ʳ   .e corner.
   B. begin slowing down when you're about a block .om the corner.
   C. gear down as you make the turn.
   D. upshift as you make the turn.

10. Over-driving your vision
    A. means the same as driving ahead of yourself.
    B. means being able to see the roadway in front of you for at least a quarter of a mile.
    C. is not possible when you're tailgating.
    D. means you can't see very much of the road ahead of you.

★ GOING BEYOND THE FACTS AND IDEAS

1. Describe a mousetrap situation that was not described in this chapter.

2. In Example Number Five (Tailgating) who is at fault? How might an accident be avoided? As it is, if the trucker can't move left, what will happen?

3. You've read about the eight most common mistakes made by novice drivers. If you aren't careful, what mistake are you most likely to make when *you* begin driving?

4. Did Ginger handle her situation as you would have handled it? If you agree with what she did, explain how it was the proper action. Or, if you feel she should have behaved differently, what should she have done?

Chapter Twenty-Four

LOG BOOKS

Figure 24-1. A sign points the way to one of the many truck stops scattered across the US. This one is on Interstate 10 between Phoenix and Los Angeles. *Photo by H. Haase*

WALT DUNCAN'S STORY | There are many ways a driver can become entangled in problems. Many of them result from not thinking. Here's a personal experience that took place at a truck stop in Yuma, Arizona.

Walt Duncan and I pulled into the Yuma stop at about the same time, pretty late one evening. We both decided to fuel up, shut down the rigs and grab a motel for the night. Trying to find a parking spot for our rigs, we wound up in an area in front of the stop, off the street and only about 200 feet from the motel where we intended to stay. We got a room and cleaned up. In about a half hour, we were showered and feeling pretty good. So we went to a restaurant where we could get a decent meal.

We were in the restaurant about two hours, talking over old times and having a few drinks after dinner. When we left the restaurant, we made another stop at a bar across the street from our motel. The music sounded pretty inviting, and, being typical truck drivers, we decided to see if we could find some companionship. Contrary to our expectations, the place was Dullsville. But we stayed and had a few drinks anyway.

By now, it was close to eleven o'clock, and we had to be on the road again by 5:30 the next morning. As we crossed the street, we noticed that all of the ten or twelve rigs that had been in front of ours at the fuel stop had pulled out, leaving only ours.

Walt said, "Hey, Ken, let's pull our rigs up to the motel."

I answered, "Walt, when I park that rig and get cleaned up, I never go back to it until I'm ready to hit the road again."

WALT DUNCAN'S STORY (cont.)

Well, Walt is one of those fellows who can't leave well enough alone. He was going to pull his rig up to the motel, even though it didn't matter. We were going to have breakfast back at the truck stop in the morning, after all. Anyway, my keys were in the motel where I had left them, purposely. But I walked with Walt to keep him company.

Figure 24-2. A couple of truck jockeys order up a meal at the Maryland Liberty Bell, a Union 76 TruckStop near Elkton. *Photograph courtesy of Road King Magazine*

Walt climbed up, fired it off and waited a minute or so for the air pressure to build up. I was standing alongside Walt's tractor, and I noticed a man in an old, white Plymouth across the street. He was watching us, so I asked, "Walt, do you know that guy over there? He's looking over here like he knows you."

Walt glanced over and said, "No, I don't know him." He proceeded to release the brakes and move down to the motel, with me alongside.

By the time Walt brought his rig to a stop, the man from the Plymouth was out of his car and following us. Just before Walt swung out of the cab, the man asked him, "Are you the driver of this truck?"

By the sound of his voice, I thought, "Ah ha! This is a man of authority."

Walt was never one to use common sense, so he answered, "Sure it's my rig. And, furthermore, what's it to you?"

That started it. It was the wrong thing to say. Another lesson for a trucker is this: When you don't know who you're talking to, be very careful how you answer a question. It always pays to be polite.

Well, the man showed us his ID. He was an ICC inspector. He turned to me and asked where my truck was. I said, "Parked."

Then the inspector turned to Walt who was getting a little hot by this time. "Let me see your log book."

Walt said, "What do you mean my log book? I'm parked."

"It doesn't look like it. You just moved your rig. It looks like you're on duty." Walt explained he was just pulling it up in front of the motel, but the inspector said, "I have no way of knowing that. You might be going on down the road."

WALT DUNCAN'S STORY   (cont.)

Walt fumbled around and finally produced his log book. Unfortunately, he had not brought it up to date when he stopped, so it didn't show him off duty. Technically, he was still on. This put him out of service for being over his legal hours. Plus, he had been drinking. The inspector had seen us coming out of the bar, heading for the truck. He had waited to see if we were going to take off after drinking.

Walt's fine was $150.00 for being in violation of his log book in hours of service. He was lucky the inspector didn't hit him for driving under the influence of alcohol. That could have been a real disaster.

The inspector seemed to be a decent sort of fellow. I found that out in a later conversation. He told me that if Walt had been polite, instead of belligerent, he wouldn't have made anything of the situation. He would just have told him not to do it again because of the dangers of driving while intoxicated.

It seems that some drivers never know when to keep their mouths shut, when to use discretion. Their mouths usually cause a lot of unnecessary trouble.

Walt's experience is an example of this: A driver doesn't even have to be moving on down the road to get into trouble. Even a standing truck can get you into trouble. There's an endless list of things that can happen. Even getting out of the cab and walking 30 feet to hand a piece of paper to a port of entry inspector can cause trouble. You may get back to the cab to find a police officer writing a ticket for leaving the vehicle unattended with the engine running.

BEFORE YOU READ ON

What is it you need to learn about log books? Perhaps you've looked through a log book at a truck stop or stationer's store. If you've been on the road, professionally, you've already used one. Your information needs depend upon what you already know. Try to write down five questions you have about log books. If you've used a log book, are there areas where you always have trouble. For example, does the recap section cause you trouble? If you've never used a log book, your questions will be different from questions from those who have used log books a lot. Whatever they are, write them down. Then, as you read, seek the answers to your questions. Hopefully, this chapter will answer your questions. If it doesn't, ask the question in class discussion. Perhaps the instructor or an experienced driver can answer it.

WHAT IS A LOG BOOK?

A log (or log book) is a *written record* of a trucker's on and off-duty time. Keeping logs is one of the facts of life for a trucker. The log shows that the driver has complied with the **Hours of Service Law**. Logs must be filled out according to certain rules and procedures. Basically, all log books look the same. But there are some differences between one style and another. We'll be discussing two styles in this chapter, and we'll teach the fundamentals of keeping logs.

THE	The Motor Carrier Safety Regulations require all drivers
HOURS OF	to be familiar with the federal Hours of Service Law.
SERVICE	
LAWS	Transportation has always been a very competitive busi-

ness. In the early days, truckers often competed for business by driving for long periods. By the 1930's, studies of truck accidents revealed an important point: Driver fatigue was a major cause of truck accidents. Obviously, the federal government wanted to reduce the number of accidents. So, they passed the Hours of Service Law which limits the number of hours a driver may be on duty.

Many states also have Hours of Service laws for their intrastate drivers. Sometimes, these laws are different from the federal regulations. If the driver operates in interstate commerce, she or he follows the federal law. If she or he operates only intrastate, the driver follows the state law. You should check with your supervisor to see which law applies if you aren't sure.

You can find the complete text of the federal Hours of Service Law in MCSR 395. For this section, we have picked out the most important parts of the law. We've also simplified the wording of some parts of the law to make it easier to understand.

● *The Hours of Service Law Says . . .*

MCSR 395.3 (a)   ...with some exceptions...no motor carrier shall permit or require any driver used by it to drive, nor shall any drive more than 10 hours following 8 consecutive hours off duty. In addition, no driver may drive for any period after having been on duty 15 hours following 8 consecutive hours off duty. However, drivers using sleeper-berth equipment, or off duty at a natural gas or oil well location, may accumulate the aforementioned total of at least 8 hours off duty in two periods of at least 2 hours each, resting in a sleeper berth, as defined in MCSR 395.2(g), or resting while off duty in other sleeping accommodations at a natural gas or oil well location.

● *In Other Words . . .*

What it all comes down to is this: You cannot continue working after 15 hours of duty. You don't just count driving hours. You count all on-duty time. For example, you count the time you spend doing your pre-trip inspection, the time you spend attending a broken-down vehicle, and the time you spend loading and unloading.

After 15 hours, you must take 8 hours off unless you're running with a co-driver. Then, the regulation is slightly different. You can split your time in and out of a sleeper berth. Many drivers work it out like this. Each driver puts in 5 hours behind the wheel. Then, the driver gets into the sleeper berth and the co-driver drives. By doing this, drivers can keep the truck moving over a 24-hour period.

Some drivers, as you know, don't have to help load and unload. These drivers will try to accumulate off-duty hours by jumping into the sleeper berth upon arriving at the loading or unloading destination. Technically, the driver in the sleeper berth is off duty and doesn't have to show his or her hours as on duty for that period. (The driver does, of course, have to log this time, just as he or she logs *all* time, both on and off duty.)

Trucking companies expect their drivers to save as many hours as possible on a stretch so the truck can keep moving. Remember, a driver who is sitting up in a moving truck is still considered *on duty*, even though the driver is not behind the wheel.

Here's an example. Your company needs a tractor in San Diego, but the tractor's up in the Los Angeles terminal. So, the dispatcher in San Diego tells you to ride up to LA with another driver. You have to pick up the tractor in LA and bring it back down to San Diego. But say you've already completed 5 or 6 hours on duty. If you sit in the seat beside the driver on the way to LA, you are on duty. And, when you bobtail on back to San Diego, you're on duty. That's not good if your dispatcher wanted you to take the tractor on a run after loading up in San Diego. You could be very close to being out of hours. What you want to do is this: Regulate your time so you don't run out of hours before you want to.

● *Definitions*

The Safety Regulations also define each duty status. They explain how various activities should be counted.

Off-Duty Time: Periods of time when the driver is *not* on duty, *not* required to be in readiness for work, and *not* responsible for performing work.

Sleeper berth: Periods of time off duty resting in a sleeper berth. "Sleeper berth" means one which conforms to the MCSR standards. It definitely *does not* include time spent sleeping in a truck seat.

Driving Time: All time spent at the driving controls of a motor vehicle in operation.

On Duty Not Driving: This status contains many possible activities. In general, on-duty time means all time from the time a driver *begins to work* or *is required to be in readiness for work* until the driver *is relieved from work and all responsibilities for performing work.*

On-duty time includes -

● All time at a terminal waiting to be dispatched, unless the driver has been relieved from duty.

● All time spent performing required equipment inspections or servicing equipment.

- All time, other than driving, spent in or on a motor vehicle, unless this time is spent resting in a sleeper berth.

- All time a driver is required to be present when a vehicle is being loaded or unloaded, whether the driver is doing work or just attending the vehicle while work is being done.

- All time spent performing the driver requirements relating to accidents.

- All time spent repairing, obtaining assistance or attending a disabled vehicle.

- All time spent performing *any other work* in the employment of a common carrier.

- Travel time undertaken at the direction of a motor carrier, during which the driver assumes no responsibility for work to be performed. However, there are two exceptions. If the driver takes 8 hours off when he or she reaches the destination, travel time isn't counted as on-duty time. Or, if the travel time was preceeded by 8 hours off duty, the travel time is considered off duty.

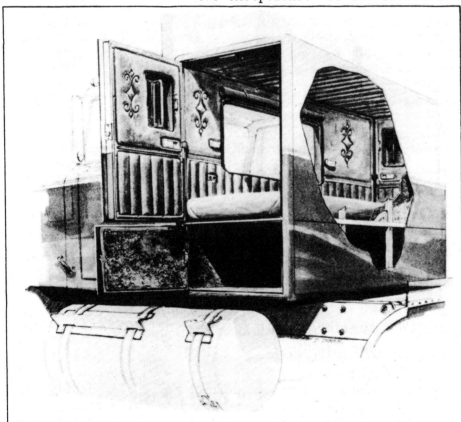

Figure 24-3. "The Bunker"® sleeper, Model 43000. This sleeper includes dual dome lights, radio speakers, and a large carpeted luggage area. *Courtesy of Brighton Metal Products, Inc.*

● *The Hours of Service Law Says . . .*

MCSR 395.3 (b)   Furthermore, except as provided in paragraph (e) of this section, no motor carrier shall permit or require any driver used
by it to be on duty, nor shall any such driver be on duty,
more than 60 hours in any 7 consecutive days as defined in
, MCSR 395.2 (c), regardless of the number of motor carriers
using the driver's service. However, carriers who operate
vehicles every day in the week may permit drivers to remain
on duty for a period of not more than 70 hours in any period
of 8 consecutive days.

(MCSR 395.3 (e) regards driving in Alaska. We will discuss
this under exceptions, below.)

The limitations of this paragraph shall not apply with respect
to any driver-salesperson whose total driving time does not
exceed 40 hours in any 7 consecutive days.

● *To Clarify . . .*

Basically, a salesperson is not considered a driver in many cases even
though she or he may be called a driver-salesperson. The limitations on hours
of service don't apply to the driver-salesperson because she or he doesn't
usually work over 40 hours a week. In most cases, such a driver would not be
subject to the DOT regulations to begin with. Usually, these drivers are considered to be local drivers. As long as the employer keeps accurate pay records, driver-salespersons don't need to log their time.

You may already have noticed an important thing about MCSR 395.3. It has
two parts. The first part, (a), limits the number of work hours *each day*.
The second part, (b), limits the number of work hours in a *7 or 8-day period*.
You can have hours available in your 24-hour period, but be out of hours in
your 7 or 8-day period. Or, you can have hours available in your 7 or 8-day
period, but be out of hours for the 24-hour period. The important thing to
learn is this: *If you are out of hours either way, you are not eligible to
drive again until you've been off duty for the required time period.*

● *Exceptions*

The next thing to notice is this: The law allows for exceptions. Here
they are:

● Drivers of trucks with *two axles or less*, with a gross weight of
*10,000 pounds or less, and which are not used to carry passengers or
hazardous materials* are exceptions. These vehicles include move-
it-yourself-type trucks, privately-owned delivery trucks, etc. In
other words, any vehicle that does not have more than two axles and
does not weigh more than 10,000 pounds is exempt from these regulations unless it carries passengers or hazardous materials.

● Drivers are exempt if they do all their on-duty driving within a
radius of 100 miles of the terminal where they report for work.

THE HOURS OF SERVICE LAWS (cont.)

That is, if you don't drive over 100 miles in any direction from your terminal, you are exempt. However, this exception *only* applies if the employer keeps accurate records, showing the total hours each driver is on duty each day.

● Drivers in the state of Alaska who encounter adverse driving conditions, may drive their truck for the time needed to complete the run. Adverse conditions means snow, sleet, fog, or unusual road or traffic conditions.

Figure 24-4. You should not keep driving if you are overly tired. Pull into a truck stop and wake yourself up. If you go off duty when you stop for a meal or rest, log out immediately. *Photo by H. Haase*

We have just listed the exceptions to the Hours of Service Law. Most heavy duty truck drivers *do not* come under these exceptions.

KEEPING LOG BOOKS | MCSR 395.8 requires all drivers who are subject to the Hours of Service rule to keep *daily logs* of their time. What happens if you don't? Here's what the DOT says: "Failure to make logs, failure to make entries therein, falsification of entries, or failure to preserve logs shall make *both the driver and carrier* liable to prosecution."

These rules are strictly enforced because drivers who are over-tired can have serious accidents. We've mentioned it in previous chapters, but let's say it again. Your log is subject to inspection by designated authorities whenever you're on duty. You may go months without anyone checking, but you had better have it up-to-the-minute when someone finally does check it. Who are these designated authorities? Traffic patrol officers, port of entry officers, special federal and state investigators, and others. All these people expect to find your log current up to the last change-of-duty status. (That's the first thing Walt Duncan did wrong. He didn't log out when he went off duty.) If your log isn't up to date, you and your employer may be found in violation of the rule regarding making required entries in your log.

The DOT prescribes a standard form for log books. You can buy logs through trucking associations and at truck stops. Sometimes, carriers will provide log books for their drivers.

KEEPING LOG BOOKS   (cont.)

Each log book page contains a chart which covers 24 hours. (See Figure 24-5.) If these charts were laid end to end, they would form one long, written document of the driver's duty status since his or her first day on the job.

⬤ *Four Duty Statuses*

The log chart allows for four possible states: Off duty, sleeper berth, driving and on duty not driving. After each status is a box for each hour of the day. Each box is divided into quarter hour periods. You don't need to record a change of duty status of less than 15 minutes.

⬤ *How to Record Your Time Spent in Each Duty Status*

Your first step in completing your log sheet is to draw lines through each appropriate duty status. Show the time spent in each status. The heavy line in Figure 24-5 easily shows what the driver's status was for each hour of the day.

Whenever you change your duty status, you must enter the place where each change occurred. Notice the words, "Richmond, VA; Fredricksburg, VA," etc. in the space near the bottom of the chart.

Figure 24-5 is an example of a one-day entry. Using a straight edge, the driver has drawn neat, straight lines, showing which hours were spent in each status.

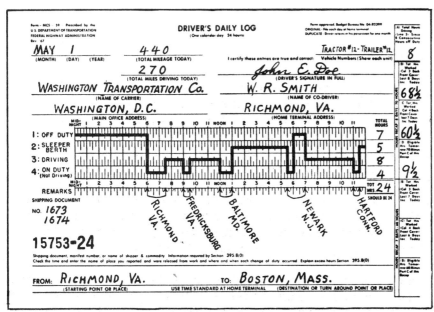

Figure 24-5. A properly-completed log book page. This is an example of one type of log book. The log in Figure 24-6 is a different type. Both types have been approved for use by the DOT. This log is available from the American Trucking Associations, Inc.

⬤ *Filling-in the Total Hours Column*

The next thing you do is fill-in the Total Hours column. You add up the hours in each status and write them on the lines to the right of each status. Then, you add all four totals to correctly arrive at 24 hours. This way, you account for each hour of the 24-hour day.

John Doe, in Figure 24-5, was off duty for 7 hours, in the sleeper for 5 hours, drove for 8 hours, and was on duty not driving for 4 hours.

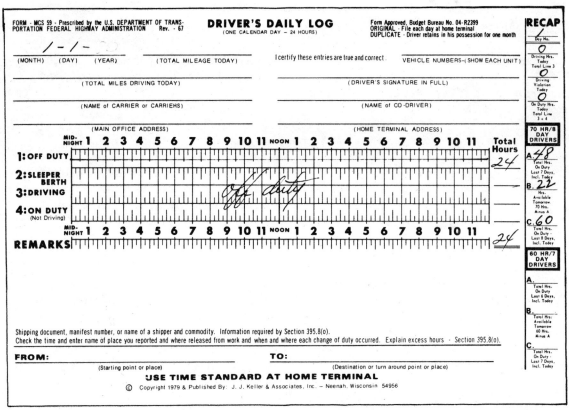

Figure 24-6. A properly completed log book page. The driver filled this page out for January 1, 1980, a day on which she did not work. Therefore, she showed the whole day as off duty. *Courtesy of J. J. Keller and Associates, Inc., Neenah, WI*

KEEPING LOG BOOKS (cont.)

● *Completing the Recap*

Now the driver has to complete the recap on the far right of the log sheet. This part of the form shows the driver how much time she or he can legally work during the next period. First, the driver records the total hours driving (from line three) where it says, "Driving Hours Today Total Line 3." Then, the driver adds the driving time and the on-duty-not-driving time together. That is, the driver adds lines three and four.

The driver in the sample arrived at 8 hours total on-duty hours for January 2, 1980. (See Figure 24-7, next page.) She added line three (driving 6 hours) and line four (on duty not driving 2 hours) together to get 8 hours. She wrote "8" above the line reading, "On Duty Hours Today Total Line 3 & 4."

Della Seward, our driver, works under the 70-hour/8-day system. So, the next thing she has to do is figure how many hours she has left in her 70-hour period. That is, how many hours can she still work before she has to take 8 hours off? Take a look at the recap column in Figure 24-7 again. Look beside the A. What did Della record in that space? _46 hours_ The space says to record "Total Hours On Duty Last 7 Days, Including Today." Della has apparently worked 46 hours over the last 7 days, including today's 8 hours.

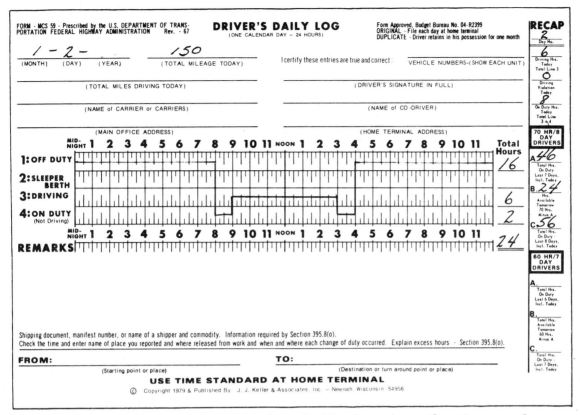

Figure 24-7. Della Seward completed this log sheet for January 2, 1980. She works under the eight-day system so she completed the center section under "Recap." Drivers who work under the seven-day/60-hour system complete the bottom section under "Recap" instead. *Courtesy of J. J. Keller and Associates, Inc., Neenah, WI*

KEEPING LOG BOOKS (cont.)

Now Della has to fill in the space beside B, "Hours Available Tomorrow, 70 Hours Minus A." She subtracts 46 hours from the available 70 hours. Her answer is 24 hours. She has 24 total hours on-duty time available for her next period.

Finally, she fills in the space after C. To do this, she adds up the total hours on duty for the last 8 days. As long as it doesn't exceed 70, she knows she will have hours available. Della records 56.

If this has been difficult for you to follow, it may be for the following reason. You have not had Della's hours for the previous 7 days in front of you. Therefore, you might have wondered how she got the number 46 to write after A and 56 to write after C. Keep reading, the whole thing may become clearer. Next, we'll be discussing the Monthly Log Summary Sheet. But, for now, you may wish to take a look ahead at Figure 24-8. It shows the recap column from Della's log sheet for January 3rd *and* the log summary sheet. On the summary sheet, at the left beside "Last 7 Days of Preceding Month," are Della's hours for the previous 7 days. This is where Della got her numbers.

MONTHLY LOG SUMMARY SHEET

Month _January_

If you operate on the period of 70 hours in 8 days, use the summary sheet on the left; if you operate on the period of 60 hours in 7 days, use the summary sheet to the right.

The figures 1 to 31 represent calendar days, and entries should be made for each day— even when driver does not work. If no work is performed, enter zero(0) in first column and compute other columns as explained below.

DAY OF MO.	HOURS WORKED TODAY (TOTAL LINES 3 + 1 ON DAILY LOG)	70 HR/8 DAY DRIVERS ONLY				DAY OF MO.	HOURS WORKED TODAY (TOTAL LINES 3 + 1 ON DAILY LOG)	60 HR/7 DAY DRIVERS ONLY		
		A TOTAL HOURS ON-DUTY LAST 7 DAYS	**B** TOTAL HOURS AVAILABLE TOMORROW (70 HOURS MINUS COL. A)	**C** TOTAL HOURS ON-DUTY LAST 8 DAYS				**A** TOTAL HOURS ON-DUTY LAST 6 DAYS	**B** TOTAL HOURS AVAILABLE TOMORROW 60 HOURS MINUS COL. A	**C** TOTAL HOURS ON-DUTY LAST 7 DAYS
LAST 7 DAYS OF PRECEDING MONTH	12					LAST 6 DAYS OF PRECEDING MONTH				
	10					1				
	8					2				
	10					3				
	10					4				
	0					5				
	10	60	10			6				
1	0	48	22	60		1				
2	8	46	24	56		2				
3	12	50	20	58		3				
4						4				
5						5				
6						6				
7						7				
8						8				
9						9				
10						10				
11						11				
12						12				
13						13				
14						14				
15						15				
16						16				
17						17				
18						18				
19						19				
20						20				
21						21				
22						22				
23						23				
24						24				
25						25				
26						26				
27						27				
28						28				
29						29				
30						30				
31						31				

70 hours - 8 days

Enter the number of working hours (on duty & driving) for each of the last seven days of the preceding month in the first seven spaces under the column headed "Hours Worked Today" in the first space under Column A the Total of the number of hours worked during the last 7 days. Subtract the figure entered in Column A from 70 hours and enter this figure - hours available for tomorrow - in Column B.

At the end of each day, complete the first three columns adjacent to the day of month in the same manner as explained above. Total the number of hours worked during the last 8 days and enter in Column C. Any number in Column C which exceeds 70 indicates a violation and should be circled for easy identification.

60 hours - 7 days

Follow the same instructions provided for completing the summary sheet for 8 days - 70 hours, except substitute last seven days and 60 hours for 70 hours; last six days for last seven days and 60 hours for 70 hours.

RECAP
for one month

Day No. **3**

Driving Hrs. Today **10** (EACH UNIT)

Total Line 3 **0**

Driving Violation Today

On Duty Hrs. Today Total Line 3+4 **12**

70 HR/8 DAY DRIVERS

Total Hours

A. **50** Total Hrs. On Duty Last 7 Days, Incl. Today — 12

B. **20** Hrs. Available Tomorrow: 70 Hrs. Minus A — 10

C. **58** Total Hrs. On Duty - Last 8 Days, Incl. Today — 2

24

60 HR/7 DAY DRIVERS

A. Total Hrs. On Duty Last 6 Days, Incl. Today

B. Total Hrs. Available Tomorrow 60 Hrs. Minus A

C. Total Hrs. On Duty - Last 7 Days, Incl. Today

Figure 24-8. Every driver has to have a record of the previous 7 days in his or her possession. This is the only way she or he can determine how many hours are legally available for work. The driver makes this record on the Monthly Log Summary Sheet. You will find this summary sheet on the inside front cover of your log book. We have shown the summary sheet beside the recap of a daily log sheet so you can see how the numbers are transferred from the log sheet to the summary sheet.
Courtesy of J. J. Keller and Associates, Inc., Neenah, WI

Figure 24-9. Tractor-trailer and bobtail trucks spotted at a loading dock. This driver has just completed his pre-trip inspection and is ready to roll. He has changed his duty status from on duty not driving to driving. In a moment, he'll be out of the terminal and moving on down the road. *Courtesy of American Trucking Associations, Inc.*

KEEPING LOG BOOKS (cont.)

● *Completing the Monthly Summary Sheet*

The Monthly Log Summary Sheet is on the underside of your front log book cover. This is where you keep track of your hours for the whole month. You will be transferring your hours from your daily log sheets to this sheet as soon as you stop driving for the day. Notice that the 7 days of the previous month are also shown on the summary sheet. See Figure 24-10.

KEEPING LOG BOOKS   (cont.)

When you complete the summary sheet, use either the left or right graph. That is, use the 70-hour/8-day graph or the 60-hour/7-day graph, but not both. We have shown both sides filled in as examples to study only. (See Figure 24-10.) Let's work through part of the 70-hour/8-day schedule as an example.

Column 1 is the calendar days of the month.

Column 2 is the hours worked from the daily log sheet (lines 3 and 4 daily). The day January 1, shows 0 hours worked. If you add up 7 days from the 0, counting 0 (January 1), you will get 48 hours. This figure appears in Column A. It is the total hours on duty going back 7 days from January 1.

Subtract the 48 hours (Column A) from 70 hours and place that sum in Column B. These 22 hours are the available hours you would have left to work over the next days coming up. As you total the hours on the cover sheet each day, be sure you also place them in the recap on the extreme right edge of each daily log sheet.

Column C is the total hours on duty going back 8 days from January 1. That is, 8 days back, including January 1. The figure in Column C for January 1 is 60 hours. This includes all the driver's on-duty time for December 25th, 26th, 27th, 28th, 29th, 30th, 31st and January 1st - 8 days. If you add up Della's hours for these dates, you get 60 hours. This is the amount she put in Column C.

● *Handing or Sending in Your Log Sheets*

Standard log books make a carbon copy of each day's log. Sometimes the copies will be printed in a different color than the original log sheets. Sometimes the copies will have the word, "COPY," printed across the face of the sheet. But one sure way to tell the copy from the original is this: The original will have the vehicle condition report on the back; the back of the copy will be blank.

The driver hands in the originals to his or her dispatcher and keeps the copies in the book. As a driver, you are required to have in your possession, a copy of your logs for the previous 30 days.

Drivers hand in their log sheet for the day *daily*. If you return to your terminal after each day's trip, you hand it in to your dispatcher upon your return. If you're out on the road for days or weeks at a time, you mail your logs in each day.

When you send in your original log sheet, your carrier will be able to follow your hours. This way, they'll know how many hours you have available for the next few days. If they have another run that requires 10 hours and your recap shows you are running out of time, they will have to send another driver - one who has sufficient time available.

MONTHLY LOG SUMMARY SHEET

Month _Jan/July_

If you operate on the period of 70 hours in 8 days, use the summary sheet on the left; if you operate on the period of 60 hours in 7 days, use the summary sheet to the right.

The figures 1 to 31 represent calendar days, and entries should be made for each day - even when driver does not work. If no work is performed, enter zero(0) in first column and compute other columns as explained below.

DAY OF MO.	HOURS WORKED TODAY (TOTAL LINES 3-1 ON DAILY LOG)	**70 HR/8 DAY DRIVERS ONLY** A — TOTAL HOURS ON-DUTY LAST 7 DAYS	B — TOTAL HOURS AVAILABLE TOMORROW (70 HOURS MINUS COL. A)	C — TOTAL HOURS ON-DUTY LAST 8 DAYS	DAY OF MO.	HOURS WORKED TODAY (TOTAL LINES 3-4 ON DAILY LOG)	**60 HR/7 DAY DRIVERS ONLY** A — TOTAL HOURS ON-DUTY LAST 6 DAYS	B — TOTAL HOURS AVAILABLE TOMORROW (60 HOURS MINUS COL. A)	C — TOTAL HOURS ON-DUTY LAST 7 DAYS
LAST 7 DAYS OF PRECEDING MONTH	12				LAST 6 DAYS OF PRECEDING MONTH	0			
	10					12			
	8					10			
	10					10			
	10					10			
	0					10	52	8	
	10	60	10						
1	0	22	22	60	1	10	62	-2	(62)
2	8	46	24	56	2	0	50	10	(62)
3	12	50	20	58	3	0	40	20	50
4	10	50	20	60	4	12	42	18	52
5	10	50	20	60	5	8	40	20	50
6	10	60	10	60	6	12	42	18	52
7	10	60	10	70	7	8	40	20	50
8	10	70	0	70	8	10	50	10	50
9	0	62	8	70	9	10	60	0	60
10	0	50	20	62	10	0	48	12	60
11	12	52	18	62	11	10	50	10	58
12	12	54	16	62	12	10	48	12	60
13	10	54	16	62	13	10	50	10	58
14	10	54	16	64	14	10	50	10	60
15	8	52	18	62	15	10	50	10	60
16	8	60	10	60	16	10	60	0	60
17	10	70	0	70	17	0	50	10	60
18	0	58	12	70	18	0	40	20	50
19	10	56	14	68	19	15	45	15	55
20	10	56	14	66	20	15	50	10	60
21	10	56	14	66	21	10	50	10	60
22	10	58	12	66	22	10	50	10	60
23	0	50	20	58	23	10	60	0	60
24	10	50	20	60	24	0	60	0	60
25	10	60	10	60	25	0	45	15	60
26	10	60	10	70	26	10	40	20	55
27	10	60	10	70	27	15	45	15	60
28	10	60	10	70	28	0	35	25	45
29	10	60	10	70	29	10	35	25	45
30	12	72	(-2)	(70)	30	10	45	15	45
31	0	62	8	(72)	31	10	55	5	55

Figure 24-10. This sample Monthly Log Summary Sheet has been filled out on both graphs, left and right, as an example to study only. Normally, the driver only fills out one side, depending on whether she or he is on a 70-hour or 60-hour schedule. Notice that our driver was in violation of the Hours of Service Law where the check marks appear. She'd better have a good excuse! *Courtesy of J. J. Keller and Associates, Inc., Neenah, WI*

KEEPING LOG BOOKS   (cont.)

● *A Few Final Notes on Keeping Log Books*

Many drivers become confused as they add up their hours. Remember this: As the days go on, you will gain or lose hours according to how many hours you worked over the last 7 or 8 days.   Your company will decide which schedule you'll be following - whether it's the 60-hour/7-day schedule or the 70-hour/ 8-day schedule. For carriers who operate every day in the week, it's strictly a matter of company preference.

When you're working in a two-person operation, your log should be the opposite of your co-driver's. While one person is driving, the other person is off duty, in the sleeper berth. You'll be in hot water if your logs don't jive. Imagine this, for example. Your log shows that you are in the sleeper berth. Your co-driver's log also shows off duty in the sleeper berth for the same period of time. Yet the truck covered 300 miles. How'd that happen? That's what the DOT inspector will want to know.

You might take a look at the driver's log for January 30th and 31st in Figure 24-10. Notice that she showed 72 total hours on-duty the last 8 days on both these dates. (See Column C.) Della was *in violation of the Hours of Service Law* on both these dates. If this happens to you, you'd better have a very good excuse for the violation. Getting back to your home instead of sleeping in the sleeper berth or a motel is *not* a good enough excuse.

Keeping your log book up to date is extremely important. Remember, the DOT requires you to keep it accurate *up to your last change of duty status.* When you jump into that sleeper berth for a few hours sleep, draw that line across your previous duty status first. Then, take your forty winks. Not only do federal and state governments require you to keep your log current, but ex-perienced truckers have agreed that it's the easiest way to do it. They've found that it's easier to keep their logs as they go than to try to figure them out at the end of a trip.   If you forget the time and place of your change of duty sta-tus, and try to fill it in two or three days later, you're really in trouble. Each figure affects each other figure on your month-ly summary sheet. You might even end up in viola-tion of the Hours of Service Law without realizing it.

We won't kid you. At times, you'll find keeping logs to be a nuisance.

Figure 24-11. Some truck stops provide a log room so that truckers have a place to keep their logs up to date. *Photo by H. Haase*

412

KEEPING LOG BOOKS (cont.)

At these times, it might be good to remember this thought: An industry which competes on the basis of *service and the safe delivery of freight* is a good industry to work in. It's much better than an industry which competes on the basis of "Last one awake at the wheel wins."

OTHER REQUIRED INFORMATION	You can see that there is room on the log sheet for other information, besides hours on and off duty. All of this is required information. This information includes the following:

- the date

- vehicle identification numbers (for *each* unit)

- the name of the carrier

- the address of the driver's home terminal

- the origin and destination of the trip

- the shipping document numbers

The name of the carrier may be *printed* on the form. You have to put *all the other entries in your own handwriting*. When you have completed the whole form, you sign it. Your signature says that everything on the log sheet is correct.

The log form also requires two mileage entries: a *total mileage* (total mileage today) and a *total miles driven* (total miles driving today). In a two-person operation, the total mileage for the day would be the sum of the miles each person drove. (That is, the total miles driven by both you and your co-driver.) Therefore, each driver shows the same *total mileage*, but each driver only shows the miles she or he drove individually on the space marked, *"Total Miles Driving Today."*

Often, carriers place additional pages in their drivers' log books. These pages may ask you to list the *trip route, junctions of Interstate Highways, entrances and exits from cities, fuel used, tire reports, etc.* This helps keep the driver from deviating from the established route. It can also prevent loss by hijacking, and solve other problems too. If the driver is paid by the mile, this information is very important. You can easily spend two hours filling in all the information in this type of log book. Be sure to leave time in your schedule for this activity.

DIFFERENT STYLES OF LOG BOOKS	As we mentioned at the beginning of this chapter, there are two different styles of log books. You have seen two different log sheets in this chapter. Figure 24-5 shows one type, and Figures 24-6 and 24-7 show a different type.

DIFFERENT STYLES OF LOG BOOKS (cont.)

There are small differences on the face of the log sheet, but both log sheets follow the form set by the MCSR. The main difference between the two log forms is on the *rear side* of each log sheet. This is the side with the inspection report or the "Driver's Vehicle Condition Report."

The reverse side of the log shown in Figure 24-5 has an itemized check list. (See Figure 8-3.) The log shown in Figure 24-6 and 24-7 has a much simpler inspection report form. (See Figure 24-12.) Here, there are just two boxes. You put a check mark in one, depending upon whether you considered the rig to be *safe* or *not safe* when you did your inspection.

But let's consider a case in point: A situation where the simplified form may cause you some grief.

Let's say you were unfortunate and were involved in an accident. You wind up in court and there is some question about whether you inspected the vehicle or not. When the accident occurred, the mechanical condition of the truck was not good. Apparently, it contributed to the accident. Just how would this cause you trouble? Here's how.

DRIVER'S VEHICLE CONDITION REPORT

AS REQUIRED BY THE D.O.T. FEDERAL MOTOR CARRIER SAFETY REGULATIONS, I SUBMIT THE FOLLOWING:

DATE:__________ TRACTOR NO.:__________ TRAILER NO.:__________

CHECK APPROPRIATE BOX

☐ I detect no defect or deficiency in this motor vehicle as would be likely to affect the safety of its operation or result in its mechanical breakdown.

☐ I detect the following defects or deficiencies in this motor vehicle that would be likely to affect the safety of its operation or result in its mechanical breakdown:

Indicate whether defects are on TRACTOR or TRAILER - Use sufficient detail to locate for mechanic

____

____

____

____

____

____________________ DRIVER'S SIGNATURE ____________________

Figure 24-12. Simplified vehicle inspection sheet, found on the rear of some log sheets. *Courtesy of J. J. Keller and Associates, Inc., Neenah, WI*

DIFFERENT STYLES OF LOG BOOKS (cont.)

You are put on the stand. The attorney wants you to state your routine for inspecting a rig. You start mentioning things, one right after the other: fuel, oil, water, headlights, etc. You figure you're doing a pretty good job of remembering everything a pre-trip inspection should cover. Finally, you finish. The attorney asks you if you are sure you have covered everything and if this is your normal inspection. You say, "Yes." After all, you know your business. Or do you?

The attorney starts naming a dozen points or items that you forgot to mention. Think about it. You've been on the stand before a bunch of people. Even if you aren't nervous, you're bound to forget something. There goes your credibility and your company loses the case. And you may find your job sliding away from you too.

You see, the easy way is not always the best way. Here again, develop a good routine and it will stand by you when you need it - regardless of what it involves, be it driving, inspecting or whatever.

SUMMARY | A log book is a written record of a trucker's on and off-duty hours. Each log book has an original and a copy log sheet for every day of the month. Each day a driver works, the driver has to fill in a log sheet and hand it in to his or her company. The duplicate log sheet (or copy) stays in the driver's book.

Since driver fatigue causes a lot of accidents, the DOT limits the number of hours a driver may be on duty without taking time off. Drivers may not drive for over 10 hours without having 8 hours off duty and they may not be on duty for over 15 hours without having 8 hours off. (There are a few exceptions, but most line-haul drivers must follow these regulations.)

The DOT also limits the number of hours a driver may be on duty in a period of 7 or 8 days. If a carrier carries freight every day of the week, the carrier may pick the 7-day or 8-day system for its drivers. Under the 7-day system, no driver may work over 60 hours in any 7 consecutive days. Under the 8-day system, no driver may work over 70 hours in any 8 consecutive days. Again, there are a few exceptions, but the exceptions don't apply to most line-haul drivers.

By law, every driver subject to the federal Hours of Service Law must keep daily logs. If you don't keep your log book up to date, you and your company can both be prosecuted. The law says that you have to keep your log up to date, up to your last change of duty status and there are four duty statuses: off duty, sleeper berth, driving, and on duty not driving. As soon as you change from one status to another, you have to show that change on your log sheet in the proper manner. You also have to show where the change took place: Janesville, Wisconsin; Tecate, Mexico; Rawlins, Wyoming, whatever. Changes of duty status of less than 15 minutes don't have to be recorded.

When you fill in your log sheet, you have to do it in your own handwriting. To show your status, you draw a line through each duty status as you come out of that duty status. At the end of your driving day, you fill in the Total Hours column and the recap. The time you spent in each status should add up to 24 hours, total. By filling in the recap, you find out how many hours of on-duty time you have left in your 7 or 8-day period. Instructions on the right-hand side of the log sheet will remind you of what you do to complete your recap correctly.

The Monthly Log Summary Sheet shows how many hours you worked each day of the month. It includes the 7 days of the previous month so you can figure out how many hours you have left to work when it's the beginning of the month. Each day, after you fill in the daily recap, transfer the numbers from the recap to the summary sheet. (See Figure 24-8.)

Log sheets ask for other information besides hours on and off duty. You are required to fill in the whole sheet, every blank. Some of the things you have to record are date, vehicle ID numbers, place you left from and place you arrived, shipping document numbers, etc. In addition, some carriers who supply their drivers with their own log books, also require other information to be recorded. They may ask for amount of fuel used, reports on your tires, your route, etc.

We displayed copies of two different kinds of log sheets in this chapter. Both are approved by the DOT and ask for the same basic information. They both have DOT-approved vehicle condition reports on the back of the original sheets too; however, the condition reports are quite different. The one with the itemized check list takes longer to complete. However, we think it may be better from one standpoint: It provides a better record of the things you checked in your pre-trip inspection than the other one does. This may be important if you wind up in court after an accident.

GLOSSARY

accumulate: To pile up; to gather or collect.

belligerent: Hostile; warlike.

comply: To yield to; to act in accordance with. If you comply with the MCSR regulations, you follow them.

consecutive: In a row; following in order; successive.

deviate: Wander from; turn away from.

discretion: Caution and politeness; being careful about what you say or do.

driver-salesperson: A driver of a delivery truck, such as a bread truck, milk truck or fuel truck. The driver-salesperson hauls display equipment around on the truck or trailer.

GLOSSARY   (cont.)

duty status: One of four types of activities, as defined by the MCSR, that drivers engage in. The four duty statuses are (1) off duty, (2) sleeper berth, (3) driving, and (4) on duty not driving.

monthly log summary sheet: A form, on the inside cover of your log book. You keep this up to date daily, by transferring your total hours worked from the recap of your daily log sheet to this form. It quickly shows how many hours you've worked each day, and how many hours you have left to work in your 7 or 8-day period.

recap: Part of your daily log sheet. The recap appears on the extreme right edge of your log sheet. This is where you figure your total hours on duty for the day and determine the number of hours you have left to legally work in your 7 or 8-day period.

sleeper berth: A bed or bunk behind the driver's seat which line-haul drivers use for sleeping and resting. Sleeper berths may be built-in when the cab is built or they may be added later as separate units behind the cab.

► CHECKING THE FACTS

Circle the letter of the phrase that best completes each sentence or best answers each question.

1. Which of the following best describes a trucker's log?
   A. a record of the miles a truck has traveled since it was serviced
   B. a record of where the truck has been
   C. a record of the driver's expenses
   D. a record of the driver's on and off-duty time

2. If a state's hours of service law sets work hour limits which are different from those set by the federal regulations, the driver should
   A. go by the state rules.
   B. go by the federal rules.
   C. check to see which law applies to his or her situation.
   D. note in his or her log book that he or she wasn't sure what to do.

3. The federal Hours of Service Law limits the number of hours a driver may drive after 8 hours of rest to
   A. 8 hours.
   B. 10 hours.
   C. 12 hours.
   D. 15 hours.

4. The federal rule limits the number of hours a driver may be on duty after 8 hours of rest to
   A. 10 hours.
   B. 12 hours.
   C. 15 hours.
   D. 17 hours.

5. The federal rule limits the number of on-duty hours in a 7-day period to
   A. 40 hours.
   B. 48 hours.
   C. 55 hours.
   D. 60 hours.

6. The federal rule limits the number of on-duty hours in an 8-day period to
   A. 50 hours.
   B. 64 hours.
   C. 70 hours.
   D. 80 hours.

7. Which of the following interstate drivers would be an exception to the Hours of Service Law?
   A. two-axle truck with gross weight of 10,000 pounds, not carrying passengers or hazardous materials
   B. heavy-duty truck operating within 300 miles of terminal
   C. heavy-duty truck operating within 400 miles of terminal
   D. heavy-duty truck operating within 500 miles of terminal

8. Who can be prosecuted if a driver fails to keep a log, makes false entries or doesn't keep a log for the previous 30 days in the cab?
   A. only the driver
   B. only the carrier
   C. both driver and carrier
   D. whoever the MCSR Bureau decides is liable for prosecution

9. A line-haul driver must bring the log book up to date
   A. after each 8 hours of on-duty time.
   B. after each change of duty status.
   C. after the completion of a trip.
   D. at the end of each month.

10. Time spent in any of the following activities -
    performing required inspections
    supervising loading of a vehicle
    performing driver responsibilities at an accident
    repairing a disabled vehicle
    riding in a truck seat -
    must be logged as
    A. off duty
    B. sleeper berth
    C. driving
    D. on duty not driving

11. In a two-driver operation,
    A. the entries in each driver's log should be opposites.
    B. both drivers use the same log book.
    C. only the lead driver must keep a log.
    D. Two driver operations are exempt from the Hours of Service Law.

12. At all times while on duty, a driver must have a copy of his or her log for
    A. that day.
    B. the previous 7 days.
    C. the previous 30 days.
    D. the previous 90 days.

13. Experienced truckers agree that it's easiest to keep your logs up
    A. as you go.
    B. whenever you get into the sleeper berth, before beginning to rest.
    C. when you finish your work for the day.
    D. immediately upon returning to your home terminal.

■ GETTING THE MAIN IDEAS

1. The first thing Walt Duncan did wrong was fail to log out when he went off duty. What else did he do wrong?

2. What is the main purpose of the Hours of Service Law and the keeping of logs?

3. What are some of the activities counted as on duty not driving?

4. In your own words, tell what this sentence means: "Trucking companies expect their drivers to save as many hours as possible on a stretch so the truck can keep moving."

5. Remember the situation in San Diego we talked about? Your dispatcher asks you to ride to LA to pick up a tractor and drive it back to San Diego. (Reread the paragraph from the chapter.) How should you regulate your time to save as many hours as possible for driving?

6. Who is exempt from the federal Hours of Service Law?

7. Look at Figure 24-5. Where was the driver when he was in the following duty statuses or changes of duty statuses? That is, what part of the country was he in?
   (1) in the sleeper berth
   (2) got into the sleeper berth
   (3) came out of the sleeper berth and went off-duty
   (4) came from off duty and started driving

8. Where do you get the information for your Monthly Log Summary Sheet?

9. How do you determine the number of hours left for work in your 7-day period?

10. Who requires you to complete your log book?

★ GOING BEYOND THE FACTS AND IDEAS

1. Write a short description of a trucker's typical day. Assume that the driver spends some time in all four duty statuses. Tell what the driver does in each status, where each change of duty takes place, and the number of miles the driver travels. The driver may be driving alone or with a co-driver, whichever you like.

2. List a good excuse for being in violation of the Hours of Service Law. (List more than one if you like and list some bad excuses if you like too.)

3. What is the difference between the recap and the Monthly Log Summary Sheet?

4. What is similar about the recap and the Monthly Log Summary Sheet?

5. Do one of the following exercises:
   (1) Outline the process of completing the recap section in your log book.
   (2) Outline the process of completing one day's portion of the Monthly Log Summary Sheet.

Chapter Twenty-Five

COMPANY RULES AND REGULATIONS

Figure 25-1. Bonny Floyd and Darryl G. Evans are co-drivers of this huge Pete. Triple T Manufacturing of Kent, Ohio customized it by adding a special, aerodynamic, vista-view addition to the sleeper. *Photograph courtesy of Road King Magazine*

INTRODUCTION | It is essential for all drivers to know what their employers expect of them. Most companies and almost every truck fleet in the United States, Canada, Australia, and throughout the world firmly spell out their basic rules to their employees. They do this through a book or bulletin, commonly called the *"Company Rules and Regulations."* No employer can hand out a book covering everything the employer wants you to do and wants you *not* to do. However, a rules and regulations book does help the company give you a *basic outline* of its desires regarding its *do's* and *don'ts*. Don't forget that the company developed these basic rules at the school of hard knocks. In giving you these guidelines, it is trying to protect the company and protect you, the driver.

The central part of this chapter is a sample company rules and regulations book. We've included it so you will know the types of rules you'll be expected to follow when you begin working for a carrier. One of the things which most companies rule out is unauthorized passengers. Let's take a moment to examine the whys. Then, we'll get into the rule book itself. We'll complete the chapter by talking about *bonding* and reading a final true life story about trucking.

HITCHHIKERS, FRIENDS AND RELATIVES | The problem of carrying unauthorized persons in the cab of a truck probably occurs wherever trucking exists. It's a problem in the semis of the US and the articulated lorries of England. The results of picking up unauthorized persons go from the comical to the deadly serious, depending upon the situation the driver is foolish enough to get into.

A few years back a driver had his eye on a particular gal at a truck stop, and every once in a while, he'd take her with him on a run to Los Angeles. One morning, the owner of the company that the driver worked for was driving up to LA on business. Up ahead, he recognized one of his own trucks. As he pulled up alongside to wave to the driver, he saw that his driver had beautiful long eyelashes and pretty, long blonde hair. It turned out to be the waitress from the truck stop, driving the rig!

Figure 25-2.

Photo by H. Haase

There is no need to explain what happened to the driver in that situation. It may have seemed perfectly okay to the driver to teach his girlfriend to drive the company truck. At the same time, he didn't realize the dangerous situation in which he had placed his company and their insurance carrier by letting an unauthorized person drive his vehicle.

Unauthorized people in the cab come about in various ways. A few years ago, my company needed a truck that was parked at the home of one of our drivers. We wanted to load it that evening so it would be ready for the early morning run on the next day. Bud, whose house the rig was at, had already been on duty a long time, and he wasn't very reliable; so we sent Phil, another driver, to pick it up.

Within a short while, Phil telephoned. Bud would not give him the keys to the truck. Bud had said he'd bring the rig in himself. Phil couldn't do anything about it, so he headed back to the maintenance shop.

While I waited for Bud to come in with the truck, I went to the coffee shop on the corner. Sitting there having a coffee, I noticed our truck come over the bridge and make a turn at the corner. Normally, I wouldn't have paid much attention to the truck. But, this evening, the engine speed seemed to be floating up and down as it rounded the corner, and I didn't hear any shifting of gears. As the truck went by the window where I sat, I noticed Bud sitting next to the window of the cab on the passenger's side. Naturally, I wondered who was driving the truck. It couldn't be Phil.

I finished my coffee, hopped in my pickup, and got back to the yard as soon as I could. As I pulled up alongside of our rig, Bud was getting out

HITCHHIKERS, FRIENDS AND RELATIVES (cont.)

on the passenger side, and, while I looked on in amazement, on the driver's side, out came Bud's fourteen-year-old son!

Needless to say, I was upset thinking that Bud had let his son drive that expensive rig back to the shop, especially late at night. He should have had better sense than to pull a dumb stunt like that.

As I walked up to Bud, he was literally hanging onto the side of the cab handle. Then I realized he'd been drinking and could hardly stand. Boy, was he loaded! That was the end of his driving job with us.

It is possible to pick up some hitchhikers and have a lot of fun. But you never know who you are picking up, and if you're unlucky, that may be the last one you'll ever pick up.

Many a driver has been fooled by this situation. You roll down the road and see a truck apparently with a breakdown on the side of the road. Being a good buddy, you want to try to help. As you come upon the truck, there is a fellow standing out in front of it, a few feet ahead, with his thumb up. You open the door to give him a ride to the nearest town. You think you have picked up the driver of the rig, when all you did was pick up a man who was hitchhiking. He figured he'd use the old ruse of standing in front of the truck, knowing that another trucker going by would assume he was the driver of the truck. All the time, the real driver may have been asleep in the cab, waiting for help from his or her own company, or just sleeping, for that matter. So, if you're going to pick up anyone, it would pay to check him or her out first. Find out if it's who you think it is.

Many drivers carry a fair amount of cash for pocket expenses. If you should happen to pick up the wrong person, you can possibly lose all your money. If it's your load the person is after, you can even lose your life.   There are many hijacked loads today. Sometimes, even when the driver is asleep in the sleeper berth, hijackers will try to steal the load if they think they can get away with it. Picking up hitchhikers is a dangerous game to play.

It is strictly against federal regulations, company regulations, and in-surance regulations to carry *any* unauthorized person in the cab of the vehicle. This includes your wife or husband. Even if you are an owner-operator, you cannot carry your wife or husband with you in the cab unless she or he has been authorized.

LEARNING TO BECOME A PROFESSIONAL

To become a real professional, a driver must apply every bit of knowledge that she or he has acquired. Then, she or he must combine that knowledge with the desires of the employer. Remember, it costs your employer time, effort, and money to train you to perform efficiently. Respect your employer. Know the rules and regulations of the company you work for, and follow them.

On the following pages, you will find a sample rules and regulations book. We have created it from typical rules and regs of many different companies.

423

SAFETY DEPARTMENT DIRECTIVE

From: Safety Director
To: All Personnel
Subject: Company Rules and Regulations

 Many rules and regulations have been formulated within our company during the past few years. To better inform you, and in an effort to cause better cooperation between all Company personnel, we are re-publishing these rules and regulations.

If you do not clearly understand any of them, you should immediately contact the Management for clarification.

 1. SPEED LIMITS: The maximum speed anyone will be permitted to drive is the legal speed limit, but not to exceed 55 mph.

Note: Speed limit in all yards is 5 mph in <u>all</u> vehicles.

 2. DRUGS: The use or possession of illegally-obtained narcotics or drugs by any Company employee is strictly forbidden and will be grounds for immediate dismissal. The use of legally-obtained narcotics or drugs for the purpose of physical stimulation is also prohibited and grounds for immediate dismissal.

Every driver, when taking medication for illness, should do so with extreme care, and under no circumstances should drive a vehicle if such drugs hamper physical or mental ability.

 You are advised by DOT regulations that possession of illegally-obtained drugs is a serious violation of the federal law and punishable by imprisonment. If any employee is suspected of using or selling illegally-obtained drugs, it will be reported to the federal authorities for whatever action they deem necessary.

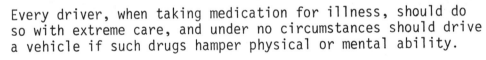 3. ALCOHOLIC BEVERAGES: The use or possession of alcoholic beverages while on duty is strictly forbidden and grounds for immediate dismissal. Under no circumstances shall a driver be required or permitted to drive a motor vehicle, be in active control of such vehicle, or go on duty or remain on duty when under the influence of any alcoholic beverage or liquor, regardless of its alcoholic content, nor shall any driver drink any such beverage or liquor while on duty. "Possession" shall be defined as any alcoholic beverage on a person, truck or trailer.

 4. LOGS: Logs must be completed and turned into the Dispatcher daily or at the completion of each trip. All logs must be filled out properly.

5. REPORTING OF ACCIDENTS: All accidents involving Company equipment shall be immediately reported to the closest Dispatcher. The term "accidents" shall include, but not be limited to, the following:

A. The <u>contact</u> of truck or trailer, truck or trailer part or accessory, or of the cargo we are carrying, with another vehicle, person, animal or fixed object.

B. The <u>unintended separation</u> of units of a combination of truck and trailer, etc., the <u>overturn</u>, <u>rolling off</u> the roadway, <u>rolling away</u> from a parked position of one of our vehicles.

C. <u>Fire</u> or <u>explosion</u> in or on one of our vehicles.

D. The <u>shifting</u> of cargo we are carrying, resulting in damage to property or damage to the cargo itself.

E. The <u>falling</u> of cargo or <u>damage</u> to cargo in loading and unloading operations.

F. The <u>injury</u> of any person, if involved in some way with our company operations.

6. TAILGATING: A distance of at least 300 feet must be maintained between vehicles operating within a city while our trucks are traveling in a forward motion at a speed of 30 mph or more at all times possible, and at least ¼ mile (1320 feet) when outside city limits at all times possible.

7. SIGNAL FOR TURNING OR CHANGING LANES: Turn signals must be flashed for a minimum of 200 feet in advance of any turn or change of lane. This is greater than the distance provided for in DOT regulations because of the length of our equipment. This is why we insist on this additional safety precaution.

8. NO RIDERS: No one except Company employees may ride as a passenger in any of our equipment unless authorized to do so by the Management.

9. DOT REGULATIONS FOR DRIVERS: All DOT rules, now in effect or as amended or changed from time to time, must be adhered to by all Company employees. All information on DOT regulations is available in the office.

10. EQUIPMENT INSPECTION REPORTS: Each driver must, at the start and completion of each run or work day, fill out in detail an inspection report of his or her vehicle <u>regardless of whether</u> or not there is anything to report wrong with the vehicle. This is a regulation of the DOT and must be accomplished each time you start and finish a run.

11. BREAKDOWNS: All drivers, in the event of mechanical failure of their vehicle on the road, must do whatever they can to help get their equipment back in operation. If minor repairs cannot be made, notify the closest Dispatcher immediately.

12. YARD ARRIVAL: When arriving at any yard, the following will apply:

A. Check over equipment, such as tires, lights, hoses, safety equipment, brakes, body defects, etc.

B. Record all fuel and oil on the fuel ticket. Turn the ticket in at that terminal. Keylock tickets and outside charges will be turned in to the closest terminal daily.

C. When picking up trailers, be sure you have the right trailers and right converter gears.

13. CALLING IN: If running late, call nearest Dispatcher, and notify said Dispatcher of your delivery time. Always check with your Dispatcher by 11:00 AM, whether loaded or not.

14. LOADING AND UNLOADING PROCEDURES: There are a few DO's and DON'TS in this business of service to the public that must be observed if a trucking concern wishes to survive:

A. Do count your freight when loading. If you are unable to physically count the number of pieces, mark all copies of the Bill of Lading "S L & C."

B. Do not sign for freight loaded by another driver unless instructed to do so by your Dispatcher.

C. Do not sign a Master Bill for more freight than is loaded on your own truck. If you are requested to do so by the shipper, call your Dispatcher.

D. Do make your delivery tag as legible as possible, and include the correct number of pieces, shipper's numbers, and any markings, if required.

E. Do not leave damaged freight at consignee's dock. Annotate your delivery as to correct number of pieces delivered; then call your Dispatcher for disposition.

F. Do not leave your truck while in the process of unloading or loading.

G. A Bill of Lading must be obtained for each shipment and must be turned in with a signed Freight Bill.

H. The aforementioned are for obtaining maximum dollar for each load hauled.

15. GENERAL REMARKS: The above listing of Safety and Operating Rules is not intended to cover completely all the "DO'S and DON'TS" of truck driving, but is merely an outline of some of the more important points that your Company believes necessary to professional operations and safe driving. All these rules must be complied with by all Company personnel. Anyone failing to do so will be subject to disciplinary action.

This Directive shall remain in full force and effect until such time as it is amended by a subsequent Directive or cancelled by such a Directive.

Dan Wright

Safety Director

Most companies today require drivers to be *bonded*. Bonding provides security for the company. The kind of bond we're talking about here is sometimes called a fidelity bond. Its purpose is to safeguard the company against losses caused by employee dishonesty.

● *Who Bonds the Driver?*

Trucking companies themselves do not bond the driver. The bond is written by an insurance carrier or underwriter that stands behind the bond. Through bonding, the trucking company can *guarantee* the driver's performance (or honesty) up to, say, $10,000. And the company can do this by paying a small fee to the bonding company. The fee is paid by the employer if bonding is more or less a condition of employment.

● *What Does a Bond Do?*

A fidelity bond is not exactly the same as an insurance policy. The bond does *protect* the company against loss by initially repaying the company for lost goods and/or equipment. But it tries to recover the loss *from the em-plyee* who was responsible for the loss. One insurance agent explained it like this: "The loss is paid by the insurer and then the insurer assumes the obli-tation to collect from the employee, including prosecution." So, while the bonding company does insure the company against loss, the bond is nevertheless not an insurance policy.

Not every driver can be bonded. If the insurance carrier feels that the driver has a record of dishonesty, or for some other reason feels that the dri-ver is "a bad risk," that driver may not get bonded. And, if she or he is unable to get bonded, she or he may lose the chance at a good job.

Figure 25-3. Refrigerated trailers can carry large amounts of meats and other products needing to be kept cool. Some companies make sure their drivers are bonded to protect their investment in the cargo. This is Trailmobile's Optimum Van refrigerated trailer. *Courtesy of Pullman Trailmobile*

WHAT DOES IT MEAN TO BE BONDED? (cont.)

● *What Does the Bonding Company Require?*

Bonds are ordinarily written with a *deductible;* that is, an amount of money which the trucking company must pay before the insurance company begins to pay. It works like the deductible on your car insurance. Most car insurance policies say that you have to pay the first, say $200 in repair bills, on your car before they will pay anything. The bonding deductible works in the same way. The trucking company must usually pay some amount of money out before the bonding company begins to pay. The amount of the deductible depends on the type of items being hauled.

The bonding companies also usually ask that the trucking companies keep some kind of control on the drivers. For instance, they may require the drivers to phone in to their employers upon arrival at their destination. This is because an entire truck and load could be stolen, and the company should know early if something fishy is going on.

Most companies have a standard bond form. The Hartford Insurance Group calls their bond a "Comprehensive Dishonesty, Disappearance, and Destruction Policy."

ANOTHER TRUE STORY | One of the first company rules you'll come across if you drive with a co-driver is this: the senior driver is boss.

In any team operation, there is always a first and second driver, or senior driver and helper. The senior driver is held responsible for the welfare and safety of the vehicle. Therefore, the co-driver is expected to follow instructions to the letter. This is unbreakable rule number one. Even though the less-experienced driver may not fully understand why, to keep out of trouble, certain instructions must be obeyed exactly. Lacking experience, the newer driver doesn't have the knowledge necessary to stay out of trouble, and the senior driver knows this.

Here's a story to illustrate this idea. Once again, the drivers wouldn't want their real names used, so we'll call them Vernon and Harry.

Vernon was a trainee from a driving school on his first trip out with a cross-country rig. For the first time, his senior driver, Harry, was asleep in the bunk. Vernon was driving on his own. Before Harry had lain down, he told Vernon to check on him if he stopped for any reason. This is another unbreakable rule: Whenever you leave the cab and return, always make sure the driver in the bunk is okay and that you haven't awakened him or her. An important rule, so Harry had reminded Vernon to be sure he knew it.

Vernon felt on top of the world. He was steaming down the road toward Phoenix where he had a regular stop on the way to Los Angeles. Impulsively, he pulled into a truck stop in Flagstaff and ran to the men's room. It was being cleaned and was out of use, so he crossed the street to a service station.

Figure 25-4. Two cab-overs and a
conventional rig at a truck stop.
Photo by H. Haase

ANOTHER TRUE STORY (cont.)

A few moments later, he returned to the cab, swung in, and went wheeling down the road to his check-in point at a Phoenix truck stop.

Arriving in Phoenix, Vernon opened the curtains to wake up his senior driver. Harry wasn't there! Vernon couldn't figure out where Harry was. Getting a little excited, Vernon went into a phone booth and called back to Flagstaff to see if there was a driver wandering around.

Just about that time, a truck pulled alongside his rig, and Harry got out. He had on slippers and a topcoat over his shorts, and that was all. He'd gotten out while Vernon was across the street. By that time, the restroom had been cleaned, and he'd gone on in.

As Vernon walked toward Harry to explain what happened, Harry just let go and hit him in the chin. The next thing Vernon knew, he was sitting on the ground. He was lucky that's all Harry did.

It's funny now, but it wasn't at the time - not to either one of them. When they got to Los Angeles at the end of the run, Vernon couldn't understand why Harry wouldn't take him as his co-driver again.

Sometimes, failure to obey orders can be more serious. Drivers may over-estimate their own abilities, so they need to rely on the professionals and follow the basic rules.

SUMMARY | Most trucking companies give their employees a rules and regulations book. This book outlines the companies basic do's and don'ts. However, it does not list every single thing it expects of its drivers.

The sample booklet which we presented is typical of the types of rules and regulations your future employer will require you to follow. Here are some of the rules and regs you may have to follow.

▷ Speed Limits: Observe speed limits.

▷ Drugs: No illegal use of drugs. Careful and controlled use of prescribed
      drugs for illnesses.

SUMMARY (cont.)

▷ Alcoholic Beverages: You may not use or be under the influence of alcohol while you are one duty.

▷ Log Books: Complete your log properly at the end of a run or at the end of each day if the run continues over more than one day.

▷ Reporting Accidents: Immediately report all accidents, of any kind, to your company's closest dispatcher.

▷ Tailgating: Try to keep a distance of 300 feet between your vehicle and another in the city, and a distance of ¼ mile on the open road.

▷ Turn Signals: Use them at least 200 feet before turning or changing lanes.

▷ No Riders: No one except another company employee may ride in your rig unless the company authorizes it.

▷ DOT Regulations: Follow all DOT rules.

▷ Inspection of Equipment: Fill out your inspection report at the beginning and end of each run or at the start and end of each day if the run continues over more than one day.

▷ Breakdowns: Try to make minor repairs; then, call your dispatcher.

▷ Yard Arrival: Make proper checks when you arrive in the yard.

▷ Calling In: Call in if you're running late.

▷ Loading and Unloading: Follow the company's rules for checking the correctness of a load.

Most carriers require their drivers to be bonded. This helps to protect the company against loss of cargo and equipment. Since bonding companies may not bond drivers who have a poor record of honesty or responsibility, it's important to be dependable and honest. Otherwise, you may lose a chance at a good job.

Remember that the senior driver is always boss.

GLOSSARY

articulated lorry: A tractor-trailer combination. This is a British term. A lorry is a truck in England and many other countries.

bonding: A method of guarding a company against losses caused by employee dishonesty. It works something like an insurance policy. The insurance company repays the employer for stolen cargo and equipment.

GLOSSARY   (cont.)

deductible: An amount of money which an insurance policy owner has to pay before the insurance policy starts paying.

insurance carrier: An insurance company.

senior driver: In a co-driver relationship, the more experienced driver who is responsible for the welfare and safety of a rig.

► CHECKING THE FACTS

Answer the following questions as if you work for the company who put out the rules and regulations book shown in this chapter.

1. Who should you contact if you don't understand the company's rules

    and regulations? _____

2. What type of drugs can you use while you are driving? _____

    _____

3. When are you required to turn in your logs? _____

    _____

4. At what distance should you flash your turn signals before turning or

    changing lanes? _____

5. What distance should you maintain between your rig and the vehicle

    in front of you in the city? _____

    on the open road? _____

Circle the letter of the phrase that <u>best</u> answers each question or <u>best</u> completes each sentence.

6. The person who schedules and controls truck pickups and deliveries is
    the
    A. manager.
    B. dispatcher.
    C. safety engineer.
    D. senior driver.

7. A method of guarding a company against losses caused by dishonest
    employees is called
    A. a deductible.
    B. coinsurance.
    C. a safety department directive.
    D. bonding.

8. Can the use of or possession of alcoholic beverages while on duty
   be grounds for dismissal? (In other words, can they fire you for it?)
   A. It depends on the circumstances.
   B. Yes.
   C. No.
   D. Not under ordinary driving conditions.

9. Should a driver turn in an inspection sheet on the vehicle before and
   after a trip even if nothing is wrong?
   A. Yes, in all circumstances.
   B. Before yes, but after only if there have been mechanical problems.
   C. Only upon completion of the trip.
   D. Only if the driver feels like it.

■ GETTING THE MAIN IDEAS

Put a plus (+) before the statement if it is true. Put a zero (0) before
the statement if it is false.

_____ 1. All interstate trucking companies use the Company Rules and
            Regulations Book which is shown in this chapter.

_____ 2. Companies don't want you to pick up hitchhikers because the
            hitchhiker might pose a risk to the cargo or driver or both.

_____ 3. Most companies allow you to take your family members for rides
            in the rig without prior authorization. Some even encourage
            you to take your spouse occasionally.

_____ 4. A helper should always follow the senior driver's instructions.

_____ 5. On a long haul across country, a driver is allowed to use
            drugs that simply enhance the effects of coffee.

For the next four questions, circle the letter of the phrase that best
answers the question.

6. What does a rules and regulations book list?
   A. all the rules a company expects you to follow
   B. the DOT regulations
   C. a basic outline of the company's main do's and don'ts
   D. guidelines you should follow to be a good commercial driver

7. When you arrive at the yard, what is the standard operating procedure?
   A. Check equipment for breakdowns.
   B. Record fuel and oil usage on the fuel ticket.
   C. Make sure you're picking up the right trailer.
   D. All of the above

8. What is proper procedure to follow when shifting cargo results in damaged goods?
   A. Note the condition on the bill of lading.
   B. Consider the condition an accident and report it immediately to the nearest dispatcher.
   C. Reload the cargo and proceed as you were originally instructed.
   D. Notify the shipper (that is, the company that sent the shipment).

9. What is the main purpose of the rules about loading and unloading?
   A. to safeguard cargo and make sure no one is cheated
   B. to follow the DOT regulations
   C. to make sure you don't exceed weight load limits
   D. to encourage the most efficient loading and unloading techniques and save company time

How about answering one final question on a separate sheet of paper.

10. Why did Bud lose his job? What things might the company have considered before firing him?

★ GOING BEYOND THE FACTS AND IDEAS

1. What do you do if you're trying to keep a safe distance of 300 feet between your vehicle and others in front and drivers keep pulling in front of you?

2. You've always followed the rule of letting the senior driver be boss. But one fine, sunny morning, Amanda, your senior, tells you the rig is overweight. She says she has a route picked out that will avoid the scales - hopefully. What do you do?

3. Write a definition of "accident" which will cover all of the types of accidents listed in the company rules and regulations book in this chapter.

4. What are some pressures that might be on a driver to encourage him or her to break a company's rules about drugs and alcohol?

5. There are some activities which a driver might engage in that would keep her or him from getting bonded. Can you think of what some of these actions might be? You might list five or six of them.

Ken Gilliland has an impressive background, and his list of credits is long. Among the positions he has held in his more than 30 years in the industry are truck driver and foreman, equipment operator, safety director, truck and forklift salesperson, cost analyst and trouble-shooter, truck driver evaluator and truck accident reconstruction expert. For the past several years, Mr. Gilliland has been actively engaged in teaching new drivers the skills he learned driving big rigs coast to coast, testing for the US Army and training and driving in Alaska during the laying of the pipeline. He is an enthusiastic teacher with a wealth of first-hand experience.

J. Millard, who holds a Masters Degree in Education, owned, directed and developed the curriculum for the first industry-recognized truck driver's training school west of the Mississippi, a school which became one of the country's largest and most important truck driver's training schools. Before that, he taught driver's training at the high school level for several years. Mr. Millard is also a past member of the Safety Supervisors' Council of the California Trucking Association, and for the last 20 years has been on the Governor's Advisory Committee for Motor Vehicle Regulations.

Michele McFadden holds a BA in English and an MA in Education. Her other credentials include California Teaching Credentials as a Reading Specialist and teacher of English and Communications. Having taught for several years at the junior and senior high school levels, both in the US and England, as well as instructed at the college level, she is aware of the problems faced by both students and teachers in the learning process. Her extensive work with authors as a textbook editor for the past eight years prompted her to do considerable research in the areas of readability and learning theory in order to prepare books designed to help students learn. The results of her research, as well as her private insights, have been applied in *Trucking: A Truck Driver's Training Course*. As Senior Editor for Career Publishing, Inc., she designed the format and organization, developed many of the pre-reading activities and questions, and encouraged the authors to write in the appealing, personal style used throughout this textbook.